Domestic
Sources
of
Foreign
Policy

EDITED BY JAMES N. ROSENAU

The Free Press, *New York*
Collier-Macmillan Limited, *London*

ACKNOWLEDGMENTS

The essays comprising this symposium were originally presented at a Conference on Public Opinion and Foreign Policy, held in Princeton, New Jersey, in March, 1965, and sponsored jointly by the Foreign Policy Association and the Center of International Studies, Princeton University.

The idea for such a conference originated with Samuel P. Hayes, President of the Foreign Policy Association, and I am grateful for his continued support throughout the planning of the conference and the preparation of this book.

The support of the Director of the Center of International Studies was also of immense value. Klaus Knorr greatly eased the task of organizing and activating scholarly endeavor by making the facilities of the Center available at several critical stages.

The editors and authors are also indebted to the distinguished scholars who attended the conference as discussants. Their criticisms and suggestions were invaluable aids in revising the papers for publication. More specifically, we are grateful to Robert C. Angell, Morton Deutsch, Harry Eckstein, Mark F. Ferber, Harold Guetzkow, H. Field Haviland, Alfred O. Hero, Samuel P. Huntington, Herbert C. Kelman, Nelson Polsby, James A. Robinson, and J. David Singer. Useful contributions were also made by three officers of the Foreign Policy Association, Norman Jacobs, Roger Mastrude, and Robert McDonald, who participated in the conference along with Mr. Hayes.

The proceedings of the Conference were ably recorded by Mr. David Blake and the subsequent typing chores were largely shouldered by Mrs. Roberta Weber. Appreciation for their efforts is gratefully acknowledged.

Finally, the many-faceted contribution of the editor's wife, Norah, needs to be recorded. Her moral support, editorial advice, and substantive insight made, as always, a big difference.

Of course, none of the foregoing persons or organizations are responsible

for the emphases and conclusions contained in the essays. This burden remains
with the authors and the editor even as they here record their appreciation for
the help received.

JAMES N. ROSENAU

New Brunswick, N.J.
October 8, 1966

FOREWORD

HUNDREDS of national and local organizations today carry on programs of adult education in world affairs. Many schools, particularly
at the secondary level, provide students with opportunities to learn about
the world and their relation to it. Colleges and universities are broaden-
ing their research and teaching in international affairs. And these educational activities are reinforced by the coverage of world events—and
by their analysis—in newspapers, magazines, and books, and on radio
and TV.

But how much effect do these activities have? How successful are
they in developing familiarity with important world events and an understanding of our international relations? More than that, how much do
they contribute to national decision-making in foreign policy by helping
to develop an informed and articulate public opinion that plays some
role in influencing national policy and in supporting—or undermining—
the implementation of that policy? Finally, how can they make a greater
contribution to the quality of the continuing foreign-policy dialogue
between government and private citizens?

These are critical questions for organizations that are engaged in
citizen education in foreign policy. Some openly build support for the
policies they advocate. Others, like the Foreign Policy Association,
concentrate on encouraging individuals to develop explicit opinions
on issues and to make their opinions heard. Even organizations that
consider their task strictly educational, and the purpose of education
as the development of the individual, have an interest in knowing what

part their students play in civic life, and how well that part is played.

As one seeks to assess the importance for the nation of education and mass communication in world affairs, one is led to ask more fundamental and precise questions about how our foreign policy is really made. How interested in foreign affairs is the general population, and what is the character of that interest? How many people have explicit opinions about foreign affairs? Where and when do they acquire their information, opinions, and attitudes? How easily and through what processes do they change? Who are those that bring their views to bear, either individually or through their organizations, on governmental de-decision-making in foreign policy, and through what processes or intermediaries? How does the public interact with decision-makers in the executive and legislative branches of government? To what extent are decision-makers really opinion leaders, or only followers — or perhaps both — in matters of foreign policy? Are these conditions and processes different for issues of foreign policy than for domestic policy?

The Foreign Policy Association (FPA) is keenly interested in the answers to questions of this kind, for they bear directly on the decisions it must make about priorities, techniques, and operating principles. Yet, as an operating agency, FPA has neither the professional expertise nor the resources required to carry on extensive research on such questions. Hence, it has turned to experts in the behavioral sciences, asking them to consider these questions, to make available and interpret the findings of studies that bear on them, and, hopefully, to undertake additional studies that will further illuminate them.

In tapping the behavioral sciences, FPA has followed a precedent set by many business concerns, government agencies, and educational institutions that seek to improve their operations by applying the results of behavioral science research and by stimulating additional studies. Developing a mutually satisfactory and productive relationship between an action agency and behavioral scientists is neither simple nor easy, however. Differences in values, objectives, styles of work and discourse, experience and knowledge of each other's field, and ways of handling ambiguity and uncertainty raise barriers. Nonetheless, making a start is half the battle.

Over the years, FPA has drawn extensively on behavioral science and scientists in defining its tasks and designing its program activities. It has utilized the published findings of research in education, communication, psychology, sociology, and political science. It has consulted with behavioral scientists individually and in conferences. And it has seen its own program through others' eyes in the results of a number of research studies undertaken by independent investigators.

As a major step in the development of its relationship with the

behavioral sciences, FPA took the initiative in the organization of a conference on public opinion and foreign policy, for which the papers appearing in this volume were originally prepared. Professor James N. Rosenau undertook the professional planning of the conference and the editing of the resulting papers. Four of the senior personnel of FPA participated in the conference. It is anticipated that this resulting volume will be of value to FPA's program and personnel, and to others professionally concerned with citizen education in world affairs.

Translation of the insights, data, and concepts presented in a volume such as this into practical recommendations for educational policy and administration is neither simple nor easy. This is a task to which FPA expects to continue devoting its own energies, and in which it hopes to engage the continuing attention of behavioral scientists like those who participated in the conference. More than that, FPA hopes that the conference, and this resulting volume, will stimulate a range of additional research investigations and interpretive studies bearing on the general topic of the conference. Clearly, as several of the papers emphasize, much still remains to be discovered about the complex interaction of public opinion and foreign policy decision-making.

SAMUEL P. HAYES, PRESIDENT
Foreign Policy Association

New York, N.Y.

CONTRIBUTORS

BERNARD C. COHEN is Professor of Political Science at the University of Wisconsin. His writings include *The Press and Foreign Policy* (1963) and *The Political Process and Foreign Policy* (1957).

JOHAN GALTUNG is Director of the Peace Research Institute, Oslo, and editor of the *Journal of Peace Research*. The author of a number of articles bearing upon the domestic sources of foreign policy, he has taught at Columbia University and held a UNESCO professorship in Chile.

SCOTT GREER is Professor of Political Science and Sociology, and Director of the Center for Metropolitan Studies, Northwestern University. Among his publications are *Governing the Metropolis* (1962) and *Metropolitics* (1963).

THEODORE J. LOWI is Associate Professor of Political Science at the University of Chicago. His work includes authorship of *At the Pleasure of the Mayor* (1964) and editorship of *Legislative Politics U.S.A.* (1965).

HERBERT McCLOSKY is Professor of Political Science at the University of California, Berkeley. His research has concentrated on the psychology of political behavior, and he has enriched that field by the publication of many pioneering studies.

LESTER W. MILBRATH is Professor of Political Science, State University of New York at Buffalo. His recent books include *The Washington Lobbyists* (1963) and *Political Participation* (1965).

WARREN E. MILLER is Professor of Political Science and Program Director of the Survey Research Center, the University of Michigan. He is author or co-author of many of the Center's pathbreaking inquiries into voting behavior, including *The Voter Decides* (1954) and *The American Voter* (1960).

JAMES N. ROSENAU is Professor of Political Science, Rutgers University, and Research Associate at the Center of International Studies, Princeton University. Among his books are *Public Opinion and Foreign Policy* (1961) and *National Leadership and Foreign Policy* (1963).

MILTON J. ROSENBERG is Professor of Psychology at the University of Chicago. A co-author of *Attitude Organization and Change* (1960), he has published the results of many innovative experiments in a wide number of professional journals.

KENNETH N. WALTZ is Professor of Political Science at Brandeis University. He is currently completing a book on politics and foreign policy in Great Britain and the United States, and among his previous writings is *Man, the State, and War* (1959).

CONTENTS

DOMESTIC
SOURCES
OF
FOREIGN
POLICY

INTRODUCTION

James N. Rosenau

As your Secretary of State I wish to talk to you about foreign relations. Let me start with a simple remark which I earnestly hope you will never forget: Foreign policy is about you. It is about your home, your community, your safety, your well-being, your chance to live a decent life and to prepare a better world for your children. Foreign policy is not a game played by "those people in Washington" with other players from far-off distant places. It is as close to you as the members of your family, or the neighbor's boy, in uniform . . . as close as the taxes you pay to sustain the struggle for freedom, as close as the prices and the markets for what you produce. Even more personal, it is as close as your highest hopes, your puzzled concern that man can be both so good and yet so evil, your own impulse to do something to build a better world, your own private and personal search for the answer to the ageless question: "What is the chief end of man?"[1]

1. Dean Rusk, address to the Farmers Union Grain Terminal Association, St. Paul, Minnesota, December 10, 1963.

HOWEVER else they may be interpreted, these exhortations succinctly illustrate both the underlying premise and the main dilemma of
this book. The premise is that domestic sources of foreign policy are no
less crucial to its content and conduct than are the international situations
toward which it is directed. The dilemma is that the links between the
domestic sources and the resulting behavior—foreign policy—are not
easily observed and are thus especially resistant to coherent analysis.

Perhaps never before have the domestic sources of foreign policy
seemed so important and been the focus of so much discussion. The
intense controversy in the United States over the struggle in Vietnam
has dramatized anew the fact that the foreign policy of governments is
more than simply a series of responses to international stimuli, that
forces at work within a society can also contribute to the quality and
contents of its external behavior.

However, it is one thing to believe that a nation's foreign policy
reflects its way of life and quite another to back up such a conviction
conceptually and empirically. It is one thing for an official to tell citizens,
"Foreign policy is about you," but is quite another for the scholar to
identify the causal processes implied in such an assertion.

In other words, greater recognition of the wellsprings of foreign
policy does not necessarily lead to greater clarity of thought about it.
On the contrary, as the discussion of why states behave the way they
do widens, so does reliance on crude and oversimplified explanations.
Explaining foreign policy has become a popular sport and everyone seems
to have a pet theory about who caused what event or what event caused
whom to respond. The crudest of these, of course, are the "devil theories,"
in which the course of events is attributed to a power-hungry individual
or to a conspiratorial group. These theories are especially attractive to
people in times of international or domestic tension, such as a war
abroad or an election at home. It is much easier to fix on a single culprit
as the cause of undesirable events than to treat such events as the cul-
mination of many factors, each of which is a necessary, though not a
sufficient, cause. Devil theories thus provide a simple and quick explanation for complexity, enabling their holders both to take a position and
to cope with anxiety.

Yet clarity is hardly a distinguishing feature of many of the more
sophisticated approaches that do not rely on the devil for coherence.
Theories which concede that events are not caused by single factors are
numerous, but all too often holders of these theories reorganize them so
as to make the complex of factors consistent with other values. Thus, for
example, many Democrats who are impressed by a Johnson or a Kennedy
will, in the case of decisions they applaud, ascribe primary causation

to the presidency and secondary causation to public opinion and the mass media, but they will reverse the strength of the factors in the case of decisions they deplore. When a Republican enters the White House, such theorists will rearrange the factors again and blame the President for events they regret, but will treat his actions as merely responses to public demands in the case of trends they approve.

Nor are professional inquiries into such matters models of clarity. How the various sources of foreign policy combine to produce various forms of behavior under various kinds of conditions is neither the subject of extensive research nor the focus of systematic theorizing. Most scholarly treatments of foreign policy are either case studies or institutional analyses; that is, they are concerned either with the effects of many sources in a particular situation or with the effect of a single source in a variety of situations. Rare is the work that traces and assesses the relative contribution made by many sources in many diverse situations.[2] Moreover, like the case studies and institutional analyses, those few inquiries that do attempt to generalize across both sources and situations tend to minimize the domestic sources of foreign policy and to stress the processes of governmental decision-making, the events abroad with which officials must contend, and the nonhuman realities—such as geographic position, resource availability, and military or economic capacity—which limit or enhance their choices. Although such inquiries usually pay lip service to the idea that events and trends within a society also impinge upon the deliberations of its officials, the literature is short on works that consider a wide range of nongovernmental variables and estimate how their interaction shapes the contents and conduct of foreign policy.[3] Occasionally, to be sure, inquiries will focus directly on the connection between public opinion and foreign policy,[4] but, since they deal exclusively with public opinion, these are also single-factor analyses rather than systematic attempts to link basic societal processes to the behavior of officialdom.

There are, of course, good reasons for this disparity between the recognition that foreign policy springs from domestic sources and the scant treatment paid these sources in research. One is that events abroad,

2. For an elaboration of this point, see James N. Rosenau, "Pre-Theories and Theories of Foreign Policy," in R. Barry Farrell (ed.), *Approaches to Comparative and International Politics* (Evanston: Northwestern University Press, 1966), pp. 27–92.

3. Some possible exceptions are Gabriel A. Almond, *The American People and Foreign Policy* (New York: Frederick A. Praeger, 1960), and Karl W. Deutsch and Lewis J. Edinger, *Germany Rejoins the Powers* (Stanford: Stanford University Press, 1959).

4. See, for example, Douglas H. Mendel, Jr., *The Japanese People and Foreign Policy: A Study of Public Opinion in Post-Treaty Japan* (Berkeley: University of California Press, 1961) and William A. Scott and Stephen B. Withey, *The United States and the United Nations: The Public View* (New York: Manhattan Publishing Co., 1958).

nonhuman realities, and governmental decision-making processes *are* the primary determinants of foreign policy and, on balance, they may well be more crucial than any and all domestic sources. In the rare instances when politicians cannot prevent the requirements of external and internal situations from coming into direct conflict, the former are likely to prevail in virtually every society.[5] So it is understandable that analysts have been inclined to concentrate on the international, nonhuman, and governmental sources of foreign policy.

However, domestic factors may be of considerable significance even if they are not primary sources of foreign policy, and on some issues they may well be dominant. It is instructive to note, for example, how McGeorge Bundy, himself a leading student of foreign policy before becoming a presidential adviser, responded to an interviewer's query about "What was different in the actual conduct of American diplomatic affairs from how it had seemed to be from the safety of Harvard Yard?" According to the interviewer, "Bundy thought that three things stood out. The first was his recognition of the powerful place of domestic politics in the formulation of foreign policies . . . "[6]

Another reason for the disparity, and one that goes farther in accounting for it, must be noted. Upon reflection, the number of nongovernmental factors that can shape a society's foreign policy is staggering and, accordingly, the task of piecing them together into a coherent whole is extraordinarily complex. Many analysts may have a sense that the structure of a society is somehow related to the way in which its officials cope with the international environment, but translating this insight into meaningful research propositions presents a theoretical challenge that few have dared to confront. What aspects of societal structure affect what kinds of official behavior? Exactly how and under what circumstances are the forces at work in society—the shared values, the unresolved conflicts, the irrational drives, the memories of the past, the

5. Such a conflict occurred in the United States on May 15, 1965. The Johnson administration, concerned about academic criticism of its policies in Vietnam, had previously agreed that one of its top foreign policy decision-makers, McGeorge Bundy, would participate in a nationally televised "teach-in" devoted to the issue on that day. As the time for the debate neared, however, a crisis in the Dominican Republic became so acute that a choice had to be made as to whether Mr. Bundy's time should be devoted to the external or the internal scene. And apparently it was an inescapable choice: to have Bundy participate in the teach-in was to remove a key adviser from a fast-moving and critical situation, but to fail to appear at the teach-in was to risk further antagonism of a critical group in the society. Unable to hedge, the administration decided that Mr. Bundy would attend to the Dominican Republic rather than Academe and sent him on a mediating mission to the strife-torn island. To interpret his trip as a ruse for avoiding the teach-in, as some ardent critics did, is to minimize the extent to which internal considerations must give way to external ones when the two cannot be accommodated to each other.

6. Henry F. Graff, "How Johnson Makes Foreign Policy," *The New York Times Magazine*, July 4, 1965, p. 17.

ever-changing dynamics of group life, the shifting composition of cities and classes, the ups and downs and changing structure of production and trade, the profound alterations in work and leisure patterns induced by technology — articulated in the actions of decision-makers? Through the latters' conscious perceptions of such forces? Through their prior socialization and training, which has made them unconsciously sensitive to societal tendencies? Through the resource opportunities and limitations that derive from societal structure and that serve as parameters within which effective choices can be made by officialdom? Through intervening institutions such as elections, mass media of communications, and organized interest groups?

1

It would be misleading to suggest that the ten essays in this volume provide definitive answers to these questions. All of them, however, are addressed to questions of this sort and, taken collectively, they provide conceptual and empirical insight into the processes whereby internal variables condition external behavior. They do so by considering a wide range of "domestic" variables, from the personality and attitude dynamics that operate at the level of individual citizens and officials to the group and organizational processes that are operative at the grosser levels of society and politics. Not every domestic variable that might serve as a source of foreign policy is subjected to searching examination. Since the essays were originally prepared for a conference on public opinion and foreign policy, they devote little, if any, attention to economic, technological, and other nonhuman variables. On the other hand, psychological, sociological, and political factors do fall within the scope of our analysis. In effect, "public opinion" is here expanded to encompass basic behavioral processes as well as the orientations of the citizenry toward international affairs.

That the symposium consists of a wide-ranging analysis of the domestic sources of foreign policy rather than a narrow concern with foreign policy itself is due in large part to the training and expertise of the contributors. Only three, Cohen, Waltz, and the editor, are political scientists who have done most of their work in the field of international politics and foreign policy. None of the other seven — a social psychologist, two sociologists, and four political scientists — received any formal training in this field, and only Galtung has done extensive research on international phenomena. Of the remaining six, Greer and Lowi are specialists in urban affairs, McClosky has done distinguished research on the psychology of political behavior, Rosenberg is known for his work

in the social psychology of attitude formation and change, and Milbrath and Miller have specialized in the domestic dimensions of interest group and voting behavior. In other words, the relevance of foreign policy phenomena to the professional concerns of most of the authors had to be derived. In several cases, in fact, the tasks of derivation seemed so complex and difficult that the invitation to participate in the symposium was resisted on the grounds that "I have never done any work on such matters." This response, however, only encouraged the editor to press for acceptance of the invitation, since it seems clear that thorough and incisive comprehension of the domestic sources of foreign policy is more likely to come from those who specialize in intra-societal phenomena than from those who study inter-societal relationships. So, if most of the chapters seem short on foreign policy analysis, this is more than compensated for by the talent that has been momentarily diverted from the investigation of more basic forms of behavior to consider the problem of how they culminate in foreign policy.

One important limitation of the symposium must be mentioned, however. For all practical purposes it is culture-bound. A preponderance of the chapters is primarily concerned with the domestic sources of United States foreign policy. Throughout, mention is made of comparable phenomena in other societies and often the analysis is cast at such a high level of generalization that the reader will have little difficulty applying the conclusions to non-American situations. Nevertheless, only in the chapter by Galtung does the analysis concentrate on another society (that of Norway).

Just as the papers range widely across a variety of phenomena, so also do they vary in their analytic techniques. At one extreme are three strictly conceptual chapters by Greer, Milbrath, and the editor that employ only a minimum of empirical data, while at the other extreme are chapters by Galtung, McClosky, and Miller that present quantitative data never before published. Between these extremes is the chapter by Lowi that employs historical data to test and extend a generalized model, those by Cohen and Waltz that use previously available materials, both quantitative and historical, to develop comprehension of a specific set of phenomena, and the one by Rosenberg that synthesizes the findings of an area of experimental research in order to elaborate a particular view of present-day world politics. This variability of method might be ascribed to the nature of symposia, but an even more valid interpretation is that it reflects both the potentialities of research into the domestic sources of foreign policy and the rudimentary state of our knowledge about them.

There is yet another important respect in which variability marks the symposium, namely, the degree to which the authors adhered to

the organizing framework that was originally suggested to them. In order to stimulate fresh thought and to insure analysis that probed below the surface of current events, each author was asked to re-examine the phenomena in his field and assess whether they function differently in the area of foreign policy than in the area of domestic policy. So as to facilitate adaptation to this "issue-area" framework, the editor supplied the authors with an initial formulation of it.[7] For a variety of reasons, however, the authors differed markedly in the degree to which they employed the framework, some fully responding to the question of whether a useful foreign-domestic distinction could be drawn and others paying only incidental attention to it. Sensitivity to the notion that attitudes and behavior can vary from issue to issue is manifest in all the papers, but not in the organized way that the editor had originally hoped would be the case. He must admit in all honesty that this volume reflects a failure of the issue-area concept to spark imaginations or organize thoughts to a significant degree.

A number of reasons for this failure might be cited. The most obvious would be to explain that the issue-area concept lacks clarifying power because individual and group behavior do not vary significantly from one area to another. A second explanation might concede some utility to the concept, but argue that international affairs do not fall within its scope. That is, it might be reasoned that the differences between foreign and domestic policy issues are not nearly as great as the similarities, that, in fact, the foreign-domestic distinction becomes blurred when subjected to empirical verification, and that therefore the issue-area concept is not applicable to the concerns of this particular volume, even though it might have utility in other areas of research.

In the absence of evidence to the contrary, neither of these reasons can be refuted and both are somewhat plausible. There is, however, a third line of reasoning that is no less plausible and is especially appealing to the editor, who is naturally reluctant to abandon a concept to which he has become committed. This is that the issue-area concept must be further refined and more extensively used before its clarifying power can be adequately tested. As it now stands, the idea of deriving both the distinguishing characteristics and the boundaries of a set of activities from the values that are being sought or contested (i.e., an issue-area), rather than from the nature of the units to which the actors belong (e.g., a nation, a legislature, and so on), is so contrary to the usual mode of analysis that it is unreasonable to expect its swift adoption. Since the concept has yet to be used widely, data that would permit systematic comparisons across issue-areas are not readily available. In effect, the authors were asked empirical questions that they could not answer

7. A revised version of the framework is presented here as Chapter 2.

without elaborate efforts to accumulate entirely new data or to reorganize and rework the existing data. Such an effort is obviously a major undertaking and one that exceeds the time and resources any of the authors could give to this momentary diversion from their primary research interests.

An obstacle even more important than the scarcity of data is the long-standing habit of thinking horizontally across issue-areas rather than vertically within them.[8] Being accustomed to treating the interaction patterns that occur within legal and/or social entities as sustained by common motives and processes, the authors understandably resisted dropping this assumption and, instead, postulating the possibility of significant variation in both the interaction patterns and their sources. In short, the editor would argue that further research may yet reveal the issue-area concept to have merit even if its use here did not prove successful.

2

Whatever the inadequacies of the concept, they did not prevent the writing of creative and insightful essays. While these were not prepared in terms of an explicit and shared framework, they do have in common a concern for a particular source of foreign policy and, as noted, they collectively cover a wide range of sources. The order of their presentation, following the editor's formulation of the issue-area concept in Chapter 2, is in terms of a scale of increasing complexity. The first essays deal with sources located in the individual actor—his personality, attitudes, and social position. The next essays focus on the instruments through which action is taken—the mass media, voting, and interest groups. These are followed by those that probe the sources operative at sites where individual and group actions converge—the urban community and the national political system.

Whether or not the reader proceeds through the essays in this order, any tendency he may yet have to view foreign policy as springing from a single source will doubtless be attenuated. In Chapter 3 McClosky demonstrates that one's orientation toward foreign affairs is closely linked to certain basic personality traits. In the next chapter Rosenberg emphasizes that although research into attitude formation and change has followed several different lines, these have all converged on the finding that people cannot tolerate discrepancies among the attitudes they hold

8. For an elaboration of this distinction between the vertical and horizontal approaches to phenomena, see Rosenau, "Pre-Theories and Theories of Foreign Policy," *op. cit.*, pp. 71–88.

and will change these attitudes in an attempt to achieve consistency. Regardless of personality, in other words, attitudes toward foreign policy issues have an inner dynamic of their own and are thus ever capable of change. In Chapter 5 Galtung presents convincing evidence that another aspect of every individual, his social position (or, as Galtung puts it, his place on the underdog-topdog scale), contributes to his posture toward international phenomena. That is to say, personality and needs for consistency notwithstanding, one's place in a society, be it in the citizenry or officialdom, exerts a significant pull on his approach to world politics.

Irrespective of all these factors that underlie the behavior of individuals, Cohen's analysis in Chapter 6 makes it clear that the mass media of communication and those who operate them perform a vital function in the process whereby people acquire information about and attitudes toward the external world. His conclusion that the mass media can only handle one main foreign policy issue at a time also has significant implications for the capacity of officials to mobilize public support for their efforts. In Chapter 7 Miller plainly indicates the existence of a relationship between American voting patterns and foreign policy that is independent of the influence wielded by the mass media. Quite apart from the impact of both these factors are the activities of countless interest groups, which in the next chapter are shown by Milbrath to be among the critical mechanisms for conveying foreign policy attitudes to officialdom. Still another set of factors are identified in Chapter 9, where Greer presents an intriguing argument for considering the expanding and troubled communities of a nation as a major source of foreign policy. In the final two chapters Waltz and Lowi demonstrate that the activities and outlooks of officials are crucial determinants of foreign policy, even as their behavior is conditioned by the nongovernmental sources analyzed in the preceding papers. Waltz focuses mainly on governmental behavior as it is shaped by the anticipation of future elections and the memory of past elections, Lowi's analysis calls attention to the subtle link between the underlying forces at work in a society and the processes through which officials establish governmental machinery for making foreign policy.

Throughout the essays two themes recur. One is a concern with the clash of interests, self, group, or national. Each author in his own way depicts foreign policy behavior as arising out of tensions between the interests of individuals or small groups and the interests of larger aggregates such as parties, communities, and societies. In some instances the tension is posited as unavoidable and in others as reducible, but all of the essays focus on the problem of identifying both the interests of actors and the conflicts generated by them. In so doing, most of the essays touch

upon a second main theme, namely, the role of the leaders who speak for the larger aggregates. These are variously conceived as perpetuators and reconcilers of the clash of interests, but whatever the results of leadership, its influence is deemed to be considerable throughout. In effect, one of the main sources of officialdom's behavior is seen as the feedback of societal responses to its previous behavior.

In sum, the essays collected together here assert that the external behavior of a society stems from an extraordinary complex of sources, each source contributing something to the behavior and no one in itself sufficient to determine it. But the fact that behavior stems from a multiplicity of sources does not mean that it is mysterious and unfathomable. The cumulative experience of reading these essays ought to provide a clearer conception of the dynamics of foreign policy and of the close interrelationship of the many factors that enter into its creation. The essays may not answer the question of how the various sources interrelate under particular circumstances, but they do provide the wherewithal for clarifying and deepening one's comprehension of how the process of interrelation works.

FOREIGN POLICY AS AN ISSUE-AREA

James N. Rosenau

THE concept of an issue plays an inconsistent and deleterious role in political analysis. On the one hand, many analysts ignore it and presume that the political process unfolds similarly with respect to any issue. On the other hand, numerous analysts accord such a prominent place to the concept that the political process is assumed to be as infinitely variable as the issues that sustain it.

"You cannot make such a statement," the latter say to the former, "it all depends on the issue."

"Sure we can," respond the former, "political systems have general characteristics that are operative irrespective of the issue being processed at any moment in time."

It is a major contention of this paper that both approaches are insufficient but that an empirically accurate and theoretically viable approach lies between them. Stated succinctly, the approach suggested here rests on the premise that it all depends on the issue-area.

1

Before examining the issue-area concept, however, it is useful to look briefly at the ways in which the two prevailing approaches hold back political inquiry. Perhaps the greatest damage is done by those who emphasize the infinite variability of issues and their effects. The notion that the outcome of an interaction sequence is dependent on the issue that precipitated it rests on the premise that each issue either encompasses different actors whose motives vary in intensity and direction or evokes different motives on the part of the same actors. Regardless of the identity of the actors, therefore, the interaction patterns that unfold with respect to each issue are presumed to be too distinctive to permit generalizing about the operation of political systems.

Such reasoning thus serves as one of the great bulwarks against inquiry. It provides a simple and effective means of cutting off any discussion of the political process. By observing that "it all depends on the issue," one can quickly halt any effort at generalization. The strength of a political party becomes unassessable because on some issues the party is unified and on others it is fragmented. The stability of an international relationship becomes incalculable because the parties to it agree on some issues and differ on others. The influence of a leader becomes inestimable because the public is responsive on some issues and not responsive on others. The effectiveness of an interest group becomes unmeasurable because on some issues it commands respect and on others it does not. Indeed, there is hardly a political phenomenon that has not been assumed to be so subject to issue fluctuation as to render futile any attempts to trace general patterns.

Perhaps in reaction to the paralyzing implications of this approach, general theorists have tended either to ignore the relevance of issue fluctuation or to assume that its impact on the political process is not sufficient to warrant theoretical attention. Models of the legislative process depict structures and functions, but these are usually posited as unvarying in the way in which they handle different types of issues. Formulations of the processes by which equilibrium is maintained in party, national, and international systems do not conceive of various equilibria constantly replacing each other as the focus of systemic activity moves from one type of issue to another. Most models of executive and bureaucratic decision-making also tend to presume an underlying uniformity and to delineate a process that is undifferentiated by the matters that are the subject of decision. Similarly, those who focus on the linkage between public opinion and foreign policy tend to ignore the differential impact of issues. Virtually every model presently available posits foreign policy as a constant, as a set of values and activities that are taken for granted and assumed to be unvarying in the motives,

interests, and processes they activate. Indeed, there is hardly a major type of political process which has not been denuded of issue fluctuation by the theory-builders.

To be sure, theorists allow for variability in the functioning of political systems. Considerable attention is devoted to both the potentialities for and the processes of change in the operation of legislatures, party systems, international organizations, bureaucracies, and all the other units that serve as theoretical foci. But the variability and the change always seem to be attributed to structural or capability components of systems and not to their functional or dynamic elements. Variability is seen to exist in the functioning of legislatures when, say, the size of the majority alters, but it is not also seen when the focus of activity shifts from one type of consideration to another. Variability in the operation of international systems is conceived to exist when the capabilities of one or another bloc increase or diminish, but variation is not also ascribed to changes in the matters that occupy the attention of diplomats.

Whatever the reason for this neglect of issue fluctuation—and many possible sources could be cited[1]—it clearly seems to be unwarranted. There is abundant evidence that motives, actors, and interaction sequences do not remain constant for all issues and that therefore the functioning of political systems can be differentiated in terms of the values that are being contested. Election campaigns in open systems are a good case in point. Most candidates or parties scour the contemporary scene in search of the one or two issues that will appeal to the electorate and bring about victory at the polls. Presumably such behavior is based on the premise that voters distinguish between issues, that they are aroused by some and bored by others, and that consequently the task of a campaign is to identify the combination of issues which is most likely to activate support.

Nor does one have to look far to find empirical support for the politician's wisdom. For years his presumption that success depends on the achievement of consonance with the changing concerns of the electorate has been amply demonstrated by nationwide poll data showing variations in attitudinal structure and intensity from one issue to another.[2]

1. One important source is the conception that a major function of political systems is that of aggregating issues, of canceling out conflicts between issues so that systems can endure without being dominated by a single issue or a single cluster of issues. In this sense, political systems are treated as being, so to speak, above issues. They are viewed as impartial arbiters of the many conflicts which are outstanding at any moment in time and which might bring about chaos if the system did not exercise supervision. In fact, of course, many political systems are single-issue dominant and they can collapse when the dominant issue is either resolved or otherwise removed. The loss of integrative potential suffered by many newly established Asian and African systems is an obvious example: when independence has removed the anticolonial issue, fragmentation has often followed.

2. V. O. Key, Jr., *Public Opinion and American Democracy* (New York: Alfred A. Knopf, 1961), Chap. 9.

Equally clear-cut are the interview data that describe the large degree to which people, in face-to-face situations, are influenced by different opinion leaders on different issues.[3]

But issue fluctuation is not confined to the intellectual-emotional processes of the individual and the resulting patterns of mass opinion. Systematic analyses of the functioning of all types of political systems — from local to national to international on the geographic scale and from party to legislative to executive at the functional level — are also converging on the finding that different types of issues elicit different sets of motives on the part of different actors in a political system, that different system members are thus activated by different issues, and that the different interaction patterns that result from these variations produce different degrees of systemic stability for each type of issue. Perhaps the most impressive data along these lines are to be found in Dahl's inquiry into the politics of New Haven.[4] Using varied and elaborate survey techniques, Dahl examined the processes of governmental and nongovernmental leadership activated by three types of issues, "urban redevelopment," "education," and "nominations." His finding is stunning: the "overlap among leaders and subleaders" on the three issues involved only 3 per cent of his sample and only half of these were leaders with respect to all three issues.[5] In effect, there are at least three New Haven political systems, and to know how the political process functions in any one of these is not necessarily to know about its operation in the others.[6]

Similar findings on legislative and national systems are reported by Miller and Stokes, who employed survey data to correlate the attitudes of congressmen, the attitudes of their constituencies, and the congressmen's perceptions of their constituencies' attitudes with respect to three major types of issues, "social welfare," "foreign involvement," and "civil rights."[7] Again the results compel reflection: the differences between the operation of the processes of representation in civil rights on the one hand, and social welfare and foreign involvement on the other, proved to be highly significant statistically, constituting "one of the most striking findings of this analysis."[8] Given such variability at the center

3. Elihu Katz and Paul F. Lazarsfeld, *Personal Influence: The Part Played by People in the Flow of Communications* (New York: The Free Press, 1955).

4. Robert A. Dahl, *Who Governs: Democracy and Power in an American City* (New Haven: Yale University Press, 1961).

5. *Ibid.*, p. 175.

6. For much additional evidence that "the pattern of decision-making" varies from issue to issue in local systems, see Nelson W. Polsby, *Community Power and Political Theory* (New Haven: Yale University Press, 1963), pp. 113–14, 124–28.

7. Warren E. Miller and Donald E. Stokes, "Constituency Influence in Congress," *American Political Science Review*, Vol. LVII (March, 1963), pp. 45–56.

8. *Ibid.*, p. 53. For another, equally impressive set of data describing issue fluctuation

of the political process, again it seems reasonable to assert that there are at least two American national systems and that to comprehend one is not necessarily to understand the other.

Comparable findings for international systems are provided by Hovet's inquiries into the patterns of bloc voting in the United Nations. Leaving aside the Soviet bloc, the degree of coherence within the other nine blocs examined was found to vary substantially when broken down in terms of some seven types of recurrent issues in the General Assembly.[9] Accordingly, it does not seem unwarranted to observe that, insofar as the functioning of international organizations are concerned, there are several international systems and that to comprehend the processes of any one of them is not necessarily to grasp how the others function.

2

But there is no need to pile example upon example. The point is that the functioning of political systems does depend on the nature of issues and that therein lies an important conceptual challenge: how to accommodate issue-generated differences without permitting their multitude to overwhelm analysis and reduce it to a fragmented and idiographic enterprise. The response is as obvious as it is difficult to implement. What is needed is a typology of issue-areas — of categories of issues that affect the political process in sufficiently similar ways to justify being clustered together. If the entire range of issues that are processed by political systems could be classified into a manageable number of mutually exclusive areas, with each area distinguished by the political dynamics it generates, then it should be possible to probe the political process without being paralyzed by idiographic description.

The construction of such an issue-area typology, however, is not a simple task. An imposing set of theoretical and operational problems must be overcome: On what bases are the many values and interests over which men differ to be clustered together into distinctive issue-areas? At what level of abstraction should they be clustered? Are the boundaries of each area to be defined in terms of the nature of the issues they encompass, the nature of the processes through which the issues are resolved, or the kinds of units in which they are activated? How many areas would be both empirically manageable and theoretically viable?

in the U.S. Congress, see H. Douglas Price, "Are Southern Democrats Different? An Application of Scale Analysis to Senate Voting Patterns," in Nelson W. Polsby, Robert A. Dentler, and Paul A. Smith (eds.), *Politics and Social Life: An Introduction to Political Behavior* (Boston: Houghton, Mifflin Company, 1963), esp. pp. 751–56.

9. Thomas Hovet, Jr., *Bloc Politics in the United Nations* (Cambridge: Harvard University Press, 1960), *passim.*

How similar must issues be to justify treating them as falling within the same area? What aspects of the political process are affected by the nature of issues and how do these issue-generated differences vary from one area to another?

While a full response to these questions cannot be undertaken here, some general guidelines can be noted. Plainly, a typology of issue-areas ought to be something more than a mere catalogue of the matters over which men are divided at any moment in time. As has already been implied, not much would be accomplished if "issue-area" came to mean nothing more than that which is conventionally designated as an "issue," namely, any conflict over values or interests among identifiable individuals or groups. Rather, a typology of issue-areas must be cast in sufficiently abstract terms to encompass past and future conflicts as well as present ones. To posit issue-areas as persisting beyond the lives of particular actors, it is necessary to conceive of them as structures of roles that derive their patterned relationship to each other from the nature of the values or interests they encompass. That is, each issue-area must be seen as comprised of certain kinds of actors whose values and interests are such that they can be expected to engage in certain kinds of behavior when issues are activated in the area. If, for example, a civil rights area were included in the typology, its structure would include minority group leaders, journalists and other civic leaders in ethnically heterogeneous urban communities, law-enforcement officers, certain governmental officials, and a variety of others likely to be sympathetic or opposed to civil rights.

It follows that several aspects of the political process can be traced to the nature of issues. The intensity and extensity of the motivation that leads citizens and officials to participate in a controversy seems to be clearly a function of the values and interests that are being controverted. Similarly, the number and identity of the roles, both in and out of government, that are politically active at any moment in time are manifestly a consequence of the nature of the issues that the system is processing at that moment. In addition to motivational intensity and role activation, and partly as a consequence of these variables, the direction and degree of the interaction through which issues are processed would also appear to be shaped by the values and interests at stake.

General guidelines are much more difficult to establish with respect to the questions of how the boundaries of issue-areas should be delineated and of how issues should be classified within them. Both the possibilities and the difficulties can be indicated through a brief examination of some of the crude categories that are generally used, often unknowingly, to denote broad classes of issues. Three kinds of issue-area typologies frequently seem to be embedded in discussions of the political process.

One might be called a *value* typology, wherein issues are clustered together on the basis of the kinds of values or interests over which controversy ensues. The widespread tendency to distinguish among, say, agriculture, labor, education, and finance issues exemplifies the employment of a value typology. Such typologies rest on the assumption that significantly different goals underlie the major activities comprising the life of a community, and thus value typologies consist of as many issue-areas as seem appropriate to account for the diverse pursuits of the community. In a second kind of typology, issues are clustered together on the basis of the kinds of processes through which they are conducted and settled. This can be designated a *process* typology and it is illustrated by the inclination to differentiate between, say, legal and administrative issues or crisis and routine issues. Underlying the use of process typologies is the premise that issues which are resolved in the same way also tap similar motives and activate similar roles. The third technique of classifying issues is what we shall label the *unit* typology. In this widely used approach, issues are clustered together on the basis of the kinds of units in or for which they are contested. The local-national and domestic-foreign dichotomizations of issues are illustrative of unit typologies and of the premise that issues processed in one (local-national) or for one (domestic-foreign) type of unit evoke significantly different motives and roles than do those processed in or for other kinds of units.

That such typologies pose complex problems for those who would use them can be readily discerned in the few systematic efforts to employ the issue-area concept as an analytic tool. Perhaps most revealing in this regard is Dahl's aforementioned inquiry. Although not intended as an elaboration of the concept, this work is illustrative of a value typology. His three issue-areas represent different aspects of life in New Haven and each consists of more than a single issue in the sense that his investigations in each area focused on more than a single conflict of values and the interaction sequence through which it was processed and resolved. In all, thirty-four major interaction sequences (or, as Dahl calls them, "decisions") that spanned different segments of an eighteen-year period were examined, and eight of these were considered to be, on the one hand, distinct from the other twenty-four and, on the other hand, sufficiently alike to cluster together into the "urban redevelopment" area. A similar process led to the clustering of another eight into the "education" area and the remaining eighteen into the "nominations" area.

While the derivation of the last of these areas presents no serious difficulty — since the motives, roles, and processes involved in contesting a mayoralty nomination arise out of clear and long established sources that presumably were operative in all eighteen of the issues classified

in the area—the first two are not so narrowly bounded and, in their greater diversity, pose troublesome conceptual and empirical problems. Consider first the eight major decisional sequences that Dahl identifies as falling within the redevelopment area:

1. Creating the Redevelopment Agency.
2. Building and extending the Oak Street Connector.
3. Redeveloping the Oak Street area.
4. Creating the Citizens Action Commission.
5. Redeveloping the Church Street area.
6. Redeveloping the Wooster Square area.
7. The Long Wharf project.
8. Negotiations between Savitt, a jeweler, and the city over the proper price for his property.[10]

Some of these issues, to be sure, are as much alike as any two mayorality nominations are to each other. Presumably, for example, the goals, roles, and interaction patterns involved in the third, fifth, and sixth issues are virtually identical, differing only to the extent that the configuration and residents of Oak Street, Church Street, and Wooster Square differed. Likewise, it is not difficult to presume similarity between the sequences whereby the Redevelopment Agency and the Citizens Action Commission came into being. On the other hand, assumptions become more tenuous and data more elusive when, say, the clustering together of the first and last of the issues is considered. The immediate values at stake in the creation of the Redevelopment Agency and the acquisition of Savitt's property were obviously disparate. Due to the legal measures that Savitt took in order to get a higher price for his property, some of the roles and interaction patterns activated by the two issues were no less disparate. Clearly, therefore, Dahl was compelled to presume that the more general goals of a modernized New Haven gave sufficient commonality to these seemingly diverse interaction sequences to justify clustering them together. Upon investigation, some support for this presumption was found. Creation of the Redevelopment Agency initiated a shorter and much less complex interaction sequence than did the acquisition of Savitt's property, but many of the same leadership roles participated in essentially the same ways in both situations. Nonetheless, to classify these two issues in the same area is plainly to make a delicate set of assumptions for which the empirical evidence is not abundant.

Much the same can be said about the eight major "decisions on public schools" which Dahl grouped into the "education" area:

10. Dahl, *op. cit.*, p. 333.

1. Selling the high schools to Yale and building two new ones.
2. Accepting or rejecting a proposal to change procedures on promotions.
3. Major appointments, particularly an assistant superintendent for secondary education.
4. An eye-testing program.
5. A proposed ratio plan on salaries.
6. Budgets.
7. A proposal to deal with delinquency.
8. Proposals to increase appropriations for school libraries.[11]

Again it seems clear that several of the issues are highly comparable but that in a couple of instances the clustering would appear to rest more on analytic presumptions than on empirical data. In drawing boundaries around such seemingly diverse considerations as, say, how to test the sight of pupils, whom to appoint as an assistant superintendent, and whether to accept the new ratio plan on salaries, Dahl again had to rely on the unverified premise that at a higher level of generalization—namely, the one delineated by the goal of perfecting the educational system of New Haven—the motives, roles, and interaction patterns involved in these issues converged sufficiently to warrant classifying them in the same area.[12]

If Dahl's inquiry suggests some of the problems inherent in the construction of issue-area typologies, the work of Theodore J. Lowi provides an exciting glimpse into their potential utility.[13] Where Dahl lacks explicitness about the motives, roles, and interaction sequences common to the issues in each area, Lowi's typology is exceedingly self-conscious in this respect. Its main focus is the national system of the United States, but it is at the same time a process typology that contains an explicit rationale for attributing similar underpinnings to seemingly different issues. Indeed, Lowi explicitly asserts that each area (his term is "arena") of the typology "tends to develop its own characteristic political structure, political process, elites, and group relations."[14]

11. *Ibid.*
12. It should be re-emphasized that in raising these questions about the clustering of issues within the same area we are not doubting the distinctions among the areas. As has already been indicated, ample evidence confirming existence of boundaries separating the areas was uncovered by Dahl when he found a startling lack of overlap between the leadership roles activated in each area.
13. The most thoroughgoing formulation of his typology, along with the promise of subsequent elaboration at book length, is presented in "American Business, Public Policy, Case-Studies, and Political Theory," *World Politics*, Vol. XVI (July, 1964), pp. 677–715. For an earlier, more restricted, and less developed version of the typology, as well as some supporting empirical data, see Theodore J. Lowi, *At the Pleasure of the Mayor* (New York: The Free Press, 1964), Chaps. 6 and 7.
14. "American Business, Public Policy, Case-Studies, and Political Theory," pp. 689–90.

Instead of subdividing the community in terms of the many activities that sustain it, Lowi starts from the premise that in politics governmental policies determine the conflicting expectations of people and that political issues therefore arise out of "the impact or expected impact on the society" of governmental policies.[15] This approach enables him to construct his typology at a more general level than Dahl's and to classify all domestic issues within three areas. One encompasses issues that arise around the *distribution* of resources; another embraces conflicts over the *regulation* of the use of resources; and the third subsumes disputes over the *redistribution* of resources. For reasons that are too complex to elaborate here, Lowi's derivations allow him to equate the interaction sequences in each of the three areas with, respectively, the coalition, pluralist, and elitist models of the political process. Indeed, so convincing is the logic of his scheme that it seems entirely justifiable for him to delineate each area in terms of the "primary political unit," the "relation among units," the "power structure," the "stability of structure," the "primary decisional locus," and the process of "implementation" that it encompasses.[16]

What Lowi's formulation lacks is the kind of quantified data that Dahl gathered as a basis for discerning the presence of different political structures within each issue-area. At best, Lowi shows how the findings of another recent study[17] take on added meaning when reinterpreted in the light of his scheme. But this weakness may be short-lived. Lowi makes a persuasive case for expecting that the findings of empirical inquiry will uphold his distinctions among the three areas. Clearly a major breakthrough in political theory will have occurred if, as seems likely, it proves possible to accommodate issue-generated differences at this level of analysis.[18]

3

For present purposes, Lowi's typology is more a source of encouragement than an instrument of analysis. It suggests that theorizing about

15. *Ibid.*, p. 689.

16. See his "diagrammatic summary," *ibid.*, p. 713.

17. Raymond A. Bauer, Ithiel de Sola Pool, and Lewis A. Dexter, *American Business and Public Policy: The Politics of Foreign Trade* (New York: Atherton Press, 1963), a review of which served as the immediate occasion for Lowi's article.

18. For three other efforts to cope with issue-generated phenomena, see the even more abstract typologies in Herbert J. Spiro, "Comparative Politics: A Comprehensive Approach," *American Political Science Review*, Vol. LVI (September, 1962), pp. 577–95; Ernest A. T. Barth and Stuart D. Johnson, "Community Power and a Typology of Social Issues," *Social Forces*, Vol. 38 (Oct., 1959), pp. 29–32; and James N. Rosenau, "Pre-Theories and Theories of Foreign Policy," in R. Barry Farrell (ed.), *Approaches to Comparative and International Politics* (Evanston: Northwestern University Press, 1966), pp. 71–92.

issue-areas is likely to pay off, but it offers no help with respect to the main concern of this chapter. Here we want to assess the validity and utility of one particular unit typology, namely, the one in which domestic policy issues are presumed to be different from foreign policy issues. The latter are not included in Lowi's scheme. He regards them as "not part of the same universe" and puts them aside as "obviously a fourth category" of issues in addition to the three domestic types.[19] Hence we must make a fresh start in our effort to determine whether foreign policy is indeed a different universe of issues and, if it is, whether it is a unified world or one divisible into several logical areas.

The task is not an easy one. Perhaps because the question straddles the fields of national and international politics,[20] it has not been systematically explored and discussion of it consists largely of either unrefined impressions or gross contradictions. Numerous observers compare, briefly and on the basis of unstated assumptions, the foreign and domestic realms in the course of launching an analysis of world affairs. Gunnar Myrdal, for example, recently noted: "After two decades of continuous study, I have come to the conclusion that foreign-policy decisions are usually less well-founded on the available facts and alternatives than domestic-policy decisions; that they are, in general, much more influenced by irrational motives."[21] Why this should be the case is, typically, not elaborated. One can readily think of circumstances that seem to contradict Myrdal's impression. Indeed, in the absence of systematic efforts to delineate how the foreign and domestic areas might differ, contradictory assertions abound. Even as issues of foreign and domestic policy are assumed to be distinct from one another, so is there also a tendency to stress that in a shrinking world, foreign and domestic matters have become inextricably linked and that only for analytic purposes can distinctions between them be drawn. Stated more concretely, not only do political scientists presume that the processes of making foreign policy are sufficiently unlike those of domestic policy to justify writing special texts and giving special courses, they are also inclined to call the attention of their students to the wisdom of the practitioner who observed that "if ever the line between domestic and foreign affairs could be drawn, it is now wholly erased."[22]

19. Lowi *op. cit.*, p. 689. In the light of the analysis that follows here, it is noteworthy that Lowi accompanies the isolation of this fourth category with the confounding observation that, "Of course, those aspects of foreign and military policy that have direct domestic implications are included in my scheme."

20. For a discussion of how and why questions straddling the two fields have been ignored, see Rosenau, *op. cit.*, pp. 27–71.

21. Gunnar Myrdal, "With What Little Wisdom the World is Ruled," *The New York Times Magazine*, July 18, 1965, p. 20.

22. Senator J. W. Fulbright, "What Makes United States Foreign Policy?" *The Reporter*, Vol. 20 (May 14, 1959), p. 19.

More importantly, regardless of whether the distinctions between the two areas are concrete or analytic, they are seldom identified, and even more rarely are their sources specified. One is hard pressed to find even a mere listing of the differences between the motives, roles, and interaction sequences that foreign and domestic issues are, respectively, likely to activate. There is no consideration of the possibility that certain kinds of foreign and domestic issues may precipitate political processes more akin to each other than to the other foreign and domestic questions with which they are usually clustered. In short, foreign policy issues may or may not constitute an area with clear-cut boundaries and distinguishable characteristics, but, whichever the case, the reasons therefor have yet to be expounded.

What follows is thus an initial effort to consider the foreign-domestic distinction in a detailed and organized fashion. Our observations are no less impressionistic than those of others. In the absence of empirical inquiries designed to contrast foreign and domestic issues, we have been forced to rely on speculation rather than data. Throughout, our assertions about the motives and behavior of individuals, groups, and governments must thus be viewed as hypotheses rather than findings. We did not start with any preconceptions as to whether foreign and domestic issues are different or similar, but the fact that we reached conclusions on the question should not be interpreted as meaning that we tested it. Our analysis, in other words, is distinguished not by its validity, but by its effort to be systematic. While no special claim is made for the accuracy of our hypotheses, we would contend that by systematizing thought on the foreign-domestic distinction we have taken a necessary first step toward empirical investigation of it.[23]

Let us specify the scope of our concern more precisely. By "foreign policy as an issue-area" we mean all the controversies within a society that, at any moment in time, are being waged over the way in which the society is attempting to maintain or alter its external environment. The attempts to exercise control over the environment constitute "foreign policy," whereas the controversies engendered by the attempts (or lack of them) comprise the "issue-area." Once an attempt is no longer controversial, either because it comes to be accepted or because changes in the external environment allow it to be modified or abandoned, then the issue-area is diminished accordingly. Contrariwise, new issues are considered to enter the area whenever developments in the environment occasion controversy within the society over how it should react. Foreign policies are regarded as issues within the area only if the controversy over them persists and extends to major segments of the society's

---

23. Indeed, quantitative data designed to test some of the main hypotheses developed here have already been gathered and are presently being analyzed.

governmental organization or to segments of its public. A brief argument over how to respond to an environmental event between, say, a prime minister and his foreign minister would not be treated as an issue in the foreign policy area. Such a sequence is part of the routinized procedures whereby all societies conduct the day-to-day aspects of their foreign relations. On the other hand, a prolonged disagreement over a proposed military strategy between, say, a foreign office and a defense establishment involves major elements of the government and would thus be considered a foreign policy issue.

In other words, our focus is on national political systems and not on international systems. We are interested in the processes through which national systems undertake to cope with their external environment and not in the processes which transpire in the environment.[24] Within this framework, we wish to consider whether the controversies over what courses of action to pursue abroad involve different motives (on the part of both citizens and officials), roles (within both the public and the government), and interaction sequences (both within the government and between it and the public) than do those controversies that are occasioned by the question of what courses ought to be pursued at home. Even more specifically, we are interested in analyzing whether foreign or domestic issues differ in the degree of involvement they arouse (motivational intensity), whether the two areas can be differentiated in terms of the number of high-arousal issues they contain (motivational extensity), whether the ranks of the citizens and officials activated by each type of issue are likely to differ in size (role number) and in social and occupational character (role identity), and whether the areas vary in the extent to which those activated must confront each other (degrees of interaction) in either equal or superior-subordinate situations (direction of interaction). Stated diagrammatically, if the cells of Table 1 represent the scope of our concern, to what extent do foreign policy issues call for different entries in the cells than do domestic policy issues?

Table 1 — The Components of an Issue-Area

	MOTIVES		ROLES		INTERACTION SEQUENCES	
	Intensity	Extensity	Number	Identity	Direction	Degree
Private citizens and groups						
Government officials and organizations						

24. Throughout, our discussion will employ examples drawn mainly from American experience, but this is only because of greater familiarity with the United States policy-making process. Presumably many of the conclusions can be applied to any national system.

4

Let us begin our analysis by making two simplifying assumptions: that the political processes of the foreign and domestic areas operate independently, and that in each area all the issues are processed in the same manner. Later we shall have occasion to relax these assumptions, and to emphasize the existence of a third area that lies between the foreign and domestic areas and that embraces issues which are a composite of the foreign and domestic policy processes. In order to trace and clarify the boundaries separating the three areas, however, it is useful to proceed at the outset as if there were only two.

Motivational Differences[25]

It does not require much thought to discern at least one major distinction between the motives aroused by foreign policy issues and those that are operative with respect to domestic affairs. For the citizenry, the former area is likely to generate motivation that is less complex and ambivalent, and therefore more clear-cut and intense, than is the domestic area. Foreign policy deals with events and circumstances outside the system and, being in the environment, these events and circumstances can appear potentially threatening to the members of the system. Whatever the differences among the members, they would seem minimal compared to the distinctions that set them all apart from the members of the other systems that comprise the environment. Fellow system members thus come to be viewed as a "we" who are constantly endangered by a "them." Hence, proposals designed to ward off and manage "them" tap motives that are relatively unfettered by cross-cutting interests and therefore remain undiluted in intensity.

Domestic issues, on the other hand, cast members of the system in opposition to each other and their common system membership is, except under revolutionary conditions, usually irrelevant as a motivational source. Instead, individuals bring a multiplicity of affiliations and loyalties to domestic issues. Goals thus become confounded by cross-cutting interests, and the maintenance of a clear-cut priority of values with respect to one's fellow citizens becomes a delicate and complicated task. Things are never so clear-cut as they are with respect to non-citizens. Motives offset each other; perhaps they even cancel each other out; and presumably the resulting complexity curbs the intensity of the feeling that is invested in domestic controversies.

25. So as to avoid undue complexity, no effort has been made here to draw sharp distinctions among the various stages in the mental-emotional process whereby actors initiate behavior and react to stimuli. For our purposes it is sufficient to subsume such psychological dimensions of behavior as intentions, drives, habits, attitudes, and perceptions under the general heading of "motives" and to use these terms more or less interchangeably.

Treason and war suggest the extent to which the simplicity and intensity of motives differ in the foreign and domestic areas. In the sense that they involve a system's relations with its environment, both phenomena can be classified as foreign policy issues. Historically both treason and war have aroused the members of national systems to heights of involvement that are rarely, if ever, matched in the domestic area.[26] Indeed, treason, the act of enriching the environment at the expense of the system, evokes such intense motives that the framers of the American Constitution went to much greater lengths in protecting the rights of those accused of it than they did in the case of any other situation they envisoned as controversial.[27]

The simpler and more solidary motives that sustain foreign policy issues are also illustrated by the large degree to which the concept of "bipartisanship" is reserved for such issues in most national systems. Even if the norm is expressed more through lip service than actual practice, its prevalence signifies a recognition of the distinctive quality of foreign policy issues. Certainly its emphasis on the thought that dealing with "them" requires greater solidarity and less ambiguity than dealing with "ourselves" is consistent with the foregoing interpretation.

Still another example along these lines is provided by the leaders in underdeveloped countries who often seem to be better able to overcome domestic strife and inertia by citing the hostility of the external environment than by stressing the need for hard work and patience at home. In effect, they attempt to solve domestic issues by redefining them as falling in the foreign policy area.[28]

Intensity, however, is not the only motivational dimension along which foreign and domestic issues seem to be differentiated. An important distinction obtains with respect to their extensity. Paradoxically, while the foreign policy area may tap simpler and more intense motives,

26. At first glance this assertion might seem dubious on the grounds that intense nationwide involvement frequently focuses on kidnappings, lost children, and other forms of tragedy. Upon reflection, however, such events seem irrelevant to the comparison. Without denying that crime and catastrophe arouse high degrees of involvement, particular instances of tragedy do not ordinarily become public issues. They are not normally the focus of subsequent controversy and thus it seems inappropriate to classify them within the domestic policy issue-area. Here we are concerned with motivation and behavior toward public issues and not toward all the events that come to the attention of the public. To be sure, the prevalence of crime can become a public issue, but there is no evidence that as a generalized concern it evokes the intense and sustained feelings that accompany war and treason.

27. In the case of treason the Constitution states (Art. III, Sec. III) that there must be two eye-witnesses to "the same overt act," a criterion of evidence that surely exceeds in its stringency that required for proof of any other offense.

28. This is not so say that the leaders of developed systems are immune to the temptation to rest the case for internal changes on the ground of external necessity. The tendency of many American leaders to cite negative world opinion as a reason to accord civil rights to Negroes is also illustrative of this point.

for the ordinary citizen these do not extend across as wide a range of phenomena as do those operative in the domestic area. Foreign policy deals with remote and obscure matters that, if they are kept under control, seem too distant from the daily needs and wants of most citizens to arouse concern. "There are enough things to worry about in one's immediate surroundings," many say, "without fretting over the arrangements whereby people abroad conduct their lives." For most citizens the external environment is simply an "out there," an undifferentiated mass that can be threatening but rarely is. It is only when rapid changes occur in the environment that this mass acquires structure for most citizens and thereby appears to be linked to their own welfare in potentially damaging ways. As long as the environment persists unaltered and inchoate, or at least as long as the changes in it are slow and localized, few persons are likely to perceive it as having a structure and thus to feel that it might threaten their interests. In short, for most citizens the intense feelings that can be directed toward the external environment usually lie dormant. Usually they are inclined to leave its management to officialdom, an inclination which is not nearly so widespread with respect to those seemingly close-at-hand, highly structured phenomena that constitute domestic affairs.

What we are trying to stress is that one's interests are linked to a variety of interaction sequences that recur among individuals and groups, but that most of these sequences are perceived to unfold within the boundaries of one's own system. Thus, for example, it becomes possible for many Americans to be concerned about racial strife in Mississippi even as they ignore similar strife in South Africa. Events in Jackson are part of their lives, but those in Johannesburg are not. The former become intimate in the sense that they are perceived to unleash a chain of events into which every American may eventually be drawn, whereas the latter remain remote because their repercussions seem far away. For the same reasons, to use a more mundane and thus even more pertinent example, Americans can become concerned about the contents and outcomes of proposals to provide medical assistance to aged Americans even as they remain totally uninvolved in the question of whether the British system of socialized medicine should be extended. The arrangements of the former potentially encompass them, whereas those of the latter do not. It follows that the ordinary citizen has few convictions about how things should be arranged abroad and many about the arrangements at home. The arrangements abroad are the business of others, but those at home are his—unless, of course, those abroad should suddenly shift and appear capable of moving across his doorstep, in which case, to repeat, they are likely to seem especially ominous.

A good measure of the concern about close-at-hand events is provided by the response of a nationwide sample of Americans to the question, "Of all the things you could hope for, what one thing, if you had to choose, do you look forward to most in your life?" As can be seen in the following breakdown, an overwhelming proportion of the reported aspirations are highly specific, material, and immediate, whereas only 5 per cent related themselves to a chain of events ("peace") of which at least some necessarily occurred in the external environment:

Table 2*

Main Goals in Life	Total Public (per cent)
Good health for self and family	23
Get ahead on job, new job	15
Live more comfortably	14
Give children good education (college)	10
Own a house	8
Get a raise	5
Peace in the world, no war	5
Want children near me	5
Want to travel	4
Go back to school	3
Raise children well	2
Retire from work	2
Move to different area	2
Get married and have children	2
	100

*Reported by Louis Harris in *The Daily Home News*, New Brunswick, N.J., December 14, 1964.

It must be emphasized that the perception of oneself as affected by the chains of events within the system and unrelated to those in the environment is not merely the result of the socio-psychological process whereby people develop a sense of community and acquire loyalties to the system. Feelings of nationalism, to be sure, can contribute to the perceived distinction and they may even lead to an exaggeration of its sharpness. It is also true, however, that the distinction has a reality of its own and that perceptions of it are in many respects accurate. One's health, house, and job, along with the health, education, and proximity of one's children, are in fact crucially dependent on what happens in the neighborhood or community. A host of legal, political, economic, and social aspects of a national system do in fact make all its members subject to events that originate within it. The simple fact that all the members of a system are subject to its laws means that whenever events in one part of the system precipitate a legal response, repercussions are bound to be felt elsewhere in the system. On the other hand, such chain

reactions do not follow when events in other systems evoke legal responses. Indeed, in many instances the boundaries of a system are explicitly designed to cut off sequences that start in other systems.

Tariffs and trade barriers constitute an obvious example of the foregoing. They allow people to ignore a steel price rise abroad even though the same people correctly expect to be caught up in the repercussions of a similar event within their own system. Likewise, an American is justified in perceiving himself as a part of the interaction sequences initiated by racial strife in Mississippi and as essentially separate from those in South Africa. The former give rise to new political forces, new legislation, and new judicial interpretations that are bound to affect all Americans, whereas comparable events in South Africa initiate sequences that are largely confined to the politics of that country. Much the same can obviously be said about the Medicare illustration. By definition, Americans residing in the United States are not eligible for benefits under Britain's socialized medicine program and thus they are not likely to experience the political, economic, and social consequences of changes in it. Alterations in the U.S. social security program, however, are eventually felt by all Americans, through either the taxes they pay or the benefits they receive.

There is still another reason why the distinction between the foreign and domestic areas fosters different degrees of political involvement on the part of the citizenry. The very fact that citizens are subject to the laws of their system also entitles them—at least theoretically—to help shape or change its legal arrangements and political balances. On the other hand, events or situations in the environment—that is, in somebody else's system—clearly lie beyond their control and jurisdiction. Consequently, it seems reasonable to presume that most citizens bring to domestic issues a much greater sense of what Almond and Verba call "subjective competence"[29] than they bring to foreign issues. That is, they feel more capable of influencing the outcome of disputes in the former area than in the latter. In turn this difference in subjective competence is likely to lead most citizens to participate more extensively in domestic political processes than in those through which foreign policy is developed. Support for this conclusion is provided by this comment of one observer who had ample opportunity to assess its validity in the American system:

> In domestic affairs, a presidential decision is usually the beginning of public debate. In foreign affairs, the issues are frequently so complex, the facts so obscure, and the period for decision so short, that the American people have

29. Gabriel A. Almond and Sidney Verba, *The Civic Culture: Political Attitudes and Democracy in Five Nations* (Princeton: Princeton University Press, 1963), esp. Chaps. 7–9.

from the beginning—and even more so in this century—delegated to the President more discretion in this vital area and they are usually willing to support any reasonable decision he makes.[30]

Quantitative support for presuming that the two areas differ in this respect is also available through an extension of Almond and Verba's finding that, in all five countries they surveyed, "the sense of subjective competence occurs more frequently vis-à-vis the local government than the national government."[31] Stated more analytically, just as Almond and Verba concluded that "one reason why individuals differ in the frequency with which they adhere to participatory norms is that the structure of government and community organization changes from one nation to another,"[32] so might we say that the citizens of one nation vary in the extent of their adherence to such norms because the structure of policy-making changes from one issue-area to another.[33]

In sum, it is not just parochialism that leads most people to have a greater interest in domestic than in foreign affairs. Good reasons for such a distinction are rooted in the structures of the two areas. But, it might be argued, the independence of national systems can be exaggerated. It is self-deception to see oneself as unrelated to environmental events or incapable of affecting them. Legal barriers do not necessarily contain all the chains of events that are forged in the life of polities, economies, and societies. On the contrary, some legal arrangements either necessitate or facilitate interaction sequences that start in one system and culminate in others. Commercial and financial treaties, for example, enable goods and currency to be exchanged across system boundaries and in so doing they also render a nation's economy vulnerable to economic trends in its environment. Security treaties go even further in this respect. They not only facilitate the linkage of systems to their environments, they also necessitate such arrangements and require the signatories to come to each other's defense in the event of external attack. Surely, for instance, a Russian attack on Turkey would initiate, both legally (through NATO) and politically (through the prevailing structure of world politics), a chain of events that would quickly extend into the lives of many Americans.

Furthermore, the argument might continue, even the legal barriers to international interdependence can be surmounted. There is the

30. Theodore C. Sorenson, *Decision-Making in the White House* (New York: Columbia University Press, 1963), p. 48.

31. *Op. cit.*, pp. 184–85.

32. *Ibid.*, p. 168.

33. Almond and Verba are not unaware of the possibility of extending their conclusions to account for variability within as well as between nations: see *ibid.*, pp. 483–84 (footnote 12).

"demonstration effect" whereby events in one system leap across the boundaries of other systems merely by being perceived and then either emulated or countered. Price rises in one system can affect the economy of another if members of the latter anticipate repercussions and act to offset them. News of race riots in Johannesburg can so impress groups in Jackson as to lead them to act in ways that sustain the causal chain despite the geographic and other barriers. It can even be argued that Medicare programs are subject to the demonstration effect. The vigor and frequency with which the American Medical Association calls attention to the defects of Britain's socialized medicine program is illustrative in this regard.

There is, of course, considerable validity to this argument that the structures of the foreign and domestic areas are not as distinct as they might seem and that more interaction sequences cross national boundaries than most people realize.[34] To assert this argument, however, is to relax our simplifying assumptions prematurely and to move on from the analysis of how citizens are differentially motivated in the two areas. As will be seen, some citizens do, under certain conditions, recognize the interdependence of environmental and system events. Likewise, as noted in the next paragraphs, officialdom is dedicated to an awareness that situations need not be confined to the system in which they originate. Nevertheless, this mode of analysis would not appear to be appreciated by the citizenry in general. Except for those who directly experience the demonstration effect and the other more intricate boundary crossings, recognition of such processes requires a capacity and an inclination to perceive the subtleties of causation that most members of most systems do not seem to possess. The subtleties, moreover, are obscured by the aforementioned reality that many interaction sequences unfold only in the environment and that still others are kept there by the protective barriers with which systems surround themselves.

In short, however extensive the interdependence of systems and their environments, it usually does not become a part of the ordinary citizen's awareness. And, since motives are aroused only by events that seem to impinge on one's interests, activities, or aspirations, there would seem to be no reason to modify the conclusion that foreign and domestic areas evoke different motivational patterns on the part of most people and that, relatively speaking, high intensity-low extensity characterizes the pattern in the former area and low intensity-high extensity distinguishes the pattern in the latter area.

34. For an interesting empirical effort to identify all the ways in which the life of a community is linked to chains of events in the international environment, see Gerard J. Mangone, *Foreign Policy and Onondaga County* (Syracuse: The Maxwell Graduate School of Citizenship and Public Affairs, 1964).

But "most people" are not "all people." Our hypothesis is clearly inappropriate insofar as officialdom is concerned. The notion that motivational intensity and extensity are functions of the real and perceived structure into which daily life fits leads to quite different conclusions when applied to those whom systems endow with responsibility for scrutinizing and managing the interaction sequences that unfold in the environment. From the perspective of policy-makers at the national level, every event in the environment is approached as if it potentially might be linked to the daily life of the system. Be he elected or appointed, the official is required to be sensitive to the possibility that causal chains forged abroad may acquire links at home. His job is to take care of the system's needs and to protect the integrity of its boundaries. His interests, activities, and aspirations all converge on the question of whether the environment is enhancing or endangering the system's welfare. Thus the extensity of his motives toward foreign policy issues is likely to be as high as that which he brings to bear on domestic issues.

This conclusion must be qualified somewhat by the fact that most national systems divide the labor of caring for their internal and external affairs between different segments of officialdom. Specialization among career civil servants is perhaps so narrow that those assigned to cope with issues in the foreign area rarely need to pay attention to domestic considerations, just as the reverse situation obtains for bureaucrats who work in the domestic area. Country desk officers in the Department of State, for example, are not likely to be alert to controversies over collective bargaining in the railroad industry; nor are their counterparts in the Department of Labor who respond to industrial issues likely to be aroused by border disputes in Asia or Africa. Similarly, low motivational extensity would presumably distinguish the professional staffs of congressional committees that process issues pertaining, respectively, to foreign and labor relations.

On the other hand, the political superiors of executive and legislative specialists cannot so easily ignore issues that fall outside their immediate jurisdiction, and thus our general point still holds with respect to top officials who hold elective or appointive posts. Their legal and political responsibilities are too extensive for them not to be sensitive to the whole range of foreign and domestic issues that can suddenly be activated. Indeed, chiefs of state and chief executives are constitutionally required by national systems to be alert to both internal and external needs. Nor is such a broad perspective any less relevant at the next level of officialdom. Although some division of the labor of caring for a system's needs usually prevails at this second level, the specialization is not so great that those with primary tasks in one area can take the management of events in the other area for granted. The specialization does not

diminish their over-all responsibility. The member of Congress who becomes chairman of his chamber's Committee on Labor does not thereby lessen his foreign policy responsibilities. Contrariwise, the Secretary of State cannot proceed to cope with the external environment without being cognizant of the possible domestic consequences of his actions. One can readily think of circumstances in which he must even apprise himself of the labor-management situation at home as he enters into diplomatic negotiations or makes a foreign policy address.

If the extensity of officialdom's motivation toward developments abroad is thus much greater than the citizenry's, quite the opposite would seem to be the case with respect to motivational intensity. Whereas citizens are capable of investing extremely intense feelings into the few foreign policy issues that arouse them, officials are not likely to direct an equivalent intensity toward the many issues in the foreign area that engage their concern. Being aware of the interrelatedness of issues and of the subtle and circuitous routes whereby casual chains forged abroad may acquire links at home, the top official tends to exercise restraint and to avoid positing any single issue as a life-or-death problem. He recognizes that system survival would be jeopardized if he reacted so intensely to an issue that he lost perspective and did not pause to consider how its solution would affect the outcome of other issues. In addition, he knows—or learns soon after entering his official role—that the habits of people are hard to change and that, consequently, issues cannot usually be solved by one dramatic action. He becomes accustomed to partial solutions and slow progress. Unlike citizens, he rarely allows himself the luxury of unqualified involvement in a foreign policy issue. The extreme intensity with which American officials are reported to have participated in the 1962 Cuban missile crisis stands out as an exception in this regard. At least history does not record any other ininstance when an American President gave his aides a special souvenir in gratitude for their help in resolving a single issue that lasted less than two weeks.

In fairness to the reader, it should be noted that this interpretation of the approach of officials to foreign policy questions is in sharp conflict with the widespread view, previously implied in the quoted observation of Myrdal, that greater "irrationality" is operative in foreign affairs than in domestic. One observer, for example, recently claimed that "In all countries foreign affairs are likely to become the object of more emotionalism and irrationality than domestic questions,"[35] while another confined his assertion of this thesis to the United States:

35. Grayson Kirk, "World Perspectives, 1964," *Foreign Affairs*, Vol. 43 (October, 1964), p. 1.

If, then, we recognize that in regard to foreign policy the Johnson admistration is under far less popular constraint than in regard to domestic policy, and if we also bear in mind that our constitutional system allows the President very large powers in conducting external affairs, we must conclude somewhat unhappily that on problems like Vietnam and the Dominican Republic Johnson has a relatively free hand. Confronting a Medicare bill he must calculate and measure; considering a proposal to send marines to Latin America he can act upon what he takes to be the national interest, or what at the moment comes to little more than his, or his advisers,' panic or pique.[36]

From our perspective, however, such an analysis overlooks the enormous constraints that the international system imposes on officials. While their own systems do permit them much greater leeway in foreign affairs, as we shall also have occasion to emphasize below, this is more than offset by the international constraints. We would contend that the opportunities for them to express "panic or pique" are much more varied and numerous in the domestic than the foreign area.

In positing officials as cautious in their approach to the foreign area, we do not mean to imply that they will be particularly vague or vacillating. On the contrary, clarity of official behavior appears to be one of the distinguishing characteristics of foreign policy issues. The price of being misunderstood in this area is much greater than it is in the domestic area. The former involves issues in which "we" are pitted against "them," and while restraint must be exercised to avoid provoking "them" unnecessarily, it can never be carried to the point where the line between "we" and "them" is confounded. So that the "we" can continue to provide support and the "them" can continue to avoid ruinous miscalculations, the officials must always let each know exactly where he stands—at least he must do so to a much greater extent than is the case on domestic issues.[37] In the latter area, in fact, there are a number of incentives that might lead him to adopt somewhat vague positions. Clearly distinguishing the "good" citizen from the "bad" can weaken the system and hinder the solution of issues, whereas, to repeat, plainly drawing the line between citizens and noncitizens can only facilitate the work of officialdom. Hence the view that in underdeveloped countries "leaders are encouraged to adopt more clearly defined positions on international issues than on domestic issues"[38] would seem to be applicable to any system.

36. Irving Howe, "I'd Rather Be Wrong," *The New York Review of Books*, IV (June 17, 1965), p. 3.
37. For an elaboration of the difficulties that confront officials who try to maintain the support of both foreign and domestic publics, see the discussion of the "dual politician" in my *Calculated Control as a Unifying Concept in the Study of International Politics and Foreign Policy* (Princeton: Center of International Studies, Research Monograph No. 15, 1963), pp. 17–18.
38. Lucian W. Pye, *Politics, Personality, and Nation Building: Burma's Search for Identity* (New Haven: Yale University Press, 1962), p. 28.

It follows from the preceding analysis that the foreign policy area is marked by a motivational gap between the citizen and the policy-maker that is not nearly so pronounced in the domestic area. Domestic issues arouse the public and the government alike, but only rarely is the public activated by questions of foreign policy. The implications of this gap are manifold. It means that on most foreign policy issues officials are likely to be far ahead of citizens in terms of their perception, comprehension, and concern. No less importantly, the motivational gap normally has the consequence of freeing officialdom from the restraints that the citizenry imposes in the domestic area. At the same time, to anticipate our discussion of the interaction differences between the two areas, the gap also means that in the foreign policy area officials are confronted with a herculean consensus-building task whenever they need domestic support for their endeavors abroad. The task is no less than that of demonstrating for an uninterested public how it is linked to the events in the environment. A succinct portrayal of the breadth of the motivational gap and the enormity of the task required to bridge it is provided by the contrast between the reactions of Algerian officials and citizens to the 1964 Belgian-American expedition to rescue white missionaries held captive by Congolese rebels in Stanleyville. That those responsible for managing the environment tend to perceive the system's boundaries as vulnerable to processes initiated abroad is plainly evident in the comment of Ben Bella, then the Algerian President: "If the Congo falls [as a result of the rescue expedition], it will be next the turn of Brazzaville, then Burundi, Tanzania, Uganda, Cairo and why not Algeria? We have lost Stanleyville but Africa remains." That citizens regard the environment as remote and causality as rooted within the system is equally clear in the reaction of a middle-aged hotel employee: "I don't want to be an Arab, a Berber, an African or anything else. I just want to be an Algerian." Similarly, after listening to Mr. Ben Bella's speech, a housewife said: "Why doesn't he talk about our problems here at home. My brother can't find work and the cost of living keeps going up."[39]

There is one respect, however, in which citizen and official orientations toward the two areas are quite similar. Like the citizenry, officialdom can be expected to have a greater sense of subjective competence toward domestic affairs than they do toward foreign policy issues. Although their freedom of action is not nearly so limited by the demands and restraints which the citizenry imposes in the domestic area, officials are nevertheless likely to feel especially constricted in their ability to cope

39. *New York Times*, December 6, 1964. For an inquiry into the elaborate efforts needed to bridge this motivational gap in the foreign policy area, see James N. Rosenau, *National Leadership and Foreign Policy: A Case Study in the Mobilization of Public Support* (Princeton: Princeton University Press, 1963).

effectively with foreign policy issues. For success in this area is crucially dependent on persons and groups who belong to other national systems and whose actions are guided by other goals, rules, and precedents. In attempting to resolve domestic issues officials can at least rely on those affected by their actions to respond in terms of the rules of the game whereby the system is organized. They can at least count on compliance with decisions that have emerged from the policy-making process.[40] In dealing with foreign policy issues, on the other hand, officialdom cannot take such factors for granted. Many of the participants play a different game and often respond half-heartedly or defiantly to the products of the policy-making process. In other words, mobilizing domestic support for foreign policy proposals may be a huge task, but it is simple in comparison to mobilizing the foreign support necessary to implement such proposals. Thus, like the citizenry, and for similar reasons, officialdom is also bound to feel more frustrated and less competent toward issues in the foreign area than they do toward those in the domestic area. This distinction is poignantly illustrated in the following response of John F. Kennedy to a reporter who asked, "As you look back upon your first two years in office, sir, has your experience in the office matched your expectations?" Without even mentioning domestic issues, the President focused immediately upon his competence in the foreign area:

> Well, in the first place, I think the problems are more difficult than I had imagined they were. Secondly, there's a limitation upon the ability of the United States to solve these problems. We are involved now in the Congo in a very difficult situation. We've been unable to secure the implementation of the policy which we've supported. . . . There is a limitation, in other words, on the power of the United States to bring about solutions. . . . So that I would say the problems are more difficult than I imagined them to be. The responsibilities placed on the United States are greater than I imagined them to be, and there are greater limitations upon our ability to bring about a favorable result than I had imagined it to be.[41]

But this is not to imply that the motivational gap between the citizen and the policy-maker that prevails in the foreign policy area is bridged by their shared lack of subjective competence toward it. On the contrary,

40. This is especially the case in large industrial societies where people are likely to develop what has been appropriately called "a *role readiness*, a predisposition to accept behavioral requirements that are legitimately sanctioned." See Daniel Katz, Herbert Kelman, and Richard Flacks, "The National Role: Some Hypotheses about the Relation of Individuals to Nation in America Today," in Walter Isard and Julian Wolpert (eds.), Peace Research Society (International): *Papers, Volume 1, 1964: Chicago Conference, 1963* (Tokyo, 1964), p. 119.
41. "A Conversation with the President," *Transcript of an Interview* (The CBS Television Network, December 17, 1962), p. 1.

it seems doubtful whether the citizen is aware that he shares this feeling with those in policy-making positions. Having accepted the division of labor that casts him in the role of citizen, he tends to assume that official-dom is able to maintain control over the external environment and therefore tends to ascribe a much higher degree of subjective competence to policy-makers than they actually possess.

While the breadth of the motivational gap cannot thus be minimized, note must be taken of two bridges that do span it. One is a temporary and fragile structure, namely, the aforementioned capacity of citizens to become intensely concerned about the occasional situation abroad that does appear likely to initiate a chain of events which will upend or otherwise intrude upon their daily lives. Under these circumstances the gap is not only narrowed, but often is actually reversed as an aroused public becomes anxious to move quicker and further toward resolution of the issue than does a cautious officialdom. The second bridge is a more solid and enduring structure. It consists of those persons in the society whose interests do lead them to perceive themselves as linked to the interaction sequences that transpire in the external environment. This small stratum of the public is comprised of two main elements: non-governmental leaders whose occupational responsibilities, like those of officialdom, require them to be attentive to the international scene, and those few citizens—such as intellectuals—whose interests are not directly linked to the environment but who are nonetheless indirectly led to an involvement in foreign affairs by a need to protect their self-images. An American, for example, who defines himself as a civil libertarian is likely to feel obliged to be as attentive to incidents of racial strife in South Africa as to those in Mississippi. In the ensuing dis-cussion of role differences between the foreign and domestic areas we shall have occasion to elaborate on the roles that form this permanent bridge between the citizenry and officialdom. Here it suffices to note that, having a longer gap to span, the bridge is much narrower in the foreign than the domestic area.

Role Differences

Our conception of the structure of a public issue calls to mind the giant wall maps that corporation executives and military commanders use to depict the distribution and utilization of their resources. Where the twinkling lights on such maps indicate the points at which resources are either located or being employed, in our image of an issue being pro-cessed by a national system the flashing lights correspond to those roles in the system that have been aroused to participate in the controversy over the issue. We conceive of the map as composed of many more lights than flash at any one time because the system is regarded as

consisting of innumerable roles that do not require continuous activity on the part of their occupants. Hence the pattern of lights on our map is considered to vary from one issue-area to another, depending upon the number and identity of the roles that are activated.

Stated less metaphorically, we see the inclination and capacity to participate in the discussion of public issues as aspects of roles rather than as characteristics of people. National political systems consist of roles, both public and private, that are filled by different persons in each generation but that nevertheless require or stimulate similar activity (or inactivity) on the part of their occupants, whoever they may be at any moment in time. In the United States, for example, labor leader, person of Polish descent, editor, intellectual, and bureaucrat are but a few of the roles out of which activity on certain issues can be expected to emanate, irrespective of the particular persons involved. In other words, behavior on an issue theoretically can be anticipated in advance of its activation. If one had sufficient knowledge of the system, for each area one could plot the set of roles that are likely to be active and that thereby form its structure.[42]

In developing this conception of issue-areas as role structures we are not ignoring our earlier discussion of motives. Obviously it is people, and not roles, who experience motivation. And clearly the inclination and capacity to participate in public debate is conditioned by personality and other individual variables as well as by those arising out of role expectations and requirements. Yet, there would seem to be two good reasons to use the analytic device of attaching motives to roles rather than to people. One is that to a large extent role variables precede individual variables as motivational sources and, consequently, limit and channel the ways in which individuality gets expressed. The expectations of others always serve as the backdrop for action and it is these expectations that constitute the foundations of a social role. Expectations, however, do not dictate every aspect of behavior and roles do allow for and even necessitate the exercise of individuality. Nevertheless, some adherence to the expectations inherent in the role must occur if occupancy of it is to continue. Thus it is that one's behavior changes after entering a new role and that in important ways so do one's motives and attitudes.[43]

Secondly, and no less important, the concept of role would also appear to underlie the crucial motivational dimension whereby the degree of a

42. For an elaboration of this formulation, see my *National Leadership and Foreign Policy*, pp. 9–16.
43. The interrelationship of individual and role variables is amplified at greater length in my "Private Preferences and Political Responsibilities: The Relative Potency of Individual and Role Variables in the Behavior of U. S. Senators," in J. David Singer (ed.), *Quantitative International Politics: Insights and Evidence* (New York: The Free Press, forthcoming).

person's participation in the processing of a public issue depends upon whether he does or does not perceive himself as a potential link in the chain of events. What in fact he perceives is the presence or absence in the chain of one of the roles he occupies. He does not know the individuals who may act in such a way as to precipitate events that lead to his doorstep. Hence, to link himself to events he must perceive a process whereby the unknown occupants of certain roles are led to impinge on other unknown role occupants who in turn affect still others — and so on until a role he occupies is affected. From a perceptual standpoint, in other words, issues and the chain of events they initiate are structures of overlapping roles. Let us illustrate. If an American is of Polish descent and a proposed foreign aid program for Poland becomes an issue, then his ethnic ties to the homeland and other aspects of his ethnic role may foster the view that his interests constitute a link in the sequence whereby aid is or is not distributed in Poland. If, on the other hand, the issue focuses around aid for India, he will probably not have such a perception nor be aroused to participate in the issue unless he perceives some other role he occupies as potentially linked to the chain of events that aid to India might initiate. Persons of Polish descent who also occupy the role of intellectual, for example, may perceive events in India as linked to them through the expectation that intellectuals should be attentive to crises anywhere in the world. Individual variables — or conflicting roles — may inhibit some intellectuals from participating in the issue, but nevertheless activity can be expected to emanate from many occupants of this role. In sum, our formulation of issue-areas as role structures can be viewed less as a contradiction than as an elaboration of the foregoing discussion of motivational intensity and extensity.

Turning now to the differences between the role structures that mark issues in the foreign and domestic areas, we must begin with one that exists virtually by definition. Stated in terms of the earlier analogy, our map is not big enough to encompass the entire pattern of lights activated by issues in the foreign policy area. Unlike their domestic counterparts, foreign policy issues necessarily include the occupants of roles that are not part of the system. Foreigners are participants in such issues because, by definition, the objects or values that are the subject of controversy exist in the system's external environment and thus the rearrangement of the objects or the restructuring of the values cannot be accomplished without the consent of those in the environment who are thereby affected. The consent may result from voluntary acquiescence, hard bargaining, or forced compliance. Whatever the basis of the consent, however, the foreigners who provide it inevitably become parties to the interaction whereby the issue is resolved. To be sure, national systems reserve the right to decide their own foreign policies and their members may resent

the intrusion of outsiders who seek to influence the policies. Yet, even if a system manages to resolve differences among its members by ignoring foreign demands and deciding independently on a course of action, such an exercise of sovereignty may not bring an end to the issue. To achieve consensus within a system over a foreign policy is not to guarantee the cessation of controversy, as it is with domestic issues. If the foreigners toward whom the policy is directed resist, then the external environment will not be altered to conform to the internal consensus and the differences will probably reappear, reopening the issue. Obviously, for example, there would never have been a Korean issue in the United States during the early 1950s if the North Koreans had accepted the American decision to intervene and immediately had withdrawn their troops to the pre-invasion boundary.

Another evident distinction between the role structures of the domestic and foreign areas is the much greater number of roles from which activity is likely to emanate in the former. The presence of foreign roles in the latter area does not nearly offset the numerous citizens and officials who can be expected to participate only in domestic controversies. Domestic issues, involving as they do the distribution of resources and the arrangement of relationships at home, impinge upon highly generalized social roles and large categories of occupational roles. The healthy and the sick, the aged and the young, the rich and the poor—these are but a few of the broad social roles that can be directly linked to one or another of the main issues in the domestic area, whereas businessmen, workers, teachers, housewives, doctors, and mayors illustrate the all-encompassing occupational roles that such issues can activate. On the other hand, issues of foreign policy, being concerned with resources and relationships that are primarily distributed and rearranged in the environment, do not normally draw their participants from such large classes of people. Rather the occupants of much more specialized kinds of roles are likely to perceive a potential linkage between themselves and events abroad. Whereas domestic issues may activate a wide variety of, say, businessmen and teachers, foreign ones are likely to energize only exporters and professors of international relations. While the role of worker or housewife may easily be coupled to domestic issues, an equivalent linkage to foreign issues cannot be experienced unless, say, the former has relatives abroad or the latter has a son in military service.

At the leadership level, too, domestic issues are likely to evoke behavior on the part of a greater number of individuals than are foreign ones. This becomes readily apparent if a distinction is drawn between multi-issue and single-issue leadership roles. The former afford their occupants an opportunity to circulate opinions and exert influence on

a variety of issues, whereas the latter limit the leadership of their occupants to the specialized set of concerns that brought the roles into being. Editors of daily newspapers are an obvious example of multi-issue leadership roles. Indeed, not only are they expected to express themselves on all issues of the day, but they are even permitted to create a few new ones. Editors of technical publications, on the other hand, illustrate single-issue roles. They can exercise leadership only with respect to matters that are covered by the specialized foci of their journals. If they attempt to use their roles as the basis for leadership on other issues, they will either be ignored by their readers (who have turned to their publications precisely because of the specialization they offer) or, eventually, they will be removed from their roles.[44]

If we now superimpose the foreign-domestic dichotomy upon this distinction between multi- and single-issue leaders, it becomes clear that the foreign area contains substantially fewer single-issue roles than does the domestic area.[45] Foreign policy issues are no less technical than domestic ones, but since they deal with resources and arrangements abroad they do not fall within the spheres of competence of nearly as many technicians as do domestic issues. Contrast, for example, the nuclear test-ban treaty and water pollution, two issues that have in common the question of the extent to which natural resources shall be poisoned. Both issues would no doubt precipitate equivalent behavior on the part of multi-issue leaders (e.g., editors, politicians, and religious figures), but the single-issue leadership evoked by the nuclear question would not be likely to include more than a handful of lawyers specializing in international law, a few geneticists, a group of engineers acquainted with the problems of detection, and perhaps some political scientists who specialize in East-West relations, whereas the water pollution issue would probably necessitate opinion-making activity on the part of comparable specialists in every medium-sized community, a group that would number well into the hundreds of thousands. Or compare the number of Americans whose special training would cast them in leadership roles on such geographically based issues as Berlin, Vietnam, or the Congo with those whose specialties would accord them access to the channels of influence on regionally oriented domestic issues such as T.V.A., poverty in Appalachia, or the St. Lawrence Seaway. Again the latter might exceed the former by hundreds of thousands. The number of African, Asian, or European experts in the United States is

44. Additional discussion of the distinction between multi- and single-issue leaders will be found in my *Public Opinion and Foreign Policy: An Operational Formulation* (New York: Random House, 1961), Chap. 5.

45. As indicated below, a similar difference also prevails with respect to multi-issue roles even though it might seem that by definition both areas would activate roughly the same number of multi-issue leaders.

infinitesimal compared to the ranks of those whose views would be sought or heeded on the question of developing the nation's resources.

Nor is the difference between the leadership structures of the two areas merely a matter of numbers. The roles comprising the domestic area are more widely dispersed as well as more numerous than are those forming the foreign area. Most domestic controversies are directly relevant to life at every societal level, from the national through the regional down to the smallest community. Consequently, such controversies are likely to activate the occupants of multi-issue roles at all these levels. Most of the issues encompassed by the foreign area, on the other hand, do not clearly bear upon day-to-day existence at every level. Rather, occupants of roles that have responsibilities of a nation-wide dimension—what we shall call the national leadership—are likely to feel the impingement of events in the environment much more extensively than are those whose leadership roles are local or regional in scope.[46] Hence the pattern of leadership activity in the foreign area will ordinarily be substantially more concentrated than is the case for domestic issues. Recurring again to our imaginary wall map, lights will be twinkling in every hamlet of the society whenever domestic issues arise, whereas for foreign policy questions there will be bright glares of light in the centers of national leadership—in the national capital and in the seats of industry, finance, publishing, and culture—and darkness elsewhere.

This distinction can be readily illustrated. Consider, for example, American politicians and government officials. Those whose jurisdiction is confined to cities and states can be expected to participate in a variety of domestic issues. Such diverse questions as federal aid to education, water pollution, automation, civil rights, farm prices, urban renewal, and tax reduction are all likely to have repercussions within their constituencies. Thus, even if the national capital serves as the main site of the controversy, domestic issues are likely to require local politicians and officials to assert their opinions and to press for appropriate solutions.[47] Rare is the foreign policy issue, however, that will generate such behavior on their part. The local politician and official neither feel nor have an obligation to urge that the government follow a particular course in a Far Eastern crisis, nor are they obliged to insist that its stance toward a United Nations stalemate be altered. On the contrary, all the requirements of their roles orient them away from such matters and they may even be subject to electoral punishment or political reproach if they become too active in the foreign area. "Mind the community's business,

46. For an operational definition of the difference between national and local leadership, see my *National Leadership and Foreign Policy*, p. 7.

47. Cf. Arthur J. Vidich and Joseph Bensman, *Small Towns in Mass Society: Class, Power, and Religion in a Rural Community* (Princeton: Princeton University Press, 1958), Chap. 8.

not the nation's" constitutes a role limitation of which local politicians and officials are bound to be aware and which they can ignore only at their occupational peril. Stated in behavioral terms, the traffic of, say, city mayors who are brought to Washington, D.C., by domestic issues is a veritable deluge compared to that which is attracted by issues in the foreign area.

And much the same pattern prevails in other walks of life. Leaders of international labor unions are likely to be much more attentive to foreign policy questions than are their counterparts at the local level. Editors of small-town papers are much more inclined to restrict the space allotted to coverage of foreign affairs than are those with cosmopolitan audiences.[48] The heads of corporations with far-flung interests are likely to feel a much greater obligation to be active on foreign policy issues than are local businessmen.[49]

Interaction Differences

In asking whether the foreign and domestic areas differ in terms of the patterns of interaction through which issues in them are sustained or resolved, two pattern variables seem especially useful. One is the *degree* of interaction, that is, the extent to which the parties to an issue act independently or in response to each other. The other is the *direction* of interaction, that is, the extent to which interaction unfolds vertically through hierarchical channels or horizontally among relatively equal actors. To anticipate the conclusion of our reasoning, differences between the two areas can be discerned with respect to both variables, with foreign policy issues tending to precipitate primarily vertical interaction, to a low degree, and domestic issues evoking mainly horizontal inter-action, to a high degree.

Let us probe first the direction of interaction. Here empirical reality can hardly be mistaken. One cannot think of any society in which the task of making foreign policy is not assigned primarily to the executive branch of government. The need for decisive and unified action in coping with the external environment has led all political systems, democratic and authoritarian alike, to concentrate responsibility for foreign policy in the hands of relatively few officials. The need for this hierarchical arrangement has long been recognized in the United States and today the pre-eminence of the President in foreign affairs is as accepted a principle as any that is formally written in the Constitution. To be sure, exceptions can be cited, and later we shall have occasion to emphasize

48. Cf. Bernard C. Cohen, *The Press and Foreign Policy* (Princeton: Princeton University Press, 1963), Chap. 4.

49. Some quantitative data bearing on this point can be found in Bauer, Pool, and Dexter, *op. cit.*, Part II.

the existence of certain conditions that foster horizontal interaction in the foreign area. Generally speaking, however, the pattern is a pyramidal one in which interaction either converges upon or is responsive to the executive officials and agencies charged with maintaining control over the external environment. Whether the purpose be that of registering protest, exerting pressure, or proffering cooperation, citizens, groups, and legislative officials must turn to the executive branch for initiative and guidance.

The structure of the domestic area, on the other hand, is not nearly so hierarchical. Every segment of the society has some claim on the resources and relationships that distinguish it from its environment. Except in authoritarian systems, responsibility for making domestic policy is thus dispersed rather than concentrated, and accommodation rather than decisiveness is the paramount need.[50] Unity results from acquiescence in the foreign area, but only bargaining and coalition can produce it in the domestic area. Both in and out of government, therefore, horizontal interaction must occur before domestic issues can be resolved. To be sure, some groups in the society are larger and more powerful than others and to this extent the interaction slants vertically. And it is also true that the executive branch is not entirely lacking in authority in the domestic area. Such discrepancies among groups and within officialdom are hardly noticeable, however, when compared to the hierarchical structure of the foreign area.

Another way of describing this difference is in terms of the useful distinction that Huntington has drawn between the executive and legislative processes of policy-making[51] (or, to adapt his terminology to our perspective, the legislative and executive processes of issue-handling). Noting that under certain conditions decision-making within the executive branch "retains a peculiarly legislative flavor," Huntington emphasizes that the "legislative and executive *processes* of policy-making do not necessarily correspond to the legislative and executive *branches* of government," that instead

A policy-making process is legislative in character to the extent that: (1) the units participating in the process are relatively equal in power (and con-

50. We except authoritarian systems from this analysis because presumably they are marked by a high concentration of authority and responsibility in both the foreign and domestic areas. Indeed, this is so virtually by definition: they are authoritarian precisely because hierarchical policy-making prevails in all walks of life. Yet, if our analysis of the domestic-foreign distinction is correct in this respect, it suggests that even in authoritarian systems the patterns of interaction in the two areas are not likely to be identical, that the claims of domestic groups cannot be totally ignored in such systems, and that the structure of the domestic area is bound to be at least slightly less hierarchical than that of the foreign area.

51. Samuel P. Huntington, *The Common Defense: Strategic Programs in National Politics* (New York: Columbia University Press, 1961), Chap. 3.

sequently must bargain with each other); (2) important disagreements exist concerning the goals of policy; and (3) there are many possible alternatives. A process is executive in character to the extent that: (1) the participating units differ in power (i.e., are hierarchically arranged); (2) fundamental goals and values are not at issue; and (3) the range of possible choices is limited.[52]

The relevance of Huntington's distinction to our discussion is obvious: interaction in the domestic area consists mainly of the legislative process, while issues in the foreign area are handled primarily through the executive process.

Having less of a need to fashion consensuses through bargaining and support-building efforts than their counterparts in the domestic area, parties to foreign policy issues are bound to be correspondingly less impelled to interact with each other. They can, so to speak, move independently up the slopes of the pyramid of executive authority, whereas those involved in domestic controversies must respond to each other in order to join the issue and move toward their respective goals. Stated in terms of testable hypotheses, it seems reasonable to presume that the actors in the domestic area are more familiar with each other's identity and more conversant with each other's views than are those activated by foreign policy issues. Applied to the United States, one could hypothesize that for every White House Conference of national or regional leaders devoted to coping with a trend unfolding abroad, ten or more are convened on situations emerging at home.[53] It should be noted, however, that the lesser degree of interaction in the foreign area is not attributed to the aforementioned conclusion that this area contains many fewer roles susceptible to activation. We are talking about relative and not absolute degrees of interaction. Our reasoning is that the more hierarchical structure in the foreign area and the greater need for accommodation in the domestic area mean that proportionately more action will converge and overlap in the latter than in the former.

But there is another and, in view of the ensuing analysis, a more important reason for this difference in the degree of interaction. This is that foreign policy issues focus primarily on resources or relationships that are to be distributed or rearranged in the environment, whereas domestic issues involve mainly distribution and rearrangement among members of the system. Members of the system do not run the risk of forfeiting or relinquishing any possessions when they participate in a foreign policy controversy. They can, under such circumstances, suffer damage to their spiritual or psychic values, but nothing concrete can be taken away from them, since the resources or relationships at issue are

52. *Ibid.*, p. 146.
53. See, for example, the cases cited in my *National Leadership and Foreign Policy*, p. 24.

located primarily outside the system. Foreign policy controversies, in short, do not require the participants to treat each other as rivals for scarce resources. What one actor or group gains, another does not give up. Each participant seeks to persuade the decision-making authority to adopt a particular solution, but none posits a solution that necessitates depriving other system members of some of their possessions or privileges. Thus, since there is nothing material to bargain over, the parties to the issue need never come together or respond to each other. Each can contest the issue independently and without regard for the others.

Let us cite some current examples. Take the question of whether the United States should give diplomatic support to Tshombe in the Congo. At least in the short run, it will not be Americans who are affected by the outcome of the dispute. All those whose status and resources will be enhanced by the outcome, as well as all those who will be deprived in these ways, will be Congolese. Some Americans will be pleased by the outcome and some will be disappointed, but none will be poorer. Similarly, the question of United States involvement in Cyprus is primarily a matter of how Cypriote wealth and prestige should be rearranged; only second-arily, if at all, does it involve the reallocation of resources and status among Americans. Or consider the 1963 nuclear test-ban treaty. Neither the proponents nor the opponents risked a diminution of their resources or status. The welfare of the unborn may have been at stake, but like persons in the external environment, future generations are remote and unable to contest issues directly.

Domestic issues, on the other hand, unfold under conditions of scarce resources. The system itself encompasses all the resources that are to be allocated and all the relationships that are to be rearranged. What one actor or group gains, another gives up or fails to gain. There are only so many tax dollars that can be raised and only so many ways to spend them. And each dollar that is collected and disbursed results in loss to some and gain to others. Similarly, statuses have historical roots within the system and to change them is to deprive some of privilege and to provide it to others. Necessarily, parties to a domestic issue must view each other as rivals, as obstacles that must be confronted, refuted, thwarted, or accommodated in such a way as to permit satis-factory resolution of the issue. In short, even though their goals may be mutually exclusive, the actors in the domestic area are interdependent. They cannot avoid each other and continue to contest the issue. They must interact, if not on a face-to-face basis, then through actions that are explicitly in response to each other.

The civil rights issue in the United States is an obvious example of this process. Actual or proposed legislative, executive, and judicial action benefitting minority groups has involved a vast rearrangement of

the society's resources and relationships. Some Americans, especially white Southerners, have correctly seen the issue as involving the loss of both material wealth and status privilege, while others, especially those in the affected minorities, have been equally accurate in their view that the issue promises them a gain in these respects. Whatever the outcome of the issue, therefore, great numbers of Americans will be directly affected and, in their own eyes, many will be poorer. Thus it is hardly surprising that the issue has stimulated interaction at all society levels, from the struggle for integrated schools in local communities to the contest for new statuses in the national legislature.

5

Summing up the analysis thus far, it seems clear that we have developed an affirmative answer to our original question of whether the foreign and domestic areas are distinguishable from each other. In terms of the motives, roles, and interaction sequences they activate, foreign and domestic issues do seem to differ in significant ways. The extent and nature of these differences are summarized in Table 3, which recreates Table 1 and adds the entries for each of the cells that our discussion has yielded.

Table 3 — Characteristics of Foreign and Domestic Issues

		MOTIVES		ROLES		INTERACTION SEQUENCES	
		Intensity	*Extensity*	*Number*	*Identity*	*Direction*	*Degree*
Private citizens and groups	foreign issues	high	narrow	few	national leaders	vertical	low
	domestic issues	low	wide	many	all strata	horizontal	high
Government officials and agencies	foreign issues	low	wide	few	national	vertical	low
	domestic issues	low	wide	many	national and local	horizontal	high

There does remain, however, one unfinished task: that of relaxing our initial assumptions and inquiring whether the boundaries between the foreign and domestic areas are as rigid as we have presumed them to be. Again the answer seems clear. One can readily think of examples of foreign policy issues that unfold in ways descriptive of the domestic

rather than the foreign area.[54] After all, it is virtually a truism that nations are becoming increasingly interdependent and that the internal life of no nation is entirely free from the intrusion of external factors.

In short, the distinctions we have discerned would seem to be generally valid, but there are major exceptions and the question is whether the deviations occur for systematic reasons, thereby permitting us to integrate them into our analysis. Once again a clearcut line of reasoning suggests itself. The conclusion reached above, that domestic issues involve the allocation of scarce resources or the rearrangement of historic relationships while foreign issues do not, serves as a point of departure for a train of thought that allows us to account for the exceptional issues and, indeed, to predict their occurrence.

The crux of this synthesizing formulation is that some foreign policy issues precipitate an exceptional degree of interaction that unfolds along horizontal lines precisely because they involve, perhaps for a variety of reasons, the utilization of a society's personnel and wealth. That is, certain efforts to allocate resources or rearrange relationships in the external environment cannot be carried out without domestic resources or relationships also undergoing change. The use or threat of force in the external environment is an obvious example. In contrast to the more normal procedure of relying on a handful of diplomats to restructure the environment through persuasion and negotiation, policies of force require a society to dispatch its own troops and supplies abroad. Consequently, some members of the society — say, the troops and those whose welfare suffers as a result of the expenditure on military supplies — are deprived while others — say, producers of military equipment — benefit. The area of controversy then widens as those who have an immediate stake in the policy of force come to view each other as rivals. At this point the executive process of issue-handling is no longer appropriate to the situation and the outwardly directed policy comes to dominate the internal politics of the society. The centrality of the issues of Indochina and Algeria in postwar French politics is, *par excellence*, an empirical instance of this process. Both issues came to dominate the domestic political scene in France precisely because Frenchmen were having *their* resources and relationships redistributed in Indochina and Algeria. In short, most foreign policy issues may not involve the diversion of substantial resources from the internal to the external environment, but some do and these are the ones that exhibit the characteristics of domestic issues.

54. Although to a lesser extent, it is also possible to cite certain kinds of domestic issues (e.g., conservation) which would seem to consist mainly of characteristics ascribed to the foreign area. However, this point is tangential to our main concern and cannot be pursued here.

Other illustrations of this formulation are readily available from recent history. Consider again the Congo situation. As has already been implied, so long as the controversy over what diplomatic line the United States should pursue in the situation involves deprivation only for some Congolese groups, participation in the issue within the United States is confined to executive agencies of the federal government, some multi-issue national leaders, and a few African specialists. Whenever there evolves the possibility or fact of committing American transports, supplies, and personnel to the situation, however, participation becomes more broadly based, many members of Congress become aroused, and, in effect, the issue is transferred from the foreign to the domestic area. Similarly, the Berlin issue has moved back and forth between the areas as the consignment of American troops and equipment has been raised and lowered. On the other hand, since the commitment of American resources to European defense would not be essentially altered by the proposed multilateral force, MLF has remained strictly a foreign policy issue insofar as its processing by the American system is concerned. For the European nations involved, however, the MLF proposal does require new allocations of men and material, and for these nations the issue has thus acquired domestic characteristics.

One other empirical case can usefully be cited to demonstrate the explanatory power of our interpretation that the manner of processing an issue is a function of the degree to which a society's resources or relationships are affected. We refer to Cohen's thorough account of the internal policy-making process through which the United States formulated, ratified, and formally adhered to the 1951 Japanese peace settlement.[55] The salient feature of this episode is that, contrary to all expectations, the conclusion of a conciliatory treaty with an archenemy of the 1940s did not provoke extended debate and intense activity throughout the country. It had been anticipated that lingering wartime hatred for the Japanese would foster widespread demands for a punitive treaty, but these never materialized and Cohen's one hundred-page account of the citizenry's reactions – in polls, the press, and interest group statements – makes for very bland reading indeed.[56] Only the question of fishing rights in the North Pacific stimulated a flurry of demands, interactions, and bargaining: members of Congress and fishing interests from the West Coast were so active that the original plan of including a single fisheries article in the peace treaty gave way to what Cohen calls "salt water politics" and was jettisoned in favor of negotiating a separate agreement – the North Pacific Fisheries Convention.[57] For Cohen the

55. Bernard C. Cohen, *The Political Process and Foreign Policy: The Making of the Japanese Peace Settlement* (Princeton: Princeton University Press, 1957).
56. *Ibid.*, Part II: "Public Opinion," Chaps. 3–6.

fisheries question is merely an exception. It emerges as a discordant note in an otherwise harmonious sequence that he ascribes to the skillful and careful way in which those responsible for obtaining foreign and domestic acceptance of the peace settlement—especially John Foster Dulles—mobilized support and diminished opposition. But our issue-area formulation suggests another interpretation. Although policy-making skills were no doubt operative and relevant, we would emphasize that most of the peace settlement dealt with the utilization of resources and the arrangement of relationships on the islands of Japan, that only with respect to fisheries were American resources at stake, and that therefore it is hardly surprising that the latter problem was distinguished by the horizontal manner in which it was processed. In effect, the Japanese peace settlement was not a single situation. It was two situations, one falling in the foreign area and the other in the domestic area.

If our conception of the two areas and of the overlap between them sheds new light on past situations, it also allows us to predict the way in which future ones will unfold. So long as an issue focuses on some aspect of the external environment, and so long as none of the proposals to resolve it require more than the normal complement of foreign office personnel, then it is likely to activate relatively few national leaders and officials and their interactions are likely to be hierarchically patterned. However, once the focus of the issue shifts to aspects of the society itself, or once proposals to handle it necessitate the expenditure of societal resources or the alteration of societal relationships to supplement the work of diplomats, then relatively large numbers of citizens, leaders, and officials can be expected to make claims and counterclaims in a process of bargaining over its resolution. Indeed, in order to account for the exceptional issues that transgress the boundaries between the areas, we can pose our conclusion in terms of a single over-all hypothesis: *The more an issue encompasses a society's resources and relationships, the more will it be drawn into the society's domestic political system and the less will it be processed through the society's foreign political system.*[58]

Note that we predict the way in which issues will unfold, not their outcomes. The foreign area would seem to be the more stable of the two

57. *Ibid.*, Chap. 12.

58. Since the writing of the first draft of this chapter in January, 1965, the conflict in Vietnam has escalated considerably and the subsequent development of the issue in the United States has closely followed along the lines predicted by the hypothesis. Indeed, in this particular case domesticization of the issue bears some resemblance to an election campaign and all the innovative and frenzied activities that accompany such episodes: besides a rash of "teach-ins", the issue has precipitated an unusual (for a "foreign policy" issue) number of advertisements contesting the wisdom of escalation, a State Department "truth team" touring American campuses, a group of Congressmen holding "hearings" on street corners, and, in general, a highly consistent one-to-one ratio between the commitment of men and materiel and the involvement of citizens and officials.

and, accordingly, issues processed in it would seem likely to prove more integrative for the society than those processed in the domestic area. To comprehend the stability and integrative potential of an issue-area, however, is not to know how long an issue will endure or whose posture toward it will prevail. Process exerts some influence on outcome, to be sure, but it is equally true that the same process can yield a variety of outcomes, depending on the interplay of a host of variables that are not structural components of issue-areas. To predict outcome as well as process one would have to know the identity, capabilities, and aspirations of the participants in an issue; and to move to this plane of inquiry would be to descend from the theory-building level of issue-area analysis to the theory-constricting level of issue analysis, a step which we have already eschewed.

PERSONALITY AND ATTITUDE CORRELATES OF FOREIGN POLICY ORIENTATION[1]

Herbert McClosky

STUDENTS of international politics have traditionally focused upon the analysis of institutions or systems in which the principal actors are nation-states, associations of nation-states, or the decision-making agencies of nation-states. Although they have in recent years devoted more attention to such "exotic" factors as public opinion, political attitudes, and personality, few of them have accorded these variables sustained or systematic scrutiny. To most students of foreign affairs such factors remain novel, uncongenial, and difficult to incorporate into the analytical framework with which they are accustomed to work. Hard data on the influence of psychological variables in foreign policy are, so

1. This is publication A48 of the Survey Research Center, University of California, Berkeley. Support for the collection and analysis of data reported in this paper has been received from the Social Science Research Council and the Institute of Social Sciences, University of California, Berkeley. This investigation was supported in part by Public Health Research Grant MH–05837 from the National Institute of Health. I am greatly indebted to Paul Sniderman, Fellow at the University of California, for invaluable assistance in the preparation of this chapter.

far, not abundant, and the obstacles to be surmounted in collecting such data are often formidable. In addition, some students of international politics, in a conscious effort to narrow the inquiry and concentrate upon the variables that promise (as they see it) the greatest payoff, exclude attitude or personality factors on the assumption that they will not sufficiently enhance the explanatory power of their model to warrant the additional complication of integrating them into their analysis.[2]

As an outsider, I cannot accurately assess the weight of these considerations. I believe, however, that the utility of psychological explanations cannot be decided by *a priori* judgments or even by appraising the rudimentary research so far completed. Whether analytical perspectives employing personality and attitude influences prove feasible and helpful in the study of international politics is an empirical question to be settled only after much more research—presumably of an increasingly sophisticated and systematic nature—has been undertaken. This research may help not only to identify important relations among variables but also to specify the conditions under which other (nonpsychological) influences are likely to be potentiated or reduced. Then, too, even if we find that psychological influences rarely if ever dominate the course of international affairs, their role at times may nevertheless be decisive: they may, for example, furnish precisely the increment that tips the scales toward one course of action rather than another.

In this paper I shall confine attention to that aspect of the problem that deals with the relation of attitude and personality factors to foreign policy orientations.[3] I shall say little about the influence of these factors on the actual formulation of foreign policy. *A fortiori*, I shall ignore such questions as the influence of psychological variables on the roles played by various publics and policy elites in the decision-making process. These are, of course, important questions, but they are not the questions to which the present research is addressed. It is concerned, rather, to explore on various fronts the utility of psychological constructs for political belief, orientation, and activity. Foreign affairs is one of those fronts.

The major foreign policy orientation on which this chapter centers is

2. See in particular S. Verba, "Rationality and Non-Rationality in Models of the International System," in K. Knorr and S. Verba (eds.), *The International System: Theoretical Essays* (Princeton: Princeton University Press, 1961), pp. 93–115.

3. Two recent works that utilize a psychological focus, although to different degrees, are O. Klineberg, *The Human Dimension in International Relations* (New York: Holt, Rinehart and Winston, 1964) and L. Doob, *Patriotism and Nationalism, Their Psychological Foundations* (New Haven: Yale University Press, 1964). A review and discussion of research on psychology and international affairs is also contained in Herbert C. Kelman (ed.), *International Behavior: A Social-Psychological Analysis* (New York: Holt, Rinehart and Winston 1965).

that contained in the isolationist-nonisolationist distinction.[4] The persons falling into these categories will for certain purposes be further divided into those with aggressive (or *jingoistic*) international orientations and those with nonaggressive (or *pacific*) orientations. The responses to foreign policy issues that reflect these tendencies will also be examined.

DEFINITIONS

Like many terms attended by political controversy, isolationism is a value-loaded concept, bearing honorific connotations in some circles and pejorative ones in others. Inevitably, perhaps, it has borne a variety of competing and conflicting meanings. It has been embraced by pacifists who abhor militarism and by jingoists who celebrate it. It has been favored as the appropriate orientation toward Europe but not Asia; toward Asia but not Europe; toward all continents outside the Western Hemisphere; or toward foreign nations anywhere. Variations are also evident in its focus, which has sometimes been military, sometimes economic, sometimes political, and sometimes all three.[5] Writers commonly find it necessary to discriminate "types" of isolationists: Walter Lippmann, for example, has recently distinguished between the "old isolationists" who regard any military commitment outside the boundaries of the two oceans as contrary to America's vital interest, and the "neo-isolationists" who favor "economic assistance, technical assistance, the Peace Corps [and] cultural exchanges," who approve collective military action to defend vital American interests, but who oppose unilateral military intervention in places like Africa and Asia, where American interests are not "vital."[6] Other writers have distinguished between older types of isolationism that focused on the "decadence" of Europe and the "danger of infection" from abroad and a current type of isolationism that is belligerently anti-Communist, prefers unilateral action, and aims to slash foreign spending.[7]

4. On the relevance of isolationism for present-day American politics see W. A. Scott and S. Withey, *The United States and the United Nations* (New York: Manhattan, 1958); G. Almond, *The American People and Foreign Policy* (New York: Harcourt, Brace & World, 1950); V. O. Key, Jr., *Public Opinion and American Democracy* (New York: Alfred A. Knopf, 1961); and R. Dahl, *Congress and Foreign Policy* (New York: Harcourt, Brace & World, 1950).

5. For a study of the roots of congressional support of isolationist policies, see L. Rieselbach, "Congressional Isolationist Behavior, 1939–1958," unpublished doctoral dissertation, Yale University, 1963.

6. Quoted in a news release, March 2, 1965.

7. See the discussions of A. Schlesinger, Jr., "The New Isolationism," *Atlantic Monthly* (May, 1952), pp. 34–8; F. Klingberg, "The Historical Alternation of Moods in American Foreign Policy," *World Politics*, Vol. 4(1952), pp. 239–73; and N. A. Graebner, *The New Isolationism: A Study in Politics and Foreign Policy Since 1950* (New York: Ronald Press, 1956).

The literature on isolationism abounds with definitions, variously shaped by the bias of the investigator, by the historical period he is studying, or by the political movements he is describing. Differences are found in emphasis, coloration, and point of view as the doctrine passes from one historcal stage to another and from one group of advocates to another. Its origins have ranged from American "nativism," on the one side, to the Marxist conviction on the other, that all American overseas activities are impelled by capitalism's search for markets, raw materials, and opportunities for imperialist domination. Some isolationist manifestations are of long standing, deeply rooted in American populism; others have been of brief, almost momentary duration, e.g. the "isolationism" of the Communist Party during the Stalin-Hitler Pact, or the short-lived support of the America First Committee in the late 1930s by the more pacifist members of the Socialist Party.

Despite variations, certain elements have been common to most public expressions of the isolationist point of view. One of these is a sense of disengagement from other nations, accompanied often by the conviction that American interests differ from and are incompatible with those of the rest of the world. To the traditional isolationist, there is no community of international interests, and Americans have little to gain by participating in international affairs. They have even less reason to be drawn into "entangling alliances," which are bound to be costly, dangerous, and incapacitating. The element of disengagement is the dominant feature of the isolationist persuasion. From it flows the desire to avoid joint action, the emphasis upon the unlimited and eternal sovereignty of nation-states,[8] and the reluctance to commit the United States to any policy that would increase its obligations to foreign nations.[9] In its more extreme form, the sense of disengagement passes from mere feelings of nonresponsibility for other nations into a ritualistic fear that sustained intercourse with them is bound to be contaminating. Not only will it diminish our freedom to act but it will debase and demoralize us. The nation's purity and vitality will be overcome by the decadence and corruption of the countries with which it is compelled to mingle. Thus the United States is portrayed, implicitly or explicitly, as innocent, naive, and trusting, a ready victim of unscrupulous foreign powers.

If variety has attended the definition of isolationism, confusion has been the mark of whatever it is that isolationism is not. The difficulty is that there is no single, logical antithesis to the isolationist persuasion. Such terms as internationalism, cosmopolitanism, world-mindedness,

8. A. Weinberg, "The Historical Meaning of the American Doctrine of Isolationism," *American Political Science Review*, Vol. 34 (1940), pp. 539–49.

9. Rieselbach, *op. cit.*

interventionism, and even globalism have been employed to characterize the orientation of those who are not isolationists. Each of these terms, in turn, has been variously conceived and defined. Internationalist, for example, has been employed to describe world federalists, pacifists, members of the Peace Corps, supporters of the United Nations, and even war hawks who favor unilateral military action to maintain American hegemony. It would be idle to attempt to untangle these terms and to furnish each of them with an appropriate definition. Nor is it necessary to our research task, for while we will doubtless find it helpful to use these terms — if only for stylistic variety — it should be understood that those who score at the lower end of what we will call the Isolationism scale can properly be designated only as "nonisolationists"; their particular form of nonisolationism cannot in the context of the present research be specified.[10]

Later in the paper we will subdivide isolationists into those who are jingoistic or aggressive and those who are pacific or conciliatory. The terms aggressive or jingoistic refer not to psychological aggressiveness — a trait we will measure separately and treat as one of our independent variables — but rather to a belligerent and bullying posture toward foreign nations. Obviously it is a term highly correlated with chauvinism — i.e. patriotism of an uncritical, zealous, and boastful type — but is not identical with it. The jingoist, as we have conceived him, is given to sabre-rattling, prefers quick and, if necessary, violent action in response to external threats, and seeks to insulate the United States from the rest of the world by sheer superiority of force. A pacific isolationist, by contrast, usually prefers to withdraw from or avoid conflict with other nations. Both typify what might be called the "perimeter" mentality. Both regard the outside world as dangerous and hostile, but one prefers to counter this danger by retreat or withdrawal, the other by a military stance and, if necessary, retaliation.

A word might also be said about the terms *attitude* and *personality*, which figure so prominently in our analysis. By attitude I have in mind the generally accepted definition of the term, excellently stated by Selltiz and Cook "as a disposition to evaluate, or to respond to, an object

10. Definitions and operational measures of nonisolationism or internationalism also abound. See, for example, D. Sampson and H. Smith, "A Scale to Measure World-Minded Attitudes," *Journal of Social Psychology*, Vol. 45 (1957), pp. 99–106; W. A. Scott, "International Ideology and Interpersonal Ideology," *Public Opinion Quarterly*, Vol. 24 (1960), pp. 419–35; W. Mackinnon and R. Centers, "Authoritarianism and Internationalism," *Public Opinion Quarterly*, Vol. 20 (Winter, 1956–57), pp. 621–30; D. Levinson, "An Approach to the Theory and Measurement of Ethnocentric Ideology," *Journal of Psychology*, Vol. 28 (1949), pp. 19–39; M. Farber, "The Armageddon Complex: Dynamics of Opinion," *Public Opinion Quarterly*, Vol. 15 (1951), pp. 217–24; and B. Fensterwald Jr., "The Anatomy of American Isolationism and Expansion," II, *Journal of Conflict Resolution*, Vol. 2 (1958), pp. 111–39.

or class of objects in a given way, this disposition being inferred from consistency of response to the object or members of the object class.''[11] By personality I mean a readiness or disposition to respond in a patterned way to stimulus objects of many different types across a range of subject areas. Whereas an attitude disposition is characteristically tied to a particular class of objects, a personality disposition may encompass more than one class of objects or behaviors and these objects need not be manifestly related. Personality is both a more general and more fundamental or genotypic term in the sense that it often underlies attitudes and furnishes the motive force that impels them. When one uses the term personality, one is talking about such things as needs, motives, affect, defense mechanisms, and the like; when one uses the term attitude, one is talking about implicit or explicit beliefs regarding a specified class of objects. One has an attitude toward foreigners, civil rights, political freedom, or international cooperation; but one exhibits a personality disposition when one's responses are marked by stimulus boundedness, a tendency to narrow the number and complexity of stimuli from the phenomenal field, premature closure and the rejection of incompatible material, cognitive restriction, a propensity for dichotomous distinctions, avoidance of trial-and-error behavior, and so forth. These will be recognized as the diagnostic responses of an inflexible personality.

There are, of course, response states that fall on the borderline, reflecting both attitude and personality dispositions so equally that one cannot wholly locate them in either category. A few of the measures considered in later sections of this paper might be classified under either heading, e.g. pessimism, social responsibility, and contempt for weakness. While dimensions of this type obviously contain elements of the personality genotype, they are also unusually dependent upon social learning and exhibit many of the characteristics of the attitude phenotype.

ISOLATIONISM: BACKGROUND AND THEORY

In the mid-nineteenth century, a large number of Americans were undoubtedly isolationists. Many had little reason to be anything else. They were citizens of a vast continental power, safeguarded against military danger by two great oceans, secure against weak neighbors to the north and south, physically and culturally remote from the world's great centers. They lived, for the most part, in small, widely separated, rural communities, where they had little access to information about the rest of the world. Some were immigrants or the children of immigrants

11. C. Selltiz and S. Cook, "Theory and Measurement of Attitudes," mimeograph, p.2.

for whom Europe was a continent marked by unceasing quarrels, decaying aristocracies, political and religious oppression, rigid class stratification, and narrow opportunities. It was obviously a place to be avoided. The objective realities, as they appeared to many Americans of that day, made the isolationist point of view a "natural" one, easily learned and internalized, and (one assumes) sustained without help from any special psychological forces.

American isolationism grew not only from geographic insularity but also from a sense of having created a unique culture that owed little or nothing to Europe. This feeling, in turn, was related to the colonial struggle for independence, the conquest of the wilderness, and the successful fashioning of a new national state. It was further reinforced by the democratic and radical features of American society. Among populist movements, for example, freedom from domination by "Wall Street" and the Eastern seaboard became identified with freedom from European domination. Not only were they protesting against industrial and commercial capitalism but also against the effete, European type of culture to which (in their eyes) Washington diplomats and the Eastern upper classes aspired. As one writer has observed, they feared "the shape which American society would assume were it to return to a broader trans-Atlantic culture."[12] Their isolationism, thus, expressed both their estrangement from Europe and their anxiety about the forms of American life.

No one can be certain whether the isolationists of the nineteenth century differed from the nonisolationists of that era in the same ways that isolationists and nonisolationists differ today. But one can scarcely ignore the contrast between America's insularity then and its "vulnerability" now. Apart from the fantastic changes in education, travel, communication, and exposure to other cultures, America's place in the international scene has been so drastically transformed as to defy comparison with that of earlier times. The United States has been engaged in wars on almost every continent, and has participated in numerous international organizations and alliances. Millions of Americans have lived or traveled abroad for extended periods of time. The oceans no longer safeguard American territory, and the lives of Americans have become interlaced with those of other nationals in countless ways.

One may wonder, then, whether isolationism is any longer a "natural," easily learned and accepted view, and whether the forces that once produced it are the same forces that are generating it now. Is isolationism today a "deviant" orientation, one that has different social and psychological meanings from those associated with it a hundred years ago?

12. Paul Seabury, "The Irreconcilables" (unpublished). This volume contains an excellent analysis of the historical sources of American isolationism.

If, in light of contemporary realities, it is a less plausible and viable point of view than it once was, is it likely to win support from anyone who is not impelled towards it by strong inner needs? To what extent, in short, must we draw upon psychological explanations to account for the holding of isolationist beliefs in mid-twentieth century America?

That personality can be an important determinant of political attitudes has been too often confirmed by previous research to require extensive discussion here.[13] Research on the relation of personality to foreign policy attitudes is less extensive, but the findings turned up on this question are consistent with those from other types of attitude research.[14] There is, indeed, no reason to expect anything else. Needs, motives, defenses, frailties, and fears color men's judgments about foreign affairs just as they do their evaluation of other matters. In some ways, foreign policy offers an especially rich field for the play of personality variables. Many of the issues confronted have been heavily invested with symbolic meanings. They have, in some instances, occasioned struggle and sacrifice and have been dramatized as rallying points for mankind's hopes and fears. Often they present a highly ambiguous set of stimuli, thereby furnishing special opportunities for the engagement of psychological needs. Since they usually bespeak some type of conflict between nations, they furnish numerous occasions for the mobilization of appropriate affect (anger, anxiety, and the like). Sometimes they are incidents in the clash of rival ideologies, one or more of which may be intemperate in its claims. The prospect they raise is often one of danger to national pride, to independence, to territorial integrity, and even to survival.

There is reason to believe that the isolationist orientation is particularly susceptible to the influence of personality. As we shall see, isolationism offers numerous opportunities for marshalling aversive and

13. There has been considerable research into this question. Among the major works is T. Adorno, E. Frenkel-Brunswik, D. Levinson, and R. N. Sanford, *The Authoritarian Personality* (New York: Harper and Row, 1956). Other relevant articles are R. Stagner, "Studies of Aggressive Social Attitudes: I. Measurement and Interrelation of Selected Attitudes," *Journal of Social Psychology,* Vol. 20 (1944), pp. 109–20; "Studies of Aggressive Social Attitudes: II. Changes From Peace to War," *Journal of Social Psychology,* Vol. 20 (1944), pp. 121–28. More generally, H. Goldhamer, "Public Opinion and Personality," *American Journal of Sociology,* Vol. 55 (1950), pp. 346–54.

14. See M. B. Smith, J. Bruner, and R. White, *Opinions and Personality* (New York: John Wiley and Sons, 1956); M. B. Smith, "Personal Values as Determinants of a Political Attitude," *Journal of Psychology,* Vol. 28 (1949), pp. 447–86; L. Queener, "The Development of Internationalist Attitudes: I. Hypotheses and Verifications," *Journal of Social Psychology,* Vol. 29 (1949), pp. 221–36; "The Development of Internationalist Attitudes: II. Attitude Cues and Prestige," *Journal of Social Psychology,* Vol 29 (1949), pp. 237–52; "The Development of International Attitudes: III. The Literature and A Point of View," *Journal of Social Psychology,* Vol. 30 (1949), pp. 105–26. For an excellent review of much of the recent literature see B. Christiansen, *Attitudes Towards Foreign Affairs as a Function of Personality* (Oslo: Oslo University Press, 1959).

appetitive dispositions, for the potentiation or projection of motives, for the activation of defense mechanisms, and for the ready translation of psychological needs (e.g. hostility) into appropriate attitude phenotypes. If it is also, as appears to be the case, a deviant view in contemporary American politics, it will be subject to those psychological factors that affect socialization, cognitive function, and the learning of norms.

It should not be necessary to state again that nothing I shall report here is meant to suggest that foreign policy attitudes are determined solely by personality. Obviously they also result from social learning, indoctrination, reference groups, ratiocination, and other nonpersonality influences. The stands men take on international questions are affected by time, geography, and social circumstance and by the configuration of forces in which personality variables are imbedded. In the present paper, however, the focus has been deliberately restricted and no attempt has been made to deal with the entire range of possible determinants.

ASSUMPTIONS, HYPOTHESES, AND PROCEDURES

Owing to the profusion of variables employed in this study, the list of hypotheses that could possibly be investigated is unusually lengthy. It would burden the reader to face him at this point with the entire list, especially as some hypotheses will in any event need to be reiterated later in the chapter. Specific hypotheses, therefore, will be presented in subsequent sections, where they can be discussed simultaneously with the relevant findings. It might be helpful, however, to indicate at this time some of the major assumptions, general hypotheses, and theoretical considerations on which the analysis proceeded and on which the findings will, hopefully, throw some light. Principal among these are the following:

Isolationism is in reality a complex political orientation that can originate in different ways and from diverse motives. It may spring from psychological needs and impulses as well as from social, intellectual, or political elements and it need not serve the same function or possess the same meaning for all persons who embrace it.

Personality variables are most likely to evoke isolationist responses when the elements of the former are psychologically close to, cognate with, or readily converted into, the components of the latter and when the stimulus objects (say, foreigners) afford adequate opportunity for the mobilization of appropriate affect (say, fear).

From a psychological standpoint, foreign policy attitudes are in principle no different from other political and social attitudes; they spring, together with other attitude phenotypes, from common

personality genotypes (or from similar cognitive styles); many of these attitudes will often be more usefully (and more correctly) understood as part of a substantively diverse network of attitudes than as a unique stance arising wholly or largely out of elements intrinsic to the domain of international politics.

Isolationist beliefs will be strongly related to aversive rather than appetitive personality dispositions (i.e. response dispositions that aim to avoid, deny, deflect, shut out, or incapacitate other persons or related stimulus objects rather than to reach out to, embrace, accept, or involve them). This disposition will clearly manifest itself in generalized hostility, suspiciousness, misanthropy, inflexibility, a tendency toward "we-they" distinctions, intolerance of differences, and so forth.

Isolationism in its traditional form is, at the present stage of American life, a deviant political orientation, possessing many of the same characteristics and correlates that mark other extreme or deviant outlooks; support for isolationism, therefore, represents in part a failure of socialization.

Whatever interferes with the learning of political norms – ignorance, political apathy, cultural impoverishment, impaired cognitive functioning, restricted interaction, and even personality disorders – will increase the strength and frequency of isolationist sentiment.

Nonisolationism is an orientation requiring, by comparison with isolationism, a greater element of sophistication and cosmopolitanism (in the intellectual and cultural sense). It will be more frequently represented among those who are, by various criteria, more participant, more informed, more mobile, closer to the articulate mainstream, more worldly – in a word, less parochial.

Isolationism is more likely to signify a posture of international belligerency than of international pacifism, and has more to do with hostility against foreign nations and disavowal of responsibility for the well-being of others than with the considered assessment of the risks arising from international entanglements; but a subgroup of pacific isolationists can be identified who will more closely reflect, though they will not match, the personality and attitude traits of the nonisolationists.

Foreign policy attitudes are more likely than specific foreign policy issues to engage other attitude and personality variables, and they will engage them more strongly; opinions on concrete foreign policy questions will be susceptible to social and economic forces and to political exigencies more than to personality influence; but among the political class especially, for whom issues are more salient and more clearly understood, correlations between personality and attitude factors on the one side and concrete issue outlooks on the other will be clearly discernible and significant.

The exploration of these and other notions was carried out through the analysis of data collected from three extensive field surveys during the middle and late nineteen-fifties. I have described the sample and questionnaire procedures in previous publications and shall refrain, therefore, from an extended discussion of those matters here.[15]

At least this much might be pointed out, however: the first of the three surveys was carried out on a cross-section sample of the population of Minnesota (n=1,082), with the cooperation of the Minnesota Poll. The second was a national cross section survey of 1,484 respondents, administered with the assistance of the American Institute of Public Opinion (Gallup Poll). The third, and most important for present purposes, was a mail survey of 3,020 Democratic and Republican leaders, ranging from office holders at the national levels of party and government to local officials and precinct workers. All had, two years earlier, served as delegates and alternates to the 1956 national Democratic and Republican conventions.

The questionnaires employed in the three studies had many similarities. All contained large batteries of attitude and personality scales of the self-administering type, together with numerous questions relating to political experience, personal background, political opinions, and social characteristics. The nature and diversity of these scales will become evident from their presentation in the next section. Approximately forty-five scales were utilized in all three studies; others, however, were employed in the Minnesota (MB) study but not in the national (PAB) studies, while still others appeared in the national but not in the Minnesota studies. Altogether, data are available for more than 70 separate scales, containing almost 550 individual items.

Isolationism was one of the scales employed in all three studies. All scales were subjected to validity and reliability tests, including, variously, empirical validation by means of criterion groups, face validity assessments by expert raters, modified Guttman reproducability checks, and an ongoing construct validity evaluation that compares our theoretical expectations with the actual results. The Isolationism scale has been subject to all but the criterion group procedure, and we are satisfied that it meets the tests of unidimensionality and other criteria of validity. In addition, the items were initially drawn from materials published by, and about, active isolationist groups, and they express the sentiments that appeared most frequently in those writings. Built, like the other scales, from a much larger initial pool of items, it was reduced to a nine-item

15. See the discussion of these questions in H. McClosky, "Conservatism and Personality," *American Political Science Review*, Vol. 52 (1958), pp. 27–45; and H. McClosky, P. Hoffman, and R. O'Hara, "Issue Conflict and Consensus Among Party Leaders and Followers," *American Political Science Review*, Vol. 54 (1960), pp. 406–27.

scale after testing and retesting.[16] The items in the Isolationism scale are presented in Table 1, together with their item difficulties for the national leader and general population samples.

In most of the analysis to follow, I have, for convenience of presentation, classified respondents as high, middle, and low on each of the scales. The cutting points for these divisions were set by finding the arithmetic thirds in the distribution for the general population on each particular scale. Thus, those who score from 6 to 9 on the Isolationism scale have been classified as high, or "isolationists"; those scoring from 3 to 5 have been called middle isolationists; and those scoring from 0 to 2 have been designated as low, or nonisolationists.

Table 1 — The Isolationism Scale — Items and Item Frequencies

Items	Percentage Agree National Leader Sample (n=3,020)	General Population Sample (n=1,484)
The best market for American goods is right here at home.	67%	51%
We almost have to restrict the amount of goods we let into this country because labor is so cheap in most other nations.	66	56
Most of the countries which have gotten economic help from America end up resenting what we have done for them.	61	54
These foreign wars America has been in are just part of the old quarrels Europeans have been having among themselves for centuries.	37	49
The federal government should be prevented from giving away any more of our wealth to foreign governments.	37	82
In spite of all the claims to the contrary, America can defend herself, as she has always done, without the aid of our so-called allies.	24	69
George Washington's advice to stay out of agreements with foreign powers is just as wise now as it was when he was alive.	23	75
By belonging to the UN we are running the danger of losing our constitutional right to control our own affairs.	17	55
Anytime American boys are found fighting on foreign shores, it is doubtful that the war is one that the United States should really be in.	17	30

16. Although some of the scales were constructed by McClosky alone, the majority of the scales in the initial inventory were built in collaboration with Professors Paul E. Meehl and Kenneth E. Clark, of the Psychology Department, University of Minnesota. They were developed initially in a preliminary survey, for scale construction purposes only, of 1,200 residents of the Twin Cities, Minnesota.

I will begin by presenting some descriptive data on the distribution of isolationist sentiments among American political leaders and voters today. I will then consider the data on isolationism as an outgrowth of aversive personality traits, as a function of psychological and cognitive deprivation, and as part of a network of attitudes. This will be followed by an examination of the personality and attitude correlates of foreign policy issue orientations, and this, in turn, by an analysis of the pacific-jingoist distinction.

FINDINGS

For reasons that will become plain, isolationist beliefs are far more common among the general population than they are among the political leaders. (See Table 2 and Figure 1.) Similarly, isolationism is more frequently expressed among the less educated than the more educated. Intellectuals, as the mean scores show, are least isolationist of all. By every criterion on which we have data, isolationism increases as political and social awareness decline: It is more common among the unthinking than among the informed segments of the electorate, stronger among the poor, the culturally deprived, and any other groups who have been cut off from the mainstreams of the articulate culture.[17] Some of the reasons for this will be considered at a later point.

Table 2 — Mean Scores on Isolationism for Three Levels of Articulateness* Among Party Leaders and Supporters

	LEVEL OF ARTICULATENESS											
	Democratic Leaders			Republican Leaders			Democratic Followers			Republican Followers		
	H	*M*	*L*	*H*	*M*	*L*	*H*	*M*	*L*	*H*	*M*	*L*
Mean Isolationism Score	1.94	3.54	5.21	3.04	4.60	6.14	2.54	4.50	5.92	2.71	4.56	5.94
Number in Sample	638	1,047	103	384	782	66	76	527	222	83	415	125

*High articulates or intellectuals (H) are defined as college graduates who also score high on the Intellectuality scale. Low articulates (L) are persons of grade school education who score low on the Intellectuality scale.

17. On the role of education and information see Almond, *op. cit.*, Key, *op. cit.*, pp. 336–8, for example; K. Garrison, "Worldminded Attitudes of College Students in a Southern Town," *Journal of Social Psychology*, Vol. 54 (1961), pp. 147–54; M. Kriesberg, "Dark Areas of Ignorance," in L. Markel (ed.), *Public Opinion and Foreign Policy* (New York: Harper and Brothers, 1949), pp. 49–64; R. Lane, "Political Personality and Electoral Choice," *American Political Science Review*, Vol. 49 (1955), pp. 173–90. Also A. Hero, *Americans in World Affairs* (Boston: World Peace Foundation, 1959). See, in addition, "Citizen Participation in World Affairs: Problems and Possibilities," a special issue of *Journal of Social Issues*, Vol. 4 (Winter, 1948).

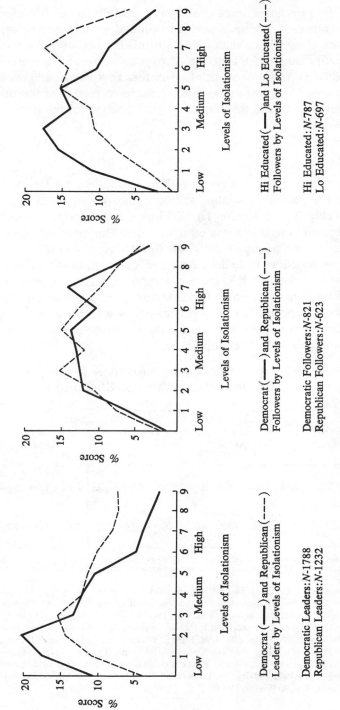

Figure 1 — Percent Scoring at Each Level of Isolationism[1]: Comparison of Democratic and Republican Leaders and Followers[2]

1. 0–2 Scorers are low on Isolationism
   3–5 Scorers are middle on Isolationism
   6–9 Scorers are high on Isolationism
2. National Samples only

Isolationism also turns out to be significantly stronger among Republican than among Democratic leaders.[18] The difference is related to the liberal-conservative differences that separate the participating members of the two parties, and will be further explored when those attitudes are discussed. Note, however, that the rank-and-file Democratic and Republican supporters differ scarcely at all on the isolationist dimension, and the small differences that can be discerned are found principally in the comparison of their most articulate members.

ISOLATIONISM AND AVERSIVE PERSONALITY TRAITS

Need Aggression

Of all the personality states that one might expect, on theoretical grounds, to relate to isolationism, *n Aggression* and its concomitant aversive dispositions should be among the most powerful.[19] The need to punish, reject, avoid, or contain others is very close to being a genotypic parallel of the values contained in the classical expressions of isolationism. Persons of more appetitive disposition are characterized by their openness to experience, their acceptance and trust of others, their tolerance of human foibles, their sympathy, and their desire to relieve human suffering. Clinical studies show that such persons carry less guilt and anxiety, impute less hostility to others, and are more willing to become involved with their fellow men. We expected, then, that persons of strong misanthropic inclinations would turn out substantially more isolationist than persons of more benign persuasion. We anticipated this correlation not because of any similarity in the substance of the values being correlated, for their content in no way overlaps. Take,

18. On party differences in foreign policy orientation—in this case attitudes toward Cuba—see P. Ekman, E. Tufte, K. Archibald, and R. A. Brody, "Coping with Cuba: Divergent Policy Preferences of State Political Leaders," in press, and Key, *op. cit.*

19. The aggressiveness trait has been paid more attention by researchers than most other personality variables. A review of a wide range of experimental research is given in L. Berkowitz, *Aggression* (New York: McGraw-Hill, 1962). See also D. J. Levinson, "Authoritarian Personality and Foreign Policy," *Journal of Conflict Resolution*, Vol. 1 (1957), pp. 37–47; H. Grace, "Hostility, Communication and International Tension: I, The Hostility Inventory," *Journal of Social Psychology*, Vol. 34 (1951), pp. 31–40; "Hostility, Communication and International Tension: II, Social Group Backgrounds," *Journal of Educational Psychology*, Vol. 41 (1950), pp. 161–72; H. Grace and G. L. Grace, "Hostility, Communication and International Tension: III, The Hostility Factors," *Journal of Educational Psychology*, Vol. 42 (1951), pp. 206–14; R. Stagner, *op. cit.*; B. Christiansen, *op. cit.* In addition, see H. P. Smith and E. Rosen, "Some Psychological Correlates of Worldmindedness and Authoritarianism," *Journal of Personality*, Vol. 26 (1958), pp. 170–83; M. B. Smith, "The Personal Setting of Public Opinions: A Study of Attitudes toward Russia," *Public Opinion Quarterly*, Vol. 11 (1947–48), pp. 507–23; and W. MacKinnon and R. Centers, "Social and Psychological Factors in Public Orientation toward an Outgroup," *American Journal of Sociology*, Vol. 63 (1958), pp. 415–19.

for example, the Misanthropy index. A seventeen-item measure, it contains statements that bear entirely on one's feelings about mankind in general and various kinds of individuals in particular. (Typical items: "You have to be pretty choosy about picking friends." "I distrust people who try to be different from the rest of us." "People ought to be satisfied with what they have.") The other scales in Table 3, such as Hostility

Table 3 — Isolationism and Misanthropy
(Percentages Down)

		ISOLATIONISM								
		National Leader Sample (n = 3,020)			General Population Sample (n = 1,484)					
					High Education*			Low Education*		
		H (643)	M (1,150)	L (1,227)	H (199)	M (359)	L (229)	H (358)	M (260)	L (79)
Scales										
	H	37	22	8	35	22	7	49	27	10
Hostility	M	48	48	38	47	42	35	41	50	41
	L	15	29	55	18	36	58	11	23	49
	H	34	17	8	51	25	10	70	34	23
Paranoia	M	36	35	24	32	35	26	21	37	29
	L	29	48	67	17	40	64	9	29	48
	H	37	15	2	45	25	5	67	42	13
Misanthropy	M	46	44	20	43	48	28	28	41	49
	L	17	41	78	12	27	67	4	16	38
F-Authori-	H	38	15	3	43	20	3	67	34	6
tarianism	M	48	49	21	48	49	29	30	57	53
	L	15	37	76	9	31	68	3	9	41
Contempt	H	36	20	8	31	19	8	47	25	8
for	M	51	56	39	50	53	45	42	57	61
Weakness	L	13	24	54	19	28	47	11	17	32
Intolerance	H	41	25	10	50	27	15	62	43	23
of Human	M	47	50	45	44	53	45	31	42	46
Frailty	L	13	24	45	6	20	40	6	15	32
					Minnesota Sample Only (n = 1,082)					
					High Education*			Low Education*		
					H (147)	M (272)	L (224)	H (203)	M (177)	L (51)
	H				9	32	48	11	32	27
Faith in	M				48	41	33	39	40	53
People	L				43	27	19	50	28	20

*On these and subsequent tables High Education respondents are high school graduates and above; Low Education respondents are those who did not graduate from high school.

and Paranoia, are typical clinical scales designed to assess the genotypic personality states suggested by their names. Nothing in the face content of their items suggests a connection with isolationism either.

The connection is as powerful as we had predicted. As can be seen in Table 3, whereas 37 per cent of the isolationists in the political leader sample score high on the Misanthropy scale, only 2 per cent of the nonisolationists are misanthropic to the same degree. For the general population, the scores range from 65 per cent high to 4 per cent. Differences of comparable magnitude are apparent throughout the entire table for every sample (educated and uneducated) and every measure. Correlations computed on the intellectuals in both the elite and general population samples (not shown in this table) yield essentially the same results. Even for intellectuals — and in some instances especially for intellectuals — the holding of isolationist beliefs is powerfully correlated with the disposition to punish, reject, and ridicule other men.

The scores on the Paranoia scale in Table 3 are equally consistent and impressive. Paranoia, of course, is a complex response disposition, but it may be understood in part as a projection of hostility. The paranoid tends to impute to others the impulses and desires to which he is himself prey. When he perceives others with suspicion, and regards them as deceptive, conspiratorial, and diabolical, the paranoid is expressing his fear and aversion of others and his desire either to shut them out or to bring them under control. The wish to dominate and to contain others is one of the elements in the megalomania and grandiosity that so often mark the paranoid personality. No great leap is required to move from these response dispositions to an orientation which holds foreigners and foreign nations to be scheming and dangerous.

The Intolerance of Human Frailty and Contempt for Weakness scales measure other aspects of the aggressive-aversive response. It may be logically inconsistent for an isolationist simultaneously to fear the demonic power of others and to scorn them for their weaknesses. It is not, however, psychologically inconsistent. While he fears their power to harm him, he loathes what he perceives to be their uncertain character, their shabby morals, and their lack of pride in seeking his collaboration and sympathy. Then, too, one who has a strong antagonism toward others is often led to reject them on any ground or pretext that presents itself. The object of the complaint is less telling in many cases than the impulse that gave rise to it.

The data collected in the present study — only a small part of which is being presented here — suggest that the relation between *n Aggression* and isolationism is not unique. Persons of hostile disposition, it seems, fasten upon various objects to vent their anger. Foreign nations are only one of many classes of stimuli to which they respond in the same way.

This is not to suggest, of course, that persons of aggressive disposition will express their anger in all contexts. A person may be manifestly kindly in his everyday life but fiercely antagonistic in his response to certain public questions. The manner of his response, after all, is a function not only of a general response disposition but of other factors as well, including the saliency of the stimulus object. If he is indifferent to the state of the nation or its place in the world, his hostility may be engaged scarcely at all. How strongly he aggresses also depends on whether it is safe to do so. A man who hesitates to disagree with his wife on any question whatever may not shy at all from expressing his rage toward foreigners, foreign nations, or any other groups outside his immediate household.

Whether hostility is expressed also depends on whether the prevailing conditions are limiting or facilitating, i.e. whether the expression of enmity is "legitimate" in the context. Hatred of Cuba or China is currently legitimate in most subcultures of the United States, and one may assail them with impunity. There are, in addition, internal restraints on the expression of such "antagonistic" attitudes as isolationism. Some individuals are psychologically less free than others to admit, much less to express, their hostility. A highly "defensed" person who cannot admit even to himself the rage that boils within him may be unable to show his anger or may express it only against targets that are safe in the sense that he can attack them without fear of arousing guilt.

Despite these qualifications, our data show plainly that *n Aggression* tends to be generalized across a range of attitudes, and that many objects can serve to satisfy it. But there is no mistaking that psychologically hostile persons will score isolationist far more often than persons who are more compassionate. The willingness to take on international entanglements or obligations plainly reflects not only ones judgment about the utility of such involvements for securing the national safety but also, in many cases, the degree to which one has concern for other people.

Psychological Inflexibility

The parallels between psychological inflexibility and isolationism are not so immediately apparent as were those shown in the case of *n Aggression*. Nevertheless, there are reasons to expect inflexibility and isolationism to be strongly and positively correlated. These reasons will become evident from a description of the inflexible personality configuration.

In a study undertaken elsewhere to explore the nature of psychological inflexibility and its significance for political belief and behavior,[20]

20. The volume reporting the results of this research is currently in progress, under the joint authorship of McClosky, Paul E. Meehl, and Kenneth E. Clark.

we have conceptualized inflexibility as an attribute of the defense mechanisms (e.g., reaction formation, rationalization, projection, denial, and the like). The inflexible person is one whose dependence upon these substitute expressions is extreme. Inflexibility, we believe, is a genotypic source trait, for the most part under aversive rather than appetitive control. Its manifest characteristics include an inclination toward black-white polarization and dichotomous distinctions, premature cognitive closure, stereotypic and automatized thought sequences, stimulus fixation, selective attention, and a narrowing of exposure to exclude unfamiliar persons and other stimulus objects. The inflexible person is also characterized by a strong need for order and autonomy, and is made acutely uncomfortable by ambiguity, uncertainty, contingency, complexity, and unfamiliarity. He tends, characteristically, to oversimplify by narrowing the phenomenal field and by assigning fixed, predictable roles to all the players. He is in a continual struggle against his own impulse life, and is rigidly constrained in the limits he imposes upon himself and others. Partly for these reasons, he is unusually susceptible both to hostility and anxiety. He is impatient with, and even angered by, differences and he accomodates poorly to novelty and change. He is severe in his judgments and intolerant of unconventionality. He is attracted to opinions that are categorical and dogmatic and he tends more than most to exclude incompatible information. Despite his elaborate defenses, he has low self-esteem, for which he often compensates by demeaning the motives and behavior of others. Individuals with this personality pattern often suffer a reduction in their capacity for interaction and an impairment in cognitive function.

Although this portrait is based on considerable evidence from our own research and the research of others, it is, of course, ideal-typical and inevitably overdrawn. Even so, we can easily see why individuals of inflexible personality might be expected to favor isolationist sentiments.[21] The parallel, it seems, is far closer than we originally had reason to think. Isolationism offers its supporters a dichotomous choice, a polarization of forces so clearly etched as to contain little or no ambiguity. The world is made simple, with "them" on one side and "us" on the other. "They"—the nationals of other countries—are irrevocably estranged from "us" by culture, politics, language, manners, skin color, customs, and national character. These variations, which might intrigue some people, merely confound and repel the inflexible. He partitions the world in an effort to make order out of diversity, simplicity out of complexity, clarity out of confusion. He also manages in this way to

21. A study concerned with personality traits related to our notion of psychological inflexibility is M. Farber, "The Anal Character and Political Aggression," *Journal of Abnormal and Social Psychology*, Vol. 51 (1950), pp. 486–89.

reduce his anxiety about "strangers" who (as he characteristically sees it) freely gratify their impulses at the expense of character, duty, integrity, and independence. Why become involved with such people? Why rescue them from the misfortunes they have inflicted upon themselves?

Since it is important for the inflexible to achieve control and make the world manageable, he resists attachments that deprive him, or his country, of autonomy and initiative. Every treaty, every alliance gives hostages to disorder and uncertainty and strengthens potential enemies. A nation that looks to its own interests without regard for the demands of others is a nation that commands fate; a nation that allies itself with others becomes fate's pawn. Not only does it lose power over the behavior of other nations, but over its own affairs as well.

The strength of the relationship between isolationism on the one side and psychological inflexibility on the other is clearly evident in Table 4. Among the political influentials, 63 per cent of the isolationists

Table 4 — Isolationism and Inflexibility
(Percentages Down)

		ISOLATIONISM								
		National Leader Sample (n=3,020)			General Population Sample (n=1,484)					
					High Education			Low Education		
		H (643)	M (1,150)	L (1,227)	H (199)	M (359)	L (229)	H (358)	M (260)	L (79)
Scales										
Intolerance of Ambiguity	H	63	42	24	53	23	13	64	43	29
	M	24	29	26	34	37	30	26	35	25
	L	13	28	50	13	40	57	10	22	46
Obsessive	H	62	51	35	54	32	25	57	38	18
	M	21	22	25	20	29	24	23	27	33
	L	17	26	40	26	40	52	20	35	49
Rigidity	H	46	32	16	53	30	21	65	48	28
	M	28	28	24	26	28	23	22	24	37
	L	26	40	60	22	42	57	14	28	35
Inflexibility Index	H	30	17	8	27	8	3	43	18	4
	M-H	42	34	26	40	30	21	32	39	24
	M-L	21	30	33	22	35	29	19	27	37
	L	7	19	32	11	27	48	6	17	35

score high on intolerance of ambiguity, compared with 24 percent of the nonisolationists. Differences of comparable magnitude hold for the general population, for Democratic and Republican leaders, and for both the educated and uneducated. The pattern is equally unmistakable

when we examine the results on the Rigidity and Obsessiveness scales, and on the Inflexibility Index. Again it should be observed that the items on these scales are free of political content. All refer to comments about one's personal habits, one's feelings about carelessness, disorder, perfection, decisiveness, the manner of organizing one's work, and so forth. Nothing in the items suggests on their face a connection with isolationism.[22]

Anxiety, Ego-Strength, and Feelings of Marginality

Both anxiety and low ego-strength are aspects of the aversive personality, for while they manifestly testify to dissatisfaction with oneself, they also carry heavy loadings of fear and rage and reflect an implicit wish to escape, avoid, or disarm others. The scales we have listed in Table 5 as measures of anxiety (Psychological Disorganization and

Table 5 — Isolationism and Anxiety
Minnesota Sample Only
(Percentages Down)

(n = 1,082)

		ISOLATIONISM					
		High Education			Low Education		
		H (147)	M (272)	L (224)	H (203)	M (177)	L (51)
Scales							
Psychological	H	36	31	19	51	37	24
Disorgani-	M	37	39	40	33	34	29
zation	L	27	30	41	16	29	47
	H	26	22	13	37	22	10
Manifest	M	53	49	46	47	53	49
Anxiety	L	21	29	42	15	25	41

Manifest Anxiety) refer primarily to constitutional states, such as restlessness, inability to concentrate, and excessive worry. So too do Guilt and Need Inviolacy (Table 6) which measure, as their names imply, profound disappointment in oneself and the fear of being found naked and unprotected before the world. The remaining scales included under the ego-strength category in Table 6 report not so much the inner life of the respondent as his ability (or inability) to accomodate to the world and command successfully the life-space in which he functions. All the

22. In reporting these results, we are not unaware of the controversy that has developed among psychologists concerning the nature and generalizability of so-called rigidity. We are satisfied that that controversy offers no difficulties for the conclusions drawn here. Part of the justification is similar to that offered in the discussion of the generalizability of *n-Aggression*. Much more can be said, but this is not the place to say it.

scales in these tables, however, register in one fashion or another feelings of frustration, fear, disappointment, self-doubt, inadequacy, or failure.

Table 6 — Isolationism and Ego-Strength
(Percentages Down)

		ISOLATIONISM								
		National Leader Sample (n = 3,020)			General Population Sample (n = 1,484)					
					High Education			Low Education		
		H (643)	M (1,150)	L (1,227)	H (199)	M (359)	L (229)	H (358)	M (260)	L (79)
Scales										
	H	68	79	87	40	41	64	19	30	42
Dominance	M	23	17	11	31	34	24	30	34	33
	L	9	5	2	29	25	12	51	36	25
	H	33	22	14	35	22	12	46	29	20
Guilt	M	32	33	26	33	32	28	31	35	28
	L	35	45	60	32	46	60	23	36	52
	H	58	62	61	25	34	48	21	29	39
Life Satisfaction	M	27	27	28	35	35	34	32	32	34
	L	15	11	11	40	31	18	47	40	27
	H	35	18	9	42	21	12	62	28	13
Need Inviolacy	M	25	24	16	29	28	19	23	30	29
	L	40	57	75	29	51	69	15	42	58
	H	23	37	53	18	32	49	8	22	42
Responsibility	M	46	48	38	39	39	44	32	45	44
	L	30	14	9	43	29	7	60	33	14
	H	16	12	8	20	14	9	35	25	14
Status Frustration	M	35	37	26	48	40	33	41	41	38
	L	49	51	66	32	47	59	25	34	48
					Minnesota Sample Only (n = 1,082)					
					High Education			Low Education		
					H (147)	M (272)	L (224)	H (203)	M (177)	L (51)
	H				35	35	45	24	15	22
Self-Confidence	M				41	42	37	44	44	41
	L				24	23	19	32	41	37

It is, of course, now well-established that such psychological states tend—through displacement, the frustration-aggression phenomenon, or the play of other defense mechanisms—to emerge in many of their victims as resentment and envy. As we have elsewhere observed,[23] those who strongly harbor these feelings "tend to project upon the external

23. H. McClosky and J. Schaar, "Psychological Dimensions of Anomy," *American Sociological Review*, Vol. 30 (1965), pp. 14–39.

world the doubts and fears that dominate their own mental life." They are likely to be disgruntled and suspicious toward the world in general. This includes the international world, which mirrors for them the uncertainty, disorder, drift, and normlessness they are inclined to find everywhere.

On this reasoning, we would expect isolationism to be embraced by some people as a way of handling their own insecurities, doubts, and frustrations. Like ethnocentrism, to which it is closely related psychologically, an isolationist orientation would permit them not only to blame others (including other nations) for the bad fate that life has dealt them, but also to satisfy their impulse to punish, reject, and demean others, partly as retribution and partly as a way of bringing other men down to an even lower, more miserable level than their own. Foreign nations, it should be observed, represent a fairly safe target for such aggression. Not only can one usually assail them with impunity, but by doing so one can simultaneously demonstrate one's patriotism.

Except for Manifest Anxiety and Life Satisfaction, which do not consistently yield correlations that are statistically significant,[24] the results from the various measures of anxiety and ego-strength presented in Tables 5 and 6 furnish strong, inferential support for these hypotheses. Even among the political leaders — where foreign policy orientations, one assumes, are more rationally calculated in response to objective international realities — the isolationists are, by a ratio of two to one, more likely than the nonisolationists to manifest strong feelings of guilt, and, by a ratio of four to one, to express anxiety about the inviolacy of their inner selves. Isolationists in all samples feel themselves less dominant or in command of themselves, tend to lack self-assurance, and, by comparison with nonisolationists, have accomodated themselves less successfully to their immediate life-space.

Similar results are found in the data on feelings of marginality presented in Table 7. Here we test more directly the hypothesis that isolationism is one expression, among others, of a general feeling of malaise or of alienation from the world as one finds it. The Alienation scale shown in that table refers primarily to feelings of personal isolation from primary groups and the absence of a nurturant environment. The Anomy scale assesses the degree to which individuals feel that the society is normless and lacking in direction and meaning. The Cruel World scale measures the tendency to regard the world as cold and indifferent, unconcerned with the respondent's fate. The Bewilderment scale, used only in the MB study, testifies to the respondent's feeling that the world is hopelessly complicated and unfathomable.

24. Unless otherwise noted, all differences reported in these tables are, by chi-square tests, statistically significant at or beyond the .01 level of confidence.

Table 7 — Isolationism and Feelings of Marginality
(Percentages Down)

| | | National Leader Sample (n=3,020) | | | General Population Sample (n=1,484) | | | | | |
| | | | | | High Education | | | Low Education | | |
Scales		H (643)	M (1,150)	L (1,227)	H (199)	M (359)	L (229)	H (358)	M (260)	L (79)
Alienation	H	25	17	12	35	26	17	54	33	24
	M	38	37	31	41	39	28	36	38	37
	L	37	47	57	24	35	55	11	29	39
Anomy	H	21	7	1	41	20	5	70	37	13
	M	48	38	18	46	46	30	25	45	49
	L	32	55	80	13	34	65	5	17	38
Cruel, Indifferent World	H	26	9	2	35	15	2	53	20	6
	M	52	44	23	33	49	27	41	52	42
	L	23	47	77	12	36	70	7	27	52

Minnesota Sample Only (n=1,082)

| | | High Education (n=643) | | | Low Education (n=431) | | |
		H (147)	M (272)	L (224)	H (203)	M (177)	L (51)
Bewilderment	H	48	22	10	58	29	12
	M	33	42	32	33	42	29
	L	19	36	58	9	29	59

The response on each of these measures is uniformly in the predicted direction. Isolationists in both the political leader and general population samples register significantly stronger feelings of estrangement, bewilderment, and moral chaos.[25] By an overwhelming margin, they are also disposed to regard the world as a hostile, dangerous, or indifferent place, populated by potential enemies and harboring innumerable threats. Similar findings turn up on a scale measuring pessimistic outlook on the world's future (not shown on this table), with isolationists scoring strongly pessimistic (in comparison with internationalists) by a ratio of approximately 5 to 1. The results on these scales are consistent for both parties and all education levels.

Whether the relationship between these personality measures and isolationism is causal or epiphenomenal is difficult to say. Like isolationism, they are all measures of dissatisfaction and fear. All refer to some imagined hostile force that prevents happiness and the realization of one's desires. That they express concern about the world or the

25. On anomy, see C. Farris, "Selected Attitudes on Foreign Affairs Correlates of Authoritarianism and Political Anomie," *Journal of Politics*, Vol. 22 (1960), pp. 50–67.

society rather than about oneself is really beside the point. Most people who score high on these measures are implicitly complaining about their own disappointments and frustrations, their feelings of being left out, and their sense of impotence and futility. They and the world have somehow diverged.

For many people, therefore, a preference for isolationism may be largely an expression of protest and resentment. I am not suggesting that no isolationist genuinely believes in the specific recommendations of the isolationist philosophy; among the political influentials, in fact, only a minority of the isolationists (approximately one-fourth) score high on the marginality measures. Nevertheless, one of the attributes of the isolationist persuasion is its association with a network of responses that bespeak frustration and disappointment.

The results on the Anomy and Bewilderment scales (and on the political alienation scales to be presented below) signify that isolationism is also related to divorcement from one's own society. Despite their jingoism and their ardently professed love of country, many isolationists are in important respect disappointed in it—even to the point of repudiating some of its most fundamental values. Possibly, therefore, the antagonism they evince toward other nations is a displacement of their dissatisfaction with their own society. Since they cannot bring themselves to reject openly a nation with which they seek so urgently to identify, their dislike of it is masked even from themselves. The same mechanisms of psychological defense (described earlier) by which an individual conceals from consciousness certain unpleasant facts about himself, also prevent him from admitting to himself his true feelings about his country. Every bit of evidence we have turned up in our research on this question confirms that isolationists, chauvinists, jingoists, or any combination of the three harbor a disproportionate share of resentment and anger against the quality of contemporary American life, against many of its fundamental values, and against the nature and performance of its institutions.

COGNITIVE CAPACITY AND FUNCTION

Isolationism, as we noted in Table 2, is found less frequently among the educated than the uneducated, less frequently still among the political influentials, and least frequently of all among politically active intellectuals. On this evidence, isolationism appears to be a deviant rather than a popular orientation among articulate Americans. This inference, of course, is also congruent with what can readily be observed in the thrust of American foreign policy since World War II. Membership in

the United Nations, participation in NATO and other defense alliances, the Marshall Plan, extensive foreign aid programs, and numerous other instances of intervention in world affairs support the conclusion that the American norm is now one of international collaboration and involvement. This, in turn, suggests that support for isolationist sentiments at this time (and perhaps in some past periods as well) is a function of articulateness as such, and of one's ability to learn and take cognizance of the norms. If so, we may have come upon an additional reason for the powerful correlations shown between isolationism on the one side and the several forms of anxiety, low self-esteem, and marginality on the other.[26] These psychological states have a crippling effect on political socialization and the learning of community norms. They tend to impede effective social interaction and to impair the internalization of a society's implicit values. We find evidence throughout our data that persons who are in command of themselves, who are not exhausted by anxiety or incapacitated by guilt, disappointments, and frustrations, who are self-assured, personally effective, and secure in their relationships with others are somewhat more likely to be aware of, and to accept, the norms of the articulate culture. While socialization, of course, is strongly influenced by education and status, the findings on this matter hold for the leader samples as well as the masses, for the educated as well as the uneducated, and for those in the upper status categories as well as those in the lower.[27]

The data presented in Table 8 bear on this matter to some degree. In addition to the findings on education, the table shows the relationship between isolationism and three other measures of articulateness. The outcome is in every instance consistent with the hypothesis: an elevation in awareness or cognitive function decreases the frequency of isolationism. Even among the political leaders, differences in orientation toward intellectual activities and the life of the mind correspond closely with outlook on foreign policy questions: 78 per cent of the nonisolationists in this sample score high on Intellectuality, compared with only 30 per cent of the isolationists. The differences are also large on the Awareness scale, an achievement measure that assesses each

26. For other research on the relationship of anxiety and self-image to social attitudes, see C. Farris, *op. cit.*; A. Brodbeck and H. Perlmutter, "Self-Dislike as an Indicator of Marked Ingroup-Outgroup Preferences," *Journal of Psychology*, Vol. 38 (1954), pp. 271-80; and H. Perlmutter, "Relations between the Self-Image, the Image of the Foreigner, and the Desire to Live Abroad," *Journal of Psychology*, Vol. 38 (1954), pp. 131-37.

27. I have not included in this paper data on the relationship between social background and isolationism. On the relationship between various foreign policy attitudes and socioeconomic status, variously defined, see Key, *op. cit.*, pp. 130-34, 140, 150; Almond, *op. cit.*, Garrison, *op. cit.*, MacKinnon and Centers, "Social Psychological Factors in Public Orientation toward an Outgroup," *op. cit.*; P. Blau, "Orientation of College Students toward International Relations," *American Journal of Sociology*, Vol. 59 (1953), pp. 205-14; and W. Miller, "Socioeconomic Analysis of Political Behavior," *Midwest Journal of Political Science*, Vol. 2 (1958), pp. 239-55.

respondent's level of information about political and social affairs. The internationalists are, to a significant degree, better informed about public affairs than are the isolationists. Other measures employed in the study, such as Mysticism and Acquiescence, furnish an indirect indication of intellectual capacity, an ability to reason from evidence,

Table 8 — Isolationism and Cognitive Functioning
(Percentages Down)

Scales		ISOLATIONISM								
		National Leader Sample (n = 3,020)			General Population Sample (n = 1,484)					
					High Education			Low Education		
		H	M	L	H	M	L	H	M	L
		(643)	(1,150)	(1,227)	(199)	(359)	(229)	(358)	(260)	(79)
Education*	H	66	74	85						
	M	27	23	12						
	L	7	3	3						
Intellectuality	H	30	51	78	23	45	72	15	29	43
	M	42	35	18	44	38	23	39	40	43
	L	28	14	4	33	17	5	46	31	14
Acquiescence	H	37	15	6	42	19	3	67	32	11
	M	41	47	29	40	43	35	25	37	32
	L	22	38	65	18	38	61	8	30	57

		Minnesota Sample Only (n = 1,082)					
		High Education (n = 643)			Low Education (n = 431)		
		H	M	L	H	M	L
		(147)	(272)	(224)	(203)	(177)	(51)
Awareness	H	24	35	54	8	7	25
	M	33	39	34	24	44	43
	L	43	26	12	68	49	31

*High Education = some college, college graduate
Middle Education = some high school, high-school graduate
Low education = grade school

cognitive consistency, and the like. These scales also yield the same basic conclusion. From whatever direction one approaches this question, then, the influentials, the educated, the informed, and what Rosenau[28] has called the "attentive public" are significantly less isolationist than the less informed and less educated members of the population.

These findings are consistent with certain inferences that can be drawn from other parts of the data. From our examination of numerous personality and other types of variables, it appears that whatever impairs cognitive function or limits cognitive capacity tends to increase

28. See J. Rosenau, *Public Opinion and Foreign Policy* (New York: Random House, 1961).

isolationist sentiments. Hence, social or cultural deprivation, remoteness from the centers of political culture, ignorance of facts, psychological disorders that have a deleterious effect on cognitive performance, or any other impediments to effective social learning tend to diminish support for the prevailing values of the society. Some people who score as isolationists are simply unmindful of the full meaning of their responses.[29] Their support for isolationism is, in part, a preference for the simpler and more easily grasped view. To favor isolationism requires only one uncomplicated intellectual operation: One simply withdraws or disengages oneself. In this way, one can avoid having to face up to the complexities associated with international cooperation, such as the appropriate amount of autonomy to be yielded, the mutual obligations imposed upon the participating nations, the proper interpretation of treaties, and so forth. Conceivably, then, articulates, and especially intellectuals, may show more favor toward internationalism than others do because, in part, they are more conversant with the substance and implications of foreign policy questions and have a greater capacity to ponder them. This superiority in awareness both contributes to and results from the greater saliency that foreign affairs possess for such people. By training, self-image, knowledge, skills, mobility, and associations, they are simply more "cosmopolitan." By intellectual capacity — or at least by functioning intellectual capacity — they are better prepared to assess information and draw conclusions about thorny international questions. Then, too, they are usually far more exposed to the intellectual products of foreign nations, which tends, on the whole, to break down stereotypes and reduce fears of what is foreign and unfamiliar.[30]

That isolationist opinions are for many people an expression of paro-

29. P. Converse, "The Nature of Belief Systems in Mass Publics," in D. Apter (ed.), *Ideology and Discontent* (New York: The Free Press, 1964), pp. 206–61; also S. A. Stouffer, *Communism, Conformity, and Civil Liberties* (New York: Doubleday, 1955); S. M. Lipset, *Political Man* (New York: Doubleday, 1960); J. W. Prothro and C. Grigg, "Fundamental Principles of Democracy: Bases of Agreement and Disagreement," *Journal of Politics*, Vol. 22 (1960), pp. 276–94; R. Dahl, *Who Governs?* (New Haven: Yale University Press, 1961); and H McClosky "Consensus and Ideology in American Politics," *American Political Science Review*, Vol. 58 (1964), pp. 361–82.

30. There is abundant data on the relationship between foreign policy orientation and the amount of information about foreign affairs. In general, those with a high degree of information are more likely to hold an internationalist orientation. In addition to the references cited in footnote 17, see B. Christiansen *op. cit.*; A. Campbell, P. Converse, W. Miller, and D. Stokes, *The American Voter* (New York: John Wiley and Sons, 1960); W. A. Scott, "Correlates of International Attitudes," *Public Opinion Quarterly*, Vol. 22 (1958), pp. 464–72; R. Schonbar, "Students' Attitudes toward Communists: I, The Relation between Intensity of Attitude and Amount of Information," *Journal of Psychology*, Vol. 27 (1949), pp. 55–72; and B. Shimberg, "Information and Attitudes toward World Affairs," *Journal of Educational Psychology*, Vol. 40 (1949), pp. 206–22. See also the summary of the literature in J. Robinson, *Public Information about World Affairs* (Ann Arbor: Survey Research Center of the University of Michigan, 1965).

chialism is suggested by various other findings in the study. For example, persons who come from rural areas, even including political leaders, are significantly more isolationist than persons from metropolitan areas.[31] Internationalist sentiments are stronger among those in both the leader and general population samples who belong to a larger number of organizations, among leaders who have held office at the national (as contrasted with local) levels of government, and among political actives who want the parties to be controlled nationally rather than locally. It may also be worth noting, though the interpretation is open to argument, that a significantly larger number of isolationists in the leader sample would prefer their party to control Congress rather than the Presidency. The explanation, presumably, lies in their greater provincialism and their conviction that Congress offers a firmer brake on international spending and involvement. There are no differences on this question among the general population. In any event, it is characteristic of "provincials" to respond less favorably to the unfamiliar and foreign, and this antipathy may find a natural outlet in isolationism.

Dichotomous Thinking

Not only the capacity, but the style of cognitive performance has a bearing upon the acceptance or rejection of isolationist views. The isolationist persuasion is one of a number of political orientations that are strongly characterized by a tendency to draw sharp we-they distinctions — to separate, in one writer's phrase, "the brother and the other."[32] This propensity is apparent in ethnocentrism, chauvinism, xenophobia, xenophilia (an inverted form of xenophobia), and the numerous caste distinctions that men have invented from the beginning of time.[33]

31. On the role of region and residence, see Key, *op. cit.*, pp. 99–120; Almond, *op. cit.*; and Fensterwald, *op. cit.* Also G. Belknap and A. Campbell, "Political Party Identification and Attitudes toward a Foreign Policy," *Public Opinion Quarterly*, Vol. 15 (Winter, 1951–52), pp. 601–23. For roll-call analyses of congressional behavior, see C. Lerche, "Southern Congressmen and the New Isolationism," *Political Science Quarterly*, Vol. 75 (1960), pp. 321–37; and L. Rieselbach, "The Basis of Isolationist Behavior," *Public Opinion Quarterly*, Vol. 24 (1960), pp. 645–57; and "The Demography of the Congressional Vote on Foreign Aid, 1939–1958," *American Political Science Review*, Vol. 58 (1964), pp. 557–88.

32. The phrase is that of B. Nelson, *The Idea of Usury, From Tribal Brotherhood to Universal Brotherhood* (Princeton: Princeton University Press, 1949).

33. For research employing these variables, see Brodbeck and Perlmutter, *op. cit.*; H. Perlmutter, "Correlates of Two Types of Xenophilic Orientation," *Journal of Abnormal and Social Psychology*, Vol. 52 (1956), pp. 130–35; and "Some Characteristics of the Xenophilic Personality," *Journal of Psychology*, Vol. 38 (1954), pp. 291–300; D. Campbell and B. McCandless, "Ethnocentrism Xenophobia and Personality," *Human Relations*, Vol. 4 (1951), pp. 185–92; T. Adorno et al., *The Authoritarian Personality*; E. Shils, *The Torment of Secrecy* (New York: Free Press, 1956); and T. Lentz, "The Attitudes of World Citizenship," *Journal of Social Psychology*, Vol. 32 (1950), pp. 207–14. For data on anti-Semitism and foreign policy orientation, see S. Crown, "Some Personality Correlates of War-Mindedness and Anti-Semitism," *Journal of Social Psychology*, Vol. 31 (1950), pp. 131–40.

In their extreme form, these divisions are usually accompanied by rituals that protect against impurity or the dilution of the ethnic or cultural strain. The sources of this propensity are now better understood than they once were, but it remains, nevertheless, a bafflling and controversial phenomenon. It seems evident that the tendency to distinguish dichotomous categories is an aspect of the inflexibility syndrome, and that isolationism, like ethnocentrism, is a phenotypic expression of the inflexibility genotype. But this is obviously not the entire story.

Certain aspects of the attachment to one's nation are easy enough to understand: the nation is the definitive, norm-giving association, in which there is a confluence of blood ties, law-making, defense and security functions, a common history and tradition, and a set of myths and symbols that together furnish an extraordinary impetus to unity. What is more difficult to explain is the tendency to exclude, by force, custom, law, or ritualistic practices those who have not previously qualified for admission. The unifying side of this behavioral phenomenon can be explained without recourse to esoteric assumptions or exotic variables. The tendency to dichotomize, however, and to reject as ineradicably tainted all those who fall on the other side of the line, is a more inscrutable form of human behavior, one that originates in the innermost reaches of the human personality. Certainly it is too formidable a question to be addressed in the context of our present inquiry.

Suffice it to recognize that we have given this tendency a name, but that we have not adequately explained it. Whatever its sources, its relationship to isolationist tendencies is overwhelmingly plain. As Table 9 clearly confirms, isolationists differ markedly from nonisolationists on measures that directly or indirectly reflect dichotomous thinking (chauvinism, ethnocentrism, anti-Semitism, and so on). Even among the political influentials, the probability of scoring high on, for example, ethnocentrism is almost ten times as great if one is an isolationist than if one is an internationalist. Similar results are found for all of the measures in the table.

Two of the scales—the We-They General and the We-They Specific— are likely to be unfamiliar, and deserve separate comment. These measures were constructed through item-rating procedures utilizing graduate students and research personnel. The We-They General scale was designed to measure the tendency to make dichotomous distinctions, without regard to any particular group or any specific set of characteristics. The We-They Specific scale was designed to assess the same trait, except that the stimuli were fairly specific and referred to particular groups or types of people. The results on both scales show an unmistakable—indeed, an overwhelming—disposition among isolationists to think in dichotomous terms. On item after item, no matter what the

Table 9—Isolationism and Dichotomous Thinking
(Percentages Down)

Scales		National Leader Sample (n=3,020)			General Population Sample (n=1,484) High Education			Low Education		
		H (643)	M (1,150)	L (1,227)	H (199)	M (359)	L (229)	H (358)	M (260)	L (79)
We-They General	H	47	25	8	43	21	11	52	38	26
	M	2	5	5	31	33	22	33	33	27
	L	52	70	87	26	47	67	16	28	46
We-They Specific	H	36	10	1	49	23	4	64	37	19
	M	54	53	22	40	47	34	29	43	45
	L	11	37	77	11	30	62	7	20	36
Chauvinism	H	40	10	1	43	10	1	70	27	5
	M	37	31	10	39	40	17	25	46	39
	L	23	59	90	18	50	83	4	27	56
Ethno-centrism	H	39	19	4	50	17	6	55	27	9
	M	46	46	22	39	47	26	37	53	41
	L	15	35	75	11	36	69	8	20	51
Anti-Semitism	H	50	33	11	58	37	16	65	48	24
	M	12	13	7	17	17	15	15	15	24
	L	36	53	80	27	46	68	19	34	52
Segregation-Integration	H	53	33	12	48	27	12	60	41	24
	M	29	40	35	27	33	29	28	31	32
	L	17	28	54	26	38	59	22	28	45

target group, the isolationists were significantly more disposed to set them apart or to identify them, implicitly or explicitly, as "different."

Further evidence of this inclination is provided by the responses to questions asking which of the groups listed has "too much power." The results for the leader sample are extremely impressive: the isolationists gave the "too much power" answer more often than the non-isolationists on nine of the ten groups listed. The only group toward which they showed hostility less frequently were the businessmen. The differences in the frequency with which the two groups expressed hostility were especially large in their responses to the foreign born (34 per cent versus 8 per cent), intellectuals (34 per cent versus 8 per cent), Negroes (34 per cent versus 10 per cent), and Jews (32 per cent versus 11 per cent). There were small differences in their responses to farmers, and large differences (87 per cent versus 56 per cent) in their responses to labor unions. Part of this difference reflects the greater conservatism of the isolationists (see below), but much of its expresses their tendency to resent any group other than their own. In the general population, the responses on this question do not hold as consistently. Even in

this sample, however, the isolationists were more likely than the non-isolationists to name foreigners, intellectuals, Negroes, and Jews as having too much power. There are smaller but significant differences for the responses to Catholics as well. The largest differences occur in the responses to foreigners: 49 per cent of the educated isolationists, compared with 10 per cent of the educated internationalists, name foreigners as having too much power. These and the findings reported earlier point not only to the greater xenophobia of the isolationists, but to their stronger disposition to regard all out-groups with aversion.

THE FOREIGN-DOMESTIC ATTITUDE CLUSTER

In the hypothesis section, we raised the question of the relation between foreign policy attitudes and other political attitudes. It was suggested there that attitudes that spring from the same personality genotypes or cognitive styles might well belong to the same attitude cluster, and might therefore be understood partly in that light, rather than as unique stances arising out of political realities. In this section we will explore the connection between isolationism and a number of political attitudes ordinarily identified with domestic politics, specifically liberalism-conservatism, attitudes toward democracy and politics, and radical attitudes of the extreme left and right.

Liberalism-Conservatism

Despite the finding reported by other investigators that the correlation is low between the orientation of voters toward domestic and foreign policy issues (a finding we will consider in the section on issues), we expected to find a strong positive relationship between conservatism and isolationism. We had no reason to believe that the connection between them, if one should turn out, was causal (and we should in any event have had difficulty deciding the direction of the causal arrows), but we did believe that the two orientations contain many elements in common, spring from similar psychological sources, and confront the human condition in similar ways and with similar values.

We have elsewhere in our research been exploring in detail the nature and correlates of the liberal-conservative dimension. This inquiry has reinforced our conviction that liberalism-conservatism is a multi-faceted dimension whose facets are only imperfectly intercorrelated. One can readily identify those elements that go with classical conservatism: resistance to change, veneration of the past, emphasis on tradition, order, status hierarchy, duty, obligation, obedience, and authority, and so on. One can also identify the elements of liberalism-conservatism that have to do with social and economic welfare, the promotion of

economic equality, the protection of property, and government intervention to redress grievances, equalize opportunity, assist the unfor-
tunate, and, more recently, regulate the economy. Other aspects of the
liberal-conservative dimension concern basic assumptions about the
nature of man, belief in human perfectability, the boundaries of social
regulation, the rational planning of human progress, and so forth. While
conservative (or liberal) orientations toward each of these subjects do
not spring with equal force from the same motives, they do reflect
underlying psychological and value dimensions and are more closely
related than one might suppose.

Most conservatives hold what is sometimes characterized as a pessimistic view of man. Whereas liberals tend to profess the inherent good-
ness and perfectability of man, conservatives typically consider him a
creature of appetite and impulse, easily tempted, often weak, and strongly
in need of firm and strictly enforced rules of conduct. A man's afflictions,
therefore, must in the conservative view be traced to his own character
faults, to his indulgence of personal weaknesses, and to his failure to
make sufficiently severe demands upon himself. Liberals are likely to
trace human misfortune to social institutions and the vicissitudes of
human existence, but conservatives are more given to blame the individual himself. It follows from this that liberals are ordinarily more
willing to use the collective resources for repairing wrongs and relieving
unhappiness. To the conservative, poverty, ignorance, and adversity
are signs of the failure of character and furnish a correct estimate of the
actual worth of the individual who is their victim. By the same token,
achievement, wealth, and success are the marks of character, signifying
a willingness to transcend one's limitations and to escape, insofar as it
is possible, from the imperfection that brands all men. The liberal believes
that human destiny can be vastly improved through rational or even
planned approaches to the distribution of life's utilities, but the conservative regards such efforts as vain, and as an interference with the
natural order, which differentiates men according to their worth.

By almost every criterion we have been able to examine, conservatives display less affection for man and less sympathy for his misfortunes. That some men have less access to life's chances must be
accepted as an inevitable feature of the human condition. Inequality
they believe, is not only endemic in human affairs, but may even be
desirable. It places men in their proper stations, furnishes estimates of
their merit, and distributes them into hierarchies that assist in maintaining
order. A certain amount of charity toward those who have failed is
appropriate, but a persistent and single-minded interest in alleviating
their afflictions and elevating their status is mere sentimentality, corrupting
both to the benefactor and the recipient.

This review of liberal and conservative beliefs could be extended, but enough has been said for our purposes. One can scarcely miss the resemblance between the conservative in this portrait and the isolationist who has been revealed in our data. They are differentiated not so much by what they believe about man and society, but by the questions to which they apply those beliefs. Conservatism says nothing about the relations between nations or the responsibility of one group of nationals for another. It has been an ideology principally of domestic politics. But little imagination is needed to appreciate the manner in which its doctrines can be applied to international relations.[34]

Some of the elements in the isolationist persuasion are nearly identical with those found in conservatism. Followers of both are reluctant to become involved with others or to assume responsibility for them. They oppose the rearranging of institutions for the purpose of correcting imbalances or promoting social and economic equality. They resist legislation that might interfere with a man's (or a nation's) autonomy and the disposition of his property, and they are, for the most part, inhospitable to social change. There is in both conservatism and most forms of isolationism the same emphasis upon frugality and the restricted use of resources, the same implicit belief that one's own good fortune — and, by extension, the nation's good fortune — is part of the natural order of things. Believers in both wish to be relieved of responsibility for the destiny of mankind and react with distaste to the "theorists" who wish to "save" the world.

The data in Table 10, and in subsequent tables, clearly confirm the strength of the connection between conservatism and isolationism. Observe that the relationship holds not only for classical conservatism (where it is very powerful), but for economic and "social-welfare" conservatism as well (especially in the leader sample). On the Liberal Issues scale, a measure composed of fourteen domestic issues reflecting attitudes toward humanitarianism and social welfare (e.g., social security, public housing, federal aid to education, minimum wages, and so on), only 7 per cent of the isolationists in the leader sample score high, compared with 40 per cent of the internationalists. Among Democratic leaders, the number of internationalists who hold strongly liberal views on these domestic issues is almost three times as great as the number of isolationists who do so.[35]

---

34. Blau, *op. cit.*, discusses the relationship between conservatism and what he calls power orientation, and Lentz, *op. cit.*, the relationship between nationalism and conservatism.

35. There are so few Republican leaders who score high on liberalism that one can appreciate the results for this sample only by examining the proportions scoring conservative. But 68 per cent of the isolationists in the Republican leader sample score conservative compared with 35 per cent of the internationalists.

Table 10 — Isolationism and Liberal-Conservative Attitudes
(Percentages Down)

		ISOLATIONISM								
		National Leader Sample (n=3,020)			General Population Sample (n=1,484)					
					High Education			Low Education		
		H	M	L	H	M	L	H	M	L
		(643)	(1,150)	(1,227)	(199)	(359)	(229)	(358)	(260)	(79)
Scales										
Pro-Business Attitudes	H	80	58	27	53	43	24	50	37	19
	M	13	20	19	28	29	26	28	28	30
	L	7	22	54	19	28	50	22	34	51
Classical Conservatism	H	38	19	4	47	21	6	70	42	15
	M	35	32	17	28	39	21	24	32	42
	L	26	49	79	26	40	73	6	26	43
Economic Conservatism	H	62	48	27	26	23	21	15	17	15
	M	30	41	48	37	51	51	45	43	47
	L	8	10	25	37	27	28	40	40	38
Opposition to Government Welfare	H	71	59	48	39	43	39	25	25	25
	M	22	27	28	37	35	37	45	45	48
	L	7	13	24	24	22	24	30	30	27
Support for Liberal Issues	H	7	17	40	18	23	28	19	27	19
	M	20	30	32	59	58	54	61	56	63
	L	69	52	27	24	18	18	20	17	13

The strength of the relationship can also be seen in the results on the Business Attitudes scale. Despite their above-average cosmopolitanism, those most identified with typical business attitudes are far more likely to be isolationists. Apparently, the conservative features of this ideology are strong enough in many instances to overcome the forces that impel businessmen toward a more internationalist outlook. Among the political influentials, as broken down by occupation, the managers and proprietors of small businesses turn out to be the most isolationist of all groups, while both large and small businessmen are significantly more isolationist than persons coming from the professions. In the general population sample, the patterns are less clear, although isolationism is stronger among small businessmen, especially if they are Republicans.

Further evidence of the relationship between conservatism and isolationism can be gleaned from the responses to other questions in the study that indirectly reflect liberal-conservative preferences. These questions refer, for example, to self-characterizations as liberal or conservative, preferences for liberal or conservative leaders, the party faction (left or right of center) with which one identifies, reference

groups from which one is likely to seek advice, party preference itself, and the response to views that characteristically differentiate Republican from Democratic leaders. On every one of these measures, those who respond in the conservative direction are significantly more isolationist than those who give liberal responses.

From whichever direction we approach the matter, then, the conclusion is plain that the conservative and isolationist orientations are highly interrelated, draw upon the same values, and—though we have not, for reasons of space, presented the data here—derive in substantial measure from similar personality configurations. It should also be noted that the correlations are stronger and more meaningful among the political influentials than among the general population—a reflection, no doubt, of their greater ideological consistency. Moreover, the nature and strength of the relationship is such as to suggest that it does not describe a fortuitous or temporary connection. Liberal and conservative groups will no doubt shift about on foreign policy questions from time to time, and may even on occasion reverse roles, but the pattern described in our data appears to be the dominant one.

Attitudes toward Democracy and Politics

Many of the observations made in connection with the liberal-conservative distinction are equally relevant for the discussion of isolationism and democratic attitudes. Little, therefore, will need to be said at this point about the findings presented in Table 11. Mainly, we need to call attention to the fact that on every measure on which we have assessed democratic convictions, the isolationists turn out significantly less democratic than the nonisolationists. When we combine items from several of these scales into a compound measure we have called the Democratic Commitment Index, the strength of the relationship is increased even further. Among the leaders, for example, only 16 per cent of the isolationists score high on the Democratic Commitment Index, compared to 76 per cent of the internationalists.

The isolationists, it is plain, have less faith in equality and popular democracy, are less committed to individual rights, and are less tolerant of people whose opinions differ from theirs. In the leader sample, modest differences show up even on Faith in Freedom, although the items in this scale are of an abstract nature and, as such, are widely subscribed to by nearly every group in the population. (In the general population the differences on this scale are not significant.) The magnitude of the differences on Faith in Direct Action are also noteworthy. This scale, which registers impatience with the democratic process, glorifies action "above all," and applauds the willingness to "take the law into one's own hands," suggests the same bullying attitude toward the rights of

Table 11 — Isolationism and Democratic Attitudes
(Percentages Down)

		ISOLATIONISM								
		National Leader Sample (n=3,020)			General Population Sample (n=1,484)					
					High Education			Low Education		
		H	M	L	H	M	L	H	M	L
		(643)	(1,150)	(1,227)	(199)	(359)	(229)	(358)	(260)	(79)
Scales										
Democratic	H	17	38	76	14	31	62	7	16	34
Commitment	M	44	93	20	43	43	30	29	44	45
Index	L	39	19	4	44	26	9	64	40	21
Elitism-	H	39	27	11	48	31	17	56	42	25
Inequali-	M	40	40	30	35	44	45	33	36	43
tarianism	L	21	33	59	17	25	38	11	22	32
Faith in	H	22	35	55	10	23	37	6	17	28
Democracy	M	53	49	39	52	53	47	53	51	54
	L	26	17	6	39	23	16	41	32	18
Faith in	H	51	30	10	55	32	13	70	42	16
Direct Action	M	26	26	20	24	26	21	18	28	20
	L	23	44	71	21	41	66	11	30	63
Faith in	H	56	59	71	50	53	55	45	43	35
Freedom	M	31	43	47	29	21	21	25	22	20
	L	54	40	39	22	26	24	30	35	44
Faith in	H	34	51	78	14	32	48	10	18	25
Procedural	M	41	35	26	47	44	37	43	50	54
Rights	L	25	15	4	39	24	15	47	32	20
	H	40	59	74	38	56	67	24	34	47
Tolerance	M	30	23	18	24	21	22	24	28	25
	L	30	18	8	38	23	11	53	38	28

others that is embodied in isolationism, especially of the jingoist type.

The isolationists not only reject democratic beliefs more frequently than the internationalists do, but they are much more cynical about politics and more impatient with politicians and the political process (Table 12). Although Americans as a people (like the nationals of other countries) are fond of complaining about "politics," the isolationists among them are far above average in this respect. They also express, as they do in their responses to international affairs, a strong sense of futility and frustration about domestic affairs. Paradoxical though it appears, they perceive their own political system in much the same way they view international organizations: both are controlled by men who are opportunistic, deceitful, self-serving, and indifferent to the people's needs.

Table 12 — Isolationism and Political Alienation
(Percentages Down)

		ISOLATIONISM								
		National Leader Sample (n=3,020)			General Population Sample (n=1,484)					
					High Education			Low Education		
		H (643)	M (1,150)	L (1,227)	H (199)	M (359)	L (229)	H (358)	M (260)	L (79)
Scales										
Political Cynicism	H	25	10	3	44	20	8	61	22	13
	M	44	42	23	46	50	34	34	49	34
	L	31	48	74	11	30	58	6	28	53
Sense of Political Futility	H	10	3	1	40	21	8	55	24	15
	M	28	17	10	39	43	35	31	40	30
	L	62	79	89	21	36	57	13	36	54
Political Suspiciousness	H	21	8	3	41	17	7	50	19	10
	M	37	29	18	41	44	29	42	50	38
	L	42	62	79	18	39	64	8	30	52

The rejection of politics and politicians is a characteristic feature of the attack on democracy — as can readily be discerned from the criticisms leveled against parliamentary government by various totalitarian movements. The line is by now familiar: politics in a democracy is characterized by talk without action, by the opportunism and self-serving of elected officials, by the wastefulness and duplicity of the competitive party system, and by a preference for negotiation, trial and error, and compromise at the expense of principle.

The similarities between these criticisms and the isolationist's opinions of international politics can scarcely be missed. As the data confirm, he finds both the domestic and international realms marked by disorder, uncertainty, "conniving," the usurpation of authority, the impotence of ordinary citizens against giant forces, and the manipulation of the masses by unscrupulous leaders. Thus, though he protests against the entanglements of world politics, he is scarcely more sanguine about the political entrapments within his own country. Here again we find evidence that isolationism is for many people an expression of disengagement and aversion that manifests itself repeatedly at many levels of interaction.

Extreme Belief

The tendency among isolationists to reject the institutions and practices of their own society can also be discerned in their responses to the doctrines of the radical right and radical left. In our brief discussion of populist movements we remarked on the persistent connection between

their isolationism and their radical objections to the prevailing system of power and the forms of American life. The evidence indicates that the two forms of protest tend to go together even today. The more one resents one's own institutions, the more one tends to dislike other nations and to resist becoming involved with them. By rational standards this may not appear to make much sense, but by psychological criteria it is entirely plausible. The needs of an aversive personality can frequently be satisfied by a variety of stimulus objects.

Table 13 contains data on the relationship between isolationism and several scales that express radical or extreme political views. The items in the Left Wing, Right Wing, and Populist scales were initially drawn from the writings and programs of political movements organized

Table 13 — Isolationism and Extreme Belief
(Percentages Down)

		ISOLATIONISM								
		National Leader Sample (n = 3,020)			General Population Sample (n = 1,484)					
					High Education			Low Education		
		H	M	L	H	M	L	H	M	L
		(643)	(1,150)	(1,227)	(199)	(359)	(229)	(358)	(260)	(79)
Scales										
	H	14	6	4	37	12	4	59	26	11
Left Wing	M	31	24	22	38	33	26	29	38	37
	L	56	70	74	25	54	70	12	36	52
	H	51	15	2	57	16	2	67	29	3
Right Wing	M	42	51	22	38	45	21	29	52	52
	L	6	34	77	5	40	78	4	19	46
	H	26	13	5	52	21	3	72	31	11
Populism	M	55	49	36	40	41	27	25	51	39
	L	18	38	59	8	38	70	3	18	49
Totali-	H	24	11	1	45	20	4	63	35	16
tarianism	M	43	37	17	38	43	31	29	46	44
	L	33	53	81	18	36	65	7	19	39
					Minnesota Sample Only (n = 1,082)					
					High Education			Low Education		
					H	M	L	H	M	L
					(147)	(272)	(224)	(203)	(177)	(51)
Fascist	H				22	10	8	38	18	4
Political	M				46	40	23	43	46	35
Sympathies	L				31	50	69	19	36	61

to promote these doctrines. The Totalitarian scale contains the values that typically identify various modern totalitarian movements, e.g. the "politicalization" of culture, desire for a "closed society," an apocalyptic and messianic visionary flavor, glorification of a single belief system, and preference for social uniformity. The Fascist scale contains statements that are drawn from or favor political regimes of the Hitler and Mussolini type. All are strongly related to isolationism.

The most powerful and, of course, least surprising of the correlations is that between isolationism and right-wing beliefs. Organizations of the radical right have usually been among the most vociferous critics of the United Nations, foreign aid, and other overseas involvements, and have led the protests against what they claimed to be American defeats in the Cold War struggle against communism. Isolationist values correspond more closely with the values of right-wing movements than with those of any other group. Both are inspired by chauvinism; both conceive themselves the nation's defenders against its enemies. Both are impatient with or suspicious of the political process, and both regard themselves as dispossessed, pushed aside by men of doubtful patriotism and questionable objectives. The supporters of both political orientations are nostalgic for an era no longer possible; they continue to yearn for a return to the simplicity of an earlier period when the nation was invincible and its own master. Xenophobia has characterized both, and their portraits of foreigners and foreign nations have been remarkably alike. Both have been given to jingoism and heroic postures, and both have repudiated the artificial, corrupt, and declining cultures of the old world.[36] Both are attracted to conspiratorial explanations of human affairs and both are inclined to attribute American reverses to softness, duplicity, or even treason.

That these similarities have a pay-off in the realities of political action was borne out in a study we conducted to Minnesota in 1954–55 on the nature and sources of "extreme belief and affiliation," including support for McCarthyism. Whereas those who were neither left-wing nor right-wing in their political sympathies had a mean score of 2.62 on isolationism (a 9-point scale), the right-wing sample – selected for their actual participation in right-wing activities – had a mean score of 5.97. Isolationism seems also to have been an element in support for McCarthy. Whereas the opponents of McCarthyism had a mean score of 3.00 on isolationism, McCarthy's supporters in the general population had a score of 4.22, while the "hard-core" McCarthyites – those who had attended meetings in his behalf, circulated petitions in his defense, or promoted his presidential candidacy – had a score of 6.10. Although Senator McCarthy himself might not be classified as an isolationist (all

36. See Shils, *op. cit.*, especially pp. 78–86.

who hold right-wing beliefs are not isolationist), the right-wing policies he advocated and the criticisms he leveled against the conduct of American foreign policy were apparently attractive to people of isolationist persuasion.[37]

The figures in Table 13, as well as our Minnesota data on left-wing sympathizers, also reveal a marked correlation between isolationism and support for left-wing values. The connection is weaker than that shown for right-wing supporters (and would doubtless be weaker still for a sample of Marxist intellectuals), but it is strong enough to be significant. It may appear to some that there is a discrepancy in the positive correlation of isolationism with *both* left-wing and right-wing doctrines. This belief, however, assumes that there is an inherent incongruity or antagonism between left-wing and right-wing movements. We cannot at this point enter upon a discussion of the many similarities between totalitarian ideologies of the left and right or of the similarities in the style and quality of political life instituted by such movements upon coming to power. Nor can we elaborate on the obvious cohabitation of left-wing and right-wing elements in American populist movements or on the remarkable process by which numerous midwestern politicians of left-wing isolationist persuasion were transformed into politicians of right-wing isolationist persuasion during the 1930s. Exploration of these matters would turn up many parallels between the extreme left and right that lead them, on various occasions, to similar foreign policy orientations.

Our findings also reveal likenesses between left-wing sympathizers and isolationists. Both are dissatisfied with the state of American life. Both are deviant in American society today, and both draw on the psychological and attitude sources that give rise to deviancy. Both carry heavy loadings of hostility and psychological inflexibility and both tend to avoid, or to be excluded from, the reference groups of the society that bear the greatest responsibility for maintaining the prevailing norms. There is a strong element of paranoia in both isolationism and left-wing attitudes, a shared suspicion of politicians, newspapers, the two major parties, and other features that are alleged to constitute the "establishment." Both points of view reflect an unusual degree of frustration and hostility. Both are given to intemperate responses, and both betray an above-average tendency to distort or misread realities. Apart from such similarities, left-wing radicals tend to portray American foreign policy as inherently imperialist and expansionist, driven by the capitalist need for markets and investment opportunities. As a result,

37. On the McCarthy supporters, see N. Polsby, "Toward an Explanation of McCarthyism," in N. Polsby, L. Dexter, and P. Smith, *Politics and Social Life: an Introduction to Political Behavior* (Boston: Houghton Mifflin, 1963), pp. 809–24.

they tend to perceive many types of international activity (though not all) as manifestations of the drive for American hegemony at the expense of smaller, weaker, or more "progressive" nations.

ISOLATIONISM AND ISSUE ORIENTATION

One of the hypotheses set out at the beginning of the chapter predicted that personality variables would have less influence on orientation toward foreign policy *issues* than on foreign policy *attitudes*, but that the stands taken on these issues would nevertheless be affected by personality and attitude factors. It was further predicted that these relationships would be stronger among the political elite than among the general population, as the elite has greater interest in these questions and is more concerned to achieve a coherent, consistent set of political opinions.

The reasoning behind these predictions was as follows: Attitudes on foreign policy differ from opinions on foreign policy issues in that the former represent a disposition to respond in a consistent way to certain classes of stimuli, while the latter are specific to particular stimuli, are more bound by time and circumstance, and are more likely to reflect group associations and interests. One's opinions about NATO or defense spending or military intervention in the Dominican uprising are not likely to be as strongly motivated by affect or the need to "act out" as are one's attitudes about, say, foreigners or the loss of national sovereignty. Being more specific, these issues do not ordinarily furnish as much opportunity for private motives to be engaged and are less likely to awaken the visceral types of response that attitudes so often awaken.

Opinions on issues, as compared with attitudes, are usually (though not always) more concrete, less symbolic, and more dependent upon factual evidence. They are more heavily influenced than attitudes by party, social class, religion, or education. Many of them are technical and require knowledge of the stimulus object before an opinion can be formed.

While attitudes, of course, are also subject to reference group and situational influences, they are less labile than issue outlooks, more deeply rooted in the respondent's value system, and more likely to be independent of the usual external influences that so often affect opinions on issues. Most of the research available on these matters[38] suggests strongly that opinions on foreign policy questions are highly unstable, and may be pushed in one direction or another by events or by other short-term influences. This happens less often to an attitude, for it is

38. See Converse, *op. cit.*, and Almond, *op. cit.*

more deeply integrated into an elaborate network of needs, motives, values, and other attitude dispositions. Hence, personality is likely to have less influence on the determination of opinions on issues than in the determination of attitudes.

There are, of course, exceptions to these generalizations, for issues can doubtless arise that are as heavily invested with affect and symbolism as attitudes are. Moreover, most foreign policy issues that have come to popular attention and that have awakened controversy (such as foreign aid or support for the United Nations) are bound to acquire significance beyond the question of their intrinsic merits – they are bound, in short, to have acquired a degree of *psychological* meaning. Often these opinions represent applications of an underlying attitude to a particular international question, and the feeling associated with the attitude is carried over in the response to the issue. In general, however, we expect personality factors to play a smaller role in the adoption of opinions than in the adoption of attitudes.

Some of the findings on the relation between isolationism and a number of foreign policy and domestic issues are contained in Tables 14 and 15. As Table 14 shows, isolationists and nonisolationists respond very differently to such foreign policy issues as immigration, foreign aid, level of tariffs, participation in NATO, and even defense spending. All the results are in the predicted direction, and the differences are in most instances fairly large. Among political leaders, for example, 55 per cent of the nonisolationists favor increased support for the UN, compared to 17 per cent of the isolationist group. The differences, it should be observed, are significantly larger for the leaders than for the general population (as predicted), and somewhat larger for the educated than the uneducated. Clearly, isolationist or internationalist general orientations tend to be carried over into the responses on specific issues,[39] especially among those who are politically participant and aware, for whom foreign policy attitudes and opinions are especially salient.

In Table 15, isolationists and nonisolationists are compared in their responses to a set of domestic issues. Some observers have assumed that there is little connection between the beliefs people hold on domestic questions and their outlooks on foreign affairs.[40] The data in Table 15 show that this assumption is, on the whole, correct for the general population. A few connections can be discerned, but they are rather weak. Some of the relationships among the general population, in fact, are actually reversals of the predicted results: isolationists, for example,

39. For an excellent study of public and congressional attitudes on a particular issue – the 1962 Reciprocal Trade Act – see R. Bauer, I. Pool, and L. Dexter, *American Business and Foreign Policy* (New York: The Atherton Press, 1963).
40. See the discussions in Key, *op. cit.*, pp. 163–68 and *The American Voter*.

Table 14 — Isolationism and Foreign Policy Issues*
(Percentages Down)

Isolationism		National Leader Sample (n = 3,020)						General Population Sample (n = 1,484)							
		Democrats (1,788)		Republicans (1,232)		Total (3,020)		Democrats (821)		Republicans (623)		High Education (787)		Low Education (697)	
		Inc.	Dec.**	Inc.	Dec.	Inc.	Dec.	Inc.	Dec.	Inc.	Dec.	Inc.	Dec.	Inc.	Dec.
Immigration	H	10	58	6	48	7	52	4	68	4	61	4	65	4	65
	M	23	36	15	31	19	34	10	49	8	43	11	45	7	48
	L	55	11	36	11	49	11	22	28	16	19	21	17	13	46
Tariffs	H	27	23	32	14	30	17	21	22	18	16	24	18	17	20
	M	18	31	17	21	17	27	18	21	15	21	19	25	14	16
	L	5	59	9	46	6	55	6	39	10	33	7	40	11	25
Foreign Aid	H	0	88	1	90	1	89	5	72	3	78	6	77	3	72
	M	9	68	4	65	7	67	9	60	9	53	10	56	8	57
	L	30	27	19	28	27	27	22	32	25	29	25	27	19	42
Reliance on the UN	H	29	41	9	67	17	57	20	24	21	33	18	35	22	23
	M	41	22	26	28	34	24	39	15	36	13	39	14	36	13
	L	61	7	39	10	55	8	53	10	50	10	52	10	49	8
American Participation in International Military Alliances	H	20	46	7	57	12	52	27	24	23	27	25	32	25	21
	M	36	20	23	18	30	19	44	9	37	10	39	10	42	10
	L	53	7	38	4	48	8	51	6	40	6	45	7	46	6
Defense Spending	H	14	55	10	52	12	54	39	22	36	23	42	26	35	22
	M	21	36	13	31	17	34	57	13	46	11	53	11	50	14
	L	23	27	19	18	21	24	16	14	61	11	60	14	57	10

*Observe that the percentages in these tables are computed across for each sample, with the middle group, those who responded "same," omitted to conserve space.

**In these and subsequent tables, Inc. signifies a desire to increase support for the issue named; Dec. signifies a desire to decrease support for the issue.

Table 15—Isolationism and Selected Domestic Issues

	National Leader Sample (n = 3,020)						General Population Sample (n = 1,484)							
Isolationism	Democrats (1,788)		Republicans (1,232)		Total (3,020)		Democrats (821)		Republicans (623)		High Education (787)		Low Education (697)	
	Inc.	Dec.	Inc.	Dec.	Inc.	Dec.	Inc.	Dec.	Inc.	Dec.	Inc.	Dec.	Inc.	Dec.
Government Control of Business														
H	9	62	1	89	4	78	17	37	10	47	12	50	16	36
M	14	49	0	85	8	64	17	33	7	47	9	45	17	31
L	28	24	1	78	20	40	24	29	5	44	16	38	18	25
Social Security														
H	49	8	15	22	29	16	68	4	64	4	63	7	67	2
M	51	5	22	9	38	6	69	2	54	4	60	4	66	3
L	71	2	31	9	59	4	72	3	51	2	59	3	75	4
Trade Union Regulation														
H	63	11	87	6	77	8	39	8	45	16	49	11	37	11
M	67	11	87	4	75	8	46	12	62	8	62	8	42	13
L	52	14	86	4	62	11	62	5	71	6	70	4	52	10
Federal Aid to Education														
H	50	26	14	55	29	43	68	8	60	12	65	16	65	6
M	59	16	22	42	43	27	79	4	65	6	75	5	69	5
L	77	7	32	32	63	14	80	5	71	7	74	7	85	1
Minimum Wage														
H	36	11	9	22	20	18	61	4	44	6	50	5	57	4
M	43	6	14	10	30	8	59	2	43	5	50	4	54	3
L	60	2	24	5	49	3	56	3	44	3	49	3	59	3
Slum Clearance and Public Housing														
H	63	12	33	32	45	24	73	7	68	14	75	10	68	11
M	75	7	39	19	60	12	84	4	73	6	79	5	77	5
L	86	3	49	13	75	6	83	6	81	2	82	3	82	8

are more opposed to trade union regulation than nonisolationists are. And there is slightly more support among isolationists than nonisolationists for increasing social security. On the other hand, the internationalists show a slightly stronger preference for federal aid to education and slum clearance. The results on this side of the table, in short, are spotty, inconclusive, and inconsistent.

The results are different, however, when we turn to the data on the leaders. Here the relationships are strong, consistent, and in the predicted direction. The correlation reported earlier between isolationism and conservatism is unequivocally borne out in these figures. Thus, whereas 59 per cent of the internationalists favor increased support for social security, 29 per cent of the isolationists favor it. Similar differences can be discerned on all of the other domestic issues in the table, except for the trade union issue, on which the differences are too small to be of significance.

We turn, finally, to consider whether the attitude and personality factors that give rise to general isolationist orientations have a similar influence on the responses to specific issues. This question is dealt with in Tables 16–21, and the answer is unequivocally in the affirmative. On all six issues in the tables, the same basic correlation patterns observed in the analysis of the Isolationism scale can again be found. On the foreign aid issue (Table 18), for example, 60 per cent of those who wish to decrease foreign aid score conservative on the Liberal Issues scale, compared with only 14 per cent conservative among those who wish to increase foreign aid. Those who are opposed to foreign aid turn out to be more chauvinistic, more ethnocentric, more hostile, more politically cynical, less socially responsible, more inflexible, and so on. The pattern is repeated on the immigration, tariff, NATO, and UN issues. Only on the defense spending issue are the results equivocal. This issue, it would appear, cuts across the divisions we have been discussing; and people with similar personality characteristics can be found with equal frequency on either side of the question.

Not only, then, does the isolationist–internationalist division reflect itself in actual stands on issues, but the forces that underlie these dispositions also underlie the corresponding issue orientations. The correlations between personality and issues, of course, are usually not as large as they are between personality and the Isolationism scale, but we did not expect them to be. As issues, they are more affected by competing influences and by some of the other factors indicated in our introductory remarks to this section.

The results in these tables do not tell us anything about the stability of issue orientations. Conceivably, there is some shifting about on these issues as circumstances change. The trends in the correlations, however,

Table 16—Support for Immigration and Selected Personality and Attitude Scales*

National Leader Sample Only
(n = 3,020)

Immigration	Liberal Issues		Pro-Business Attitudes		Faith in Democracy		Calvinism		Need Inviolacy		Chauvinism		Economic Conservatism	
	L	H	L	H	L	H	L	H	L	H	L	H	L	H
Increase	21	50	53	29	9	55	44	20	67	14	87	3	25	27
Decrease	61	11	17	64	23	25	19	33	51	26	40	27	13	49

Immigration	Elitism		Ethnocentrism		Political Cynicism		Responsibility		Hostility		Obsessive	
	L	H	L	H	L	H	L	H	L	H	L	H
Increase	58	12	75	4	65	5	11	49	52	12	37	37
Decrease	27	33	24	33	39	17	21	30	23	27	22	55

Immigration	Paranoid		Pessimism		Right Wing		Rigidity	
	L	H	L	H	L	H	L	H
Increase	62	12	48	6	73	5	58	18
Decrease	37	27	20	21	21	33	33	39

*Percentages computed horizontally for each scale. Those scoring in the middle range of the scale named have been omitted. The percentages therefore add up to less than 100.

Increase: n = 973
Decrease: n = 851

Table 17 — Support for Tariffs and Selected Personality and Attitude Scales*

National Leader Sample Only
(n = 3,020)

Tariff	Liberal Issues		Pro-Business Attitudes		Calvinism		Chauvinism		Economic Conservatism	
	L	H	L	H	L	H	L	H	L	H
Increase	57	16	19	62	21	33	42	26	13	50
Decrease	35	38	46	37	40	20	81	5	23	34

	Elitism		Ethnocentrism		Faith in Democracy		Need Inviolacy		Hostility		Obsessive	
	L	H	L	H	L	H	L	H	L	H	L	H
Increase	30	29	31	23	18	28	54	24	27	28	25	51
Decrease	50	17	63	10	12	48	65	15	47	14	34	42

	Paranoid		Pessimism		Political Cynicism		Responsibility		Right Wing		Rigidity	
	L	H	L	H	L	H	L	H	L	H	L	H
Increase	40	23	23	19	44	14	23	33	22	32	34	38
Decrease	58	14	40	11	61	8	11	47	64	10	56	21

*Percentages computed horizontally for each scale. Those scoring in the middle range of the scale named have been omitted. The percentages therefore add up to less than 100.

Increase: n = 469
Decrease: n = 1,094

Table 18—Support for Foreign Aid and Selected Personality and Attitude Scales*

National Leader Sample Only
(n = 3,020)

Foreign Aid	Liberal Issues		Pro-Business Attitudes		Calvinism		Chauvinism		Economic Conservatism	
	L	H	L	H	L	H	L	H	L	H
Increase	14	64	71	14	53	16	87	3	38	16
Decrease	60	14	17	64	22	31	51	19	10	51

	Elitism		Ethnocentrism		Faith in Democracy		Need Inviolacy		Hostility		Obsessive	
	L	H	L	H	L	H	L	H	L	H	L	H
Increase	60	12	79	4	8	53	68	14	58	9	40	38
Decrease	33	28	32	25	18	32	55	22	28	25	26	52

	Paranoid		Pessimism		Political Cynicism		Responsibility		Right Wing		Rigidity	
	L	H	L	H	L	H	L	H	L	H	L	H
Increase	63	13	49	8	68	6	10	52	80	4	60	18
Decrease	46	21	38	16	47	14	19	35	29	26	39	34

*Percentages computed horizontally for each scale. Those scoring in the middle range of the scale named have been omitted. The percentages therefore add up to less than 100.

Increase: n = 413
Decrease: n = 1,673

Table 19—Support for United Nations and Selected Personality and Attitude Scales*

National Leader Sample Only (n = 3,020)

United Nations	Liberal Issues		Pro-Business Attitudes		Calvinism		Chauvinism		Economic Conservatism	
	L	H	L	H	L	H	L	H	L	H
Increase	25	44	48	33	37	23	74	7	26	28
Decrease	70	83	12	72	20	33	46	22	8	59

	Elitism		Ethnocentrism		Faith in Democracy		Need Inviolacy		Hostility		Obsessive	
	L	H	L	H	L	H	L	H	L	H	L	H
Increase	49	19	59	12	12	45	66	15	43	17	31	45
Decrease	29	31	29	26	18	33	53	25	27	24	28	49

	Paranoid		Pessimism		Political Cynicism		Responsibility		Right Wing		Rigidity	
	L	H	L	H	L	H	L	H	L	H	L	H
Increase	52	18	40	9	60	7	13	45	63	8	49	27
Decrease	44	22	21	22	43	16	21	32	19	38	38	31

*Percentages computed horizontally for each scale. Those scoring in the middle range of the scale named have been omitted. The percentages therefore add up to less than 100.

Increase: n = 1,176
Decrease: n = 743

Table 20 – Support for Defense Spending and Selected Personality and Attitude Scales*

National Leader Sample Only (n = 3,020)

Defense Spending	Liberal Issues		Pro-Business Attitudes		Calvinism		Chauvinism		Economic Conservatism	
	L	H	L	H	L	H	L	H	L	H
Increase	30	33	42	37	31	25	62	12	19	33
Decrease	53	23	25	59	28	39	58	17	16	44

	Elitism		Ethnocentrism		Faith in Democracy		Need Inviolacy		Obsessive	
	L	H	L	H	L	H	L	H	L	H
Increase	43	21	51	15	15	43	60	18	31	47
Decrease	38	25	41	21	16	35	57	21	28	50

	Paranoid		Pessimism		Political Cynicism		Responsibility		Right Wing		Rigidity	
	L	H	L	H	L	H	L	H	L	H	L	H
Increase	49	17	37	11	58	10	15	40	47	15	46	31
Decrease	47	20	30	16	49	13	26	36	39	24	41	30

*Percentages computed horizontally for each scale. Those scoring in the middle range of the scale named have been omitted. The percentages therefore add up to less than 100.

Increase: n = 538
Decrease: n = 1,030

Table 21 — Support for NATO and Selected Personality and Attitude Scales*

National Leader Sample Only (n = 3,020)

NATO	Liberal Issues		Pro-Business Attitudes		Calvinism		Chauvinism		Economic Conservatism	
	L	H	L	H	L	H	L	H	L	H
Increase	27	39	47	33	34	24	74	8	22	30
Decrease	64	13	17	67	22	31	41	27	12	55

	Elitism		Ethnocentrism		Faith in Democracy		Need Inviolacy		Obsessive		Hostility	
	L	H	L	H	L	H	L	H	L	H	L	H
Increase	50	19	59	11	11	46	66	16	33	45	43	16
Decrease	27	32	29	28	20	28	50	26	25	52	28	28

	Paranoid		Pessimism		Political Cynicism		Responsibility		Right Wing		Rigidity	
	L	H	L	H	L	H	L	H	L	H	L	H
Increase	55	16	43	9	61	8	12	45	59	10	48	28
Decrease	41	26	22	22	39	18	23	31	25	36	39	25

*Percentages computed horizontally for each scale. Those scoring in the middle range of the scale named have been omitted. The percentages therefore add up to less than 100.

Increase: n = 1,022
Decrease: n = 631

are so strong as to suggest that even these opinions are part of the personality and attitude network to which we referred earlier, and that the pattern of responses revealed in these tables is the characteristic one.

PACIFIC VERSUS JINGOIST ISOLATIONISM

We began our analysis of isolationism on the assumption that, within the terms of our general definition, two basic sub-types could usefully be distinguished: the pacific and the aggressive (or jingoist) isolationists. While both, we believed, would seek to disengage themselves from the outside world, the pacific isolationist would prefer to have the nation withdraw into its own shell, safeguarding itself by having as little to do as possible with other nations and by avoiding the threat or use of force, while the jingoist isolationist would display a more bullying, sabre-rattling attitude toward other nations, and would rely for protection on superior military force and the threat of using it unilaterally. We expected to find that while both types would differ significantly from nonisolationists in their rejection of other nations, and while neither would exhibit an above-average concern for the maintenance (or achievement) of peace, the pacific isolationists would more closely resemble non-isolationists in their personality and attitude characteristics. Their isolationism, we thought, would be less motivated by aversive psychological needs, and would not to the same degree be associated with other attitudes that reflect intolerance and obduracy toward other men, political and economic conservatism, or disillusionment with the forms and quality of American institutions.

To test these notions an attempt was made to construct a jingoism scale from items already in the questionnaire pool. A number of possible items were submitted to a group of judges (graduate students and research workers at the University of California, Berkeley) to be rated according to the degree to which they expressed a jingoistic stance in the conduct of foreign policy. Six items that were most frequently and consistently rated as highly jingoistic were selected for initial inclusion in the scale. Of these, we eventually selected only the two that contained on their face the content of the jingoist concept.[41] The three isolationist categories (isolationist, middle, and nonisolationist) were then subdivided high, middle, and low on jingoism, and the resulting nine groups were compared on various personality and attitude characteristics. The results on a

41. The two items retained were: "A nation faced with a bunch of really dangerous enemies might be better off to 'shoot first and ask questions afterward'"; and "Let's face it, the only way to bring peace and order back to the world is to make America the one powerful nation on earth."

selected group of representative scales are presented (in the form of percentages high only) in Table 22.

A word of caution is appropriate concerning the interpretation of this table. The use of so short a measure for so major a classification contains some risks both for validity and reliability. That the two items discriminate and are in some instances very powerful can readily be observed from the table. But the number of misclassifications and the danger of picking up spurious influences on the correlations is of course greatly increased as the number of items in a scale diminishes. A more serious difficulty, however, is the absence of an adequate measure of the pacific or conciliatory spirit in international relations. There were unfortunately no items in the item pool that could be used to measure this orientation, and we have therefore classified a respondent as pacific not by what he asserts or *affirms* about this matter (as we would have preferred) but by what he *repudiates*. Hence, a pacific isolationist (or a pacific nonisolationist) is one who rejects both items in the jingoist measure; an aggressive isolationist or nonisolationist is one who embraces both items.

These qualifications aside, the data in Table 22 tend on the whole to bear out our general expectations: Both pacific and jingoist isolationists differ from their nonisolationist counterparts in precisely the ways that isolationists and nonisolationists were shown to differ in the earlier sections of this chapter. In comparison with pacific nonisolationists, pacific isolationists are significantly more inflexible, hostile, and alienated in their personality characteristics, and significantly more ethnocentric, conservative, business oriented, undemocratic, and politically cynical in what they believe. With a few exceptions (the results on the Alienation and Business Ideology scales are exceptions in the leader sample), jingoist isolationists show up as even more extreme on these measures than the pacific isolationists do. Both types of isolationists, however, would have to be classified as comparatively aggressive in their international orientations—an inference buttressed by the correlations between Isolationism and Jingoism of .41 for the leader sample and .46 for the general population.[42] This is consistent with the strong indications in the data reported earlier that present-day isolationism represents, as stated in our hypothesis, a posture of belligerency rather than pacifism in international affairs, and that it "has more to do with hostility against foreign nations and disavowal of responsibility for the well-being of others than with the considered assessment of the risks arising from

42. These correlations, it should be noted, do not appear to be spuriously influenced by the tone or flavor of the items in the isolationism scale, for most of these items were adjudged by our raters as free of belligerency—in fact, as falling on the pacific side of the distinction.

Table 22 — Percentages High on Selected Personality and Attitude Scales, by Isolationism and Jingoism*

Isolationism	National Leader Sample (n=3,020)				General Population Sample (n=1,484)		
	Jingoism				Jingoism		
	H (356)	M (959)	L (1,705)		H (295)	M (556)	L (633)
			Alienation				
H	25	25	26		60	44	33
M	22	16	16		42	32	22
L	7	16	11		0	19	19
			Intolerance of Ambiguity				
H	70	65	53		75	55	44
M	61	44	36		51	33	24
L	31	39	20		0	25	15
			Pro-Business Attitudes				
H	84	79	78		52	51	50
M	59	61	55		40	37	44
L	48	39	23		0	20	24
			Ethnocentrism				
H	53	41	24		67	49	39
M	33	23	11		43	21	13
L	10	8	2		0	13	4
			Faith in Democracy				
H	10	23	29		6	5	13
M	18	34	41		11	17	27
L	28	44	58		0	34	35
			Classical Conservatism				
H	57	37	25		75	58	46
M	36	22	12		44	35	21
L	14	9	2		0	19	4
			Hostility				
H	49	39	23		60	41	24
M	38	26	15		46	26	15
L	28	16	5		0	9	7
			Political Cynicism				
H	38	24	15		64	53	43
M	20	11	6		37	20	17
L	17	5	2		0	5	11

*Percentages middle and low have been omitted from this table to conserve space. All the figures in the table represent the proportion of each of the nine types of jingoists–isolationists who score high on the personality and attitude scales named.

international 'entanglements.'" There appears to be little spirit of reciprocity in the isolationist orientation—in any of the forms in which we, at least, have observed it.

All this, of course, does not abrogate the fact that there are differences between the pacific and jingoist isolationists, and that there are reasons for the difference. We have not yet been able to carry the analysis far enough to account adequately for the distinction, although we do know that the two groups differ somewhat in certain social characteristics (the jingoist isolationists, for example, are somewhat older than the pacific isolationists, and less educated) and in the personality and attitude characteristics suggested by the scales in Table 22. At the moment, however, we do not know which, if any, of these factors is most critical, and our uncertainty about the quality of the jingoist-pacifist measure has discouraged the more sophisticated analysis that would be required to answer the question. The question, however, will be explored in future research.

SUMMARY

This paper has focused upon the personality and attitude correlates of foreign policy orientation, with special attention to the isolationist-nonisolationist orientation. Isolationists and nonisolationists were compared on a large battery of personality and attitude scales, as well as on other measures. The samples employed in the surveys from which the data were taken included a national sample of 3,020 political leaders, a cross-section national sample of 1,484 adults, and a cross-section statewide sample of 1,082 Minnesota adults. A number of hypotheses were tested and the results evaluated.

It was found, among other things, that isolationism is a complex attitude that can be arrived at by different routes and understood in different ways. While it is obviously a political attitude influenced by political circumstances, reference groups, demographic factors, and other such determinants, it is also shaped to a considerable extent by a complex set of personality variables, primarily of an aversive nature. Such personality states as misanthropy, psychological inflexibility, manifest anxiety, and low self-esteem have a powerful influence on the attitudes one adopts toward other nations and toward foreign policy. Such personality factors, together with social opportunity and intellectual endowment, affect cognitive capacity and function, and these, in turn, further influence one's disposition to favor withdrawal from, or entrance into, international involvements.

Isolationism was also found to be part of a network of attitudes that

are related to common underlying personality dispositions. Among these are classical and welfare conservatism, radical doctrines of the extreme right and extreme left, and attitudes critical of democratic beliefs and practices. Despite its strong chauvinistic overtones, isolationism is frequently associated with feelings of disappointment in one's own society and disaffection from the political institutions of one's country. The isolationist orientation parallels closely other forms of belief that rely heavily upon dichotomous thought processes, that lack breadth of perspective, and that seek to exclude whatever is different, distant or unfamiliar. It also parallels other attitudes that are marginal or deviant in relation to the society. Like other deviant orientations, it signifies for some of its proponents a failure of socialization and an inadequate internalization of the norms. It is more common among those who are, by any criterion and for any reason, parochial and less common among those who are open to experience and are cosmopolitan in their perspective.

Although isolationism manifestly appears as a peaceful withdrawal from international entanglements and frequently has been interpreted as a simple desire to keep one's country from becoming militarily embroiled, it is characteristically xenophobic and belligerent in its posture toward foreign affairs. It represents, for the most part, a rejection of other men rather than a concern for them, a disavowal of responsibility and a strong urge to disengage oneself from obligations toward others. One can scarcely begin to understand the phenomenon, therefore, if one confines his analysis to the familiar political categories.

A subgroup of so-called pacific isolationists was located and analyzed. While this group possesses characteristics closer to those of the non-isolationists and displays less of the bullying militancy that marks the jingoist isolationist, its members possess many of the same personality and attitude characteristics found among the jingoist isolationists, though in lesser degree.

The responses of isolationists and nonisolationists to a number of foreign policy and domestic issues were also examined. It was found that one's attitude toward isolationism has a marked effect on one's opinions on issues, particularly among the political influentials, for whom issues are more salient and ideological consistency is more valued than for ordinary citizens. The influence of personality and attitude variables on specific foreign policy issues was also examined. The results closely paralleled those found for the isolationist-internationalist dimension: those personality and attitude variables that correlated strongly with isolationist sentiments were likewise found to be correlated with opinions on specific foreign policy questions. The paper furnishes evidence for believing that our understanding of both attitudes and issue opinions on international matters can be significantly enhanced through the examination of psychological variables.

APPENDIX A

Since all nine items in the Isolationism scale have an "agree" scoring direction, a number of operations were carried out to check for the possibility of bias arising from the acquiescent tendency. In one of these operations, a sample of isolationists and nonisolationists were, by a random procedure, exactly matched on acquiescence, and each of the matched samples was then compared on a selected set of variables. An illustration of the results is contained in Table 23. The results make it plain that the differences reported in the body of the paper are not the spurious products of acquiescent response set. This procedure, it should be noted, imposes a much more severe restriction on the data than is necessary or justified. Nevertheless, differences reported in the paper remain substantial and significant when acquiescence is controlled in this way.

Table 23 — Isolationists and Nonisolationists Matched on Acquiescence and Compared on Selected Scale
(Percentages Down)

Intolerance of Ambiguity	ISOLATIONISM			
	National Leader Sample		General Population Sample	
	H (444)	L (444)	H (186)	L (186)
H	54	34	42	18
M	28	27	39	37
L	18	39	19	45
Pro-Business Attitudes				
H	78	37	48	23
M	15	20	27	39
L	8	44	25	48
Ethnocentrism				
H	29	7	41	10
M	51	30	43	31
L	20	63	16	59
Hostility				
H	29	14	22	9
M	52	45	52	40
L	20	40	26	52
Responsibility				
H	37	43	22	46
M	32	44	42	44
L	31	14	36	10
Tolerance				
H	45	73	40	62
M	29	18	23	21
L	26	9	37	17

ATTITUDE CHANGE AND FOREIGN POLICY IN THE COLD WAR ERA

Milton J. Rosenberg

A common intention in the formulation of a nation's foreign policy is to alter the attitudes of foreign elites and sometimes of foreign publics as well. Frequently for some nations and occasionally for others the prosecution of foreign policy also requires attempts to affect the attitudes of their own internal domestic publics.

Illustrations of these related generalizations might be drawn from many different areas in the history of international relations. However, in the first major section of this chapter I shall restrict myself to demonstrating their applicability to the history and current status of the Cold War, particularly as it has involved attitude-changing interactions between the Soviet and American elites and between each of these and its respective domestic publics. In later sections I will attempt to show how these relationships might be more sharply viewed, and more effectively utilized, in the light of certain recent gains in the social psychological study of attitude dynamics.

In choosing to focus upon the Cold War, I do not mean to suggest

that its dynamics are identical with those of all other conceivable areas of foreign policy; nor do I mean to suggest that from a full, close analysis of it (which, in any case, is certainly not attempted here) we can even learn all we need to know about that subclass of international systems whose hallmarks are conflict, distrust, and persisting competition between states. However, I am convinced that analysis of the Cold War does disclose many important and general aspects of the relationships between foreign policy and the attitudes both of mass publics and of various, more specialized and powerful ones. As I proceed, in the context of an interest in the Cold War system, to consider the role of attitude change in foreign policy, it is my hope that this examination may yield some insights of use in analyzing coming developments in international relations. A second justification for this inquiry is simply that the Cold War, though changing in its scope, content, and stability, still persists and that its resolution is a goal toward which the behavioral sciences must remain sensitive.[1]

1. The decision to restrict the present analysis largely to the U.S.–U.S.S.R. inter-action has limiting consequences for this chapter. The most pertinent of these, as seen from the vantage point of the summer of 1966 (when this chapter—originally written in the spring of 1965—received its final editing), is that little is said here about certain issues, events, dilemmas, and nations that, at the moment, are commonly seen as adversely affecting the prospects for the reduction of international tensions.

In the light of these developments, one could not contend that the trend toward international conciliation which has been evident in the recent history of American–Soviet relations is irreversible, or that it will inevitably prosper. Geopolitical adventures such as the Soviet attempt to place nuclear missiles in Cuba and the American attempt to achieve an advantageous hegemony over Southeast Asia are clearly still attractive to important members of the policy elites of these nations; and such adventures can freeze or even reverse effective movement toward settlement of outstanding international issues. Furthermore the policy elites of other nations can sometimes disrupt, by their own undertakings, the comparatively becalmed state of American–Soviet relations. More problematic still is the increasingly apparent fact that even if the U.S. and the U.S.S.R. were to achieve settlement of all the outstanding issues between them, even if they were to achieve true *détente* and were to move beyond to *entente*, international security and balance would not necessarily be guaranteed. To the contrary, it is conceivable that either or both of these national giants may yet find itself inextricably engaged in unstable conflict with some other emerging (or decaying) national power.

Presently, as pessimists, "realists," and Armageddon fanciers see it, China is the leading and obvious candidate for this role. But the problems of U.S.–Chinese relations (or for that matter Soviet–Chinese relations) seem to be open either to exacerbation or reduction; and whether we shall in coming years see the one or the other depends, among many other things, upon future changes in the attitudes of the relevant policy elites toward one another and toward the issues they contest, and upon their perceptions of each other's intentions and attitudes. Already some State Department personnel are urging that Chinese endorsements of the inevitability and desirability of full international war should be read as expansive rhetoric which obscures, but does not alter, an essentially prudent foreign policy. The Western policy elite appears, then, to be in the process of revising its view of its Chinese counterpart. Also, at the time of writing, intense intra-elite competition is raging within China and this is being interpreted by some qualified observers as evidence that a significant sector of that elite is now advocating modification of its erstwhile hard-line in foreign affairs.

Can such presently figural aspects of international politics be understood in terms of

ATTITUDE CHANGE AS AIM,
RESOURCE, AND LIMIT

Shortly after World War II it became clear that a new constellation of international competition had taken shape and that the United States and the Soviet Union had emerged as the respective leaders of two contesting arrays of powers. The relations between these two nations confirmed one great historical regularity and partially violated another.

As commonly has been the case in sustained international competition, each contestant was committed to the pursuit of economic and political advantages that it saw, whether correctly or not, as accessible only if the other could be brought to accept a complementary state of disadvantage. In keeping with a pattern well established since the emergence of conscience in human affairs, the quest for national advantage and for limitation of the kind of disadvantage that could be imposed by the antagonist was justified by ideology. Indeed, the celebration of ideological differences in the playing through of the competition has tended to further energize that competition and to define much of its focus and style.

Whereas all of this has followed forms rendered easily recognizable by virtue of their historical recurrence, one additional historical regularity has been transmuted, if not completely lost. What is now missing, in the sense that it presently lacks its former clear pertinence, is the Clausewitzian axiom that war is the appropriate and inevitable continuation of policy by nondiplomatic means. It is now the case that otherwise intractable international disagreements cannot be as readily unfrozen as once they were by recourse to war or by one or the other of the antagonists giving "credible" evidence that it is prepared to defend or advance its interests by going to war.

This change in the dynamics of international competition has, of course, been due to the development of the nuclear technology of destruction. The paradox that it has imposed upon the elites of the contesting powers is that they must at one and the same time, or in rapid sequential alternation, work to influence each other in two different directions. To retain leverage and control in the continuing diplomatic

---

the considerations that are developed in this chapter? Rereading it somewhat more than a year after it was written, I have managed to persuade myself that a positive answer to this question is defensible. It does seem reasonable that, within limits, the attitude processes that are revealed through analysis of the interactions between the American and Soviet policy elites and between each of these and its relevant domestic publics, might afford some principles and propositions that can be generalized to the Chinese case and to other international and intranational situations. At any rate the analytic scheme and the various tentative recommendations offered here can be "tried on for size" by the reader. In doing this he will need to judge for himself how close they come to fitting other current and foreseeable developments in the realm of international conflict and conciliation.

confrontation each must work to create in the opponent an attitude of apprehension; of anxiety over the possibility that by pressing the quest for national advantage too hard and too far they will foster nuclear retaliation—or the kind of conventional retaliation that may, either by plan or inadvertence, escalate to the nuclear level.

At the same time, and apparently on both sides, there has developed increasing concern over the uncontrollable and grossly dysfunctional aspects of this pattern. Particularly there is now full appreciation for the paradoxical fact that actual recourse to the kind of nuclear assault whose *threatened use* provides the standard that ultimately anchors the whole Cold War system will probably destroy the system itself, obliterating not only its issues but also its institutions and actors.[2]

2. A basic conceptual problem is whether this apprehension and its aggression-inhibiting consequences should be considered part of the "Cold War system" or considered as a force external to the system and yet exerting influence upon it. Despite occasional passages that may suggest that I have followed the former choice, my basic conceptual strategy has been governed by the latter one. This is in some part a mere expository convenience, for the behavior of the main protagonists in the Cold War has certainly oscillated between evocation of the threat of nuclear response and increasingly frequent assurances of commitment to the distant goal of "denuclearizing" the international process.

The view taken in this chapter is that international relations are presently processed not only through the Cold War system (which is a modern, nuclearized version of international competition conventionally anchored in the threat of recourse to arms), but also that such relations are affected by a desire to move beyond the Cold War system itself and toward some new patterning of the international process. Continued reliance upon the Cold War dynamic, as this reliance has interacted with the motivation to avoid its ultimate implications (and to assure one's antagonist of this motivation), is perhaps the source of much of the confusion, and some of the inhibition, that has characterized the Soviet–American partial *détente* of recent years. Basically, the main task of this chaper is to examine speculatively the attitudinal processes that have impeded effective movement away from the Cold War system and toward an emerging international system whose potential availability has already affected the conduct of relations between the American– and Soviet–dominated portions of the world. I take the gross lineaments of this potentially emergent system, as now discerned, to include expanded arms reduction and control arrangements, ultimate reduction or perhaps dismantling of nuclear destructive capability, balance of power and sphere of influence settlements, and, finally, the partial pooling of sovereignties under expanded world law.

This chapter assumes, then, that some such perspective—held with whatever insecurity and conflict—is now affecting the performance in the policy process of at least some central members of the Eastern and Western governmental elites. That significant barriers exist to effective movement in pursuit of this perspective is obvious. Some of these are "attitudinal" in nature, whereas others are keyed to significant and "realistic" considerations of national interest. While this chapter is addressed primarily to analyzing the sources and possibilities for alteration of the former, it is at the same time guided by the author's conviction that national interest, in the broad sense, will also be well served by more rapid movement toward revision of the international system.

The foregoing comments should not be taken as comprising a denial of the interpretation that some of the basic interests of the competing powers are served by the present pattern of international competition. Clearly there are some major disparities of interest between the U.S. and the U.S.S.R. and the blocs (though these grow increasingly polycentric) that they respectively lead—and, just as clearly, the Cold War is in part a structured expression of the clash of those national interests. If any prescriptive assumption underlies

In the face of this dilemma each of the competing elites,[3] attempting to move beyond the restrictions and dangers of the Cold War system, has sought ways to create in the other an attitude of trust. Washington strives to persuade Moscow that it is "responsible," that though it will defend, and indeed pursue, its legitimate interests even to the point of nuclear retaliation if assaulted, it will never initiate a nuclear assault. Further, Washington attempts to convince Moscow that its guiding aspiration is for the achievement of international stability through just settlements of outstanding issues and through arms control arrangements that look toward disarmament as their ultimate, but far distant, goal. Discounting differences of rhetoric and pace, Moscow continues to communicate much the same sequence of messages to Washington.[4]

To describe this situation as one in which each of the two ruling, policy controlling groups is attempting to influence the attitudes of the other is simply to introduce a basic social psychological perspective into an analytic framework that has already been elaborated by representatives of other disciplines. But this intrusion has useful consequences, particularly in suggesting the applicability of a body of theory that has been rather closely developed and heavily researched in recent years. I speak, of course, of the energetic endeavor by social psychologists to construct a detailed understanding of the processes by which attitudes are developed, stabilized, and altered, and also of the processes governing the relationship between attitudes and overt behavior. Though there is competition and debate within this area of social psychology and, thus, though there is more than one theory of attitude dynamics presently

---

this chapter, it is simply this: Movement beyond the Cold War system toward a less dangerous form of international order (and a related clearing away of the misperceptions and attitudinal distortions that have fostered and been fostered by the Cold War) will enable some significant reduction in the intensity and number of apparent conflicts of interest, and the remaining conflicts may then be pursued more openly because they have been rendered less dangerous.

3. In current writing much is obscured by the too ready or too vague employment of the term "elite." As used in this chapter, the term should be taken as designating those persons within government (and those with direct advisory access to them) who actually contribute to the definition of policy alternatives or to the choice between them. It is, of course, so obvious as to hardly require iteration that the policy process involves many other subelites and special interest groups who, though positioned beyond the framework of official government, do exert important influence upon the shaping of policy or do render crucial service in its execution and popularization.

4. This is not to say that actual recourse to war is now impossible. While the occasional "eyeball to eyeball" confrontations of the U.S. and U.S.S.R. have not led to any significant exchange of military blows, they may yet do so. Moreover, when these nations have been able to exert partial control over conflicts between other non-nuclear nations—or over conflicts within such nations—they have sometimes been willing to use such surrogate wars as instruments of policy. At the time of writing, the war in Vietnam, however complicated its background, is the most salient example. However, as in the Korean conflict (and unlike the earlier conflicts in Azerbaijan, Greece, and the Congo), at least one of the background parties is committed to direct, undisguised participation in the contest of arms.

available, scientific consensus has been established on a number of major variables and relationships. Later I shall attempt to show how some portion of this body of work may help to clarify certain features of the interaction between competing elites. Also I shall presume to offer some prescriptions about how attitudes of international trust and cooperation, attitudes of the sort that would facilitate the transformation of the international system so as to reduce its present level of high risk, might be more effectively fostered. However, before turning to such matters it is necessary that we examine, in far closer detail, some of the possible relationships and interactions between public attitudes and foreign policy.

The exact nature, scope, and direction of the interaction between a nation's various domestic publics and its foreign policies have been submitted to considerable speculative examination and debate. If there is one item holding that debate within manageable limits it is that those who have some direct control over the shaping of policy do not take it as their primary obligation to simply interpret and execute the "will of the people." Miller and Stokes[5] have reported evidence that seems to confirm the common judgment that legislators who have some voice in policy design and revision do not typically conform to a simple version of the "instructed delegate" model. Nor do foreign policy specialists and those in executive positions to whom they report (and who exert ultimate power over foreign policy decisions) willingly submit to much direct instruction by delegates. Indeed, the foreign ministry as a governmental institution is protected more than many comparable departments from legislative encroachments. This protection is achieved not only by frequent iteration of claims to technical competence and privileged information, but also by the intervention of highest executive power when those claims are seriously challenged. In fact, excepting the Eisenhower-Dulles period, it has been characteristic in recent decades in the United States for the President to take so large a role in the shaping and maintenance of foreign policy as to place the State Department rather securely under his protective wing.

Yet it would be grossly mistaken to conclude that the formulation and execution of foreign policy in nations like the United States, or even in the Soviet Union, is uninfluenced by public opinion. The contrary view that guides the analysis presented in this chapter is that national elites do have some control over the shaping of public opinion on issues of foreign policy—but that subsequent attempts at policy alteration are in turn influenced, or at least constrained, by the very public opinion that they have sought to create and control.

5. Warren E. Miller and Donald E. Stokes, "Constituency Influence in Congress," *American Political Science Review*, 57 (March, 1963), 45–56.

If we may turn again to the Cold War epoch for contemporary data bearing upon the relationship between foreign policy and public opinion, we find a number of relevant and supporting facts. The first is that on both, or all, sides during the twenty-year confrontation significant effort has been expended in attempts to affect the content, intensity, and evocability of domestic public opinion. Until rather recently these efforts have been mainly directed toward the creation and reinforcement of a distrusting and hostile view of the competing national power. Often, of course, such efforts have been facilitated, or even stimulated, by actual or perceived hostile actions on the part of the competing power.[6]

In the Soviet Union, and also in many of the nations within its sphere of influence, "agitprop" specialists and agencies seem to have worked rather effectively to influence mass attitudes in the anti-American direction. The United States has been represented as a nation dominated, though not without significant internal opposition, by military-industrial cliques. To these cliques and the government they are said to control, Soviet propagandists have in the past attributed intentions such as these: to reverse the gains achieved by the "socialist nations"; to frustrate the ambitions of those peoples who have been grudgingly allowed to slip the "yoke of colonialism"; to preserve and restore the inequitable capitalist economic order; and, in the service of all these goals, to plan for an eventual total victory, one that may be sought through massive armed assault if the vigilance of the "peace-loving nations" is ever relaxed.

In the United States, and with somewhat greater complexity in most of the nations allied with it, a similar view has been propagated as regards the Soviet Union. While control of media content is more informal and less uniform in the Western world (and while more often than in the Soviet Union it is based on a "voluntary" alignment of the views of media specialists with those that the policy elite desires to have propagated), the extent of that control has been sufficient to create considerable uniformity concerning the mass image of the Soviet Union.

The content of this attitude cluster is well known. Through the Truman and Eisenhower years (with the possible exception of the brief "Camp David period"), it included all of the following themes: The Soviet Union seeks increased dominance in all sectors of the world.

6. It is generally credited that the Cuban missile crisis was the peak confrontation in the history of the Cold War. Since then there has been a significant increase in the intensity and frequency of interelite communications stressing the intention to limit the dangers of nuclear and other forms of military confrontation. But, at the same time, both nations and their partners have, in the main, continued their dependence upon the basic Cold War principles of "prudential distrust" and deterrence. The significance of such pronouncements as President Kennedy's speech at American University and the atmospheric test-ban treaty is that open avowal of the desire for revision of the international system is now more permissable than it was during the first decade and a half of the Cold War.

Unlike the Western states that oppose its malign plans, it is politically immoral and its pledges "are not worth the paper they are written on." It is committed to the destruction of capitalism and the democratic political institutions of the West. Unless it is vigilantly opposed and constantly confronted with the prospect of militarily effective counter-attack, it may unleash massive nuclear assault, either when its particular ambitions for extended hegemony are blocked or in a fanatic gamble for a single-stroke total victory.

The fact that some such parallel training in attitudes of international hostility and distrust has been essayed on both sides of the Cold War conflict requires interpretation, even if in recent years there has been introduced the additional theme that realism and perhaps even humane concern are also at work within the opposing camp and are tending to modify, however unreliably, the more intemperate aspects of its aggressive proclivities. Functionally viewed, the pattern of attitude-shaping communication that I have been describing may well have had a number of different kinds of utility. What these may have been (or are now) can only be approached by the method of informed conjecture. Perhaps the least obvious possibility (though it is one that is recommended by generalization from basic principles of psychodynamics) is that the propagation of attitudes of international distrust and hostility has helped to reduce the intensity of an individual psychic dilemma that may well have been experienced by many of those in elite positions who have helped to shape and maintain the internationally competitive, war-risking policies of their governments. To be a sort of advance man for Armageddon cannot but be psychologically taxing, except for that rare personality in which a core of sadistic impulse and fantasy exists unaffected by any species of ethical sensibility. Despite speculative appraisals of the relation between psychopathology and politics (and rejecting the hypothesis that amoral psychopathy often marks the public man of power), it is reasonable to assume that when a leader shares in the responsibility for policies that risk holocaust this must often be provocative of painful guilt and self-doubt.

Such dysphoric states require release or reduction, and in this as in other instances of major intrapsychic conflict there is available a repertoire of ego-defensive strategies. Certainly one route out of the particular dilemma that I have attempted to describe is to search for further *justification* for the war-risking policies that one has helped to develop and to which one remains tied by role-based responsibilities.

Probably one of the most readily available ways to achieve such an increase in justification is in the further elaboration and rationalization of the assessment that the competing power is dangerously antagonistic and constantly given to duplicity. As men who enjoy power over policy

decisions have pressed this judgment in their own public pronouncements, and as they have urged media specialists to "get the facts about
the enemy" across to the public or to present "a realistic picture of the
difficulties and dangers of our international situation," they have probably
experienced some consoling diminution of self doubt. Furthermore,
this effect has probably been fostered not only by the iteration of such
views but also by the waves of resonance and approving feedback from
the publics to which they have been communicated.

I have described one way in which the propagation of pessimistic
and untrusting attitudes toward the competing power may have had
some direct psychological value for those in high leadership during the
Cold War epoch. In doing so I have not meant to suggest that the
emotional conflicts encountered by leaders comprise either the sole
source or even the main source of the mirror-image pattern of attitude
training to which publics on both sides of this international competition
have been exposed. On the contrary, I am persuaded that in the analysis
of international politics and policies it is important to avoid the lure of
excessive "psychologism." Though the personalities of men in power
are of some relevance, and though even greater relevance may be found
in the emotional hazards that they encounter in making difficult choices,
inquiry into the characteristics of the institutions and systems that
organize and process the relations between states will probably account
for a larger portion of the variance. Certainly this seems to be the case
as one attempts to understand why and how the publics of East and West
were so heavily showered with anti-American and anti-Soviet propaganda
respectively from the end of the World War II until the early years of
the present decade.

One of the more obvious and important of a group of system-related
functions that seem to have been served by such campaigns has been to
justify, and thus render acceptable to the public, the costs for continued
prosecution of the Cold War. These costs might be reckoned in terms
of the capital outlay that has been deflected from other uses that would
have afforded more immediate general benefit. It seems likely that this
has been more intensely felt in the Soviet Union, where economic
deprivation has probably been more severe, and where delays in meeting
needs for housing and consumer goods have been publicly attributed to
the priorities of national defense. But on both sides of the international
competition other costs have been exacted which, if less tangible in
economic terms, are felt to be no less onerous. The maintenance of large
military forces requires of many that they must accept the difficult
burden of separation from family. To the extent that individuals identify
with their nations they are likely to suffer some real frustration and
bitterness over the fact that after many years the Cold War has not

been won. Still larger numbers must somehow reconcile themselves to a world which, as they are led to perceive it at times of actual or threatened military confrontation, may be momentarily blown out from under them. No matter how apathetic the mass public may seem toward the detailed issues of foreign policy, the over-all direction of that policy, if it imposes high costs upon the public, cannot be maintained unless those costs are somehow justified. The maintenance of national morale during the Cold War era has thus been served (though, to be sure, not always consciously served) by something rather similar to what is required in the prosecution of hot wars: that is, the maintenance of morale has been facilitated by continuing campaigns that have tended to keep national publics suspicious of and hostile toward the visible antagonist.

The creation and stabilization of the cross-national attitude pattern of hostility and distrust has afforded yet another specific utility for the maintenance of the Cold War as the basic system through which East and West have prosecuted and regulated their continuing competition. I have suggested that resort to nuclear arms is the final standard to which all instances of the Cold War conflict have at least implicitly referred. The danger of stumbling into, or provoking, nuclear war is salient not only when diplomatic conflicts are being played through, but also when the major powers have taken on supervisory roles in limited and peripheral wars that are fought with nonnuclear weapons.

In evoking and relying upon the prospect of armed conflict carried forth at the full present capacity, the Cold War dynamic is, as we have seen, comparable to most earlier types of competitive international systems. Where it has differed is that in any particular situation, the intention to take resort to arms is now considerably less credible than it was in the prenuclear era. To render the incredible credible has been a major tactical difficulty for the nations caught up in the seemingly inflexible dynamic of the Cold War system. The main attempt to do so has involved the mounting and display of complex arms systems, ever more potent in their presumed overkill capacity and in their first- and second-strike capabilities.

At the same time the display of human, rather than technological, resources has also been important. Thus the proficiency and dedication of military personnel have often been celebrated in ways that seem intended to provoke notice on the opposing side. Similarly, saber-rattling pronouncements by military leaders are not infrequent. In some part such pronouncements must be presumed to be beyond the full control of the governing political elite; for an important consequence of the Cold War has been that it has provided the military with easier access to the attention and deference of the mass public, and in certain ways this has led to a widening of the sphere in which official spokesmen for the

military services, as well as individual deviates within the military structure, may presume to greater autonomy.

On the other hand, one cannot resist the interpretation that both the hard-line general who embarrasses the State Department with a speech arguing the possible necessity of a "preemptive assault" and the Soviet air marshal who publishes an article suggesting something of a similar order may often be acting out roles that have planned tactical significance. Nothing might better work to create in the opposing elite an attitude of apprehension about the response that is being readied by its antagonist if its interests are challenged too far or too insistently in some current confrontation.

No less significant as a human resource that fosters credibility is the display of a pattern of public opinion that is geared to a condemning and untrusting view of the competing nation. For just as the governing elite knows that its militant commitment to the long Cold War conflict depends upon some necessary degree of broad public consent, it expects the elite of the opposing power to know this as well. As long as the Cold War system continues to function, leaders in Washington will expect that their intention to resist aggrandizement from Moscow (or from Peking) will seem more credible if, in both of the latter capitals, American public opinion is perceived as inflexibly and insistently "anti-Communist" and "anti-appeasement." Comparable expectations are, no doubt, held by the elites of these latter nations as regards the meaning that the Western elite will give to evidence about the content and force of public opinion in the Communist world.

It is not likely, of course, that either elite will expect of the other that it can be driven by the force of public opinion to military or other action that it deems inadvisable. But more reasonably it may interpret evidence of an aroused and antagonistic pattern of public opinion as indicating that the options available to the elite of the competing power include the taking of forceful initiatives, or the mounting of militantly resistant responses to initiatives that have been taken against them.

A related value that is achieved by maintaining a pattern of public opinion that is organized around hostility and distrust for the competing power is that it lends itself to certain kinds of dramatic manipulation at points of "crisis" in the continuing Cold War interaction. An American public that remains basically convinced that the Soviets intend "to bury us" will, for example, be more likely to accept government-initiated calls for a program of fallout shelter construction. Though in 1961–62 the actual number of private shelters built was not great, the amount of public interest and endorsement that was expressed may well have been sufficient to add to the credibility of the resistance that the United States was then taking in the face of a new wave of aggrandizing

pressure brought by the Soviet Union. Similarly, expressions in North Vietnam and neighboring states of "mass solidarity" against the United States (if those expressions are not perceived as "staged" by local governments) may have worked in the past, and may yet work again, to limit the scope and duration of the "toughening" of the American position in Vietnam.[7]

7. As this book goes to press the Vietnam situation holds considerable interest. This conflict highlights the importance of further aspects of the relationship between public opinion and the Cold War policy, aspects that cannot be encompassed unless we move beyond the limits of the crudely simplified model that I have so far employed. In attempting a sort of systems analysis of the Cold War, I have treated it as essentially a Soviet–American conflict, a treatment that may convey the undesired implication that other nations have been involved only as dependent and obedient allies. Of course this is not the case. There is considerable differentiation and competition within both the Eastern and Western blocs. One of the areas in which this situation has important consequences is the interaction between the policy and public-opinion processes. Especially does this seem to be the case as one pursues the specific problem now at hand—the role of dramatic expressions of the opinions of particular publics at crisis junctures in the Cold War.

The relevance of the Vietnam situation in the summer of 1966 is that of an illustrative and highly instructive case. Publics in the Communist and "ex-colonial" worlds beyond the Soviet Union seem to have become enraged by American initiatives in escalation and they have occasionally given direct and dramatic expression to demands that these initiatives be punished. As viewed from Washington, these expressions are likely to add to the credibility of Soviet warnings, for they evoke the concern that the Soviet elite, motivated by its competition with China and cognizant of China's actual military and economic limitations, may come to view the Vietnam situation as one in which it must demonstrate to the aroused publics of the subsidiary Communist states and of the "developing nations" that it is, after all, their main guardian against the "forces of imperialism."

This situation suggests that the content and intensity of public opinion beyond its national boundaries may foster (or diminish) the severity of a position taken by one of the main competing powers working through some major crisis. If the trend toward polycentrism in the Communist world continues, there is reason to expect that this problem, and thus the importance of expressions of public opinion from outside the boundaries of the United States and the Soviet Union, will become still more significant in their influence upon the American-Soviet patterns of Cold War interaction.

Another aspect of the Vietnam situation is of considerable interest as regards the dynamics of the interaction between public opinion and foreign policy. I have in mind the strenuous effort on the part of the U.S. government to justify its involvement in Vietnam to the American population and to win active support for that involvement. The protest mounted by American academics, peace movement organizations, and various liberal political groupings has been of sufficient intensity to rouse in the policy elite a concern that the firmness of the U.S. commitment will not be believed in Hanoi and Peking. At the same time, at least until the summer of 1966, one could not help pondering whether the mobilization of this pattern of critical opinion had not helped the American policy elite in resisting the demands of those other organized groups who were pressuring for still less restrained warfare against the Viet Cong and North Vietnam. At the time of writing, those who have been actively critical of the aggressiveness of United States policy in Vietnam have reason to be both disappointed and enraged. Yet they may have achieved, at least during 1965 and the early months of 1966, far more indirect braking control over policy than they now suspect.

However, in late June of 1966, the U.S. policy elite took yet another significant step up the escalation ladder by initiating bombing assaults against oil facilities near Hanoi and Haiphong. This seemed to be motivated, among other considerations, by a concern to demonstrate to the North Vietnamese government and to the nations supporting it that they

In the foregoing comments I have attempted to show that within the systemic limits of the Cold War there is functional value in creating and maintaining patterns of public opinion that are hostile and threat-oriented in their attitudinal view of the competing power. However, this "functionality" is of a decidedly restricted order; what is served is the maintenance of the Cold War system as a way of processing the issues and crises that arise as the major contesting powers continue to try to work their wills, each upon the other, in their respective quests for advantage and security.

However, as I suggested earlier, we are now living through a period whose prime significance in histories yet to be written may well be that it was the beginning of the end of the Cold War itself. For the Cold War system seems to have been becoming more dysfunctional than functional. Or perhaps it would be more accurate to say that though it has always been a poor and dangerous way of ordering the affairs between international competitors, this is now more fully appreciated at levels where such an understanding can have consequences for the future of the system itself. Perhaps a still more judicious interpretation would be that the dysfunctionality of the Cold War has long been apprehended by members of policy elites but that only recently have they come to believe that it is not an inevitable and presently unchangeable system.

At any rate, major governmental leaders, and those who influence them or speak for them, are now directly declaring certain insights and hinting at others. The most manifest and frequently voiced theme of concern and disillusion is simply that the risk of blundering or miscalculating into a full nuclear exchange remains quite high, and that this risk can only be reduced by changing the final standard against which international confrontations are "settled." To do this means to find some effective substitute for the process in which competitive initiatives and resistant responses are backed by the threat of recourse to nuclear arms. The search for such a substitute remains an insistently pressing issue

---

had no right to take heart over expressions, by many Americans, of opposition to their country's military intervention in Vietnam. Indeed, during much of the first half of 1966, increasingly irritated criticisms of "Nervous Nellies" (i.e., Americans opposing their nation's Vietnam policy) were heard from the President and his close associates. As congressional elections approached and as poll data continued to reflect considerable disaffection toward the President and his Vietnam policy, it seemed likely that failure to achieve "victory" or "settlement" in coming months might yet increase the danger of electoral punishment. Thus while the U.S. policy elite was willing to run political risks, there was reason to believe that its further decisions would be affected by awareness of these risks. In fact some interpreters viewed the escalations of June, 1966 (which included not only bombings at the periphery of North Vietnamese cities but also a further, sizeable increase in troop committments) and the related new wave of reassurance by officials of a noteworthy decline in North Vietnamese military prospects and morale, as the beginning of a last major effort to bring the conflict to completion before it exacted an unacceptable degree of domestic political loss.

between the main protagonists of the Cold War, though it is counterpoised by a reluctance to abandon the "security" of deterrence as well as by an uncertainty as to whether national interests can be properly served and protected if gross changes are introduced into the structure of international relations. But against this background of confusion and uncertainty there yet appears to be some serious commitment on the part of the major protagonists in the Cold War to finding some way of ending it, to constructing some alternative system that will regulate the competitive struggle at least as well, but without the load of high risk that must currently be borne.

The one expedient in this direction that continues to receive the greatest attention is, of course, the possibility of arms control and disarmament arrangements. While doubt persists that absolutely effective inspection and control measures could be developed, it is nevertheless felt that some "defusing" of the present Cold War technology is urgently required. The motivation behind this growing conviction is not solely the fear that the major Cold War protagonists, through accident and miscalculation, may blunder into an exchange of nuclear blows. Another quite salient apprehension is that unless the Cold War dynamic is reversed to the point where there can be negotiated some effective multilateral treaties that limit nuclear arms production and development, "proliferation" will soon be upon us and, once under way, will be extremely difficult to reverse. In essence, the insight now agitating those who have been caught up in the latter concern is this: As a system involving essentially two protagonists, the Cold War, despite the high risks it has involved, has been somewhat viable, particularly as the protagonists have gained experience in the delicate art of using it. But with a multiplicity of nuclear powers, with little Cold Wars between China and India, Egypt and Israel, Ghana and Guinea, or Yugoslavia and Albania, the probability of catalytic ignition of holocaust will rise.

Another force impelling elite interest toward some sort of international restructuring through which the Cold War might be ended is the awareness that its national economic cost is far too high. In the Soviet Union, in England, and less obviously in the United States, the need to radically reduce defense investments and to free capital for other uses seems now to be widely appreciated within governmental and managerial elites and also within some sections of the national publics.

Perhaps yet another and less easily specified, force is also at work. This is the growing suspicion that in the major nations the rise in violence and in other manifestations of social and individual pathology is due not only to continued urbanization and bureaucratization and their attendant disorienting stresses, but that it is fostered also by the themes of assault, anxiety, distrust, and disloyalty that are conveyed through

the very institutions and imagery of the Cold War system. While in the United States this is probably not a matter of immediate concern for those who shape and regulate foreign policy, it has in recent years become more salient within certain intellectual and professional publics, some of whose members do have influence upon members of the policy-controlling elite.

I have tried to suggest some of the forces and problems that are presently working to impel policy-makers, particularly in the United States, on one side, and in the Soviet Union, on the other, toward a dismantling of the Cold War system. Implicit in this interpretation is a proposition that some interpreters might question, but which to me seems well supported by a close reading of the analyses and programmatic statements by spokesmen and leaders of the policy elites of these nations. That proposition is that many of the policy objectives that now are openly declared on either or both sides (i.e. arms control and reduction, extension of the nuclear test ban, possibilities for stabilizing contested national boundaries, creation of a potent international police force, disengagement plans, increased cultural and scientific exchange and cooperation, and so on) are intended as instrumental to the eventual achievement of a general settlement and to the transformation of the processes by which international competition is now conducted.

In short summary, and risking both the audacity of extreme simplification and the label of "wishful optimist," I am persuaded of this: that in Washington and Moscow, the elites who presently dominate the shaping of foreign policy (though, to be sure, that dominance is contested) are now motivated in some significant degree toward a continuing process of conciliation that has as its ultimate aim to discard the Cold War system and to erect some other system in its place.

But if this be so, why has movement in this direction been so inconsistent, so unrhythmic, so halting, so fragmentary? One main and obvious reason is surely the shared attitudes of deep distrust between the elites of those major nations around whose competition the Cold War system has developed. This we shall have occasion to submit to closer analysis below. Another part of the explanation may be found in the issue-area concept developed by Rosenau in Chapter 2. Some of the issues that make up the "agenda" of the Cold War are probably perceived by the protagonists as involving presently irreconcilable oppositions of important national interests, while others may be perceived as permitting conciliatory bargaining and yielding. Yet another part of the explanation may well lie in the fact that neither the Soviet nor American policy-elite groups are uniform in their views. Though the evidence is persuasive that the prevailing view in both groups does favor conciliation and eventual reorganization of the international system, it is also certainly the case,

as I have already noted, that this view is contested at policy elite levels. Beyond these considerations at least one other answer is possible within the limits of the general interpretive approach taken here. It is that the presently dominating policy planners of the contesting powers are sensitive also to certain major "domestic" barriers and risks that may be encountered as they pursue the possibilities for international conciliation and system revision. This latter sort of concern involves, most particularly, the prospect of public rejection and indignation toward certain kinds of policy changes, and we will examine this matter also in closer detail below. But at this point a summary judgment will suffice: possibly for a number of reasons, the elites of the major Cold War powers cannot advance with unqualified directness toward the goals of "issue settlement" and reorganization of the international system; rather they are lured toward this goal state and yet, as they move toward it, are anxiously driven back. The situation is not unlike the sort of individually experienced ambivalence that psychologists have in mind when they speak of approach-avoidance conflict.

The persistence, in the face of the anxieties it generates, of the orientation toward the goal state of international tension reduction and institutional revision may well be interpreted as it would be in the individual psychological parallel; that is, as evidence that the "approach" motivation has reliable strength. But, again as in the individual psychological parallel, energetic and direct movement toward the goal state will not be possible unless the intensity of the anxiety can be reduced. This necessitates a close examination of the particular foci of anxiety, of the separate risks and losses that are feared. Such an analysis discloses different types of anticipated risks. Some of these have little to do with attitudes and attitude change. But others, as I have suggested, do appear to refer to the attitudes that the policy elite attributes to the elite groups of other nations, and yet others seem to refer to the attitudes attributed to publics with which the elite is involved as it seeks to protect its control of the policy process and its very security in ruling status.

ATTITUDE ATTRIBUTIONS AS OBSTACLES
TO INTERNATIONAL CHANGE

The characterization that I have given of the current situation in the Cold War has been that it is a system still in operation, but one that has been found dysfunctional by its major actors. Further, I have suggested that those actors are now seeking to alter that system or to replace it with another. To do this they must conciliate many outstanding issues between them and then they must go on, in the design of new international

institutions and problem-processing arrangements, to a kind of cooperation that they have never before attempted. Also, I have suggested that one type of major barrier that stands in their way is based upon the kinds of attitudes that they attribute to one another.

Each seems to have persuaded the other that its attitude toward the utilization of available nuclear assault power is one of anxious dread. In this the pattern of shared attitudinal attributions facilitates, or at least keeps alive, the ambition to get beyond the Cold War system and its dangers. However, various other attitudinal attributions that lay behind the original emergence of the Cold War system and that have kept it going still do persist. Basically the elites of the United States and the Soviet Union still seem to perceive one another as holding to attitudes of hostility and to ambitions for achieving degrees of aggrandizing gain that have not been available to them during the period of nuclear standoff. Furthermore, each group knows that it is so perceived by the other. In consequence each approaches the other with a prudential distrust that tends to confirm the very pattern of shared suspicious attributions that has fostered that distrust. On some such basis substantive progress in reorganizing the relations between these states is largely blocked and, in many of the areas that both major powers have hoped to be negotiable, frustration is encountered. Particularly notable have been failures with regard to further arms-control arrangements, territorial adjustments, UN reform and, perhaps most immediately important, the development of informal agreements to cease contesting certain outstanding issues or to avoid competition for dominance over certain unstable areas of the neutral world.

In essence, then, one of the reasons why the policy elites of Washington and Moscow find it difficult to proceed from limited *détente* to a more active process of international conciliation is that they are possessed by apprehensions of this order: that the opposing side, given its persisting attitudes will use conciliatory arrangements to "seize advantage," that it has "some dirty tricks up its sleeve;" and that, at any rate, even if it wanted "to play the game honestly" it would not be able to do so because "they don't trust us any more than we trust them."

The hopeful aspect of this situation is that the frustrating power of this pattern of attitudinal attribution is now recognized at elite levels, and it is now more frequently and openly acknowledged that ways must be found to "change their attitudes toward us." To this it might be added that effective reduction of the pattern of mutual distrust would be further advanced if the policy elite of each of the contesting nations were to attempt to more systematically submit its "attitudes toward them" to the sort of critical scrutiny that fosters change in those attitudes wherever the "data" seem to require it. How both types of attitude change might be

facilitated is one of the main matters to be treated in the next section of this chapter.

However, even if change in the attitudes of these elites toward one another were fully achieved, other kinds of attitudinal attributions, especially those involving elite conceptions of mass opinion, would probably operate to inhibit many phases of the required process of international conciliation and system revision. Earlier, and in some detail, I dealt with the ways in which the attitudes of broad national publics have become relevant to the conduct of the Cold War. I suggested specifically that the shaping of a pattern of public opinion that was hostile toward, and distrustful of, the competing national power was functional for the effective utilization of the Cold War system itself, at least for as long as the leading nations feel bound to that system as the basic structure through which their competitive interactions are to be conducted. Implicit in that earlier discussion was another proposition that must now be examined. It is that the erection of this pattern of public opinion has imposed upon the elites of the competing powers a demanding constraint as they consider moving beyond the limits of the Cold War system toward the goals of conciliation and institutional revision and as they endeavor to discover means toward those goals.

The basis for this interpretation can be presented more simply in the case of the United States than in that of the Soviet Union. This, of course, is because in the United States the security of the political elite is far more directly dependent upon the electoral process. Thus, whenever any major foreign policy changes or innovations are being considered, members of the policy elite (and intermediaries who link them to the power concerns of the political parties) are likely to ask: How will the public respond? How will this affect electoral prospects nationally and locally? What use will the opposition party be able to make of this in arousing public indignation? More particularly, and in the light of the presently conflicted and uncertain movement toward conciliation with the Soviet Union and its European allies, the political and governmental sectors of the American elite must ask whether the general pattern of anti-Communist public opinion will be grossly violated by such measures as further arms control agreements, increased economic aid to certain Balkan states, Soviet-American multilateral economic and technical aid to developing nations, settlement of the Vietnam conflict by including the National Liberation Front in a coalition government and formalization of the reality of two Germanies.

My argument is not that any policy change that violates the earlier hard-line commitment will be rejected within elite circles because of apprehensions over domestic political consequences. Clearly this has not been so. Rather, the dynamic seems to be a quite complex one

in which policy undertakings that arouse such apprehensions are designed, "trial-ballooned," advocated, and then withdrawn, revised, or carried forth, in ways that tend to be influenced at many points by a concern over public response. And since that concern tends to be keyed to a reading of public opinion as essentially anti-Soviet and anti-conciliatory in its attitudinal basis, the consequence, more often than not, is that conciliatory and system-revising courses of policy are pursued less directly, less unambiguously, less effectively than would otherwise be the case. Also, as if to placate and reassure the general public, when clearly conciliatory policy steps are taken they sometimes seem to be followed by some increase in visible severity, some apparent intensification of Cold War competitiveness, in a contiguous issue-area.

Such accommodation to anxieties about the punitive consequences that might be encountered if public opinion is violated has a number of clearly dysfunctional aspects. One of these is that it hampers the integrated design and revision of policy, and thus it sets limits upon what may be achieved at any particular juncture in the continuing interaction between the contesting nations as they search for mutually advantageous ways to limit and redefine their contest. A possible case in point is that on the crest of the atmospheric test ban the United States might well have gone on to examine the possibilities of central European "disengagement" or other confrontation-reducing arrangements, but if this was privately considered it was not publicly pursued or even expressed. In the view of some "inside dopesters,"[8] the prevailing attitude at top levels of the policy elite was one of relief, mixed with some surprise, at how little public indignation had been aroused by the test ban. Under these circumstances it may well have been deemed judicious by those policy-makers who must keep a worried eye on electoral prospects, that they had better not press their luck.[9]

Yet another consequence of the constraining influence of public opinion upon the policy process might be noted in regard to the Cold War situation. This involves second-order influence upon the perceptions

8. Cf. Sander Vanocur, "Kennedy's Voyage of Discovery," *Harper's*, 228 (April, 1964), 41–45.

9. Again the issue-area concept seems to have some applicability, at least as a way of sharpening the questions that might be asked. Was the test-ban issue viewed by interpreters within the American policy elite as one that the general public approached in the special and possibly isolated terms of a concern over the health hazards of fallout? Was this the actual cognitive-affective meaning of the issue for those portions of the public that did express rather clear and enthusiastic endorsement of the treaty? Or was that endorsement an expression of a generalized public readiness to accept a dismantling of the Cold War system? It seems likely that at elite levels the answer to the last question was taken, whether correctly or not, to be negative. The importance of public-opinion poll data in the shaping of such estimates and the problems posed by the frequently unsuspected bias and invalidity of such data deserve special consideration. See the last section of this chapter.

of the elite of the competing power. I have argued that one major attitudinal obstacle to international change is the persistence of attitudes of distrust as between the policy elites in question. Where steps toward conciliation are taken in rhythmic sequence, in impressively patterned extension, they will probably have far more effect in dispelling the distrust of the opposing elite than when each such step is taken haltingly, or is followed by immobility or, still worse, by a step sideways or backwards.

Though I have cast these comments in terms applicable to the situation in the United States I do not mean to suggest that the dynamic I have described obtains only in nations whose political institutions permit open electoral recall. Loss of governing political power and insecurity over the possibilities of such loss seem to be important features of all modern political systems, and in virtually all states, opinions of publics are somehow relevant in the competition for power. In the Soviet Union, with its lack of institutions guaranteeing high office for a fixed term, leadership must remain sensitive to the opinions of sub-elite, specialized publics such as the military hierarchy, managerial cadres, and the provincial satraps of the party system. Also, it must remain sensitive to the opinions of Communist publics beyond the Soviet Union. To the extent that these Soviet and extra-Soviet publics continue to hold attitudes of implacable competitiveness and distrust toward the nations of the Western alliance, the Soviet elite, sensitive to the possibility of internal challenges, is bound to be constrained by this attitude pattern in its approach to foreign policy issues.[10] Furthermore, the claims of a rather inflexible ideology impose still additional limits upon the possibility for open declaration of new policy choices and open implementation of such choices. In consequence, the Soviet elite, despite its celebration of the desirability of coexistence (and despite the fact that it seems basically persuaded that conciliation and revision of the international system are required) at times has seemed to move even more guardedly than the United States toward the dismantling of the Cold War.

For the foregoing and other reasons it seems reasonable to suggest that the possibility of speeding the movement toward revision of the international system, and toward conciliation of the basic conflicts of interest that are now prosecuted through the Cold War system, is somewhat more open to American than to Soviet initiatives. In the United States the constraining influence of apprehensions over electoral

10. However, it should be noted that, if one can estimate main trends in Soviet public opinion by shifts in the positions and views articulated by the Soviet "intelligentsia," recent years have been marked by a considerable strengthening of the proconciliatory orientation.

consequences of violating public opinion may well be less of a barrier than many policy elitists think it to be (and more of a barrier than many policy scientists think it to be). At any rate, it does seem possible to examine this question by reference to recently developed knowledge about attitude structure, dynamics, and measurement.

Before turning to these psychological matters, however, it should be noted that in these last comments I have broached some aspects of a central problem that is shared by a number of the chapters in this volume — that of how public opinion and foreign policy affect one another. In the light of this concern there is visible yet another special value in focusing upon the Cold War. It is that in recent years the Cold War has supplied those issues of foreign policy that have been most often treated in the mass media, most often presented as ones in which "liberal" and "conservative" alternatives can be discerned, most commonly and most dramatically commended to the public as engaging their basic interests and welfare. Thus, questions about the extent to which public opinion is capable of encompassing issues of foreign policy, questions about the modifiability of public opinion and its interaction with the policy-making process, might well be most profitably examined in this area of foreign policy rather than in some other. Data and analysis concerning public opinion on Cold War issues should, then, be of particular value in formulating generalizations that could be tested over a far wider range of issues.

On the other hand, separate issue-areas, even within the broad area of foreign policy, may well possess some distinctive, nongeneralized features. Indeed there is some evidence that this may be so as regards the role of ethnic, religious, and personality factors in disposing members of the general public toward acceptance or rejection of the Cold War "hard line." Some of this evidence is presented below. Apart from their direct bearing upon the policy-opinion interaction in the Cold War issue-area, these data suggest the need for developing theoretical propositions that will clarify, for all issue-areas, the balance between general and issue-specific relationships.

ATTITUDE CHANGE AND CLARIFICATION IN THE SERVICE OF INTERNATIONAL CHANGE

In the preceding sections I have often referred to recent developments in attitude theory and research, and I have said that aspects of this work have potential value for clarifying and altering the attitudes of the Cold War elites toward one another. Also, I have suggested that recent work on attitude structure and dynamics might be applicable to the task of

comprehending and revising the relationship between the attitudes of mass publics and the conduct of foreign policy by the elites that are in some part dependent upon those publics. Hence, it is necessary now to focus upon some of the relevant major developments in the recent social psychological study of attitudes.

Attempts to develop detailed and systematic theories of attitude acquisition and change began only some twenty years ago. Before then research was rather concretistic, seeking usually to answer untheoretical and often crudely practical questions about persuasion (e.g., Is "emotional" propaganda more effective than "rational" propaganda?), or seeking to discover how particular social attitudes were correlated with certain personality or social-identity characteristics.

In the last two decades at least three major theoretical approaches have been developed. Each of these has been able to generate testable propositions and some of those have been submitted to rather close laboratory investigation. One of the three approaches is essentially an instrumental learning model of attitude dynamics; the second has been labelled the "functional" approach; the third consists of a group of models which, taken together, are now usually called the "consistency" approach.

The instrumental learning model was developed by Hovland and his associates, first in field experiments conducted for the Army[11] and then at Yale.[12] It treats the attitude dynamic process in terms kindred to those used by Hull[13] in his analyses of animal and human learning and then applied to personality development and psychotherapy by Dollard and Miller.[14] At the core of the theoretical model elaborated by Hovland and his associates is the proposition that an opinion (defined as some habitual judgment or prediction) or an attitude (defined essentially as an habitual evaluative orientation) *becomes* habitual though the fact that its expression or internal "rehearsal" is followed by the experience of positive reinforcement. But whereas reinforcement in the animal learning laboratory is conveyed by food pellets, cessation of electric shock, and the like, in any human process involving symbol manipulation other kinds of reinforcers become particularly relevant: namely those that are rendered accessible through anticipation, through the uses of imagination and through the capacity for thinking about relationships.

Speaking of "incentives" rather than "reinforcements," Hovland

11. Carl I. Hovland, Arthur Lumsdaine, and Fred D. Sheffield, *Experiments on Mass Communication* (Princeton: Princeton University Press, 1949).
12. Carl I. Hovland, Irving L. Janis, and Harold H. Kelley, *Communication and Persuasion* (New Haven: Yale University Press, 1953).
13. Clark L. Hull, *Principles of Behavior* (New York: Appleton-Century, 1943).
14. John Dollard and Neal Miller, *Personality and Psychotherapy* (New York: McGraw-Hill, 1950).

and his colleagues have contended that attitude change is achieved by communications which, if adequately designed, force the "target-person" to examine, or otherwise experience, the incentives available through adopting the new, advocated attitude position. Of various classes of incentives, two seem to have received the greatest research study. The first concerns the utilities directly available if the attitude is changed (e.g., reduction of anxiety over health if some advocated hygienic practice is adopted, the promise of individual economic gain if some candidate or proposal is viewed favorably and voted for). The second concerns gains in social acceptance that may be anticipated if it can be demonstrated to the person that his present attitude varies significantly from those held in his reference groups or by respected, prestigeful figures, and that the new, advocated position will bring him closer to these normative standards.

It is recognized that existing attitudes are already bolstered by coordination to a set of supporting incentive considerations, and that communications intended to alter attitudes will be resisted on this basis. Thus the attitude change process is analyzed into a sequence of steps that must be successively and successfully transacted. Roughly these steps are: to capture the attention of the target-person or group; to establish the "credibility" of the communicator; to direct to the person a well-designed communication that calls into doubt the incentive supports for the original attitude and offers compelling arguments which highlight the positive incentives associated with the advocated attitude; to direct the person or group toward rehearsal of the new attitude so as to make the associated incentives more tangible and to provide vivid anticipatory experience of them.

Within this framework it becomes possible to identify many variables that might affect the success with which one or another of these stages is negotiated. The systematic manipulative testing of these variables has comprised the major portion of the large experimental program carried out by the Yale group and the programs of others influenced by it. Among the many variables that have been experimentally studied are these: "communicator credibility" and its sources; aspects of the organization of persuasive communications (particularly the comparative efficacy of "one-sided" versus "two-sided" appeals); anxiety arousal as a method for altering incentive supports; role-playing as a way of fostering consideration of incentive aspects of the advocated attitude; intensity and content of group memberships and reference group orientations; personality factors making for "general persuasability" and for "topic-bound persuasability."

Findings about the relations between such variables and the achievement of effective attitude change have by now been fairly well replicated and they seem to have affected some aspects of propaganda practice,

particularly in their application to commercial advertising. But as Hovland himself suggested, greater and easier attitude change is achieved under laboratory conditions than in mass-persuasion campaigns. In a recent paper, Janis and Smith[15] have examined the barriers to effective application of such laboratory findings, particularly as regards mass communication campaigns designed to affect attitudes on foreign relations issues. They have been able also to develop, in impressively dexterous detail, a number of recommendations for circumventing these barriers. Their paper might well be recommended as the best effort to date at showing how the findings of the Hovland group (and also of the "functionalist" school with which Smith has been associated) might contribute to the reeducation of public opinion so as to ready it for required revisions in the relations between East and West and for revisions in the international system that controls those relations.

We are now in a position to ask what relevance the instrumental learning approach to attitude change has for the problem of altering the attitude pattern of conflicted distrust that seems to inhibit both the American and Soviet policy elites as they confront the necessity for major conciliation and for ultimate revision of the international system. These are not mass publics low on information and highly variable in their attentiveness to Cold War problems. On the contrary, these groups are composed of men playing roles that bind them to the issues, and to their present stands on the issues, in ways that reduce flexibility. Particularly limiting is the fact that their roles have been defined during the Cold War era as requiring considerable "prudential" distrust of the opposing power and thus of the assurances offered by its elite. Yet on both sides it is recognized that the opponent's attitude of distrust must be converted at least toward provisional trust, if anything more than a guarded, uncertain, and easily upset *détente* is to be achieved. Specifically what is required is that each elite persuade the other that it is willing to forego all opportunities for resort to nuclear surprise and the uses of nuclear threat and that in implementation of this willingness it will abide by all arms control and disarmament agreements that it may enter, even when it is technologically impossible to arrange for fully effective policing. Also, each elite must find ways to build its opponent's trust in its intention to closely adhere to sphere-of-influence and delimitation-of-competition agreements as these are developed. And as new and powerful international institutions are constructed, each elite must be able to elicit from its competitor a basic trust that it will continue to accept necessary limitations upon its sovereignty.

    15. Irving L. Janis and M. Brewster Smith, "Effects of Education and Persuasion on National and International Images," in Herbert C. Kelman (ed.), *International Behavior: A Social Psychological Approach* (New York: Holt, Rinehart and Winston, 1965).

The point at issue, here, then is rather close to what is comprehended in the use by the Hovland group of the concept of communicator credibility. As has been found in their studies with individual persons, so in the international area as well it should prove true that high communicator credibility makes for readier acceptance of the communicator's messages. But what will affect the level of credibility itself? In the experimental studies, the main influences are the communicator's apparent status and his apparent issue-related expertise. In the Soviet-American relationship these criteria have no particular pertinence. Instead there seems to be a more direct, but also extremely difficult, route toward enhanced credibility—one that must be taken even as each elite continues (for as long as separate sovereignty is maintained) in its efforts to preserve and advance its national interests. That route, if one may speak most directly, is to stop lying, faking, and posturing.

Is it at all possible, or even conceivable, that in their relations with one another, modern states can abandon the disingenuousness and deceit which, since Machiavelli, have seemed an inevitable part of the necessarily amoral art of statecraft? Particularly, can such a transformation in the style of international behavior be achieved in those special issue-areas that seem to involve basic opposition of significant national interests? I am aware that a simple affirmative answer will seem radically naïve to many specialists in international relations. Yet it seems to me that this question deserves a fresh look, one that does not hesitate to persevere beyond the limits of those studies that, by describing the modes, roles, and methods of international relations, sometimes suggest, or are misread to suggest, that "As it has been so must it ever be." In essence I am suggesting that it may be possible, under the motivating power of the continuing and dangerous inadequacy of the present international system, for elites to get beyond the limits of *realpolitik* and to impose some form of moral order upon their relationships with one another. I am also suggesting that if this radical change is to be explored, this exploration might well begin with a direct assault upon the attitudinal barrier of international distrust. There are probably many ways in which the behavioral sciences might facilitate such an assault. One, for example, would be the use of inter-nation gaming and simulation techniques to test the operating characteristics of a system based upon a principle of generalized trust. Such simulation studies might clarify just how feasible, how resistant to breakdown a system of this sort would be, and if found feasible, how it might be instituted.

As it is my intention in this section to touch with gadfly lightness upon a number of possible implications of the data and theory on attitude change, I will resist further pursuit of the matter treated above, except for one additional point. Initiatives in honesty and self-revelation are

presently available to any policy elite group that desires to seize them. While there is much that must yet remain "classified," while the international system yet remains more closed than open, there is nevertheless much that could be revealed to the antagonist under conditions that would allow him the opportunity for verification. I have in mind, for example, direct revelation of data about arms technology, economic affairs, the policy formulation process itself. Such candor might well invite reciprocation. If properly planned it might well set in motion cycles of reciprocation, which will expand their range so as to gradually encompass most of the matters upon which the contesting elites presently do not allow themselves to trust one another. Still another way to work toward altering the attitudes of distrust felt by the opposing elite is, simply, to seek occasions that will require promises to be given, particularly ones that seem to incur some disadvantage to the promiser, and then to fulfill them scrupulously and with full, incontrovertible display of one's scrupulosity.

The foregoing comments do not exhaust the directives that can be derived from the work of the Hovland group. Another concerns the rather obvious matter of incentive-manipulation. The most generally applicable part of the Yale approach is its insistence that persuasion is achieved by disconfirming the links between the old attitude and the rewards that it affords or promises, and establishing that the commended attitude, instead, yields such rewards. Thus much research has shown that in the case of the individual one can achieve persuasion by getting him to examine the motives that will be satisfied by action based upon the advocated attitude, or by social rewards that follow directly upon the expression of the attitude. How does this translate to the situation of one elite communicating with another? It highlights the importance of structuring the content and style of diplomatic interaction so as to make clear to the other side the gains that are available if it will undertake an accommodating shift on some issue under negotiation.

This last recommendation is applicable not so much to the goal of reducing attitudes of distrust as to the conciliation of more specific issues. If, for example, the U.S. could persuade the Soviet Union that it stands to gain by supporting all UN police actions (or if the Soviet Union could persuade the U.S. that it stands to gain by guaranteeing that Germany will not be allowed any access to nuclear arms), then conciliatory yielding might be likely. Such yielding would be due to change of attitude on the particular issue. But an exchange of such yieldings, if with it was associated the recurring experience of realizing the promised gains, would in turn alter the more basic attitudes of distrust that currently restrict the relationship between these two elite groups.

Why, then, has this sort of pattern not developed? One reason is

that the underlying, though conflicted, attitudes of mutual distrust do inhibit rapid exploration and exchanges of conciliatory shifts. Another is that the incentive conditions offered by each elite to the other are usually negative ones. They refer to threats that will be carried out, pressures and harassments that will be intensified unless the other agrees to yield. Such yielding is sometimes obtained, but often at the cost of fostering, rather than diminishing, attitudes of hostility and distrust—and also, of course, yielding of this type fosters the intention to take retribution by employing similar pressure or threat.

Attempts at control of the competing elites' attitudes and actions by use of negative incentives are bound to persist so long as those elites conceive of their relationship as a kind of extended zero-sum game, so long as each defines its gain as necessitating that the other accept loss. While some present issues do force a zero-sum relationship, many others could be structured in other ways so as to highlight the possibilities for mutual gain. For example, even on so seemingly resistant an issue as the Soviet Union's rejection of frequent inspection of atomic facilities or on the United States' commitment to some form of joint nuclear force within NATO, arguments mustered by the U.S. and the Soviet Union respectively could more often be turned toward demonstrating perspectives for mutual gain.

But this is not the strongest illustration of my point. More readily conceivable would be a systematic, rather than merely sporadic, reliance upon the cross-issue trading of gains; that is, upon altering a particular issue attitude of the opposing elite by intruding into that attitude structure incentives referring to still another issue attitude. For example, the Soviet Union might well consider whether acceptance of frequent inspection of its nuclear installations might be offered for permanent cancellation of MLF or kindred plans. The opportunities for this sort of strategy are vast. A systematic and continuous exploration could be undertaken in which the United States, the Soviet Union, and their allies could develop exhaustive specifications of their aspirations for particular policy changes. Concomitant with permanently maintained trade-off negotiations, both sides could regularly revise their rankings of how strongly they desire to elicit particular yieldings and how willing they are to offer others in trade. Through such a procedure, if rationally designed and structured, there might well be achieved not only a series of simple two-issue trade-offs, but also large and rather thoroughgoing patterns of settlement.

Furthermore, a cyclic effect might be induced; the mutually experienced gain in tension reduction and the beneficial domestic changes that successful trade-off would make possible would probably foster significant change in the attitudes of competitiveness and distrust that presently inhibit major progress in conciliatory negotiations. And this

in turn would be rather likely to produce, on both sides, over-all perceptions that the trade-off negotiations do yield gain rather than loss, even though they involve for each side some abandonment of earlier policy aims.

It should be added that there would also be great value in expanding the search for shared problems that do not engage the apparent or fundamental issues of the Cold War; problems in such comparatively manageable areas as technological development, scientific techniques, urban design, educational methods, crime control, administrative organization, and so on. A fully institutionalized framework that could foster greater East-West cooperation in the solution of such problems would add greatly to the number of mutually beneficial solutions achieved and would thereby be bound to further invalidate basic attitudes of competitiveness and distrust. This in turn would foster further progress in resolving issues that have arisen and persisted in the framework of the Cold War competition.

Among a number of other directives that might be drawn from the instrumental learning model of attitude change, one has especially attractive specificity. In some early studies by members of the Yale group[16] it was shown that role playing had the potential for inducing considerable attitude change. In these studies the role that is usually played is that of an advocate of an attitude position that deviates significantly from the individual's own. Usually the experimental subject is required to improvise a speech or write an essay in support of the new attitude position. This, according to Janis, exposes him to the most effective considerations in support of the new position and, with the additional influence of his ego-identification with the product of his improvisation, the person begins to see the issue in quite different terms. While Festinger and other proponents of dissonance theory[17] have offered an alternative interpretation of the process that mediates this effect, there is general agreement on the potency of the effect itself.

The implication for altering the attitudes of elites toward one another is clear. Whenever it is recognized that one's ability to negotiate with the elite of the competing nation is hampered by attitudes of distrust, or for that matter by difficulty in comprehending the interests, appre-

16. Irving L. Janis and Bert T. King, "The Influence of Role Playing on Opinion Change," *Journal of Abnormal and Social Psychology*, Vol. 49, (1957), 211–18; Bert T. King and Irving L. Janis, "Comparison of the Effectiveness of Improvised Versus Non-improvised Role-playing in Producing Opinion Changes," *Human Relations*, Vol. 9 (1956), pp. 177–86; Herbert C. Kelman, "Attitude Change as a Function of Response Restriction," *Human Relations*, Vol. 6 (1953), pp. 185–214.

17. Leon Festinger, *A Theory of Cognitive Dissonance* (Evanston: Row, Peterson, 1957); Jack W. Brehm, "A Dissonance Analysis of Attitude-discrepant Behavior," in Milton J. Rosenberg, Carl I. Hovland, *et. al.*, *Attitude Organization and Change* (New Haven: Yale University Press, 1960).

hensions, and points of view of that elite, the role-playing technique might prove valuable. Particularly, this could serve as a basis for reexamining and, where necessary, revising the attributions that one elite makes toward another.

Though I have not seen any published reports confirming it, I have heard that some systematic use of the role-playing technique has been attempted in certain closed and unofficial international meetings. According to this account, Soviet and American scientists and intellectuals have reversed roles and argued each other's positions and interests in continuing discussion. Formal research on this process and on other inventive applications of the role-playing procedure would comprise an extremely valuable contribution to the development of a technology of conciliation. A sizeable literature on the uses of role playing in industrial human-relations and group-dynamics programs might supply some valuable guides for further research.[18]

In reviewing some implications of the instrumental learning model of attitude change, I have hoped to show that it affords a useful perspective from which the problem of altering cross-elite attitudes might be approached. The functional theory of attitude dynamics, though equally significant as a theory, highlights variables and relationships that are probably less open to manipulation in the situation involving continuing interaction between competing elites.

As developed by Smith, Bruner, and White,[19] and Katz, Sarnoff, and McClintock,[20] this approach comprises a systematic extension and elaboration of an earlier insight generated through use of the psychoanalytic style in social analysis. That insight was that a social attitude might be viewed as "manifest" content that both expresses and imposes order upon repressed conflicts and motives. The best example of an empirical program designed to study a specific functionalist hypothesis was that of the California group whose well-known studies have established that ethnic hostility (particularly when it is not based upon strong normative prescriptions) serves the function of expressing and reducing large reserves of conflictfully repressed aggressiveness.[21]

However, ego-defensive functions are not the only ones specified in the contemporary functional theory. Attitudes may also serve such functions as expressing the person's values, helping to organize his

18. For a useful review of some of these techniques see Norman R. F. Maier, *Psychology in Industry* (Boston: Houghton Mifflin, 1965).

19. M. Brewster Smith, Jerome S. Bruner, and Robert W. White, *Opinions and Personality* (New York, John Wiley & Sons, 1956).

20. Daniel Katz, Irving Sarnoff, and Charles McClintock, "Ego Defense and Attitude Change," *Human Relations*, Vol. 9 (1956), pp. 27–46.

21. Theodore W. Adorno, Else Frenkel-Brunswik, Daniel J. Levinson, and Nevitt R. Sanford, *The Authoritarian Personality* (New York, Harper & Row, 1950).

knowledge of his world, or smoothing his approach toward utilitarian goal states. Katz[22] has attempted to specify the types of functions most commonly served by attitudes in different issue-areas and has also suggested the methods that might be most effectively employed in attempting to change them. While this is a highly valuable set of propositions and seems to provide the core of a more complex functionalist approach, in the main it has not yet been submitted to detailed empirical test. One exception is a group of related studies in which it was purportedly shown that attitudes of ethnic hostility serving various ego-defensive functions could, as predicted, be significantly reduced by fostering insights about the underlying psychodynamic processes through which repressed hostility has been displaced onto minority group members.[23]

Apart from this work, most research uses of the functionalist approach have involved close case studies of the interaction between personality themes and defensive processes, on the one hand, and the content of social attitudes, on the other. By far the most impressive undertaking along these lines has been the study by Smith, Bruner, and White of the functional articulation of the attitudes toward the Soviet Union of a number of individuals who were also submitted to very extensive personality study.[24]

I have suggested that the functionalist perspective, particularly in its emphasis upon ego-defensive bases of attitudes, is not easily applicable to the task of altering the attitudes of policy elites toward one another. This is because the personality processes and structures of major elite figures are simply not available for close, clinical scrutiny. Yet there is, to be sure, the possibility of studying personality from a distance. Biographical material, the protocols of journalistic interviews and diplomatic conversations, the content and style of public pronouncements might all have some value in attempts to map the character structures and ego-defensive styles of world leaders and other important members of policy-shaping groups. And this in turn might have some utility in suggesting just how communications directed at such figures might be styled so as to maximize the chances for influencing their attitudes. But it would first be necessary to conduct much additional preparatory work addressed to the question of how available techniques for close personality analysis could be put to use without direct access to the personalities being studied.

Perhaps a more immediately feasible expedient would be to aim for some simpler and more generalized characterization of the patterning

---

22. Daniel Katz, "The Functional Approach to the Study of Attitudes," *Public Opinion Quarterly*, Vol. 24 (1960), pp. 163–204.

23. Daniel Katz, Irving Sarnoff, and Charles McClintock, *op. cit.*,

24. Smith, Bruner, and White, *op. cit.*

of emotional and ego-defensive processes in typical members of the policy elites and bureaucracies of different nations. It does seem possible, for example, to ask whether there are some outstanding personality elements that are shared by members of the Soviet and Chinese foreign ministries respectively and that differentiate those two groups from one another. If such characterizations of modal personality can be developed (again, through study from a distance and employing secondary materials), and if a seemingly reasonable speculative account can be constructed showing how these personality patterns might contribute to the germination and stabilization of certain policy attitudes, then some related attitude-change experimentation could be attempted. Such experimentation would, of course, have to be conducted in the field; that is, communications designed on the basis of the hypothesized patterns of modal character, could be employed, and their attitude-altering effects upon the policy elite groups for which they were and were not designed might be capable of at least indirect assessment.

Before turning to the third general approach to attitude change, one further judgment about the functionalist approach should be made clear: while it does not seem capable of easy or highly profitable application to attitude change in the cross-elite situation, it does have considerable value in interpreting a good deal of the data on the personality and social identity correlates of public opinion on Cold War issues. Thus I shall have occasion to refer to the functionalist approach again when I examine (below) some of the available correlative findings.

In the field of social psychology, the consistency theories of attitude dynamics recently have aroused more interest than either the instrumental learning approach or the functional approach. This in itself does not indicate that they are superior theories, but it probably does reflect an aspiration on the part of many social psychologists for theories that abandon discursiveness for formal simplicity.

The various theories that may be grouped together as representing the consistency approach share, in at least loose similarity, a set of basic propositions. They conceive attitudes, or constellations of related attitudes, as organized according to one or another type of internal order (i.e. "balance," "congruence," "consonance"). Such states of inner order they view as self-conserving, in that any sizeable disruption of the initial structure will be an unstable state of affairs and will tend to generate symbolic activity through which inner order is reestablished. Attitude change is seen as one possible outcome of such a homeostatic process, though a more common one is restoration of the original attitude after rejection or reinterpretation of the inputs that served to temporarily disrupt it. Thus it might be said that for all the consistency models the prerequisite for attitude change is the arousal of internal inconsistency,

and the process of attitude change is a kind of consistency restoration. It goes virtually without saying that all these models are reared upon one necessary motivational assumption: that intra-attitudinal and inter-attitudinal inconsistency are motivating states, or, more simply, that human beings have a need for the achievement and maintenance of such consistency. Where the separate consistency theories differ from one another is in the actual ways in which they conceive and represent the states of consistency and inconsistency, in the methods of inconsistency reduction that they take to be basic, and in the number and type of psychological elements that they assume to be involved in inconsistency arousal and consistency restoration.

It does not fall within the scope of this chapter to examine more closely the differences in conceptualizations and propositions that separate the consistency models developed by Heider,[25] Newcomb,[26] Osgood and Tannenbaum,[27] Festinger,[28] Rosenberg[29] and Abelson and Rosenberg.[30] Rather, to advance the present inquiry it will be expedient to go further into the details of one of these formulations and then attempt to show that it has some bearing upon the cross-elite attitude change process, both in suggesting certain prescriptive applications and in raising certain pertinent questions.

The model that I shall use for this purpose is my own, though at points my exposition of it reflects aspects of a related approach developed in cooperation with Abelson. The use of this model here does not imply that it is offered as superior to the other consistency formulations. If it has any special value for the present purpose, this is largely because it can be rather easily presented and because it does provide categories that impose a certain ready order upon some aspects of the problem of cross-elite attitude change.

In this model, an attitude is conceived as a comparatively stable affective-cognitive structure. The affective core of the attitude is simply the person's habitual positive or negative evaluative orientation toward

25. Fritz Heider, "Attitude and Cognitive Organization. *Journal of Psychology*, Vol. 21 (1946), pp. 107–12, and *The Psychology of Interpersonal Relations* (New York: John Wiley & Sons, 1958).

26. Theodore M. Newcomb, "An Approach to the Study of Communicative Acts." *Psychological Review*, Vol. 60 (1953), pp. 393–404.

27. Charles E. Osgood and Percy H. Tannenbaum, "The Principle of Congruity in the Prediction of Attitude Change," *Psychological Review*, Vol. 62 (1955), pp. 42–55.

28. Festinger, *op. cit.*; Brehm, *op.cit.*

29. Milton J. Rosenberg, "Cognitive-Structure and Attitudinal Affect," *Journal of Abnormal and Social Psychology*, Vol. 53 (1956), pp. 367–72, and "An Analysis of Affective-Cognitive Consistency," in Rosenberg and Hovland, *op. cit.*, pp. 15–64.

30. Robert P. Abelson and Milton J. Rosenberg, "Symbolic Psychologic: A Model of Attitudinal Cognition," *Behavioral Science*, Vol. 3 (1958), pp. 1–13, and Milton J. Rosenberg and Robert P. Abelson, "An Analysis of Cognitive Balancing," in Rosenberg and Hovland, *op. cit.*, pp. 112–63.

the attitude object: that is, toward some other person, issue, proposal, institution, event, and the like. The cognitive component is the total set of beliefs about that object's relations to other objects of affective significance. When the object of the attitude is some issue, proposal, or event, these beliefs typically connect the object to the attainment or blocking of positive or negative goal states. When the attitude object is some other person or group, the beliefs are typically concerned with the positive or negative attributes of that person or group.

Some examples are required. Assume a senator within, but not central to, the American policy elite shortly before the ratification of the atmospheric nuclear test-ban treaty. He is highly favorable toward the treaty and plans to vote for it. This reveals the affective component of his attitude on this issue. In public debate he reveals a number of beliefs about the proposed test ban. Some of these are: "The ban will reduce the pace of nuclear proliferation. It will protect us from further radioactive pollution of the atmosphere. It will prove to the world that we urgently desire peace." In private conversation he adds: "It will probably freeze the nuclear development race and conserve our advantage in that race. Also it may ultimately open up some East European markets to which we need fuller access." And as concerns voting for the treaty, he may privately acknowledge: "From what the last polls show it should go over well with the liberal church and women's groups back home. Anyway it will get the White House off my back and maybe get me better support from the National Committee in 1966."

If each of these cognitions is reduced to a binary code in which the attitude object, the object or goal to which it is related, and the nature of that relationship are each classified as either positive or negative, a meaningful fact is immediately disclosed. The affectively positive object "test-ban treaty" is believed to be positively related to positive goals and negatively related to negative ones. This, in the present model, is an operational exemplification of consistency within an attitudinal cognition. It is not contended that positively evaluated attitude objects will be embedded in a structure of beliefs which are all of the +++ or +-- form. Nor is the complementary contention intended, that negatively evaluated attitude objects will be embedded in a structure in which all the beliefs are of the form --+ (the disliked object blocks access to a positive goal) or -+- (the disliked object fosters a particular negative state). But what is contended is that in the main such beliefs will be found in association with comparatively stable affective orientations. Furthermore, as research has shown[31] the actual extremity of the

31. Cf. my "Cognitive Structure and Attitudinal Affect," *op. cit.*, and William A. Scott, "Cognitive Consistency, Response Reinforcement and Attitude Change," *Sociometry*, Vol. 22 (1959), pp. 219–29.

affective response toward the attitude object will be closely correlated with the degree of certainty that characterizes the cognitive supports for that affective response.

From this point of view, what is the basic nature of the attitude-change process? It begins with the attempt to induce or increase inconsistency within the affective-cognitive structure of the attitude. Most often this is attempted by the presentation of arguments and data from prestigeful or "expert" or otherwise credible sources. The aim of such inputs is to invalidate supporting attitudinal cognitions (e.g., "We can't be sure of our test-detection system, and thus the test-ban treaty will give the opponent the chance to get far ahead of us in the nuclear race") or to introduce new cognitions that will be inconsistent with the original affective orientations toward the object (e.g., "If we have to stop testing we simply cannot develop a good, low-yield anti-missile nuclear missile").

With significant intrusion of such cognitions into his fairly consistent affective-cognitive structure the person will, at some point, be brought to a level at which his threshold of intolerance for inconsistency is transgressed. People vary in their mean threshold levels and the actual threshold level probably varies for the same person from one situation to another and from one issue to another. But when sufficient discrepant input has been received and at least provisionally accepted, a motivating state is aroused. The characteristic effect of this state is that it will set going new symbolic activity. This activity will persist until any one of three basic resolutions is achieved. One resolution is to find a way of disregarding the whole issue-area in which affective-cognitive inconsistency has been generated. A second is to reject the attitude-discrepant cognitions that were temporarily internalized, and thus to restore the initial attitude. A third is to yield to the import of the new inconsistency-generating cognitions and, by changing the sign of one's affective response to the attitude object, restore the total situation to consistency. This last type of restructuring is, of course, what is usually meant by attitude change.[32]

Having come this far we may now specify a number of variables that seem to affect the likelihood that intra-attitudinal inconsistency of a motivating intensity will be resolved by over-all attitude change. Some of these variables have been experimentally studied; predictions about others are based only upon extrapolation from more basic theoretical

32. The consistency theory view also predicts that attitude change can be produced by direct manipulative alteration of attitudinal affect which will be followed by spontaneous, consistency-restoring reorganization of the cognitive content of the attitude structure. Though this has been confirmed experimentally (see Rosenberg, 1960, *op. cit.*), the sequence beginning with cognitive change and leading to affective change is by far more common in real-life persuasion.

propositions. One such group of variables has to do with the initial structure of the attitude. The attitude will probably be more open to inconsistency arousal and ultimate change to the degree that any of the following conditions obtain: the absolute number of affect-supporting cognitions in the initial structure is small; the intensity of the affects elicited by the goal concepts represented in the structure is low; within the structure there are already present at least some few cognitions that are inconsistent with the over-all attitude; the original attitude structure stands in isolation from most of the other attitudes of the individual – it is either at the periphery of some matrix of interdependent attitudes or is not at all included in any such matrix.

Another group of variables influencing the likelihood that intra-attitudinal inconsistency can be generated and that it will subsequently be reduced through attitude change concerns the relationship of the original attitude to the motives and role-requirements felt by the person. The less the original attitude serves (in the functionalist sense) to reduce basic needs and conflicts, the more open it will probably be to inconsistency arousal and to attitude change. The same would probably be true of attitudes that are not required by prescriptive aspects of the roles the person plays or the groups to which he adheres.

From the foregoing considerations we can gain a new comprehension of why attitude change through cross-elite encounter has proved so difficult during the Cold War era, even with the apparent desire on both sides to find a way out of the Cold War impasse and to move toward conciliation and some form of reorganization of the international system. In both elites the core attitudes of distrust, hostility, and competitiveness have been so thoroughly elaborated by supporting cognitions (whether or not these are, in final terms, veridical), so closely fitted to a web of more precisely focused attitudes of distrust and hostility on particular issues, so strongly supported by role requirements, as to render them decidedly resistant to change. This is not to say that inconsistency-generating cognitions cannot be intruded into these structures as one elite gives evidence of its good will or pacific intentions. But what is likely to happen is that these inputs are most usually reinterpreted so as to diminish their inconsistency-generating power. For example, the Soviet elite will be prone to interpret the American offer of wheat sales as intended to help the U.S. economy rather than the Soviet people; the American elite will be prone to interpret Soviet desires for pooling of information on industrial nuclear technology as intended to circumvent the costs of research rather than to foster more general cooperation.

This has probably been less true in recent years than it was earlier. The main positive value of the few highly dangerous confrontations between the U.S. and the U.S.S.R., particularly the Cuban missile crisis,

may have been that they established in the views of each of the major policy elites an appreciation of how deep and desperate was its opponent's desire to permanently close off the paths by which they might stumble or miscalculate into an exchange of nuclear blows. Since then a number of measures of danger limitation have been taken, and these have probably had some real value in building into the over-all structures of the shared attitudes of distrust some highly inconsistent elements.

Thus there is greater potential now than there has been for some time for the interacting elites to direct at each other further inputs that might ultimately generate gross attitude change. But how might this best be done? The consistency approach outlined above offers some leads that may be worth examining.

One clear prescription is that as the competing elites undertake to revise each other's attitudes they would profit considerably from closer scrutiny of the detailed cognitive structure of those attitudes. Too often both the American and Soviet elites seem to be confused as to the perceptions and goal choices that might lie behind a surprising policy position enunciated by the competing power. Where these appear to be "mysteries cloaked in riddles wrapped in enigmas," the failing is probably on the part of the observer rather than the observed. Surely from the stream of policy justifications, white papers, and diplomatic conversations that express and justify Cold War policy attitudes, there can be constructed some mapping of the opponent's affective-cognitive structuring of particular issues. Though such structures may vary in their details, there is usually so much pressure toward the coordination of individual views with established policy that a generalized map of the cognitive supports of particular policy attitudes could be constructed. Such study could help to locate the issues on which receptiveness to inconsistency-generating inputs would be likely to be highest.

To be sure, these issues would tend to be at the periphery of major policy-attitude matrices. But for either elite to succeed in persuading the other that it really does favor cultural exchange for its tension-reducing, rather than for its propagandistic, value—or for either to persuade the other that its interest in Central European disengagement is to reduce the dangers of confrontation rather than to seize some unrevealed political advantage—would increase the acceptability of comparably discrepant inputs at the crucial core of the attitudinal web of distrust and competi. eness.

Yet, ultimately, the comparatively intractable core attitudes must be modified if effective conciliation and international system revision are ever to be achieved. How is this to be done? The relevance of the consistency approach here is that it suggests this principle: *There are no truly intractable, unchangeable attitudes.* A highly resistant attitude

is one with a large and detailed supporting cognitive structure and with many additional supports from role-requirements and normative standards. For such an attitude to be changed, it will have to be assaulted with a continuing, unrelenting stream of inconsistency-generating inputs while, at the same time, the more peripheral attitudes to which it is linked must also be exposed to change pressures. Thus, for either the Soviet or American elite to affect the core attitudes of distrust with which each approaches the other, and through which each is prone to interpret evidence of trustworthiness as its opposite, either or each elite must undertake an unflagging display of evidence of its trustworthiness and of its sincere desire for reconciliation. In this light Osgood's GRIT strategy takes on clear significance, particularly in its advocacy of a long schedule of unilateral initiatives that must be executed before any sign of reciprocation is forthcoming.[33] Also, his stress on the communicative, inconsistency-generating power of overt actions as compared to verbal assurances appears quite correct, for in this regard actions do often speak far louder, or less ambiguously, than words.

More briefly I should like to suggest two other prescriptive points that might be derived from two respective variants of the consistency-theory approach. Heider[34] and, similarly, Newcomb[35] have been particularly interested in interpersonal consistency over "shared attitude objects." Among other things that their theories have asserted and their researches have demonstrated is the high generality of this proposition: Individuals bound together in personal or role relationships are driven toward attitudinal convergence on issues in which they share an interest. If inconsistency is introduced between their attitudes, it is more likely that the formally subordinate (or emotionally subordinate) person will alter his attitude toward that of the other person than that his attitude will influence the other. This proposition is not surprising but it does have useful applicability. It suggests that efforts at cross-elite attitude change would be more successful if, in advance, one learned as much as possible about both the formal and informal structure of the competing policy elite. The identification of crucially placed persons in that elite (often they will not be particularly visible to public scrutiny), particularly of persons whose central positions in intra-elite influence networks are due to their reputations for analytic and strategic acuity, may suggest the most effective channelling of communications about intentions or actions that are commended as disconfirming the elite's present attitudes. If such persons can be persuaded, or even mildly influenced, this may

33. Charles E. Osgood, *An Alternative to War or Surrender* (Urbana: University of Illinois Press, 1963).
34. Heider, *op. cit.*
35. Newcomb, *op. cit.*

have sizeable effects across the range of other policy elite members from whom they tend to elicit deference.

Another quite fascinating consideration emerges when we focus upon a central tenet of Festinger's theory of cognitive dissonance.[36] This approach has stressed a type of attitude change in which the initial inconsistency is between the attitude as cognized by its holder and a counter-attitudinal action that he has somehow performed. The less the "justification" for that counter-attitudinal action the greater the assumed need to find justification for it—and thus the greater the possibility that the attitude will be altered so as to fall in line with the overt action. I shall not attempt here to suggest how such counter-attitudinal actions could be elicited. Instead I shall merely suggest in passing that it might prove quite profitable if, on either side of the Cold War competition, attempts were made to find ways of eliciting "poorly motivated" conciliatory acts from the opposing elite.

In the foregoing comments I have not dealt with the practical limits imposed by the role systems that govern the policy process and that set tight controls upon adventurousness in such matters. However, in the light of such limits, one must, of course, acknowledge that much that has been said here might not be readily accepted by the elite communities of either of the major contesting nations. On the other hand, desperation over the impasse imposed by the Cold War system and the generation of a willingness to reexamine one's attitudes about the attitudes and intentions of the opposing elite have actually progressed quite far in recent years. And a willingness to launch upon more radical programs of cross-elite attitude rectification may well have risen to a higher level than many academic specialists are willing to credit. What does, in fact, seem to be the case is that on both sides there has developed a commitment toward limited conciliation and toward finding ways to defuse if not yet to dismantle the Cold War system. As previously suggested, the main barrier to more effective pursuit of this provisional commitment may well lie as much in apprehensions about the domestic mass public as in unrelenting doubts about the intentions of the opposing elite.

MASS OPINION AND ATTITUDE CHANGE

Thus the last major task to which this chapter will address itself is one that was noted earlier: to examine more closely, and in the light of the attitude theory perspectives reviewed above, the interaction between the public opinion and policy processes. Particularly I shall argue in support of these interpretations: Policy innovation in conciliatory

36. Festinger, *op. cit,*; Brehm, *op. cit.*

directions need not defer as much as has sometimes seemed the case to hard-line patterns of public opinion on Cold War issues. Those patterns of opinion may be less intensely held and less uniformly distributed than they appear to be. Where such patterns of opinion are in fact strong and do impose certain electoral risks, their correlates can be discerned and often their dynamic bases can be estimated. Considerations such as these suggest, in turn, various strategies for producing attitude change in publics whose opinions, as perceived by the elite, have heretofore seemed to limit the possibilities for straightforward attempts to revise the attitudes of the opposing elite and to foster international conciliation and institutional revision.

To disclose the bases of these conclusions it will be necessary first to recall some rather general problems and then to submit them to analytic discussion. It must be emphasized at the outset, however, that throughout this section the focus is restricted to the public opinion-foreign policy interaction as it occurs in the United States. To the extent that the ensuing analysis does illuminate aspects of the policy process in the United States, portions of it will probably be readily applicable to those other democracies where general literacy has been achieved and where urban-industrial forms of social organization predominate. Nondemocratic states that have reached comparable levels of literacy and social organization lie beyond the focus of this discussion. This is not to say that I consider public opinion in such nations to be solely a dependent variable, merely available to easy manipulation by the elite and thus lacking in any influence upon the way in which the elite performs its policy functions and makes its policy choices. Indeed, in an earlier section I have already indicated a quite different estimate on these matters. But the considerable differences between the political structures of the "Western democracies" and the "peoples' democracies" require that the present inquiry be clearly restricted to the case of the former.

From these comments, as from much that has gone before, it is probably quite apparent that I share with many others the conviction that in attempting to achieve systematic comprehension of the processes through which foreign policies are shaped, executed, and revised, a core problem is to specify the exact role of public opinion in these processes. Consensus is growing among political scientists, particularly those attuned to survey data, around the conclusion that the general public is extremely uninformed on the details of foreign policy issues, is often unaware of the very existence of many of these issues, and is basically uninterested in them. In effect, the characterization implicit in some recent commentaries is that on foreign policy the general public "knows little and cares less." The first part of this characterization seems to me incontrovertibly established. If one retains hope for the realization,

through modern mass democracy, of the ideal of *civitas* one cannot but feel chastened and disheartened by the import of survey data on foreign affairs. But whether knowing little about foreign policy issues renders the general public willing to accede to whatever choices and directions are set for it cannot be directly answered from data that merely demonstrate the dismaying extent of public ignorance. However, from various perspectives, including the theories of attitude dynamics that have been discussed in this paper, it may be possible to reorganize this question so as to render it more answerable. We must clarify the relationships between, on the one hand, the degrees of ignorance, intensity, and interest that people bring both to particular and highly general issues of foreign policy and, on the other hand, the probabilities that people will respond with acquiescence, indignation, or active support to policy decisions bearing upon such issues.

Yet one other extremely important question is provoked by the contention that the general public is prone to passive acquiescence in the face of foreign policy decisions. This is not the question of whether the contention is true, but of whether the policy elite thinks it to be true. I have already indicated in an earlier section my impression that in the main the policy elite does not expect full acquiescence: rather its "backings and filings" in the development and execution of conciliatory policies seem to be due, in part, to expectations that public disapproval and indignation over conciliatory undertakings may lead to electoral losses and other imposed disadvantages.

The foregoing considerations suggest that among the questions most worth asking are these: What kinds of elite members, in what roles, with what responsibilities, tend to be persuaded that the general public will be acquiescent or resistant to particular foreign policy decisions and revisions? Equally pertinent to any inquiry into the relationships governing the public opinion-foreign policy interaction is a set of questions concerning those members of the policy elite who do judge the public, however ill-informed, to be responsive to foreign policy choices and changes. Just how do they develop their views about the content and strength of public opinion on foreign policy issues? When they do perceive or expect public opposition to policy innovations, how does this affect their role performances in the policy process itself? Do they most often undertake to modify or discard policies so as to court public approval or to avoid ultimate electoral retribution? Do they more often undertake to educate the public, to change its attitudes? Or do they often seek to keep policy changes veiled from public notice?

At a time of boom in behavioral research by political scientists, it is surprising that such questions have not received more thoroughgoing empirical investigation. In the absence of close and replicated research

on these matters, one must necessarily fall back upon impressions and deductions. The impression that has guided my own thinking about the set of problems delineated in the preceding comments is that members of the policy elite who have been involved in the Cold War policy process have often allowed themselves to be *constrained* by public opinion as they have perceived it.

Though I have at a number of points in this paper reflected this common judgment about an important aspect of the public opinion-foreign policy interaction, I have not attempted to support it with data or detailed anecdote. Yet evidence that this is the case could be adduced in various ways: the large discrepancy between programmatic statements of intentions for policy revision (as, for example, in President Kennedy's American University speech) and subsequent delays and hesitations in policy performance; the frequency with which trial balloons are launched and then lost; and, most directly, the fact that policy specialists, and those in high office who coordinate the total policy process, do so often acknowledge (though perhaps more to journalists than to visitors from the Brookings Institution) that some particular measure of conciliation or settlement is desirable but that "We can't move on it until after the election," or "It will take a lot of time to get the public ready for this."

A properly mechanistic or systemic understanding of how such constraint occurs would go beyond its ultimate basis in anxieties over electoral prospects and would consider the kinds of persons, groups, and institutions that foster the dramatization of these anxieties and the linking of them to particular policy issues and programs. Figuring importantly in this category, at least as regards the constraints that have been imposed upon policy movement toward further conciliation and international system revision, would be the well-organized conservative and radical right pressure groups. At least of equal importance are the managers and technicians of the party in power. These, with their special role-based concern over electoral prospects, will usually urge the importance of not providing the opposition with opportunities for "stirring up the public." Similarly, critics representing the opposing party are likely to be extremely important in this process when, in response to early evidence of new conciliatory directions in policy, they attempt to arouse public indignation. Also, of course, within the broad policy elite itself are those who, out of conviction, are likely to oppose further conciliation.

However, such groups could have little influence were it not for the tendency of important figures within the policy elite to attribute to large sectors of the public a pattern of hard-line attitudes, a general distrust of the Soviet Union and its allies, a pervasive irritability over policies "that smack of appeasement," and a desire to see the Cold War successfully prosecuted rather than compromised. Assuming that this

pattern of attribution is prevalent, how did it first come to be made? Why does it persist, at least to an extent sufficient to exert some continuing constraint upon the freedom with which policy development and revision are conducted?

Most obviously, the policy elite may have learned to hold these expectations about the general public's attitudes because it had played a large and initiating role in training the public in these very attitudes. Within a few years after the beginning of the Cold War, evidence of success in having shaped a militantly anti-Soviet pattern of public opinion was already abundant. Such evidence came, and continues to come, from various sources: the constant resonance in much of the American press of the hard-line view of Cold War issues; the frequent electoral successes of candidates for legislative office who have asserted such a view; and, probably most important, the findings of public-opinion polls that have focused now on one, now on another separate component of the general issue-area of Soviet-American relations and have generally reported large majorities favoring hard-line positions.

In their dependence upon public-opinion poll data the policy elite has been sometimes naïve and undiscriminating, but this is a failing that they share with many of the pollsters. There is now good reason to believe that a major contaminant operates in polls on matters of foreign policy. Many respondents who are essentially apathetic on foreign policy issues, who lack clear awareness of the very existence of some of those issues, may well characterize themselves invalidly when asked how they regard, say, the admission of Communist China into the UN, wheat shipments to the Soviet Union, scientific cooperation with the Soviet Union, or even resumption of diplomatic relations with Cuba. More precisely, they are prone to report themselves as far more resistant than they actually are toward the mounting and execution of such conciliatory policies.

Elsewhere I have attempted to provide close analysis of a number of different processes that may move individuals toward such false or exaggerated self-report.[37] A main factor is that for many Americans there persists the perception, vague on detail but assured in direction, that the general position held by the government and shared by the public, is one of hard-line intransigence. Deflection of self-characterizing attitude reports toward this perceived consensus is likely to be fostered by such varied factors as uncertainty and anxiety over the possibility that the public opinion interview is some kind of disguised test of loyalty; embarrassment that one's basic apathy toward foreign issues

37. Milton J. Rosenberg, "Images in Relation to the Policy Process: American Public Opinion on Cold War Issues," in Herbert C. Kelman (ed.), *International Behavior: A Social Psychological Approach* (New York: Holt, Rinehart and Winston, 1965).

will be visible and will earn the interviewer's disapproval; and, more subtly, a need on the part of persons who have been rendered politically confused and disoriented to demonstrate to themselves that they are not really so.

It would be excessive to argue that the anticonciliatory responses of most poll respondents are of the type I have described, but that this is so for some sizeable portion of typical national samples is, I think, demonstrated in a number of ways. One is that when structure-disclosing investigation of such attitudes is undertaken they are often found, just as the academically based surveyors using other methods have sometimes also shown, to be rather lacking in clear cognitive content. Such "attitudes" are marked, as the consistency theories described earlier would predict, by considerable instability over time and by comparatively easy modifiability in the face of persuasive communications.

Yet another kind of support for the view recommended here is that when occasional conciliatory policy commitments have been made, the public has sometimes surprised the elite with the amount of acceptance it has shown after exposure to a few weeks of explanation and justification. The most obvious recent case in point was the generally positive public response (reflected in poll data) to the nuclear test-ban treaty.

The over-all import of these comments, then, is the recommendation that if the policy elite did more openly pursue those conciliatory goals that national and humane interest may require, it would be likely to encounter more public acceptance than leaders often seem to expect. But by holding back on the basis of apprehensions over electoral punishment, particularly when the political opposition stands ready to seek such electoral consequences by accusations of "softness on communism," the policy elite often fails to put those anxieties to an overt test that might correct them.

However, one must not conclude, as certain political scientists seem to have done, that lack of knowledge on foreign policy issues will always foster simple acquiescence to policy revisions. A persisting danger, despite a general tendency toward such acquiescence, is that by virtue of the very incoherence and inconsistency that characterize the foreign policy attitudes of many persons, they are likely, when artfully aroused by right wing "brokers of indignation," to accept a promiscuous anti-Communist militancy. The importance of this point is that passive, unprepared acquiescence is not to be expected, but that consent to conciliatory policy initiatives and responses can probably be obtained if these initiatives and responses are effectively presented, justified, and backed by prestige endorsements.

As regards the general problem of clarifying the structure, and thus the modifiability, of foreign policy attitudes, a major service could be

rendered by social scientists. This would require that they themselves undertake or stimulate more useful national sample studies of attitudes on Cold War issues; studies in which the deeper, more structure-oriented kinds of measurement procedures would be used. This would be likely to further confirm that for significant portions of the general public the hard-line point of view is not held with heavy emotional investment, but rather is held with low interest and with an easy readiness to accept considerable restructuring when that restructuring is effectively presented through the mass communication process.

Yet for other sectors of the broad, national public such studies would probably reveal something of a quite different order; something that has already appeared in many investigations that, though employing more restricted samples than those used in the national polls, have at the same time plumbed American attitudes on Cold War issues more deeply, more extensively, and more correlatively. These studies have revealed, first of all, that even at higher educational and socioeconomic levels, respondents do vary considerably in the degrees of interest and internal coherence that characterize their attitudes on Cold War and related issues. A second finding of considerable pertinence for the policy community is that among those who do seem to show truly attitudinal (that is, stable, integrated, and motivated) orientation toward Cold War issues, there are discernible certain major correlates of the positions that they take. Some of these correlates indicate the types of social groupings in which patterns of hard-line militancy or of endorsement for conciliatory approaches, respectively, have taken on normative significance and power. Other correlates seem to indicate that certain differences in social ideology and, for that matter, in personality, tend to be associated with hard-line or conciliatory attitude patterns.

Since these studies are all correlative one cannot, of course, reach final judgments about the causal configurations that may underlie their data. Nor can one, in short compass, disentangle the overlap and inter-penetration of the variables that have been assessed.[38] Thus I will not

38. Also, one must note that the tendency to deflect attitudinal self-reports away from neutrality and toward the perceived national consensus may operate as a partial contaminant in some of these studies as it does in the more superficial polls. However, some of these "deeper" studies have concentrated upon respondents drawn from educational levels or from the kinds of interest groups in which one may reasonably expect less intrinsic apathy toward issues of foreign policy. Furthermore, by their use of more detailed and probing forms of attitude measurement, such studies often seem to make possible some meaningful differentiation of true attitudes from pseudo-attitudes. Thus it is not injudicious to estimate that studies such as the ones reviewed in the remaining pages of this chapter are less burdened by the problem of undetected apathy than are the comparable national sample polls. At the same time it would be excessive to claim that one may approach the findings of the present studies without any concern for this particular methodological difficulty.

presume here toward an integrative, synthesizing analysis of these studies.[39] Instead I shall simply list some major correlative findings[40] and suggest how these might best influence the design of communications intended to foster public acceptance of the kind of international conciliatory effort that seems to me to be the necessary and coming development in American policy toward, at least, the non-Chinese sectors of the Communist world. I shall restrict my suggestions about attitude-change implications to comments about the selection of persons and groups at whom persuasive communications might be directed and to the kinds of themes and values that might be emphasized. Having earlier shown how the current theories of attitude dynamics dictate certain general strategies for efforts at persuasion, I need only add that those same strategies should be as applicable in attempts at mass persuasion as in attempts at cross-elite influence. Indeed, they should prove more efficacious in this kind of application, if only because the person far outside elite circles is less bound by his role commitments and past performance to resist change in his attitudes about foreign policy issues.[41]

39. Elsewhere I have attempted a close review and extrapolative analysis of them (1965, *op. cit.*).

40. Particularly I have relied upon findings reported in the following sources: Alan Barton, "A Survey of Suburban Residents on What to do about the Danger of War," *Council for Correspondence Newsletter*, No. 24 (1963), pp. 3–11; Mark Chesler and Richard Schmuck, "Student Reactions to the Cuban Crisis and Public Dissent," *Public Opinion Quarterly*, 28 (1964), 467–82; L. Farber, "The Anal Character and Political Aggression," *Journal of Abnormal and Social Psychology*, Vol. 51 (1955), pp. 486–89; C. D. Farris, "Selected Attitudes on Foreign Affairs as Correlates of Authoritarianism and Political Anomie," *Journal of Politics*, Vol. 22 (1960), pp. 50–67; Bernard Fensterwald, "The Anatomy of American Isolationism and Expansionism" (parts 1 and 2), *Journal of Conflict Resolution*, Vol. 2 (1958), pp. 111–39, 280–309; Henry Gleitman and Joseph J. Greenbaum, "Hungarian Socio-political Attitudes and Revolutionary Action," *Public Opinion Quarterly*, Vol. 24 (1960), pp. 62–76; Morris Janowitz and Duane Marvik, "Authoritarianism and Political Behavior," *Public Opinion Quarterly*, Vol. 17 (1953), pp. 185–202; Robert E. Lane, "Political Personality and Electoral Choice," *American Political Science Review*, Vol. 49 (1955), 173–90; Jerome Laulicht and J. Paul, "Some Major Findings of the C.P.R.I. Attitude Study," *International Social Science Journal* (1965), pp. 472–86; Daniel J. Levinson, "Authoritarian Personality and Foreign Policy," *Journal of Conflict Resolution*, Vol. 1 (1957), pp. 37–47; William J. MacKinnon and Richard Centers, "Authoritarianism and Internationalism," *Public Opinion Quarterly*, Vol. 20 (1957), pp. 621–30; Snell Putney and R. Middleton, "Some Factors Associated with Student Acceptance or Rejection of War," *American Sociological Review*, Vol. 27 (1962), pp. 655–67; Peter I. Rose, "Citizens Opinions on Civil Defense," *Council for Correspondence Newsletter*, No. 24 (1963), pp. 25–37.

41. Though this section is addressed to the implications for mass persuasion of certain findings on the correlates of Cold War attitudes, I do not mean to suggest that members of elites need limit their interest in public opinion only to the question of how it may be manipulated toward acceptance of new policies. On the contrary, I am persuaded that unless public apathy and ignorance concerning foreign policy are significantly reduced, the winning of public consent for policy changes is merely of limited and temporary value. The ideal of an informed, interested, and thoughtful citizenry, unrealizable as this may now seem, is basic to the social philosophy upon which democratic governments are reared, and, as such,

One other preliminary point should be made clear. The various studies that I have grouped together deal with many different Cold War issues—some with only three or four and some with fifteen or twenty. In the main, high intercorrelations between issue positions are obtained so that hard-line and conciliatory patterns do indeed appear. The person who believes the Soviet Union to be inflexibly committed to world domination, when compared to the person who rejects this view, finds nuclear war and the use of nuclear threat in defense of United States interests more acceptable, fallout shelters more feasible and desirable, the international behavior of the United States more exemplary, and so on. In the following summary I shall restrict myself to correlates that, with different degrees of reliability, have been found to differentiate between persons who hold to the over-all hard-line or conciliatory approaches respectively.

The first major finding, and one of the most thoroughly replicated, concerns sex differences. Women are decidedly less given to internalizing the pattern of Cold War severity than are men. This may be due to value differences based upon sex-role training, or perhaps to the fact that women are typically less engrossed in, perhaps less in contact with, over-all normative standards of their society as these touch upon "distant" issues. One clear recommendation for those in the elite who must be concerned with fostering public acceptance of international conciliation would be simply this: other factors equal, they will find easier receptivity from women. Furthermore, explanations of policy changes might well stress values of greatest concern to women, particularly values that, in the familial context, are shared by their husbands.

Among group differences, one that stands out rather clearly is that certain ethnic bodies tend to be committed, on a normative basis, to an endorsement and defense of hard-line severity. Not surprisingly, these groups mostly derive from nations of Eastern and Central Europe that are now within the Soviet sphere of control. As such nations as Hungary and Poland continue to achieve greater autonomy within the context of their continuing commitment to lend general support to the Soviet Union, this may make feasible a particular kind of appeal to these groups: namely, that they abandon their opposition to economic and technical

---

it cannot be too long neglected in mass democratic states without great risk to their very functional integrity as social systems. Furthermore, as I have said elsewhere (Rosenberg, 1965, *op. cit.*), "the potential threat that public opinion poses for the pursuit of rational policy is in part due to the fact that governmental and communication elites have been so ready to hide the facts, and to misrepresent or oversimplify the actual justifications for policy choices ... Given a chance to know what is really happening 'out there' and given an opportunity to consider policy alternatives in their true complexity, much of the public would be able to achieve deeper interest in policy problems and a fuller appreciation of the necessity that policy decisions be guided by ultimately humane purposes."

aid to, and cultural exchange with, their countries of origin; for such programs, it could well be argued, will facilitate the further movement toward national autonomy of these nations.

A type of group difference that many studies have shown to be related to Cold War attitudes is the religious one. One rather common finding is that Jews are somewhat more pro-conciliation than other religious groups, though of course this is likely to be due not so much to their religious precepts as to their generally liberal political tradition. Among Protestants one finds a difference between fundamentalist and liberal denominations, the former being the more hard-line. Among Catholics there is the suggestion, in a few studies, that the better educated and more clearly middle-class are more disposed toward hard-line policies. This contrasts with the tendency toward a reverse class difference among Protestants which is, to be sure, confounded with the difference between fundamentalist and other denominations.

But more impressive than all of these findings, and more clearly replicated than most of them, is the finding that "religiousity" in general is associated with the hard-line approach.[42] Churchgoers, self-described believers, whatever their denomination, are more hard-line than those who are detached from religious institutions. This finding seems to me a fascinating one and suggests many hypotheses, though most of them, unfortunately, are untestable from the present data. But surely one clear directive implication is that such agencies as the State Department might look to the problem of improving their lines of communication with the ministry and church hierarchy. Perhaps we see here the need to abandon the easy Cold War propagandistic stress upon *our* Godliness and *their* "Godless atheism."

Regional differences appear to have persisted for many years. The midwest and mountain states in some studies seem to remain most clearly pro-Cold War, while the greatest degree of conciliatory preference is found, as indeed the 1964 Republican presidential candidate rather angrily insisted, in the states of the eastern seaboard. The allocation of communications resources when attempting to justify conciliatory programs will obviously require some coordination to these regional differences.

While little clear difference is found between the labor and middle-class sectors (when factors of religion, region, and so on are held constant), some interesting intra-class differences are noted. One of these is an

42. This finding stands out clearly in the studies by Laulicht and Paul (*op. cit.*) and by Rose (*op. cit.*). I have obtained the quite comparable finding of a very strong relationship between scores on a "Cold War Attitudes" scale and answers given to three questions concerned respectively with church attendance, belief in the truth of religion, and belief that "human life is an expression of divine purpose."

unsurprising trend toward greater Cold War militancy in the business, as contrasted to the professional sector of the middle class.

Another quite interesting failure to discover a simple difference concerns adherence to the two political parties. Democrats and Republicans as such (and with factors of education, religion, and the like controlled) do not differ on Cold War issues, but self-designated "liberals," whether loyal to one or the other of the two parties, are definitely more conciliatory in foreign policy orientation than are self-designated "conservatives."

At the level of personality and related differences very little research has involved the use of truly clinical measures. However, the F scale of authoritarianism[43] has been widely employed and there can be little doubt over this major finding: those scoring high on authoritarianism are much more pro-Cold War, more anti-conciliation, than those scoring high on equalitarianism. What renders this particularly interesting from a theoretical point of view is that ten to fifteen years ago the authoritarian person was clearly more isolationist than the nonauthoritarian one.[44] This fosters a hopeful suggestion about how the authoritarian person's underlying aggressiveness and disposition toward projective disavowal of his own or his nation's faults may find a number of different, functionally serviceable outlets. If earlier the authoritarian found fulfillment in adhering to once-popular isolationist views, and if he finds it now in what is, after all, a kind of anti-isolationist position, then he is obviously capable of being directed toward new attitudinal outlets for his underlying and conflicted needs. A significant challenge is to find ways of disconfirming for the authoritarian person the functional fulfillment he presently derives from the hard-line pattern of aggressiveness and its captivating implications of gross holocaust.

Many other findings might be summarized, but those already reviewed give the general import of the available research. Those members of the public who are truly invested in either the hard-line or conciliatory positions probably are so by virtue of the functional value such positions afford them; either they serve to confirm and support important aspects of the individual's social identity and group life or they serve the deeper demands set by ego ideals and by repressed and conflicted aspects of the individual's impulse life.

I shall resist, or perhaps evade, the opportunity to summarize, except to say that in my view the attitudinal aspects of the problems that have been addressed in these pages are ones that I would commend to nonpsychologists as requiring representation in their formulations of the nature of the foreign policy process. And I would add that the over-all intended import of this rather discursive essay has been to

43. Adorno, *et al., op. cit.*
44. Particularly, see the studies by Lane (*op. cit.*) and by Janowitz and Marvik (*op. cit.*).

convey just this particular note of limited optimism: Though movement toward conciliation and ultimate system revision seems to be required, perhaps even as a condition for human survival, and though such movement seems impeded in part by attitudinal barriers, these barriers are not impenetrable. Indeed, I think the chances are fair that they can be mastered, and I am rather sanguine that theories of attitude dynamics can be of some significant service in this effort. As for the barriers set by the apparent opposition of important interests of the competing powers, one might close on this further note of optimism: With elimination or reduction of the attitudinal barriers there could come a new openness in international negotiation, a readiness to submit interest conflicts to novel and radically searching examination. In consequence, some of these particular conflicts might be found capable of resolution. As concerns those interest conflicts that are discovered to be presently irreducible, the achievement of basic attitude change and partial conciliation might yet enable a repatterning of the international system, and this, if far-reaching enough, should significantly reduce the possibility that the continued prosecution of such conflicts will bring universal immolation.

SOCIAL POSITION, PARTY IDENTIFICATION AND FOREIGN POLICY ORIENTATION:

A Norwegian Case Study[1]

Johan Galtung

IN an earlier article[2] a theory about the relationship between an individual's social position and his foreign policy orientation was developed and this chapter is an effort to explore this theme further. This attempt is motivated not by the traditional effort of sociologists

1. This is a revised version of a paper presented at the Conference on Public Opinion and Foreign Policy and I am indebted to all the participants at the conference for their helpful comments. In particular, I am indebted to Professors Robert C. Angell and J. David Singer, who also contributed their advice when the paper was presented at the Mental Health Research Institute, University of Michigan. The data collection was supported financially by the Norwegian Council for Research in Science and the Humanities and the Norwegian Council for conflict and Peace Research, and it was carried out by Norsk

to stress that structural variables are more important than personality variables as a source of attitudinal variation. Rather, the model tries to explain attitudes by means of both structural variables as well as simple personality variables operating as intervening variables. In so doing, it seeks to take advantage of the enormous qualities of poll data on various issues, found in all parts of the world where pollsters have not feared to tread, usually reported with breakdowns by background variables such as age, sex, income, education, occupation (both branch and position), urban vs. rural, a geographic periphery or center, and party identification if the society is sufficiently open to permit that. Most of these data lie virtually unexplored and little prospecting is done for theoretical ore that can be enriched. The runs against background variables are usually carried out with no theory in mind at all, as a ritual and for its possible news value.[3] The theorizing that is done is usually *ad hoc* and fragmentary if it is compared, say, to the excellent theory constructions raised on the basis of the idea of cognitive dissonance reduction.

In the present study three kinds of variables, indicated by the title of the paper, will be used. They are: (1) *Social position variables*, all of them rank dimensions, (2) *Attitudes toward ten foreign policy issues*, and (3) *Party identification*. The data are from a Norwegian Gallup sample of 1,000, collected for this purpose in November-December, 1964. The exact wording of the questions and the marginals for the answers will be found in the Appendix. The sample was found to be sufficiently representative to permit generalizations to the universe of Norwegians aged eighteen and above.

First, the social-position index will be discussed, using the social position of the respondent as independent variable, and a theory for change in the opinion structure will be outlined. Second, the same will be done for the correlations between the foreign policy attitudes. Third, the parties will be introduced relating them to social position and a typology for political parties will be developed. Finally, the joint influence of social position and party identification will be predicted and explored.

Gallup Institutt A.S. The data processing was carried out by the Institute for Social Research and Norsk Regnesentral. For their help in gathering and processing the data, I am especially grateful to B. Balstad, director of Norsk Gallup Institutt A.S and cand. psychol. B. Alstad, also Norsk Gallup; to Ørjar Øyen of the University of Oslo; and to magister Nils Halle, Birgit Elvant, and Øystein Sande, all of the Peace Research Institute, Oslo. The paper is published here as PRIO publication No. 16–2.

2. Johan Galtung, "Foreign Policy Orientation as a Function of Social Position," *Journal of Peace Research*, Vol 1 (1964), pp. 206–31.

3. A typical example is the regular section of the *Public Opinion Quarterly* entitled "The Polls," which is highly informative and highly unexploited theoretically.

THE INDEX OF SOCIAL POSITION

This index has been described elsewhere[4] as a one-dimensional measure of the *total rank* of an individual's status-set, counting the statuses in eight systems: age, sex, income, education, job, branch, ecology, and geography. The components are defined in Table 1. The index is a simple additive one based on the items in Table 1, and consequently ranges from 0 to 8. We shall refer to the lower ranges as the "periphery" (or the generalized underdogs) and to the higher ranges as the "center" (or the generalized topdogs) of the society. The rationale behind the index is in terms of reward and prestige, or more precisely, in terms of mobility preferences expressed when people are exposed to any one of the eight dimensions and asked, "Choosing freely, where would you like to be located?" All eight dimensions have more or less steep gradients in the sense that the degree of expressed desire for upward mobility varies, but all gradients are different from 0.

Table 1 — The Definition of the Index of Social Position

	UNDERDOG (Score 0)	TOPDOG (Score 1)
Age	young, old	middle age
Sex	women	men
Income	lower half	upper half
Education	lower half	upper half
Job	blue collar	white collar
Branch	primary	secondary, tertiary
Ecology	rural	urban
Geography	periphery	center

In the earlier article a number of derivations are made from the simple idea of rank, and particularly of total rank, leading to predictions about differential knowledge, differential opinionation, and differential participation. All of them should decrease relatively monotonously with decreasing social position, and even though this has been demonstrated before, revalidation does no harm, particularly when it is done on the data to be used in the present study (Table 2). The trends in Table 2 are as expected, and particularly impressive when a composite measure such as a knowledge index (with the location of the United Nations as one of the items) is used.[5] In this case social position accounts for 76

4. Galtung, *op. cit.*, pp. 216–18.

5. "1" in the table and in the following tables stands for "0 or 1", since there were so few respondents at the 0 level. Typically, this curve for Norway shows a general tendency towards concentration in the middle and avoidance of the extremes.

per cent of the maximum variation possible. But this is actually only
what was to be expected when so much of the social structure is expressed
in one variable.

Table 2 — Validation of the Index of Social Position
(in percentages)

				SOCIAL POSITION				
	1	*2*	*3*	*4*	*5*	*6*	*7*	*8*
Ignorance about where United Nations is located	24	12	11	8	5	3	1	0
"Low" on knowledge index	79	66	54	41	36	24	18	3
Read foreign news more than once a day	0	3	6	10	7	13	15	28
Talk with somebody about international situation	3	12	11	15	23	24	26	38

Table 3 presents the extent to which "don't know" responses increase toward the periphery when we asked the sample for opinions
rather than information. Again the gradients are there for all ten items,

Table 3 — Failure to have Opinions as a Function of Social Position
(in percentages)

				SOCIAL POSITION					
Ignorance rates	*1*	*2*	*3*	*4*	*5*	*6*	*7*	*8*	*Total*
Military service form	9	11	9	6	4	4	4	0	6
Closer ties for Norway	18	9	9	5	2	6	2	3	5
Attitude toward NATO	12	19	9	4	3	3	1	0	6
Attitude toward atomic arms	12	6	4	1	4	3	1	0	3
Attitude toward EEC	27	32	29	24	23	19	11	8	8
Attitude toward Khrushchev	27	11	9	4	7	8	8	8	23
Attitude toward Peace Corps	48	33	31	20	17	14	12	5	21
Merchant marine	21	10	10	14	9	10	3	8	11
Buy textiles	30	13	11	10	9	10	7	3	10
Higher coffee prices	27	9	9	11	5	8	6	5	8

as predicted, but they are neither so steep nor so regularly monotone
as for the indicators of lack of knowledge and lack of participation.
Thus, the rows of percentages should ideally never show increases,
but they nevertheless do so in thirteen out of the eighty possible cases,
inverting twenty-six of the 280 relationships in the table. The trend
is unmistakable, but it must nevertheless be concluded that the periphery
is more deprived of knowledge and participation than of opinions.

A number of authors report findings that correspond to what we report
here for the global index, but their findings concern the separate items,
one at a time. Thus, when it comes to political participation, which is

what interests us most, Berelson and Steiner,[6] summarizing the work
of several authors (but mainly Lipset and Linz[7] and Lane[8]), state:

> The higher a person's socioeconomic and educational level—especially
> the latter—the higher his political interest, participation and voting turnout.
>
> Men are more active politically than women.
>
> Middle-age groups are more active politically than young adults or the old.
>
> Urban residents are somewhat more active politically than rural residents,
> especially with regard to national affairs.

Included in these four points are seven of the eight variables of the index,
all in line with the general findings of Tables 2 and 3 and the previous
article. The eighth dimension, which refers to geographical region in
Norway, is obviously not immediately generalizable (besides, it yields,
relatively speaking, the lowest correlations for the Norwegian data).
For the Norwegian data, education is also found to be particularly
important. And the fourth point is especially relevant to the present
study, since it deals with foreign policy issues that by definition are
national even though they may have differential regional impact.

As regards "opinions, attitudes and beliefs," Berelson and Steiner
mention *residence* ("geographical region and urban-rural location"),
ethnic status ("different nationality, racial, and religious groups"), *class*
("whether measured by income, occupation, education, inherited status
or some combination thereof"), *age*, and *sex* as strong determinants.[9]
In that list the reader will find all eight items in our social position index,
provided one splits "occupation" into its two components, "job" and
"branch." Cited in addition to these items are ethnic criteria (which are
irrelevant in such a highly homogeneous country as Norway[10]) and
inherited status (which could have been included by adding the job and
the branch for the father to the index). If these criteria are included,
perhaps along with one for religious domination, a corresponding index
for the United States would be available. On such an index the legendary
WASP (White Anglo-Saxon Protestant) would get the topdog score
that is his due. Thus we do not believe that the United States is protected by some kind of pluralism that is not accounted for by these rank-

6. B. Berelson and G. Steiner, *Human Behavior, An Inventory of Scientific Findings*
(New York: Harcourt, Brace & World, 1963), pp. 423–24.

7. S. M. Lipset and J. Linz, "The Social Bases of Political Diversity in Western
Democracies," unpublished MS., 1956.

8. R. E. Lane, *Political Life: Why People Get Involved in Politics* (New York: The
Free Press, 1959).

9. Berelson and Steiner, *op. cit.*, pp. 570–74.

10. Thus, in B. Russett, *et al.*, *World Handbook of Political and Social Indicators*
(New Haven: Yale University Press, 1964), Norway is listed as the culturally most homogeneous nation of sixty-six nations or territories, using "speakers of dominant language
as percentage of population" as an indicator (pp. 134–37).

dimensions; rather we would predict the same general findings if a corresponding index is constructed for U.S. data.

What the index does is to give a total picture of the situation of an individual in his society, contrasting the generalized underdog with the generalized topdog. A vivid description of the former is given by Genevieve Knupfer in her "Portrait of the Underdog":[11]

> Closely linked with economic underprivilege is psychological underprivilege: habits of submission, little access to sources of information, lack of verbal facility. These things appear to produce a lack of self-confidence which increases the unwillingness of the low-status person to participate in many phases of our predominantly middle-class culture.

Negate all this, and one gets the generalized topdog. Join underdog and topdog in a web of affiliations and one gets, strangely enough, a functioning society, although not necessarily a perfect one from a value perspective. The problem we are concerned with is how they relate to each other in connection with, for instance, foreign policy issues, and to explore this problem we turn to the general problem of attitude propagation between topdogs and underdogs, between center and periphery.

A STRUCTURAL THEORY OF ATTITUDE PROPAGATION

There are a number of reasons why we may assume that the general direction of influence in an integrated society is from the center to the periphery.[12] The center has many obvious advantages: it has easier access to the means of communication, both as sender and receiver; it has the education necessary to perceive, understand, and interpret; it knows how to communicate ideas and has training in doing so.

But there are also more structural reasons. Imagine a person who is located in the "middle" of society in the sense of the index and who receives two messages with the usual mixture of cognitions and evaluations, one from a sender in the center and one from a sender in the

---

11. In *Public Opinion Quarterly*, Vol. 11 (1947), pp. 103–14.
12. Thus, Sorokin, following Tarde, states: "The upper-urban-civilized classes are, as a rule, the centers from which emanates the diffusion of the new and finished products. *Only in the periods of decline of these classes or groups, as mentioned before, is this uniformity reversed or broken.* In such cases the lower classes become the center of the emanation of the new values as the finished products, and the declining upper-urban-civilized strata adopt them with some lag." Pitirim A. Sorokin, *Social and Cultural Dynamics, Vol. 4: Basic Problems, Principles, and Methods* (New York: The Bedminister Press, 1962), p. 221.

periphery. If he is the receiver R of the message M from the sender S, the following cognitive triangle is produced:[13]

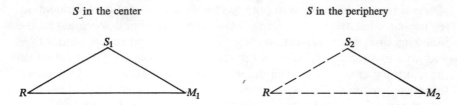

Since we assume that R perceives the position link between S and M, evaluation of M will depend on evaulation of S as depicted in the graphs if we make the following assumptions: (1) there is no independent evaluation of M, (2) R has internalized society's evaluation of S, as expressed by S's score on the index of social position, and (3) there is a drive towards cognitive balance. We accept the third premise as axiomatic, but not necessarily the previous two. The first premise is obviously disputable since independent information often is available. But to the extent it is true, it should apply more to foreign policy items than to domestic policy items precisely because so few independent cues exist, except for topdogs who have their own ties and links to the international system. But we can safely assume that only a very minor fraction of the population has a sufficiently independent basis for evaluation of the veracity, credulity, or general soundness of a foreign policy message. Hence, most people have to rely on other sources of evaluation, such as evaluation of the sender. Of course, there are also other possibilities: R may evaluate M relative to other elements in his total world outlook or ideology, be it domestic or international, and let the acceptance depend on degree of fit with his ideology. And he may evaluate it relative to his surroundings and accept it if people he accepts accept it and reject it if it is accepted by people he rejects, and so on. The latter, however, is only a generalization of the general model above, and the former neither contradicts, nor corroborates the general thesis about flow of influence; it is simply another dimension.

To what extent, then, is premise 2, above, valid? Validity is certainly not always the case: In ascription-oriented societies with blocked channels of mobility the rejection of senders from the center may be of such magnitude as to cause automatic rejection of everything emanating from the center. But in achievement-oriented and relatively well-integrated societies it is probably safe to buy the assumption, since the

13. The general idea is taken from R. E. Lane and D. O. Sears, *Public Opinion* (Englewood Cliffs: Prentice Hall, 1964), p. 43.

person closer to the center will, in general and by definition, be the person who embodies more of the values of the society—in our case, in terms of the eight items in the index.

As a test of this simple hypothesis about the flow of communication, let us see what the respondents themselves say. They were asked the following question: "Would you say that you yourself receive more than you give in such conversations [about foreign policy], or is it rather on the contrary that you contribute more than you receive?" Obviously, there were receivers and contributors at all eight levels of social position and there were people who said "even" at all levels. But when we constructed the ratio of receivers to contributors for all levels, we got confirmation (Table 4) of the general hypothesis. In the sample

Table 4—The Ratio of Receivers to Contributors in Conversations about Foreign Policy

	SOCIAL POSITION								
	1	2	3	4	5	6	7	8	Total
Percent receivers / Percent contributors	11.1	9.5	6.3	5.8	9.4	3.5	5.7	1.3	6.0

as a whole there were six times as many receivers (36 per cent) as contributors (6 per cent) but, as can be seen in Table 4, this figure is differentially distributed: the ratio is more than eight times as high in the periphery as in the center.

This can now be related to the celebrated two-step flow hypothesis of Lazarsfeld and Katz. In a sense this hypothesis is about groups as intermediaries between sources of communication and individuals, with opinion leaders within the groups who filter cognitions and evaluations and decide what shall be propagated further to rank and file members. Obviously, this filtering effect of the intermediate stage breaks down if there is independent access to the communication and independent sources of evaluation of its content. But in the case of foreign policy issues, we know from Table 2 that those in the center read more than those on the periphery and from Table 4 that those on the periphery receive more than they contribute in private conversations, relative to the center. In other words, we have every reason to believe that, in general, the two-step flow of communication in this field is from the mass media to the topdogs and from the topdogs to the underdogs. Thus the index of social position gives an instrument, however imperfect, that can be used to locate the intermediate step in the communication process: In any group look for the member with the highest social position score.

In the family he is the father, in a circle of women the woman of highest class or with most education, and so on.[14]

Thus, if these were the only factors operating, we would predict that any new foreign policy measure, if accepted at all, is accepted when it comes from levels closer to the center and rejected when it comes from levels closer to the periphery. This does not imply any kind of automatic acceptance, for, as mentioned above, the individual at any level may be protected by the joint operation of cognitive polarization and social polarization that tends to filter away messages that cannot be absorbed without provoking too much dissonance in the personal system or the social system.[15] But if we assume this factor to be of about equal importance at all social levels (although the principle of cognitive organization may vary from more "refined" in the center to more "primitive" in the periphery and from a more cognitive basis in the center to a more social basis in the periphery), some conclusions can be drawn.

Imagine that a new issue appears on the foreign policy opinion market. It may come from the outside or from within the nation itself, but in order to be propagated it will have to be identified with somebody or with some group in the center of society. It is most likely to originate in the center, since only the center has the contacts and insights necessary to give the issue a cognitive basis of knowledge. It also may originate anywhere else, for instance, in heavily ideologized sectors of the periphery, but in order to "surface" in society it has to reach the center (and here a party that is strong both in periphery and in center will have obvious advantages, as will be developed later). Hence, once the issue is accepted by some sector in the center, it may be propagated to the periphery and it will be accepted, if necessary, with a time lag.

Thus, in the early life history of an issue, before the propagation has really started, the proportion of acceptance will be steadily decreasing from center to periphery. Then, when the propagation really starts there will be more to gain in acceptance lower down in society since the center has known the issue for some time and may already have exhausted its acceptance potential. But lower down, where the social position of the sender is more important, there are still gains to be made, which means that the acceptance curve may flatten out and show equal acceptance levels in periphery and center.

From here on, a number of things can happen. The acceptance by lower levels may serve as a positive feedback on the center and increase its acceptance level ("since we have the support of the people"). This

14. See E. Katz and P. F. Lazarsfeld, *Personal Influence* (New York: The Free Press, 1955).

15. In the list given by Lane and Sears (*op. cit.*, p. 53) of sources of resistance to opinion change, *ideological integration* is, curiously enough, missing from an otherwise very complete and fine inventory.

again may feed into lower-level acceptance and gradually lead to a national consensus, which means that the issue is absorbed in the general culture and no longer is an issue. But the issue may also have another trajectory because the center discovers new issues which, expressed in sociological jargon, may be the functional equivalents of the old ones, loses interest in the old issues and ideas, and focuses on the new ones. Foreign policy issues are particularly vulnerable to this effect, since the nation is a member of an international system and subject to the influences of this system, which, in turn, is mainly perceived by the center.

But the loss of concern with the issue in the center does not automatically imply a corresponding decrease in the acceptance ratio of the periphery. If this were the case, society would return to the *status quo ante* insofar as that issue is concerned. The periphery and the middle sectors have invested some mental energy in the acceptance of the issue and its integration in their ideology and, since they think less in instrumental terms, they will question less the adequacy of the policy they accept. Moreover, the center may not be interested in issuing any explicit declaration to the effect that it has changed its policy orientation: this would imply an admission that it had been mistaken. Hence, the underdog will have to find out himself, perhaps via some middledogs, that "The center no longer thinks in these terms" (as happens, for example, when intellectuals from periphery nations discover that such and such an intellectual fashion in which they have laboriously acquired belief and training is no longer *en vogue* in Paris, London, or New York). But if he does not find out because of faulty communication or lack of visibility of what really happens in Paris, etc., acceptance may continue to grow in the more peripheral ranges of the social structure while at the same time it is decreasing in the center. And when the periphery at last discovers that it is cultivating values very different from the ones found in the center it may be too late: the values are integrated and internalized, and are now turned against the center as a weapon. The center is defined as a traitor, the periphery as the true believer, and what was once the gradualism of the center may be turned into the absolutism of the periphery. And as such it may mix with issues and values that never surface in society, that never leave the periphery but always bear the unmistakable imprint of periphery social cosmology.

Thus, we have essentially developed the nucleus of a typology of opinion structures, where by the latter term we do not think in the usual terms of intra-personal organization of attitudes but in terms of how the attitudes are distributed in the social structure. The point of departure is the model of the genesis of attitude distribution as a dialogue between center and periphery. More particularly, as indicated in Table 5, three

phases have been used corresponding to three actions in this dialogue: one of the two parties starts by accepting the policy suggested, the other one follows up by accepting or rejecting, and the first one reacts to this again by accepting or rejecting the policy. In the first phase we assume that the issue has been accepted in the sense that it is favored by a sizeable proportion of the group. We also assume that there is communication between center and periphery. From that point on the rest is dialogue, and the simple taxonomy yields eight types.

Table 5 — A Three-Phase Model of the Dynamics of Attitude Distributions in the Social Structure

PHASE I	PHASE II	PHASE III	
Attitude accepted by center or periphery	Reaction by the other party: accept or reject	Reaction by the initiators: accept or reject	Probability that the pattern will not occur
1. *Center*: accept	*Periphery*: accept	*Center*:accept	0
2. *Center*: accept	*Periphery*: accept	*Center*: reject	0
3. *Center*: accept	*Periphery*: reject	*Center*: accept	1
4. *Center*: accept	*Periphery*: reject	*Center*: reject	1
5. *Periphery*: accept	*Center*: accept	*Periphery*: accept	2
6. *Periphery*: accept	*Center*: accept	*Periphery*: reject	3
7. *Periphery*: accept	*Center*: reject	*Periphery*: accept	1
8. *Periphery*: accept	*Center*: reject	*Periphery*: reject	1

Since this taxonomy is exhaustive it says nothing about social affairs: to get from the logically possible to the substantively important we have to be bold and hypothesize the exclusion of some types. The candidates for exclusion are obvious according to the reasoning above: we think it unlikely (1) that the periphery will reject wholesale something initially accepted by the center, (2) that the center will accept wholesale something initially accepted by the periphery, and (3) that the periphery will initiate anything at all. If we now apply these three simple principles to the patterns in Table 5, and assume that they have roughly the same influence on the probability of the pattern, we arrive at a measure of the number of counts against a pattern. Thus pattern 6 has three counts against it and is highly unlikely, and pattern 5 is also rather unlikely.

The two most likely patterns according to the model are pattern 1, which leads to *national consensus* with a center that retains its interest in the policy, and pattern 2, wherein the center loses its interest while the periphery accepts the policy more and more. We shall refer to this latter as the *social propagation* pattern, or with less veneration as the pattern of *social digestion*. The metaphor we have in mind comes from

Antoine de Saint-Exupéry's lovely *Le Petit Prince*,[16] where two of the personages are a *serpent* and an *éléphant*. The former is depicted as swallowing the latter and the poor *éléphant* appears as a phenomenal bulge right behind the mouth of the *serpent*. Used as a metaphor the snake, which is a relatively one-dimensional animal, would correspond to the one-dimensional presentation of social structure given by the social position index, and the elephant represents an outside issue. It is swallowed (accepted) by people in the elite and then accepted by the center, and from this point on the digestion starts whereby the elephant is flattened out (more acceptance in the periphery, less in the center). To complete the analogy one should assume a certain cumulation at the rear end of the snake before elimination—if the reader will pardon the analogy with what happens when bits and parcels of center ideology or behavioral patterns (e.g. fashions, where clothing and furniture are concerned) attain a certain periphery accumulation before they finally disappear from the culture of the society.

Thus, patterns 1 and 2 are very different. Compared to a romance, pattern 1 leads by positive feed-back to mutual love and consensus, whereas pattern 2 corresponds to topdog seduction of the underdog: the center shows itself interested, the periphery falls in love, whereupon the interest of the center cools down and, eventually, love withers away from the periphery too. The net result is 100 per cent acceptance in pattern 1 and 0 per cent acceptance in pattern 2. But the time-span between the first beginning in the center and these final outcomes may by considerable: months, years, decennia, centuries, depending on the issue and on the rapidity of the communication process in the social structure. Hendrik Ibsen once said that a truth only lasts twenty years, and although he hardly did what modern social science would do to back up such a statement, there may be a good deal of truth in that idea (truth which, in this case, would last more than twenty years) if we limit ourselves to the center. The periphery will lag behind, some ideas will never reach it, although they accumulate steadily in the center (pattern 3), other ideas may die out and be short-run center fads because of lack of response from the periphery (pattern 4). Correspondingly, there may be short-run periphery fads that never touch the center (pattern 8), and there may be hard-boiled nuclei of resistance against the center, built around issues and attitudes that are kindled and nourished precisely because of the impenetrability of the center (pattern 7).

Although the theory (and it is a theory, not merely a taxonomy, because of the probability levels) is assumed to have general validity, it should be remembered that we are here dealing with foreign policy

16. Antoine de Saint-Exupéry: *Le Petit Prince* (Numerous editions, e.g. Paris: N.R.F. Gallimard, 1946).

issues, which makes the three factors that differentiate between the probabilities *a fortiori* valid (the *éléphant* comes from the outside, it is not generated within the *serpent*). Nevertheless, although we believe in the prevalence of patterns 1 and 2, we only reject as highly unlikely patterns 5 and 6. This gives us a typology of six types of foreign policy issues, which can be added to any theory that purports to classify political issues or other issues according to some kind of "homogeneity within, heterogeneity between" principle. Other principles of classification would be: according to *how issues cluster in individual minds* (arrived at by factor-analytic or other methods to analyze the correlation matrix); according to *content* (arrived at by content analysis of the verbal manifestations of the ideas behind the policies); or according to *political process* (arrived at by analyzing how the issues are handled by the body politic). Obviously, these classifications do not coincide. But we shall not systematically elaborate the similarities and dissimilarities here. We wish only to emphasize that intra-individual correlation between two issues does not necessarily imply that the issues are absorbed by the social structure in the same manner; for intra-individual correlations in social science are usually synchronic, whereas the phenomena we refer to take place in time. For instance, at one point in time, two policies may be favored by the center and rejected by the periphery, thus producing a substantial correlation. But, then, one issue may be absorbed by the social structure according to pattern 1 and the other issue according to pattern 2, which would affect the correlation considerably. Or some other combination of patterns might occur, depending on the issue.

And that is the problem: can we say anything general about the relation between the *content* of an issue and its *social process*? We think this is possible through the use of the idea of center culture vs. periphery culture developed in the preceding article.[17] Thus, the more moral and absolutist the issue, the more likely its acceptance in the periphery; the more pragmatic and gradualist the issue, the more likely its acceptance in the center. Moreover, the more recent the issue, the more likely that the distribution will be according to pattern 4 (if the issue is pragmatic/gradualist) or pattern 8 (if the issue is moralist/absolutist), since there is less opportunity for a dialogue to develop in the case of recent issues. Finally, if the issue is very old, we would expect either a national consensus or an accumulation in the periphery depending on whether the process has been according to pattern 2, 7, or 8.

In order to illustrate all these propositions relating content and process, let us look at the distribution profiles of allegiance to one very old institution, the Norwegian state church as expressed by "both belief

17. Galtung, *op. cit.*, pp. 210 ff.

and practice where religion is concerned," and to one very new institution, "the integration of a part of the armed forces of your country into a permanent, international force under United Nations command," as well as desire to serve in the international force oneself. The latter idea is so new that it almost does not exist, so we would expect a heavy acceptance bias in favor of the center, and the former is so old that we would expect a corresponding acceptance bias in favor of the periphery, with the center practicing without believing, or believing without practicing, or doing neither. And this is indeed what we find (Table 6). The trends are unmistakable and consistent, respectively, with the last and the first phases of Pattern 2. It is particularly convincing since we have two indicators for each institution, one giving the attitude to the institution

Table 6—Attitudes toward Religious Belief, Religious Practice, UN Forces, and Service in the International Force
(in percentages)

	SOCIAL POSITION								
	1	*2*	*3*	*4*	*5*	*6*	*7*	*8*	*Total*
In favor of state church	42	32	26	23	17	14	13	3	21
Belief and practice	18	10	13	10	13	6	11	5	11
In favor of UN forces	9	26	34	43	49	51	66	80	45
Would like to serve oneself	3	11	11	14	13	18	28	45	16

in general and one tapping more personal commitment (the latter, of course, being lower in both cases than the general acceptance level). But Table 6 does not provide proof that pattern 2 has been operative, since we do not have data for the last centuries showing a primary phase of topdog acceptance of the state church and subsequent phases with a dislocation downwards of the point of gravity for the allegiance. Nor do we have, as yet, information about how attitudes to the UN forces will distribute in the future. In both cases there may actually be a combination of patterns 1 and 2 at work: consensus is reached, and then broken down, first in the center and much later in the periphery.

If time were the only factor of importance here, the distribution of the UN issue would represent the first phase of any social absorption process and the indicators of religious belief *and* practice the last phase. But the distributions could be equally well explained in terms of cultural compatibility. Religion, also in its institutionalized form, is a moral issue more compatible with periphery ethos; the UN forces have a moral element sufficient to explain that they already are to some extent accepted by the periphery but are essentially highly gradualist measures towards, for instance, a world state that would be more according to the thinking

of the periphery.[18] The data in Table 6 are actually compatible with both explanations and also with a possible interaction between the two factors: an issue may start in the center as a gradualist issue, but by the time it reaches the periphery it may have been reinterpreted in more absolutist terms.

Let us now see, after this long excursion into taxonomy and theory, whether our formulation can shed any light on the distributions of the attitudes towards the ten foreign policy issues for which we have data (Table 7). Ideally, we should have trend data over a relatively long time-span in order to make a diachronic analysis that would correspond to the nature of the theory, but we have to content ourselves with some inferences based on synchronic analysis.

Obviously, it would be foolhardy to claim to explain all the variations in the 208 percentages given in Table 7. But if we use the two dichotomies introduced in our theory above, new vs. old and gradualist vs. absolutist, we get, roughly, the classification of policies depicted in Table 8. Here it can be seen that by "new" issues we mean essentially ideas that have arisen since World War II, which means that there are relatively few old ideas in the list. Military service and conscientious objection are both old, and so are the "Nordic line," Scandinavism, and its counterpart, isolationism. But we have also divided the total of 18 ideas according to the second axis, and here the division is more difficult. The moral content in the four forms of technical assistance listed in Table 8 is easily argued: they consist in giving things away without asking for remuneration, and, consequently, are the opposite of calculative, commercial technical assistance which the center probably would favor, both because it is new and because of its pragmatic content. The invitation to Khrushchev was also, to a large extent, a moral gesture, and, indeed, so would be closer ties with the nonaligned nations and the socialist nations.

At any rate, there is a contrast between these measures and the idea of tying Norwegian foreign policy to the UN, to NATO, to EEC, and of stationing (U.S.) atomic weapons on Norwegian territory in times of peace. The difference is not only along the leftist-rightist political continuum or the soft-tough approach to foreign policy. In the gradualist column of Table 8 are policies that have been suggested as relatively small extensions of already existing policies, not as any kind of reorientation or implementation of a new ideology. Of course, they can also be given absolutist formulations. (A defense policy based on atomic weapons might be the most absolutist of all policies, for instance. But there has

18. This is further elaborated in Johan Galtung, "Attitudes Towards Different Forms of Disarmament," paper presented to the International Peace Research Association, July 3–5, 1965, and printed in the *Proceedings*.

Table 7—Attitudes toward Some Foreign Policy Issues as a Function of Social Position
(in percentages)

	SOCIAL POSITION								
	1	2	3	4	5	6	7	8	Total
1. Military service									
under UN	3	11	11	14	13	18	28	45	16
under NATO	0	1	2	6	5	8	1	8	4
Norwegian command	46	44	50	52	53	53	53	45	51
refuse any service	42	32	27	22	25	17	14	3	23
2. Closer ties with									
Nordic countries	33	38	31	30	39	32	37	33	34
NATO countries	12	17	14	23	17	15	11	23	17
nonaligned countries	3	5	7	6	6	8	9	10	7
socialist countries	6	0	0	0	0	0	0	3	0
United Nations	18	18	26	28	30	30	34	30	28
less participation	9	14	14	9	7	10	5	0	9
3. Attitude toward NATO									
in favor of	33	35	37	55	59	58	62	65	52
against	21	24	24	16	20	20	21	18	20
4. Attitude toward atomic arms									
in favor of	0	1	4	7	7	6	3	13	5
against	73	80	80	75	77	78	84	75	78
5. Attitude toward EEC									
in favor of	24	32	36	44	43	53	59	68	44
against	49	37	35	32	34	28	30	25	33
6. Attitude toward Khrushchev									
in favor of	61	77	82	82	80	80	86	73	80
against	12	11	9	14	12	12	6	20	12
7. Attitude toward Peace Corps									
in favor of	49	60	61	70	72	74	81	80	69
against	0	4	7	6	8	12	6	15	8
8. Merchant marine assistance									
in favor of	27	33	29	33	36	37	59	48	36
against	52	56	61	53	54	53	38	45	53
9. Buy textiles assistance									
in favor of	21	20	15	22	20	27	43	53	24
against	49	67	74	68	71	63	51	45	66
10. Higher coffee prices									
in favor of	12	29	23	26	31	31	39	35	29
against	61	62	67	64	63	60	56	60	63

Table 8 — A Classification of Issues

	GRADUALIST/PRAGMATIC MEASURES	ABSOLUTIST/MORAL MEASURES

New issues	service under UN
	service under NATO
	in favor of NATO
	in favor of atomic
	   weapons
	ties with NATO
	ties with the UN
	in favor of EEC
		merchant marine assistance
		buy textile assistance
		higher coffee prices
		in favor of Khrushchev
		in favor of peace corps
		in favor of ties with nonaligned
		   nations
		in favor of ties with socialist
		   countries

Old issues	service under Norway in favor of ties to Nordic countries	refuse any service isolationism

been no suggestion to use atomic weapons in a preventive war, whereas the other side, the pacifist side, has repeatedly suggested the unilateral disarmament of Norway.)

The methodological difficulty at this point is that we do not know whether these gradualist policies are gradualist because they are accepted by the center or, whether as we shall show, they are accepted by the center because they are gradualist. Actually, both propositions are probably true: an issue is brought in and is accepted by some people in the center, but in order to gain further acceptance, the policy must be presented in a more gradualist and pragmatic style, and so on. And correspondingly for the periphery: the more it is accepted the more absolutist and moralist will it have to be, and vice versa.

However this may be, the predictions from the theory are now clear: Old, absolutist policies should be overselected in the periphery and new, gradualist policies overselected in the center. This predicts nine out of the eighteen cases in Table 8, and predicts them correctly in all cases (see Table 7). For the other nine cases we are in the difficult position that the two factors may lead to opposite predictions. However, in our theory *time* has been the dominant variable with the general idea of a process from center to periphery, which means that old, gradualist policies should be on their way towards an accumulation at the periphery but not as much as old, absolutist policies, since the pragmatism involved will not be sufficiently dear to the periphery political culture. In short, one would expect a distribution that is flattening out, and this is precisely what we find in the two cases.

This leaves us with seven issues that have been classified as absolutist/moral and also as new. The distributions may perhaps give some idea as to which factor is stronger, issue age or issue content. As mentioned, we feel age is the overriding consideration and this is certainly borne out by the data: in all cases except one there is a clear overselection

by the center. In that last case, the idea of tying Norwegian policy more to the socialist countries, periphery acceptance shows up, as it should since the idea is certainly the most absolutist one of the seven policies.

From this partly deductive, partly inductive procedure used thus far, we conclude as follows:

$H_{3,1}$: New, gradualist/pragmatic policies will be overaccepted by the center.

$H_{3,2}$: Old, absolutist/moralist policies will be overaccepted by the periphery.

$H_{3,3}$: New policies that are not of the obviously gradualist/pragmatic variety will have to be highly absolutist/moralist in order to be overaccepted by the periphery, or else tend to show an even distribution.

$H_{3,4}$: Old policies that are not of the obviously absolutist/moralist variety may show an even distribution, or else an accumulation in the periphery.

$H_{3,5}$: Whether new or old, gradualist or absolutist, there is the possibility of national consensus, in which case the issue would no longer be an issue but a part of consensual national culture.

Since the last part pertaining to the relative weight of age and content may appear so *ad hoc* as to need at least some additional support from other data, let us, in conclusion, compare the distribution of the acceptance of two policies that certainly satisfy the criteria as to types of content and that have in common the factor of age. Presented in Table 9, they represent new (to the respondents) ways of approaching the problem of aggression after disarmament, the first one highly pragmatic and the second one highly moralist. Both policies have the same total adherence, 38 per cent, but their location in the social structure is almost as opposite as possible: pattern 4 as against pattern 8, as predicted.

Table 9—Attitudes toward a Pragmatic and a Moralist Approach to the Problem of Aggression after Disarmament

(in percentages)

	SOCIAL POSITION								
	1	2	3	4	5	6	7	8	Total
If the world had disarmed but a nation nevertheless started an attack, then there should be a permission to arm again.	18	33	31	42	41	40	39	58	38
One should meet an attack with a non-military defence, so-called non-violence.	52	39	43	36	42	39	33	15	38

We let this suffice as illustration of the general theory and now turn to the more complicated problems of predicting not only "marginals" for one attitude, but also correlations between two attitudes as a function of social position.

RELATIONS BETWEEN THE ATTITUDES

That attitudes come in clusters is so well documented in social science that we shall not even bother to present a separate table of intercorrelations, but will proceed immediately to the task of testing the major hypotheses about the dependence of these correlations on social position. These hypotheses presuppose a distinction between "tough" and "soft" policies in foreign affairs: we take the former to mean force and big-power oriented policies (in other words, policies 3, 4, and 5 in Table 7) and the latter to mean contact and technical assistance oriented policies (in other words, policies 6, 7, 8, 9, and 10). Policies 1 and 2 contain a mixture of tough and soft issues and for this reason have been omitted from the analysis, since we need clear attitudes for *or* against a policy that can be classified as tough *or* soft to test these two hypotheses:

$H_{4.1}$: With increasing social position the correlation between a tough attitude and a soft attitude will decrease monotonously.

$H_{4.2}$: With increasing social position the correlation between two tough attitudes or between two soft attitudes will remain constant or increase; it will not decrease monotonously.

As the hypotheses stand, they are taken almost verbatim from the preceding article where the theory is outlined, so what we present below (Table 10) is, first of all, a replication of earlier tests on a new sample and on some new variables. Altogether twenty-eight pairs of variables are examined, fifteen of the same kind and thirteen of different kinds. There are six possible patterns where relative arithmetic size is concerned (the second can be higher or lower than the first, and the third can be higher than both, between them, or lower than both). $H_{4.1}$ is a strong hypothesis since only one of the six will verify it, whereas $H_{4.2}$ is a weak hypothesis since five of the six patterns will verify it. We get verification of the general hypothesis in twenty of the twenty-eight cases, or in 72 per cent. But then it should be noted that in two cases $H_{4.1}$ is almost verified; if we accept these cases (since more than half of the predictions of relative size of correlations are correct), we get verification in 79 per cent of the cases. At any rate, we consider this sufficient to warrant attaching credibility to the theory, and thus we now want to look more closely into the matter.

Table 10 — Attitude Intercorrelations as a Function of Social Position (Yule's Q)

	SOCIAL POSITION			
	Periphery (0–2)	Medium (3–5)	Center (6–8)	Hypothesis verification
Tough/soft				
NATO/Khrushchev	0.11	−0.23	−0.67	+
NATO/Peace Corps	1.00	0.56	0.05	+
NATO/merchant marine	0.11	0.17	−0.27	(2/3)
NATO/buy textiles	0.10	0.00	−0.17	+
NATO/higher coffee prices	0.13	0.07	−0.22	+
ATOM/Khrushchev	*	−0.38	−0.54	+
ATOM/Peace Corps	*	−0.23	−0.42	+
ATOM/merchant marine	*	−0.07	−0.38	+
ATOM/buy textiles	*	−0.08	−0.08	(0)
ATOM/higher coffee prices	*	−0.15	−0.51	+
EEC/Khrushchev	−0.49	−0.36	−0.48	(1/3)
EEC/Peace Corps	0.33	0.47	0.13	(2/3)
EEC/merchant marine	0.32	0.17	−0.10	+
EEC/buy textiles	0.75	0.19	0.10	+
EEC/higher coffee prices	0.50	−0.14	−0.23	+
Tough/tough				
NATO/ATOM	*	0.53	0.74	+
NATO/EEC	0.59	0.57	0.74	+
ATOM/EEC	*	0.67	0.48	−
Soft/soft				
Khrushchev/Peace Corps	1.00	0.14	0.69	+
Khrushchev/merchant marine	0.26	0.08	0.47	+
Khrushchev/buy textiles	0.33	0.43	0.61	+
Khrushchev/coffee prices	0.01	0.22	0.50	+
Peace Corps/merchant marine	1.00	0.73	0.64	−
Peace Corps/buy textiles	1.00	0.65	0.67	+
Peace Corps/coffee prices	−0.70	0.68	0.64	+
Merchant marine/textiles	0.98	0.84	0.91	+
Merchant marine/coffee prices	0.76	0.66	0.63	−
Buy textiles/coffee prices	0.82	0.81	0.61	−

*Since no respondents wanted atomic weapons at this level, no correlation measure could be computed.

What thinking can we bring to bear on the relation between attitude correlation and social position? Here is a short list of factors:

1. With increasing social position increasing *predominance of an evaluative mood* in political affairs: items are accepted or rejected according to ideology, whether they are liked or disliked.
2. With increasing social position decreasing *predominance of a cognitive mood* in political affairs: items are accepted or rejected less according to perception, whether they are perceived or not perceived.

3. With increasing social position *increasing ability to obtain consistency.*
4. With increasing social position *increasing tolerance of ambiguity.*
5. With increasing social position *decreasing response-set.*

The first three form the basis of the original theory. Respondents in the periphery will accept any initiative provided they have perceived it at all and reject it if it is not perceived; they are either generally engagement-oriented or isolationist, depending on whether they perceive initiatives or not. Respondents in the center will accept or reject not according to cognitive, but according to ideological affinity; they may accept tough issues and reject the soft ones, or vice versa. If the issues are of the same kind (both soft or both tough), then correlations will be positive both in center and in periphery (but for different reasons: in the periphery because both are perceived; in the center because they are ideologically compatible). This is illustrated in Table 10, where all except one of the thirty-seven correlations of this kind are positive. It is only when one issue is soft and the other tough that the theory will predict differently: in the periphery the correlations will also tend to be positive in this because of cognitive predominance (this holds in nine out of ten cases) and in the center they will tend to be negative because of evaluative predominance (this holds in twelve out of fifteen cases, with all three exceptions being close to zero). The medium category should be a mixture (this is also the case as seven correlations are positive and eight are negative). Thus, the closer we are to the center, the more are politically discrepant attitudes kept apart in the minds of the respondents, for they, even more, master the problems of perception and knowledge, have some measure of ideological clarity, and possess ability as well as training in obtaining consistency.

Thus the first three factors listed above together explain the hypotheses that predict correctly in seventy-two or seventy-nine per cent of the cases. What about the four wrong predictions for the cases in which we have items of the same kind (tough/tough and soft/soft)? Of course, one could try to explain these deviations on the basis of the remaining two principles on the list above (increasing tolerance of ambiguity and decreasing response-set), since they both predict decreasing correlation with increasing social position (this time in magnitude, not arithmetically). But if we based our theory on these two factors alone we would only get confirmation in four out of thirteen cases, which is low enough to warrant the conclusion that one, two, or all of the other three factors must also be at work. Moreover, we cannot assume that the first three factors suddenly become inoperative. Hence, we have to think in terms of some factors that tend to increase and some factors that tend to decrease the correlations, and to conceive of the data as the net result. And since we

know nothing about the relative importance of these factors, we do not obtain a perfect basis for prediction.

However, we can make an educated guess about the relative importance of the last three factors if we study Table 10 more closely. For the tough/tough and the soft/soft comparisons, all correlations should be relatively high since factors 1 and 2 combine to produce positive correlations both in the periphery and in the center. But in addition to this, factor 3 should lead to increasing correlation with social position, and factors 4 and 5, as mentioned, to decreasing correlations. If we accept 0.50 as the limit, then twenty-eight or seventy-six per cent of the thirty-seven correlations are "relatively high." If we then make all possible horizontal comparisons from lower to higher social position, we discover that in sixteen of the cases we do get an increase and in nineteen of the cases a decrease in the correlations: in other words, parity. Thus, all we can derive from these data is that ability to obtain consistency roughly balances tolerance of ambiguity and the possible effects of response-set. It should be mentioned that out of the thirty-five comparisons in the tough/soft part of Table 10, thirty or eight-six per cent are in the expected decreasing direction. Thus the detailed examination gives a new set of figures that confirm the general hypothesis of monotonicity, or order, for tough/soft combinations and no monotonicity, or disorder, for tough/tough and soft/soft combinations.

Hence, we have one more element in our general picture of the difference between political thinking in the center and in the periphery: Not only do the two groups accept different issues and enter the issue-market at different phases, they also organize the issues they absorb in a different way. This, of course, is not to say that there are not also personality factors at work that may cut across the social position axis, but it looks as if the consistent and sizeable differences in attitudinal organization are at least relatively well explained in terms of social position.

Concluding this section, then, let us have a look at where the two questions we left out fit into the general picture, questions 1 and 2 in Table 7. These questions are of a slightly different kind, insofar as they present the respondents with a larger variety of choices. However, even though all answer categories are potentially interesting, we are particularly concerned with the last (and absolutist) categories in both questions: those who would refuse any kind of military service and those who feel that Norway should participate less in international cooperation. We shall refer to them again as *pacifists* and *isolationists*, respectively, and analyze them relative to the other respondents. Since these questions were constructed the way they appear in order to yield relatively pure categories of pacifists and isolationists by giving the respondents a variety of alternatives, we feel the analysis will be meaningful.

What, then, do they believe? We already know how they distribute on social position, so we know that the political culture in the periphery is among the social conditions that are particularly favorable for the emergence of these attitudes. But what other opinions do the respondents hold? This is best seen when social position is also taken into account (Table 11), since there are very meaningful variations. That they are in favor of the Peace Corps and the Khrushchev invitation and more than average

Table 11 — Value-Profiles of the Pacifists
(in percentages)

	SOCIAL POSITION		
	Periphery (0–2)	Medium (3–5)	Center (6–8)
Nordic cooperation	41	35	28
NATO cooperation	8	11	8
Nonaligned nations	5	7	15
Socialist nations	2	0	0
United Nations	18	31	29
Less participation	18	11	15
Against NATO	36	34	21
Against atomic arms	75	88	90
In favor of EEC	41	40	54
In favor of Khrushchev	72	82	80
In favor of Peace Corps	51	66	80
Merchant marine assistance	38	32	46
Buy textiles assistance	33	21	41
Higher coffee prices	31	32	33

against NATO and atomic weapons is certainly not strange; it is more interesting that they are so remarkably similar to the rest of the population. One reason for this similarity is certainly that most of them are women, opinionwise linked to their husbands and kinship groups scattered all over the society. Another reason is simply that these pacifists are relatively well integrated in society: their value-profiles do not differ that much from other people's, nor do they change much from one social level to another. Thus, periphery pacifists do not see much further than to the Nordic countries, whereas pacifists in the center ask for orientation towards the UN and the nonaligned countries; but they all have in common that they are not isolationists.

But, as can be seen in Table 12, the isolationists are to some extent pacifists, especially in the periphery. Table 12 also shows a low level of consistency. True enough, there is less acceptance of any kind of participation than in the general population, but the differences are not overwhelming, with the resistance against NATO as the single possible exception. This may indicate that NATO has served as a stimulus toward withdrawal from any kind of international cooperation, particularly in

Table 12 — Value-Profiles of the Isolationists
(in percentages)

	SOCIAL POSITION		
	Periphery (0–2)	Medium (3–5)	Center (6–8)
Military service under the UN	0	5	10
In a force under NATO command	0	0	10
Under Norwegian command	35	63	48
Would refuse any kind of service	50	29	32
Against NATO	57	51	32
Against atomic arms	65	88	95
In favor of EEC	0	34	58
In favor of Khrushchev	86	83	79
In favor of Peace Corps	29	39	53
Merchant marine assistance	21	10	42
Buy textiles assistance	14	10	26
Higher coffee prices	43	12	21

the periphery, where none among the isolationists is in favor of the EEC or NATO service. But in the center isolationism seems to be much more specific and not so generalizable to other areas as in the periphery. As a matter of fact, it can be shown to be a periphery ideology for members of all parties except the conservative, where it is turned into a center ideology and (probably) coupled with strong nationalist sentiments.

In general, the trends in the data are the same for pacifists and isolationists as for the sample as a whole, which confirms the general findings of center acceptance and periphery rejection (with some exceptions) for foreign policy issues.

THE ROLE OF POLITICAL PARTIES

No psychologist would base his science on "Tell me with whom you associate (and particularly to whom you are married) and I shall tell you who you are." Although he would have considerable empirical and theoretical basis for doing so, he would also explore personality traits unaccounted for by reference to significant others and the impact these others may have, even if they are not mirror images of the person himself. Similarly, the political scientist would be ill-advised were he only to base his explorations of the role of political parties on the social composition of their parliamentary groups, or their staffs, or their members, or their voters, not to mention of people who say in a poll that they would vote for the party "if there were a parliamentary election tomorrow." On the other hand, since the last category is at least very heavily correlated with the category of real voters "tomorrow," and the latter are

the people with whom the leaders of the party interact symbolically and will have to depend on for further support, at least some important information can be gathered from the data on the social distribution of the sympathizers. This, of course, is indeed done in any analysis of party-identification; the only thing to be added here is the use of an index of social position instead of the traditional run of background variables one or two at a time.[19]

The social profile of a party can be defined (1) by calculating for a given party the proportions that come from different social groups, and (2) by calculating for each social group the proportions that identify with a given party. Technically this is a question of the direction of percentages; theoretically it is a question of what kind of theory one wants to construct. Both profiles give interesting information, the former about the atmosphere that is likely to dominate within a given party, the latter about its impact on society. Thus, if a party recruits almost 100 per cent of its members from the center, it is likely to be gradualist and pragmatic in a change-oriented society, and perhaps conservative; but if at the same time it takes only 10 per cent of the voters from the center it is not likely to have very much impact. We shall refer to the two profiles as the *composition profile* and the *recruitment profile*, respectively, and mainly make use of the latter.

The recruitment profile of a party can be found by comparing the three percentages for the three social groups, periphery, medium, and center. If we assume that there are no ties, then the second percentage can be either higher or lower than the first one, and the third one can be either higher or lower than the second, which gives us the typology of four profiles presented in Table 13 (if we correct for ties we would get nine profiles). Thus, we get four types of political parties according to this simple typology of recruitment patterns. The idea is simply that if one or more of the three sectors into which we have divided society — center, middle, and periphery — is overrepresented, then the implication

Table 13 — A Typology of Recruitment Profiles for Political Parties

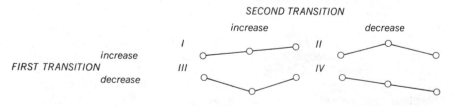

SECOND TRANSITION

increase   decrease

FIRST TRANSITION   increase

decrease

19. See Johan Galtung, "A Structural Theory of Aggression," *Journal of Peace Research*, Vol. 1 (1964), pp. 108–9.

is that this sector shows a particular predilection for the party and, hence, will color the party's activity. And vice versa: if a party launches ideas that correspond to the political culture of one sector more than to those of the others, then this sector will be attracted so that a positive feedback circle of mutual causation results.

A party is an issue-bundle and it is also an aggregate of people, so ideally we should be able to predict both from the general content of the issue-bundle (in terms of age and content of issues) to the recruitment pattern and from the recruitment pattern to the issue-bundle, i.e. to the ideology. Since the former has already been done in hypotheses $H_{4,1-5}$, we shall only do the latter explicitly:

Type I: *The center party*. Since this party is overrepresented in the center, it will be gradualist in its approach in an achievement-oriented society and *status quo* oriented in an ascription-oriented (traditionalist) society. It may accept new ideas, but only provided they have a sufficiently gradualist formulation. In other words, it will tend to be a *conservative* party.

Type II: *The unimodal party*. Since this party is overrepresented in the middle sector, it represents a combination not dealt with in the theory so far. This party avoids both the extreme moralism/absolutism of the periphery and the extreme gradualism/pragmatism of the center. Its ideas are neither particularly old nor particularly new. In other words, it is the ideal middle party, a sort of middle-of-the-road *"people's party"*.

Type III: *The bimodal party*. Since this party is overrepresented both in the center and in the periphery, it represents a complex pattern ideologically. We suggest a subtypology:

IIIa. If the center dominates, it will be more like the center party, but with an emphasis on old issues with a more moralist tinge (for instance of the nationalist or religious varieties).

IIIb. If the periphery dominates, it will be more like the periphery party, but with an emphasis on new issues that can be reconciled with an absolutist/moralist ideology. This combination is particularly important for revolutionary parties.

In either case it is safe to predict that the party will be heavily concerned with manifest and latent dissensus and conflict between the center and periphery factions of the party.

Type IV: *The periphery party*. Since this party is overrepresented in the periphery, it will be absolutist in its approach in both achievement and ascription oriented societies, revolutionary in the former and transcendental in the latter. It may accept new ideas, but only provided they have a sufficiently absolutist formulation. It may be change oriented (revolutionary) or *status quo* oriented like the periphery in general (but not evolution oriented), and it may be difficult or impossible to predict from the recruitment pattern which is which.

With this typology of parties much can be done. For instance, one may derive propositions about the relation between *social structure* (shape of the distribution on the social position index), *party structure* (which combination of parties is present in the society) and *political structure* (structure for decision-making) in a nation.[20] But we shall only use it here to classify Norwegian political parties, and then see how party identification combines with social position to shape foreign policy orientation.

The classification problem is easily solved, since we are commited to the operational definition in terms of recruitment profiles and not to the standard impressionistic account of the "ethos" of a party or its operational counterpart in terms of the outcomes of content analyses. The recruitment profiles of Norwegian parties are given in Table 14. The patterns displayed therein show a remarkable consistency over time and over samples. The classification of each party should, of course, be treated with caution. Nevertheless, it looks as if Norway has one typical center

Table 14 — Recruitment Profiles and Classification of Norwegian Political Parties

(in percentages)

Political Party	SOCIAL POSITION									Type
	1	2	3	4	5	6	7	8	Total	
Labor party (DNA)	27	32	45	37	36	33	14	10	34	*Unimodal*
Conservatives (H)	6	11	10	18	19	23	36	53	20	*Center*
Christian party (Kr. F)	15	6	6	4	6	6	6	3	6	*Periphery*
Agrarian party (SP)	21	8	5	6	7	1	2	0	5	*Periphery*
Socialist party (SF)	0	5	6	3	7	6	4	10	5	*Bimodal*
Liberals (V)	5	6	9	9	7	12	12	13	9	*Center/bimodal*
Communist party (NKP)	3	0	1	1	1	1	0	0	1	*Periphery*

party, the Conservatives, and three periphery parties: one *status quo* oriented (SP, which often cooperates with the Conservatives), one revolutionary (NKP, although it now has a more revisionist ideology), and one Christian (Kr. F., with visions of God's kingdom on earth). Then there are two bimodal parties, the Socialists and the Liberals (we classify

20. For a description and discussion of the Norwegian system of political parties in such terms, see Daniel Katz and Henry Valen, *Political Parties in Norway* (Oslo: Universitetsforlaget, 1964).

21. Johan Galtung, "Center and Periphery in Norway" (forthcoming).

the latter as bimodal with center domination; this is the only case where we use our knowledge of data from other samples that indicate a classification as bimodal party). Finally, there is the unimodal middle party, the Labor party, the largest of them all, which has dominated Norwegian politics from 1935 to 1965 and has held governmental power most of the period. The Labor party's strength may perhaps be seen as an expression of the circumstances that (1) it is the *only* middle party, which means that it can monopolize and exploit fully the kind of middle ideology described above, and (2) that the opposition parties are split into social extremes located at the periphery or at the center (in some cases this split is even found within the parties themselves). As can be seen in Table 15, both change-oriented and *status quo* oriented groups can be found in both the center and in the periphery. Some of the classifications in Table 15 may be disputed. The change orientation of the Christian party in the periphery is less of a political and more of a moral kind. Nevertheless, it represents a kind of latent radicalism, and the total picture presented in Table 15 is one of disarray and factionalism if one thinks of the "opposition" as potentially one group. Superimpose on this the homogeneity of the Labor party and its numerical strength, and one has the structural basis of Norwegian politics 1935–1965 in a nutshell.

Table 15 — Classification of Nonlaborite Political Groups in Norway

	CENTER	PERIPHERY
Status quo oriented	Conservatives	Agrarian party Liberal party, periphery
Change oriented	Liberal party, center Socialist party, center	Christian party Socialist party, periphery Communist party

But our concern is with the role of parties in shaping foreign-policy orientation. In order to examine this relationship, the responses for each party (except for the Communists, there being too few of them in the sample), for each of the three levels of social position (periphery, middle, center) and for each of the ten issues were contrasted. As can be seen in Table 16, the resulting patterns were those predicted by the general theory: new, gradualist issues were overaccepted in the center, old absolutist issues were overaccepted in the periphery regardless of party, color, and so on. But out of the total of sixty patterns, there are of course exceptions to this general trend. Twenty of them are U-shaped or A-shaped, rather than J-shaped as predicted by the theory. Moreover,

Table 16 — Distribution of Responses on Ten Issues by Foreign
Policy Attitude, Party Identification, and Social Position
(in percentages)

Issue	Social position	Labor party	Conser-vatives	Christian party	Agrarian party	Socialist party	Liberals
Refuse	periphery	36	27	40	31	50	70
military	medium	20	22	31	20	50	26
service	center	14	15	0	0	29	12
Less inter-	periphery	14	0	10	8	25	10
national	medium	11	7	6	9	16	4
participation	center	8	9	0	0	6	9
In favor	periphery	43	46	40	54	0	20
of	medium	52	74	47	60	16	52
NATO	center	49	78	71	100	6	67
Against	periphery	83	100	80	69	100	70
atom	medium	83	64	84	74	87	78
bombs	center	83	69	78	100	94	88
In favor	periphery	31	46	30	15	25	60
of	medium	38	55	47	40	31	38
EEC	center	46	75	79	0	18	70
In favor	periphery	69	82	80	62	100	90
of	medium	90	69	66	74	90	82
Khrushchev	center	89	67	79	67	100	88
In favor	periphery	52	73	50	62	50	80
of	medium	73	75	56	63	59	78
peace	center	81	77	78	67	82	88
Merchant	periphery	26	46	40	54	25	10
marine	medium	34	34	44	34	16	44
assistance	center	35	46	57	67	76	61
buy	periphery	19	36	20	23	25	20
textiles	medium	17	20	28	20	19	20
assistance	center	28	38	43	33	53	45
coffee	periphery	29	27	10	31	25	30
prices	medium	28	23	34	43	31	56
assistance	center	43	28	43	67	41	42

even though the general pattern of overselection in center or periphery
is as predicted in fifty-three of the sixty patterns, the seven exceptions
are important. Finally, even though the three groups, periphery, middle,
and center, are the same for all six parties, it is obvious that the degree
of homogeneity/heterogeneity between center and periphery will vary
with the parties. In some parties the center may be very different from

the periphery; in others, it may not. Our task now is to bring some order into this source of variation, and into the deviations from the general trend in the data.

To start with the seven cases where the trends from periphery to center are reversed: *these should be cases where the natural tendency as hypothesized in the theory is counteracted by very strong party stands on the issue.* We say "very strong" because there are very many cases where the trend from periphery to center is against the policy of the party because of the prevalence of the general tendency over weak party stands. Thus, the seven cases that deviate from the trend should be found in heavily debated issues with clear polarization in policies advocated, and this is indeed the case for six of them: the four "bourgeois" parties from periphery to center show decreasing acceptance of inviting Premier Khrushchev to Norway, and the same tendency is revealed in the attitude of the two parties that most violently opposed the European Economic Community (Common Market), the Agrarian party and the Socialists. The seventh case is the case referred to previously, the Conservatives in the center who are in favor of isolationism.

As to the degree of heterogeneity in the party (as measured by subtracting the percentage favoring a policy in the periphery from the corresponding percentage for the center) and the twenty A-shaped and U-shaped distributions, our theory is very simple. It is that the unimodal party will have a homogenizing effect and that the bimodal party will be particularly heterogeneous with a tendency toward A-shaped and U-shaped distributions, since these patterns are already built into the recruitment structure of the parties. What we are saying, in other words, is only that the recruitment structure will condition the attitude pattern. The unimodal party serves as a channel between center and periphery and literally forces them together, so that gross differences in political outlook are reduced; whereas the bimodal pattern may institutionalize and freeze and even increase these differences. In between, we expect,

Table 17 — The Interaction Between Social Position and Party Identification in Shaping Foreign Policy Attitudes

	Average number of A- and U - shaped distributions	Average percentage difference between center and periphery
Unimodal party	0.0	13.2
Center and periphery parties	3.3	17.9
Bimodal parties	5.0	20.9
Total sample	3.3	18.2

are the pure center and periphery parties. The data seem to confirm this

thinking (Table 17). More particularly, in Table 17 it can be seen how bimodal parties force more heterogeneity than there is in the sample in general and how the unimodal party, with its more homogeneous recruitment base, serves as a homogenizer between center and periphery.

CONCLUSION

It is clear from our elaboration of the theory of how social position influences foreign policy orientation, and more particularly of how it interacts with party identification in shaping the foreign policy mood of a nation, that the theory is not, as such, limited to foreign policy issues and that it has a much wider range of applicability. However, as far as foreign policy is concerned, a relatively high predictive power is claimed for the theory, as is the ability to predict changes over time with mobility or psychic mobility of the respondents (change of membership groups or reference groups in other terms) and with changes in social structure. Obviously, further elaboration and testing of this theory will require comparative data from nations with other social structures. Work of this kind is in progress.[22]

APPENDIX: QUESTIONS ASKED
WITH ANSWER DISTRIBUTIONS

1. IF YOU SHOULD DO MILITARY SERVICE TODAY, WHAT KIND OF SERVICE WOULD YOU THEN PREFER?

   16 In an International Force under UN.
    4 In a Force under NATO Command.
   51 In a National Force under Norwegian Command.
   23 Or would you refuse to do any kind of military service?
    6 Do not know.
    0 No answer.

2. WHAT DO YOU THINK NORWAY SHOULD DO TODAY? SHOULD WE ESTABLISH CLOSER TIES WITH

   34 The Nordic Countries.
   17 The NATO Countries.

22. In a three-nation study involving France, Norway, and Poland, with the data being supplied by the Institut Français d'Opinion Publique in Paris, the International Peace Research Institute in Oslo, and the Public Opinion Center of the Polish Radio in Warsaw.

    7 The Nonaligned Countries and the Developing Countries.
    0 The Socialist Countries.
  28 UN.
    9 Or do you feel that Norway should participate less in international cooperation?
    5 Do not know.
    0 No answer.

3. EVERYTHING TAKEN INTO CONSIDERATION, DO YOU CONSIDER IT AN ADVANTAGE FOR NORWAY TO BE A MEMBER OF NATO, OR WOULD IT BE AN ADVANTAGE IF NORWAY WERE NOT A MEMBER OF NATO?

  52 Advantage to be in NATO.
  22 Depends, both.
  20 Advantage not to be in NATO.
   6 Do not know.
   0 No answer.

4. EVERYTHING TAKEN INTO CONSIDERATION, DO YOU THINK IT WOULD BE AN ADVANTAGE TO HAVE ATOMIC WEAPONS IN NORWAY, OR DO YOU THINK IT WOULD BE AN ADVANTAGE NOT TO HAVE ATOMIC WEAPONS IN NORWAY?

   6 Advantage to have atomic weapons.
  13 Depends, both.
  78 Advantage not to have atomic weapons.
   3 Do not know.
   0 No answer.

5. DO YOU OR DO YOU NOT THINK THAT NORWAY SHOULD TIE ITSELF TO THE COMMON MARKET?

  44 Yes, Norway should join in.
  33 No, Norway should not join in.
  23 Do not know.
   0 No answer.

6. DO YOU THINK IT RIGHT OR WRONG THAT PREMIER KHRUSHCHEV MADE A STATE VISIT TO NORWAY?

  80 Right.
  12 Wrong.
   8 Do not know.
   0 No answer.

7. DO YOU THINK IT IS RIGHT THAT A PEACE CORPS WAS ESTABLISHED IN NORWAY, OR WOULD YOU HAVE PREFERRED THAT IT HAD NOT BEEN ESTABLISHED?

  69 Right that it was established.
   8 Would have preferred that it was not established.
  21 Do not know.
   2 No answer.

8. IMAGINE THAT A DEVELOPING COUNTRY ASKED NORWAY FOR ASSISTANCE IN BUILDING A MERCHANT MARINE THAT WOULD TAKE FREIGHT FROM NORWEGIAN SHIPS: DO YOU THINK THAT NORWAY SHOULD GIVE SUCH ASSISTANCE OR NOT?

   36 Norway should assist.
   53 Norway should not assist.
   11 Do not know.
    0 No answer.

9. IMAGINE THAT THE BEST WAY TO HELP A DEVELOPING COUNTRY WOULD BE TO BUY MANUFACTURED GOODS FROM IT, FOR INSTANCE TEXTILES, BUT THAT THIS WOULD LEAD TO DIFFICULTIES FOR NORWEGIAN FACTORIES. DO YOU THINK NORWAY SHOULD BUY SUCH PRODUCTS OR NOT?

   24 Norway should buy.
   66 Norway should not buy.
   10 Do not know.
    0 No answer.

10. IMAGINE THAT A DEVELOPING COUNTRY ASKED NORWAY TO BUY COFFEE AT A PRICE WHICH WOULD GIVE THE WORKERS A DECENT STANDARD OF LIVING AND THAT THE COFFEE WOULD BE TWICE AS EXPENSIVE. DO YOU THINK WE SHOULD BE WILLING TO PAY SUCH A PRICE OR NOT?

   29 We should be willing to do so.
   63 We should not be willing to do so.
    8 Do not know.
    0 No answer.

MASS COMMUNICATION AND FOREIGN POLICY

Bernard C. Cohen

THE media of mass communication, despite their great diversity, have in common the inability to communicate everything that happens and to communicate in one undifferentiated mass. First they must make their choices of the things they consider important. Then they must present these subjects either serially, as in the electronic media, or all at one time but in separate packages, as in the printed media. Thus the media might be regarded as a giant prism, separating the huge mass of public affairs into discrete and salient items—individual beams, so to speak, that illuminate particular areas of public policy. These individual items, or stories, are apparently important connecting links among the primary actors in these events, as well as being the major linkages between them and the much larger number of observers and even would-be participants elsewhere in the political system. Before we can begin to explore the causal connections that may exist between patterns of news coverage and the political processes they help give rise to, or sustain, or alter, we have to know more about such patterns—that is, about the way the

prism operates, how the media separate the mass of public affairs into discrete beams. We shall look, first, at the way the media distinguish between policy questions of internal ("domestic") and external ("foreign") import, and then at the way the media differentiate among the foreign policy issues. After that, we can consider some further steps required to understand the nexus between media behavior and the political processes of foreign policy formulation.

1

Reasonably precise comparisons of media treatment of foreign and domestic policy questions do not exist. The most important reason why they do not, perhaps, may be the difficulties involved in any attempt to define "domestic policy" in a consistent, meaningful, and operational manner. It is hard enough to define "foreign policy" for such purposes — most studies of foreign policy coverage are based on definitions that are *sui generis* — but the variety of internal policy questions and their modes of coverage are even greater. One can more easily compare news of foreign and domestic origin or news of external policy relevance with all other news, but in neither case is one attacking directly the question of the differences and the similarities between the treatment of foreign policy issues and domestic policy issues by the media. In attempting the latter, we have to rely on data that are only suggestive. We have also to rely more on data pertaining to the press than to radio and television, since the difficulties in measuring the content of oral programs and the scant attention the electronic media pay to public policy are both reflected in the paucity of such studies.

The space allocated to foreign affairs news is a minor proportion of the total news space in the average American newspaper. Various studies made at various times have put this figure at between 5 and 8 per cent, and the average number of columns of such news at between 4.4 and 8.[1] While this looks like second-class treatment for foreign affairs, it is not so clear that foreign policy issues are more discriminated against than issues of domestic policy, if by the latter we mean substantive policy problems, proposals, or alternatives under discussion at the national level. Table 1 comes close enough to separating these classifications of news coverage to suggest that news of national public policies of all kinds is limited in comparison with news of other kinds and other political arenas. What are some of the conditions or circumstances that lead to a similar functioning of the media in the cases of foreign and domestic policy issues?

1. For a summary of these figures see Bernard C. Cohen, *The Press and Foreign Policy* (Princeton: Princeton University Press, 1963), pp. 115–18.

Table 1*—Average Number of Column Inches
Published in fifty-one U.S. Daily Newspapers

Local news	253
Sports news	178
International news†	106
National news	97
Washington, D.C. news	64
Society news	55
State news	42

*Adapted from a table in *The Flow of the News* (Zurich: International Press Institute, 1953), p. 63. The fifty-one newspapers and their manner of selection and their dates are listed on pp. 240–42.
†Includes news of an "international character" originating in Washington, D.C.

Firstly, there is, in the general orientation of newsmen toward news, a perspective that conceives of news as being a single commodity, as it were, irrespective of its source or subject matter, and a comparable orientation toward the reader as an average type having homogenized interests. In this context, any single item of news is in competition with all other items for the passing interest of all readers, and so all news items must be judged by the same general criteria. In this competition, news about foreign policy and national domestic policy problems suffer some of the same disabilities: They are frequently complex in nature and slow to take shape and run through their course, so that the "news values"—conflict, drama, and so on—they might contain are rarely sharp. In these circumstances, one more postponement of the United Nation's dues-and-voting problem or the latest thoughts on ways to alleviate the United States' balance-of-payments problem are less newsworthy than the latest accident or murder, or even the vagaries of the weather.

Secondly, there is no special avenue of recruitment, or type of training, or path of experience that differentiates the reporters and editors who handle foreign policy news from those who handle domestic affairs. If a man is a good performer in one arena, it is generally believed that he will be a good performer in another, and so the skills and orientations and "news sense" that have developed in one field of public affairs are subsequently transferred to another. Men have come to foreign policy reporting from diverse backgrounds, and, although movement out of this field has, on the whole, been less frequent than movement in during the past two decades, they also leave foreign policy reporting for other fields of reporting or editorial work. Some recent shifts on the staff of *The New York Times* are illustrative: A. M. Rosenthal, from a succession of posts as a foreign correspondent to the metropolitan editorship; Anthony Lewis, from years of reporting on the Supreme Court and on developments in constitutional law to be head of the London Bureau;

E. W. Kenworthy, from approximately eight years of covering the State Department, to the Congress.

Thirdly, the allocation of "beats" among newsmen results in a specialization of *institutional coverage*—what Rosenau has called "horizontal political systems"—rather than a specialization of *issue coverage*—"vertical systems."[2] Reporters handle issues chiefly as these swim in and out of the institutions it is their responsibility to cover. For the State Department correspondent these specializations converge, in the sense that only foreign policy questions come up in that place. But when a foreign policy question also involves the White House and the Congress, and in certain circumstances the Pentagon, the convergence is slight. Foreign policy is covered at each of these sites by different correspondents who are mixing foreign and domestic policy reporting in various proportions. A comparable lack of specialization is found among foreign correspondents, as well. The reporter who is stationed abroad, usually in a capital city, is in somewhat the same position as the Washington correspondent for an American newspaper. Where the bureau has only a few men, they are all generalists who cover the full range of the news that comes out of that capital. While all news from London, for example, is by definition "foreign," it is not all relevant to foreign policy questions of interest to either the British or the American government. The coverage of the Churchill funeral is a case in point, and the coverage of a steel nationalization debate would be another. Here, too, is a mixing of foreign affairs news with domestic, an assimilation of both to a common standard of news and thus to a common functioning of the media.

These, then, are the factors that lead to similar treatment of foreign and domestic policy questions in the media. But we should not stress the similarities so much that we overlook some important differences in the handling of these two policy arenas. Although, as we said earlier, newsmen conceive of news as, in one sense, a single commodity, there is simultaneously a conviction among them, seemingly much stronger, that foreign policy is the "big story"—as the war was the big story from 1939 to 1945, and as the Roosevelt years in Washington were, before that. This judgment about foreign policy in our time is made repeatedly by reporters, and it is given tangible expression by editors in the form of prominent and extensive front-page newspaper space and leading spots in broadcast news. This greater salience and visibility of foreign policy issues in the media is in fact its chief distinguishing feature, for, as we have seen, foreign policy is not the acknowledged big story in

2. James N. Rosenau, "Pre-Theories and Theories of Foreign Policy," in R. Barry Farrell (ed.), *Approaches to Comparative and International Politics* (Evanston: Northwestern University Press, 1966), p. 74.

terms of the volume of coverage. This juxtaposition of acknowledged importance and continued prominence with comparatively scant volume suggests that some restraint is being exercised on the production of foreign policy news that is not also being applied to other kinds of news. The apparent sources of this restraint are found not in any one place but rather at every major stage in the production of news, through the shared and interacting expectations of the news producers.

In the first instance, the editors and publishers and station-owners who determine the make-up of newspapers and the kind and amount of broadcast news operate, for the most part, in the belief that the average reader's homogenized interests have only a marginal place for foreign policy. Partly this is intuitive—a feeling that people's interest in the problems of the environment decreases steadily as the arena enlarges from the core of the local community; partly it is projective—most of these men are themselves locally oriented, politically, economically and socially, and so they assume everyone else is, also; and partly it is intellective—the evidence that circulates among owners and news managers concerning exposure patterns confirms that reading, listening to, or watching foreign policy coverage is an activity of a very small minority.[3] The balance sheet is a matter of some importance to the owners and managers, and so the preferences of the greater number most often prevail. (What are generally called the better newspapers in the United States, and the broadcast programs having the greatest critical esteem, are those directed not at the average reader but at the minority who is interested in public-affairs questions.)

Because there is not a mass market for foreign policy news, there are few reporters who are paid to gather it—and these are keenly aware that they are working at a competitive disadvantage so far as readership is concerned. The American correspondents who cover foreign countries and those who cover foreign policy developments in the United States are employed largely by the national radio and television networks, the major telegraphic news agencies, and a dozen or so large metropolitan newspapers. And all but a very few of them are in constant competition with the more entertaining or diverting features of their medium. Their job is additionally complicated by the fact that they confront fewer sources than do reporters who work in the domestic policy area. Issues of domestic policy arise in agencies throughout the executive branch and have their supporters and opponents scattered through the Congress and in private interest groups, whereas foreign policy questions usually have a narrower set of sources in the White House, State Department, or Defense Department–i.e., a more clearly defined and restricted

3. Cf. Alfred O. Hero, *Mass Media and World Affairs* (Boston: World Peace Foundation, 1959), esp. pp. 80–81.

"establishment"–and a narrower base of informed and specialized legislators in the Congress. Furthermore, on domestic questions, coverage by
the media is sought as an important adjunct to one's political strategies,[4]
while publicity in the foreign policy field is on the whole rather more
likely to be shunned on grounds of security or national-interest considerations.[5] The output of foreign policy coverage thus has its constraints,
too, to match the inhibitions of the managerial personnel.

The interacting and reinforcing nature of these pressures on foreign
policy coverage show up in the disproportionate attrition to which it is
subject in comparison with other kinds of news. In a study of the flow of
AP news from its start on the trunk wire to its finish in the hands of the
reader, Scott Cutlip discovered that foreign news of all types sustained
larger cuts at all points in the transmission process than did other classifications of news.[6] And we saw earlier how the process of attrition continues at the hands of the average reader, supporting the editors in their
preferences for other kinds of news. Thus, despite those factors in the
news-gathering business that lead to a failure to differentiate foreign
from domestic policy questions, there is strong evidence that rather
different standards, expectations, and judgments are in force throughout
the news-evaluation process in a deliberate effort to minimize differences,
to keep foreign policy coverage generally in the same ballpark as domestic
policy news.

2

Like the prior distinction between foreign policy and domestic policy
news coverage, distinctions within the foreign policy news area have
not been uniformly pursued in studies of media behavior. Such studies
generally refer to "foreign" or "international" news inclusively; and
where some attempt is made to differentiate among kinds of international
news, the classifications employed tend to be the ones commonly used
in the analysis of domestic news – i.e., foreign relations, politics, religion,
education, and the like – rather than issue-oriented categories. Almost
as wide of our mark are the comparisons made of the national origins of
foreign news,[7] since the news from each country may span the full reach

4. Cf. Douglass Cater, *The Fourth Branch of Government* (Boston: Houghton
Mifflin Co., 1959).

5. Cohen, *op. cit.*, pp. 169–207. Cf. also Sanford H. Winston, "The Generals and the
Press," unpub. M.S. thesis, School of Journalism, University of Wisconsin, 1965, esp.
pp. 106–53.

6. Scott M. Cutlip, "Content and Flow of AP News – From Trunk to TTS to Reader,"
Journalism Quarterly, Vol. XXXI (Fall 1954), 434–46.

7. See, e.g., the data reported in *The Flow of the News* (Zurich: International Press
Institute, 1953), pp. 214–16.

of news classifications. This approach would permit us to draw a map of the world as it is perceived by any communications medium in any given time period and to compare the maps of different media and of different time periods. Such comparisons could serve some useful purposes — e.g., they could test for persistent geographical biases — but in themselves they would not shed much light on the variability of media behavior from one type of foreign policy issue to another. Here, too, then, we are obliged to work with fragmentary and suggestive data; but what there is indicates that coverage varies greatly from one foreign policy issue-area to another and from one time period to another, and for reasons that suggest coherent patterns.

Table 2 shows a comparison of the coverage of a number of post-World War II foreign policy issues in both *The New York Times* and the Philadelphia *Inquirer*. Despite the large differences in the amount of space given to foreign policy by these two quite different kinds of news-papers, we can see a striking similarity in the relative emphasis each

Table 2 — Coverage of Selected Foreign Policy Issues in The New York Times *(NYT) and the Philadelphia* Inquirer *(PI) for Nine Months Prior to Legislative or Executive Action**

Issue	Column Inches		Percentage of coverage on front page	
	NYT	PI	NYT	PI
Recognition of Israel, 1948	18,728	6,062	14.4	30.0
Greek-Turkish Aid, 1947	14,519	2,736	11.2	38.6
European Recovery Program, 1948	11,740	4,453	19.3	31.8
North Atlantic Treaty, 1949	7,955	2,012	22.0	28.1
Aid to China, 1948	6,458	733	7.4	32.3
Mutual Defense Assistance Pro-gram, 1949	4,820	1,536	25.8	31.8
First Renewal of ERP, 1949	4,198	1,185	17.3	26.1
Renewal of Reciprocal Trade Agreements Act, 1949	1,124	174	9.5	19.5

*This comparison includes news, editorials, and columns; it omits texts, digests, letters, Sunday supplements and other special features. These data were compiled by the members of the Graduate Research Seminar of the Wood-row Wilson School of Public and International Affairs, Princeton University, during 1951–52. The data in the first column appeared in Bernard C. Cohen, *The Political Process and Foreign Policy: The Making of the Japanese Peace Settlement* (Princeton: Princeton University Press, 1957), Table VII, p. 113. Also included there is a comparable figure for *The New York Times'* coverage of the Japanese Peace Settlement, 1952: 3,894 column inches.

paper has accorded to the several issues. Furthermore, we find from Table 2 that while front-page coverage may give a slightly different rank order to issues than total coverage does, it does not greatly alter the range of emphasis given to the various issues. In addition, to the extent that the salience of an issue in the political community is a function of its display on the front page as well as of the total amount of space given

to it, we might note that the high proportion of front-page coverage in the Philadelphia *Inquirer* gave these issues a prominence in that paper more nearly like their prominence in *The New York Times*.

If media attention to foreign policy issues has any significance for the political processes that develop around these issues, then the timing of that attention is likely to be significant also. In the lifespan of any single issue, there is likely to be great variability in media attention over time. Table 3 shows the distribution of coverage of one issue, the Japanese peace settlement, in two newspapers over a period of a year. The high point in coverage came in September, 1951, during the San Francisco Conference at which the treaty was signed; but during the following six months, which preceded the Senate's hearings and ratification debate, media coverage almost disappeared. It is not being suggested that the distribution of events and of coverage in this case are in any sense typical; rather, greater effort is needed to discover how the timing of press attention to a variety of issues relates to the optimum formal opportunities to participate in the development of those issues.

Table 3 — Coverage of the Japanese Peace Treaty Issue, by Month, in The New York Times *and the* San Francisco Chronicle*

	Total Column Inches	
Month	NYT	SFC
1951		
April	659	161
May	370	133
June	475	103
July	670	319
August	1,391	745
September	3,312	2,939
October	162	89
November	93	33
December	63	33
1952		
January	306	139
February	184	47
March (to 21st)†	177	81

*Adapted from Cohen, *The Political Process and Foreign Policy*, Figure 1, p. 115.
†i.e., to end of Senate ratification debate.

It is important for our purposes to know whether these differences and similarities in the extent, character, and timing of coverage of foreign policy issues within and between newspapers are more or less accidental—i.e., unrelated to any consistent judgments about issues or audiences—or whether they have their roots in fundamental, persistent, institutionally related phenomena. It is our contention here that the latter is the case; that the treatment of different foreign policy issues by the media is ultimately predictable because its sources lie in coherent and

comprehensible patterns of attitudes and behavior regarding these issues and public interest in them. We are, to be sure, a long way from the requisite understanding of these patterns and their mechanisms; here we can only sketch them as they now seem to look. In the final section of this chapter we will discuss the research necessary to sharpen our understanding of them and to clarify the circumstances and conditions under which they become relevant. We will start with those factors that appear to be the most stable and persistent and conclude with those that are subject to greater short-term fluctuations.

News Values

On their face, news values would seem to be too dependent on the intuitions and subjective judgments of newsmen to be treated as a stable factor accounting for media differentiation among foreign policy issues. Paradoxical as it may seem, however, the conventions about what is news and about what subjects people are likely to be interested in, imprecise as they are, run so deeply through the news business as to constitute its central unifying element. There is first of all the convention — or mystique — that helps to determine what is the chief news at any given point in time. We noted earlier that foreign policy as a large classification was regarded as the "big story" in the post-war years. In a similar fashion, there are common judgments about what is also called the big story within the foreign policy classification; this is the foreign policy subject that generally commands prime space over varying periods of time, with specific headlines and news stories being written about the day-to-day events within that issue-area. The corollary of the big story is that other problems are smaller stories, assigned to subordinate, if not inferior, position for the duration of the cycle. If we go back a half-dozen years, we may recall that for many months after the Soviet's six-month "ultimatum" in November, 1958, about returning sovereignty to East Germany, Berlin was the big story and anything connected with it — or anything that could be made to look as if it were connected with it — was almost automatically news.[8] Before that, for some time, it was Formosa, Quemoy, and Matsu, so that for months we were able to keep book on the shelling of Quemoy from the mainland — an event that still takes place, unnoticed. Subsequently it was the Congo, then Cuba, and for some time now it has been Vietnam. Developments in other places and concerning other

8. Cf. the following exchange, from a television program, "Washington and the Press," number 2 in the series, "The Press and the People," produced by WGBH-TV, Boston, Mass., with a grant from the Fund for the Republic:

"Man: . . . What would you say is the number 1 source of important information right now? What is the big running story at this time in Washington?

"(James) Reston: The primary story at the present time, of course, is Berlin."

Edited transcripts of these television programs have been published by the Fund for the Republic.

matters do get published, of course, but the volume and prominence of their coverage is a function of "who is on first," so to speak.

Secondly there are the general conventions as to what is news at all points in time. These judgments are not generated spontaneously in men who are recruited to or accepted for the news business; rather, there are ample mechanisms in the profession that encourage, refine, and sustain them.[9] It is this professional institutional support for these news values that makes them such an important factor in the differential treatment of issues. The conventions themselves help to define what will be the big story at any one period, and what will replace it, and when; they also shape the content of the news on a day-to-day basis, both within the context of a particular big story and independently of it. We can look at these conventions most appropriately in the context of the issues whose coverage is compared in Table 2. Twenty-one foreign affairs reporters, columnists, and broadcasters were asked about these issues during 1951–52, some two to five years after they had taken place. Eighteen of them discussed at least one of the issues in terms of its appropriate, manifest, or relevant news criteria. These *post-hoc* judgments are few in number, and are less reliable, to be sure, than judgments obtained in a process of determining why newsmen are currently choosing to report A in preference to B. Nevertheless, they are useful because they do bear directly on issues of different magnitude and salience, and they were offered in ignorance of the quantitative differences that were reported in Table 2. The eighteen interviews contain sixty-six codable references to news values in these eight foreign policy issues; these are combined into six major classifications in Table 4. The entries in each

Table 4 — News Values Perceived in Eight Foreign Policy Cases
(in number of references)*

News Values	Israel	G-T Aid	ERP '48	ERP '49	NATO	MDAP	China Aid	RTA, '49
Reader interest	3	1	2	0	0	0	3	6
Conflict	3	1	0	0	0	1	2	2
Novelty	0	1	4	1	0	1	1	1
Importance	0	1	4	0	1	0	2	1
Drama	0	5	2	0	0	0	0	1
Difficulty	1	0	0	0	0	0	1	5
Other	1	3	0	0	1	0	3	1

*These data were derived from interviews conducted by members of the Graduate Research Seminar of the Woodrow Wilson School of Public and International Affairs, Princeton University, during 1951–52.

new-value category are both positive and negative — that is, they include, e.g., both the presence of conflict situations as reasons for covering a

9. Cf. Cohen, *The Press and Foreign Policy*, pp. 54–104.

story, and the absence of conflict situations as reasons for not covering a story. Bearing these dimensions in mind, Table 4 suggests that the correspondents' judgments about news values conform rather closely to the judgments implied by the comparative coverage figures. The three cases that received the greatest coverage in both *The New York Times* and the Philadelphia *Inquirer* were the recognition of Israel, the Truman Doctrine, and the initiation of the Marshall Plan. In the case of Israel, the criteria most often mentioned were conflict and reader interest — which in this case was explicitly defined as the interest of the Jewish population in the metropolitan areas. In the case of the Truman Doctrine the dominant news value was the sudden, dramatic development of the issue. And in the case of the European Recovery Plan, the novelty of the policy departure and its basic importance were the features most often stressed by reporters. There were thirty-two references to news values for these three issues; twenty-seven were positive in character, citing the presence of the news value as the reason for treating these as big stories.

At the other end of the scale in terms of coverage was the 1949 renewal of the Reciprocal Trade Agreements Act. Here the chief criteria were the difficulty of explaining the issue and the presumed low level of reader interest; of the seventeen references in this one case, fifteen were negative. Aid to China, which was fourth from the bottom in *The New York Times'* coverage and next to the bottom in the *Inquirer's*, reflects a similar split in the news judgments of reporters: eight of the twelve references were negative. The remaining three issues were scarcely remarked upon by the reporters. Two of them, the Military Defense Assistance Program and the first renewal of the Marshall Plan in 1949 were at the lower end of the coverage scale, suggesting that they may represent a type of foreign policy development which has routine coverage precisely because it is a foreign policy development (i.e., part of the big story) and not because it has any specific character as news. (The only remark directed by a correspondent toward the renewal of the Marshall Plan was that the issue "was not new.")

The reader can scarcely overlook the subjective nature of these news values. In varying degrees, these represent personal judgments by correspondents concerning the specific tastes and interests of the reading public and the import of specific foreign policy developments. The most pervasive of these news values is "reader interest," not only because it shows up most often in the references of newsmen, but also because several of the other criteria, notably "conflict," "difficulty," and "drama," themselves contain implicit judgments about the reading tastes of the American people. We noted earlier that both editors and reporters work in the belief, for which there is much empirical support, that foreign

policy is in general a peripheral interest of the average newspaper reader and that his attention can be gained, however briefly, only by playing on the basic human emotions or involvements. But these assumptions about aggregate reader interest in foreign affairs do not give the reporter many guides to the specific variations in reader interest in different kinds of foreign policy issues. Thus, the correspondents are obliged to interpret the general assumption in all specific policy cases. The point to be made here is that the specific interpretations and applications acquire a large measure of substantiation from past experience because they are, in an important way, self-confirming. Most interested persons do not respond to public affairs until the media have made them into events, and the hypothesis may be hazarded that the response is in some measurable way directly related to the size and shape of the event thus created. Where journalists decide that there is insufficient public interest to warrant even low coverage of a foreign policy question (as in the Reciprocal Trade Agreements case, above), the public response to the "nonevent" can hardly help but be low, confirming the newsmen in the wisdom of their judgment. In this way the general belief that the public is only peripherally interested is translated into widely shared understandings among newsmen about the particular foreign policy issues that should be given the big-story treatment and those that should be given only a passing glance. But this only narrows the problem of choice, it does not eliminate it. What other factors help to account for the treatment of issues that are not so unequivocally disposed of by their "inherent news values?"

Pressures for Standardization

The news media in the foreign affairs field involve hundreds of people working in a decentralized news-gathering system, independently making judgments about the appeal and the importance of passing events. The variety of their product is theoretically almost boundless, yet each of them believes that "the news" is a reasonably determinate and objective quantity that he can recognize and report. This is so because the theoretical variety is reduced by some built-in devices and procedures that standardize the treatment of news in the thousands of news outlets; and the very processes of standardization help to cast foreign policy issues into molds that further differentiate them.

The means of standardization succeed precisely because there are pressures for standardization—that is to say, because newsmen believe that news is objective and recognizable. This belief flourishes because there is only one authoritative definition of news: news is what appears in the newspapers and goes out over the air waves. Newsmen thus are obliged continuously to measure their sense of what is important and appealing against the yardstick of the latest edition; if it is already "in

the news," or "at the top of the news," then it commands their attention. This pressure to conform is both the cause and consequence of the news agencies' greatest contribution to standardization, the "news budget." This is the agency editor's prediction of what will be the most important stories among the day's (or the night's) crop. Such a prediction, once in the hands of people who are looking for the professional standard, becomes a self-fulfilling prophecy. The editors thus publish these stories in the predicted order, and the correspondents, recognizing the news, make their rounds and write their stories accordingly.

Without denying the claims of new issues to break in on this cycle, it is clear that they suffer at least a temporary disadvantage. (And if the new issue is not a persistent one, the disadvantage becomes permanent.) When reporters respond to a manifest definition of the important issues and send confirming evidence back to the news agencies and the editorial desks, a process akin to Rostow's "take-off" occurs: The big story gets even bigger because reporters flock to it in increasing numbers, editors have more of it to print and continue to give it a big play, and reader interest has been created or stimulated by the coverage. The period of self-sustaining flight varies greatly, as we can see by the coverage data presented above, but while it is going on, other flights have been cancelled, or are sitting on the runway waiting for their chance to take off, or they are already flying but are off the radar screens.

We do not know the decision-rules that govern these crucial standard-setting and priority-establishing choices; but in the absence of such knowledge we can assume that they include in some way the application of familiar news values to the range of foreign policy subjects being written about by correspondents at any point in time. One can even hypothesize that these predictions, too, are based in part on an extensive scrutiny of already-published news—why should news-agency editors be immune to the culture of their trade, even though they play a large role in shaping what they subsequently scrutinize?

There is an important sense in which this whole process of standardizing news judgments is circular: Reporters write stories after taking their cues from the newspapers; editors make up their newspapers from cues supplied by news-agency gatekeepers; the latter supply their cues, presumably, after seeing what reporters and editors have been doing; and each of these groups makes independent judgments about newsworthiness by applying news values that will conform to the news values applied by the others.

But the news process is not totally circular, of course. A given news story does not survive forever. Nor are news values simply projections of what one's professional colleagues think is news, in an infinite regression. On the contrary, there is a steady stream of inputs which derive,

in the first instance, from reporters applying news values to—i.e., making intuitive judgments about the drama, novelty, reader interest, and so on, in—events or developments that are current within his beat, and, in the second instance, from gatekeepers who subject these accounts to their own independent and more authoritative, though equally subjective, application of the same general standards. Each member of the profession is free to make his own translation of news values in specific circumstances, but the product does not become news in any generally accepted sense until these translations or judgments have been reciprocated, and the circle of standardization has been closed.

Geographical Distribution of Correspondents

Another source of the differential treatment of issues lies in the distribution of foreign correspondents around the globe and in the distribution of *expertise* that results. This particular factor is less stable than those discussed above, since the distribution at any point in time is the result of preferences, convenience, or even governmental actions, rather than of slower moving doctrines and attitudes within the journalism fraternity. (Furthermore, it should be noted that the geographical factor does not seem to have accounted for much of the difference among the issues that are reported in Table 2 above.) What is important from our point of view are the patterns of concentration and of omission that seem to have a bearing on the public perception and discussion of foreign policy questions. and, through these, on the governmental allocation of policy attention.

Without going into great detail, we can note several structural features of the contemporary distribution of U.S. correspondents who are working for American media abroad. First, there is a large concentration of American correspondents in the capital cities of Western Europe; a recent estimate puts the proportion of American foreign correspondents located in Western Europe at about 50 per cent of all full-time U.S. correspondents abroad (about 515 in 1963).[10] Second, there are relatively few such correspondents in Latin America, Africa, and the Middle East— about 25 per cent in all three areas. Third, there is the total absence of U.S. correspondents in Communist China, for reasons of governmental policy at both ends. One can understand the attractions that Western European cities hold for American correspondents and can recognize their familiarity with Western European languages and political insti-

---

10. John Wilhelm gives detailed figures on the distribution of overseas correspondents in "The Re-appearing Foreign Correspondent: A World Survey," *Journalism Quarterly*, Vol. 40, No. 2 (Spring, 1963), pp. 147–68. See also Frederick T.C. Yu and John Luter, "The Foreign Correspondent and His Work," *Columbia Journalism Review*, Vol. 3, No. 1 (Spring, 1964), pp. 5–12.

tutions. One can also appreciate the extraordinary difficulties that reporters, who are for the most part untrained generalists, have in learning
to understand and describe unfamiliar and complex political systems
and political situations in terms that are meaningful to American audiences, as well as to get along in exotic foreign languages. But this
situation poses the problem, so far as the comparative treatment of issues
is concerned, that we are not getting alerted to the developing issues of
the developing world (not to speak of the Communist world, or parts
of it) so much as we are getting filled in on them after the situation
"breaks" and correspondents are then flown in from their more comfortable berths elsewhere.

Idiosyncratic Factors

Least stable of all the factors that account for the differential treatment
of foreign policy issues are the personal interests and predilections
of the correspondents and editors, and of their sources in government
offices. It is difficult to specify the level of importance to attach to these
idiosyncratic factors; they are too obvious to be ignored, yet it is possible
that they largely cancel out in the total processes of news production
in the United States. Foreign policy reporting in the United States is
chiefly the work of large news bureaus, where men are permitted at least
some luxury in indulging their special area or policy interests. Despite
their general foreign policy assignments, one man will pay special
attention to the Near East, another to the Soviet Union, another to trade
problems, and so on. Each of these will do so at a time when the relevant
sources of information in one State Department office will talk freely
to reporters, while those in another will talk to no one. It is hard to
avoid the conclusion that insofar as these personal predilections account
for a reporter's product on any given day, their ultimate impact on
policy coverage cannot be systematically accounted for; too much additionally depends on the prominence given to issues by news-agency
and newspaper editors and on the pressures for standardization that
quickly establish the first or early statement or interpretation of an issue.
We can safely conclude that these personal factors are important, in
the sense that experience shows that governments may become deeply
absorbed in questions that the media seized on as the result of the whim
or the interest of a single correspondent and his possibilities of access;[11]
but we cannot predict which reporter or which whim will rise to the top
on which day. We might, however, after further study, be able to specify

11. For example, Herbert Matthews' celebrated interview with Fidel Castro in the
mountains of Oriente Province in February 1957 and his subsequent coverage of the
Cuban rebellion, and E. W. Kenworthy's report, in October 1958, of the flow of critical
mail to the State Department on the Quemoy issue, both in *The New York Times.*

the conditions or circumstances that seem to favor the idiosyncratic; but the problems connected with such research would be enormous and the payoffs slight.

3

Our discussion so far should have made it clear that the media treat foreign policy issues differently from one another and that a number of identifiable factors contribute to this variable treatment. We are properly more interested in specific causal relationships, however, and in their larger policy consequences, and on these scores we can only conclude that the land is virgin and inviting. Some of the more important problems, both of conceptualization and of empirical research, can be spelled out here.

1. There is a pressing need for good data on media coverage. Comparative data on the content of, and the space and play given to, foreign policy and domestic policy news, over a large range of issues and of media, are called for in order to get extensive and reliable measures of the processing of different kinds of issues. The necessary research enterprises would be assisted by—and it would in turn help substantially to refine—a typology of issues that would bring purpose to and impose limits on the study of individual cases. As is true of all work with particular cases, the first requirement is to move, via a typology, from the level of unique instances to the level of aggregative experiences so that generalizations properly may be drawn.

2. We also need to address ourselves to the question, "What difference does it make if the media work differently in different issue-areas?" At the least, we need to know with some confidence the policy-process consequences of differential media treatment of issues. We need to explore the concept of "salience:" to study the causal relations between different kinds of coverage—different in terms of content, timing, location, headlines, and so forth—and different levels and degrees of awareness of issues. The data on the Japanese peace settlement case suggest that where the volume of coverage is low and where the layout has no prominence, the public is hardly aware of the issue,[12] but this hypothesis needs to be tested more widely and systematically—and, if possible, experimentally.[13] We also need to know more about the systemic con-

12. Cf. Cohen, *The Political Process and Foreign Policy*: *The Making of the Japanese Peace Settlement* (Princeton: Princeton University Press, 1957), esp. Chaps. 3 and 6.
13. It would also be of some interest to compare the results of AIPO's periodic question, "What do you regard as the biggest issue, or problem, facing the government in Washington today?" with the character and extent of representative media coverage of policy issues for a specified period in advance of each survey. Or perhaps the responses in particular sampling units might be compared with the content of local media outlets, for more reliable results.

sequences at the governmental level of varying degrees of press attention and of public attention to issues. One way of doing this might be to spot some developing issues before they have qualified as news stories, and then, with the necessary cooperation of the relevant government agencies, to observe the impact on policy-making institutions of substantial qualitative and quantitative changes in media treatment of those issues. (It is hard to believe, for example, that policy making in the Bureau of African Affairs in the State Department is the same since Africa has been regarded as a place where news is happening, as it was prior to that development.)

3. The above discussion treats the content of media coverage as one dimension among many in the variable treatment of issues. Such an assumption needs to be scrutinized closely: What is the relative importance of content as against volume, location, headlines, and so on, in shaping awareness of and reactions to issues? In their study, *American Business and Public Policy*, Bauer, Pool, and Dexter argue that the content of private representations to Congress has little direct substantive effect on congressmen. "We find that the net effect of communications was to heighten attention to an issue, rather than to convey specific content about it."[14] It would be important to know if the same were true in the area that concerns us — i.e., that the precise content of news stories is less important than a host of other characteristics of coverage in determining its impact on the policy-making process.

4. A special aspect of the systemic relationship between the news media and the foreign policy-making process that deserves attention is the way that relationship functions in those issues we call "crises" (or do the reporters themselves attach the label?). The assumption above was that the more elaborate and extensive the media discussion of a policy issue, the more elaborate and extensive the policy process involved in its resolution. We know, however, that issues carrying extremely high costs and risks ("crises"?), while they draw reporters like flies, simultaneously disengage both Congress and the public in a political sense, leaving initiative and discretion in the hands of officials in the executive branch. The relationships here among policy-makers, media, Congress, and the public need to be examined in detail — not least of all to discover what differentiates such a crisis-type issue from a noncrisis-type issue, and the possible role that the media themselves might play in the process of differentiation.

5. Additional research of an increasingly precise nature is required into the perspectives and behavior of both newsgatherers and policy-level

14. Raymond A. Bauer, Ithiel de Sola Pool, and Lewis Anthony Dexter, *American Business and Public Policy: The Politics of Foreign Trade* (New York: Atherton Press, 1963), p. 413.

news sources.[15] With respect to the reporters (and we can include newspaper and news-agency editors here also), we want to know more about the way issues are perceived, and the processes by which news values are deduced from or imputed to them. Some effort will have to be made to adapt the survey instrument to this purpose. A major problem arises from the fact that the processes involved in news-gathering and news-determination are not wholly conscious ones, and thus they do not easily lend themselves to discovery by standardized, direct-answer questions. As for news sources, we need, among other things, to identify and locate in the political establishment those policy officials who systematically cultivate contacts with correspondents. It would be important to discover, for example, whether certain offices in the State Department customarily attract or even recruit personnel with this predisposition, just as organizations of other kinds attract and recruit members possessing like orientations or personality characteristics.

6. Earlier we described the leading issue at any given moment as having a period of self-sustained flight, when all the pressures combined to keep it on the upward or level portions of its track. But the flight paths or trajectories are not the same for all foreign policy issues; some are very short, others are long, some peak rapidly and then fall away, others trace a relative smooth arc. Are these differences largely unpredictable, i.e., attributable chiefly to the accidents of competition from other stories, or are there discernible patterns bearing on the characteristics of the issues themselves? There is a need to relate types of issues and their periods in flight with other characteristics in order to learn more about the life-cycle of foreign policy issues.

7. Finally, it seems appropriate to point out how useful it would be if there were increased areas of collaboration between students of journalism and of political science. The descriptive literature of journalism is enormous, and journalism students are constantly producing new studies that come close to bearing on the questions raised above. A closer relationship between these two disciplines might well produce answers a great deal sooner than political scientists are likely to produce them acting alone.

15. Dan D. Nimmo's *Newsgathering in Washington*, (New York: Atherton Press, 1963), despite its limitations, points in the right direction.

VOTING AND FOREIGN POLICY

Warren E. Miller

I N an age not lacking in challenges, the conduct of foreign policy today constitutes the greatest challenge for the American ideals of popular self-government. Each year of the nuclear age has seen an increase in the potential for ultimate disaster stemming from miscalculations in foreign policy. Each year has also seemingly marked an increase in the complexities surrounding foreign policy decisions. But rising stakes, increasing odds, and the accompanying demand for better comprehension of larger quantities of information have not been preceded or followed by any very apparent change in the society's capacity for self-government. To be sure, the media of mass communications now bring news from afar—be it Washington or Moscow—more swiftly and in a form palatable to more people. Less dramatically, the presumed advantages of more years of formal education are possessed by more and more citizens, and rates of participation in national elections are rising slowly from the ebb of the war years. However much these and other indicators of political well-being are cause for rejoicing, there is little assurance that

they are changing the quality of American electoral politics at a pace commensurate with the challenge.

In a strict sense there is, of course, little firm evidence for evaluating the fit between challenge and response. Rosenau has aptly observed that decision-making and opinion-making are conceptually separate components of the opinion-policy relationship that presumably characterizes our process of government. He wisely suggests that the functioning of either component, as well as the existence of more than a null relationship between them, need not be assumed but should be the object of empirical study.[1] Events may prove that American foreign policy decision-making in the middle of the twentieth century was up to the mark in meeting an awesome challenge. It is possible that other events may prove that this essential success was the result of the functioning of a political system in which a mass electorate actually exercised crucially relevant evaluations of policy and policy-makers and wisely chose the needed alternatives. However unlikely the second possibility, the family of events involved in the popular determination, or nondetermination, of public policy are not of the same manifest, self-evident order as those of the first statement.

Understanding the role of an electorate in the authoritative allocation of values must rest on information describing the interaction of electors and elected. If the elected choose to support wise policy alternatives while thinking their constituents are urging contrary decisions, some version of self-government is operating—but it is not a version extolled in works of democratic political theory. Wise decisions by policy-makers who are mistaken in assuming they are deciding in accord with popular sentiment are doubtless more numerous, no less wise for their incidence or incidental perversity, but, again, poor evidence of the "proper" functioning of representative government. Nevertheless, knowing something of the fit between the electoral intent of the mass public and the subsequent authoritative act of the elected official is necessary as a part of any assessment of the functioning of public opinion in the formulation of public policy—foreign or otherwise.

The appraisal of electoral intent, in turn, may embrace the full range of antecedents of the electoral act. The developmental sequence may be held to begin with the formation of public opinion on matters of foreign policy, then to proceed to the consequences of such opinion for mass electoral behavior, to move on to the impact of elections on foreign policy decision-making, and to conclude by beginning again with the influence of foreign policy events on the subsequent evolution of public opinion.

1. James N. Rosenau, *Public Opinion and Foreign Policy*, (New York: Random House, 1961), Chap. 3, see especially page 21.

The following analysis is intended to illuminate only the second stage, the contribution of opinion on foreign policy to the electoral decision.

Major resources for the systematic empirical study of our topic have existed for little more than two decades. Prior to the development of survey research we have only data relevant to the third theme—the impact of the electoral decision on foreign policy-making. Instead of relatively direct evidence of voter perceptions, beliefs, values, and intentions, we have reports of others' perceptions and understandings of these phenomena. The brief time span covered by crucial data elicited from the voters themselves constitutes another major limitation on what is known. Even if the modern era is essentially similar to other eras, we still have been able to observe only a limited part of the range of theoretically pertinent phenomena. Despite total national involvement in two world wars within the past fifty years, we have only limited evidence for our understanding of the impact of impending and actual war on voting behavior. Although foreign policy is now widely seen as a necessary and permanent part of our national life, Americans past the age of fifty came to their majority in a time when it was national policy not to have a foreign policy—but the recency of our analytic material leaves us too little informed about the earlier times or about the changing times that saw foreign policy emerge as a persistent object of political attention. This obvious point is worth making because it anticipates our inability to make definitive statements about some important matters.

PUBLIC OPINION AND FOREIGN POLICY

Building on important pioneering work of the 1940s, the first major election study by the Survey Research Center of the University of Michigan was executed in 1952. That study provides our best available example of data gathered in a context in which voting behavior was crucially influenced by the electorate's concern over foreign policy. And, although we here must recognize the possible dangers of our limited perspective, the election of 1952 also seems to illustrate the chaotic nature of the connection between public opinion on foreign policy and the electoral behavior of the same public.

The Korean conflict, by 1952, had laid a massive burden of frustration on the people of the United States. Relief was sensed and sought through the election of the man who had been for ten years the symbol of national military prowess. So far so good. Even more reasonably, the supporters of General Eisenhower preferred policies sharply different from those Governor Stevenson proposed to continue. In 1952 the partisan division on the internationalist-nationalist dimension was every bit as sharp as

the counterpart liberal-conservative division on the domestic social welfare dimension. On the specific question of Korean policy, the prime disagreement within Republican ranks was between those who would end the war by bombing Red China and those who would end it by withdrawing American forces from Korea. The internationalist commitment to peace without victory, through negotiated settlement, was the unchallenged and unpopular pre-election monopoly of the Democrats.

Mr. Eisenhower's election was followed neither by an extension of aggression nor by submissive retreat. Under the General's leadership a settlement was negotiated — and on terms certainly no more favorable to the United States than those that could have been obtained by Mr. Truman. It seems fair to conclude, however speculatively, that Mr. Truman did not terminate the Korean conflict by seeking and obtaining comparable terms only because of many manifestations of hostile public opinion. The President and his party had been successfully caught between charges of being the war party ("Three wars in my lifetime, all got started when we had a Democrat in the White House") and being the party of appeasement ("Commie coddlers"; "600 Million people have been enslaved by atheistic communism during twenty years of treason"). Free of such burdens, Mr. Eisenhower was able to obtain peace without victory and to grow in popularity for having done so. Moreover, during the ensuing years his leadership virtually reshaped partisan preferences on matters of foreign policy. By 1956 and on into 1960, the policy preferences of rank-and-file Republicans gave slightly more support to an internationalist-interventionist posture than did those of their Democratic counterparts.[2] In sum, Mr. Eisenhower's election was made possible because of dissatisfaction with Democratic foreign policy, he immediately rejected the policy preferences of his supporters and by doing so gained the uncritical gratitude of the same supporters who forthwith accepted the tenets of the opposition and became more like Mr. Stevenson's supporters than Stevenson's supporters themselves.

There are many possible interpretations of this tale. The test of democratic leadership is met by combining wise decision-making with popular support for the decision — inability to command the support of public opinion is a fatal flaw properly repaired at the polls. The test of democratic leadership is met by gaining acceptance for unpopular policies.

2. Unless otherwise noted, all specific references to public attitudes or beliefs throughout this paper are based on data collected by the Survey Research Center, The University of Michigan, in its series of national political studies. The major studies were conducted at the time of national elections in 1952, 1956, 1958, 1960, and 1964. Information about technical details of the studies and access to the original data may be obtained upon request to the Inter-University Consortium for Political Research, Box 1248, Ann Arbor, Michigan 48106.

The test of democratic followership is met by rejecting leaders who have not produced desired results and by responding to appeals for support made by a leader who does achieve desired goals. Or, perhaps, popular evaluation of policy is myth and popular response to results is the only reality. With appropriate aid from partisan predispositions, the observer may read the events of 1952–53 as a testament to the system or as a demonstration of its bankruptcy.

At the time of the second Eisenhower election, Americans apparently viewed the international scene with relative equanimity. In September and October of 1956, confident and optimistic views of our chances for staying out of war outnumbered fearful and pessimistic ones by ratios of 3 and 4 to 1. Neither the Suez crisis nor the drama of the Hungarian revolt caused more than a ripple on the sea of tranquility.

Four years later, the combined events of national and international politics had produced a substantial deterioration of mood. The proportion of people who could be classified as "pretty worried" about the chance of our country getting into war had risen from 11 per cent to 21 per cent; those "not at all worried" had decreased from 44 per cent of the total to 31 per cent. Even more dramatic than this change in mood was the shift in assessments of the probability of war. By 1960 only 19 per cent of the people thought our chances of staying out of war had been improving; four years earlier some 42 per cent had professed to see comparable change for the better. In 1960, 36 per cent thought our chances of avoiding war had been getting worse, this against 13 per cent in 1956.

The change in mood was matched by changes in appraisals of the efficiency of American foreign policy. In 1958, expressions of satisfaction with the United States' dealing with foreign countries outnumbered critical comments by a ratio of 3 to 2. Two years later criticism outweighed approval; the level of critical comment was up 50 per cent (from 28 per cent of the population to 41 per cent) and those who viewed our recent conduct of international relations with satisfaction had declined (from 42 per cent to 36 per cent). Evaluations of the strength of our position in the world followed the same pattern of a declining sense of well-being. In 1958, those who thought our world position had been maintained or strengthened over the recent past totalled some 60 per cent of the population; by 1960 this figure had dropped to 52 per cent in the face of an increase from 23 to 31 per cent on the part of those who saw our position as having become less strong.

The vignette that was our review of the election of 1952 suggested that policy and the consequences of policy are not necessarily one in the mind of the citizen. An inspection of changes in specific foreign policy preferences between 1956 and 1960 provides further evidence of the

point. Voters' attitudes of support or opposition for the specific components of a policy of internationalism did not change commensurate
with the changes they perceived in our international relations. There is
evidence of a modest continuation of the drift toward internationalism,
but it is a movement of two or three percentage points—not the ten- and
twenty-point changes just reviewed. It seems fairly clear that growing
apprehension over what was thought to be a deteriorating international
situation did not provoke panic nor any tendency toward repudiation of
national policies of military and economic aid and of continuing involvement in problems in the international scene. By the same token, there
is little to indicate widespread understanding that new policies might
be adopted to cope with a newly threatening world situation. The popular
mood of optimism had been replaced with a pervasive sense of pessimism
without any apparent diminution of support for a continuation of the
nation's foreign policy commitments.

The transition from Republican to Democratic leadership between
the summers of 1960 and 1964 witnessed shifts in the public mood no
less interesting than those of the preceding four years. Having reviewed
earlier changes, the state of affairs in October, 1964 can be easily summarized: each of the indicators of public mood referred to above had
returned to almost exactly the same position we first observed in 1956.
Fear of war had receded from the 1960 high to the 1956 level, confidence in the probability of peace had been largely restored, approval
of the nation's international activities had risen, and perceptions of
increased national strength actually outnumbered perceptions of growing
weakness, whereas even 1956 had produced no more than an even
balance between these popular assessments.

On the policy front we may turn to a single indicator, the distribution
of attitudes toward foreign aid. Despite the rather substantial shift in
congressional sentiment during this period, a shift against continuation
of aid programs, popular sentiment supporting foreign aid apparently
did not diminish at all. This datum on stability is of a piece with that
observed for the more extended assessment of policy alternatives in
1956 and 1960.

Despite all of this, 1964 was neither 1960 nor 1956 in one crucial
respect: the linkage of mood or opinion with the parties and party leaders
was significantly different. On the question of foreign aid, posed in both
studies, there was no consensus in 1960 as to which party was more
likely to support a policy of sending American aid abroad. Almost 70
per cent of those with opinions on the policy question itself professed to
know of no difference between Democratic and Republican plans to
support aid programs; those who saw a difference between parties,
divided precisely in equal parts between thinking one party rather than

the other was more likely to support a policy of aid. In 1964, the proportion seeing no difference in the parties' positions had dropped to 50 per cent; within the other half, at least 40 out of the remaining 50 per cent believed the Democrats were more likely to favor a national policy of foreign aid.

More generally, in 1960 none of the several expressions of policy preference which we can examine could be easily translated into expressions of partisan electoral preference because of the persistent lack of consensus as to which party was more likely to enact which policy. Four years and two presidential candidates later, foreign policy joined social welfare and civil rights as a domain in which partisans of virtually all persuasions agreed on the policy differences that separated the parties. On each of three questions posed in the 1964 SRC election study (foreign aid, negotiations with Communist leaders, and trade with Communist countries), those who saw Republicans as favoring the specified action were outnumbered by ratios of 6 and 7 to 1 by those who understood the Democrats to be more supportive. The potential significance of such a change can scarcely be overemphasized. When Mr. Eisenhower led his followers out of the wastelands of political defeat he also led many of them into the ranks of the internationalists. Moreover, with the force of convinced example he made it virtually impossible for popular partisan politics to do other than stop at the water's edge. From Korea on, he eliminated the cues by which citizens could be guided in choosing a political instrument to further their policy goals. As far as most voters were concerned, his successor would have continued in the same broad path, and it was not until 1964 that a choice replaced bipartisan echoes. Without anticipating the impact of foreign policy preferences on electoral behavior, Mr. Goldwater was eminently successful in communicating the new availability of a real choice between policy alternatives in American international relations.

The partisan implications of changing moods underwent an even more dramatic transformation between 1956 and 1964. The Korean war, with some aid from the Republicans, encouraged the belief that the Democratic party was the war party. For many people this meant no more than the deadpan observation that all three wars of this century had occurred when a Democrat was President. The more articulate critics charged failure of policy and were attracted to the theme that Republican statesmen were more likely to be able to achieve peace. So pervasive was the theme that in 1952 and even in 1956 some followers of the Republican banner actually understood the charge to mean that Democrats wanted wars and deliberately pursued policies calculated to embroil the nation in conflict ("Roosevelt had to get us into war to end unemployment"). In 1956, sanguine appraisals of our international

position were bolstered by the widespread conviction that Mr. Eisenhower and the Republicans were best equipped to handle the problem of keeping us out of the war. The growing apprehensions of 1960 were accompanied by (if not the cause of) a visible drop in confidence in Republican leadership. By 1964, popular evaluations had been completely reversed and with a margin of better than 3 to 1 it was the Democrats, rather than the Republicans, who were thought to be better able to keep us out of war.

Table 1 — Evaluations of Relative Partisan Capabilities in keeping the United States out of War*

(in percentages)

	1956	1960	1964
The problem would be handled:			
Better by Democrats	7	15	38
Same by both parties	45	46	46
Better by Republicans	40	29	12
Don't know	7	8	4
Not Ascertained	1	2	**
	100	100	100
	(N=1,762)	(N=1,954)	(N=1,571)

*Now looking ahead, do you think the problem of keeping out of war would be handled better in the next **four** years by the Republicans, or by the Democrats, or about the same by both?
**Less than ½ of 1 per cent.

　　With this turn of political events, the Democrats enjoyed a rather complete reversal in all of the aspects of public opinion on foreign policy which had weighed against them twelve years earlier. The policies they supported were by and large well received, it was generally understood that they rather than the Republicans were the party likely to implement popular policies, and they rather than the Republicans were thought able to avoid war and secure peace for the nation.

PUBLIC OPINION AND ELECTORAL CHOICE

　　In an earlier and less well-endowed age, all but the most cautious observer might well use our narration of the ebb and flow of public opinion for a direct explanation of the accompanying changes in presidential politics. We are constrained to follow a different course. In addition to restraints imposed by various methodological canons, such as pertain to univariate analyses, we have a substantial backlog of information and theory that must be accommodated in any explanatory scheme, and we have an array of technical operations at our disposal with which to proceed in a much closer investigation of our data. One source of analytic power, in particular, derives from an important

technical attribute of a major subset of date: the material from 1956 and 1960 are part of a panel study of national voting behavior. We are not only able to proceed with the inclusion of additional variables in a more comprehensive analysis, we can study change in attitudes and behaviors by following each individual who contributes to the change.

By now it is almost to assert a truism to note that the marginal distributions of a bivariate array conceal as much as they disclose. Nevertheless, even experienced analysts are still open to some shock when first exposed to the information revealed by panel data arranged so that detailed changes over time can be examined for single variables. A reasonable case in point is provided by 1956–60 data measuring public opinion on policies that contribute to a national posture of involvement in foreign affairs. We have already noted that voter attitudes on the interventionist dimension were apparently among the most stable of any explored in this analysis. Even when we extend the definition of our analytic population to include all citizens, voters and nonvoters, who held opinions on our foreign policy questions in both years, the apparent stability between 1956 and 1960 is evident. The 1960 array could have resulted from post-1956 changes of opinion by no more than

Table 2 — Attitudes on American Foreign Policy, 1956 and 1960
(in percentages)

	1956	1960
Supports action in each of three policy areas	22	32
Supports action in two of three areas	36	33
Supports action in no more than one area, or in none	42	35
	100	100
	(N=1,118)	(N=1,118)

10 per cent of the population (7 per cent moving from bottom to top and 3 per cent from the middle to the top) or, perhaps more realistically, by some 17 per cent (with 7 per cent moving from the bottom to the middle and a different 10 per cent moving from the middle to the top). In fact, by our sample estimates, more than 50 per cent of the population changed positions between the two election years. While one-third of the people were increasing their support for internationalist policies, close to one in five was moving out of sympathy with the same policies.

Comparable inspection of change through time in the various measures of mood and evaluation of foreign policy reveals similar configurations. In 1960, 34 per cent of the population reported greater personal apprehension over war than they had four years earlier; another 15 per cent

Table 3 — Stability and Change on Three Questions of Foreign Policy, 1956–60*

(in percentages)

	1956				
	Supports three	Supports two	Supports one or none	1960 Distri-bution	
1960:					
Supports three policies	11	12	9	32	(N = 359)
Supports two policies	5	16	12	33	(N = 367)
Supports one or none	6	8	21	35	(N = 392)
1956 Distribution	22	36	42	100	
	(N = 242)	(N = 405)	(N = 471)		(N = 1,118)

*Tau beta rank order correlation of .167.

reported less concern (see Table 4 below). Assessing the probabilities of war, a full 50 per cent were less sanguine about our changing fortunes in 1960 than they had been in 1956; an additional 10 per cent assessed the world situation with increased optimism (see Table 5 below).

The gross amount of change in attitudes, perceptions, and beliefs merits further comment, but for the moment we must move on in pursuit of our central objective: the assessment of the contribution that public opinion on foreign policy makes to the electoral decision. In the analysis of panel data, the ability to identify the individuals whose opinions create the change in public opinion is, of course, matched by an ability to identify the individuals whose votes create the changes in electoral results. The intersection of these two kinds of change, change in opinion and change

Table 4 — Stability and Change in Personal Concern about War, 1956–1960*

(in percentages)

	1956				
	Not at all worried	Somewhat worried	Very worried	1960 Distri-bution	
1960:					
Not at all worried	20	9	1	30	(N = 408)
Somewhat worried	18	25	5	48	(N = 655)
Very worried	6	10	6	22	(N = 300)
1956 Distribution	44	44	12	100	
	(N = 602)	(N = 597)	(N = 164)		(N = 1,363)

*How about the chances of our country getting into war? Would you say that at the present time you are pretty worried about this country getting into another war, somewhat worried, or not worried at all?
Tau beta rank order correlation of .289.

Table 5—Stability and Change in Assessment of the Probabilities
of Peace, 1956–1960*

(in percentages)

	1956				
	Getting better	Stayed the same	Getting worse	1960 Distribution	
1960:					
Getting better	12	4	2	18	(N=238)
Stayed the same	20	22	4	46	(N=596)
Getting worse	13	17	6	36	(N=470)
1956 Distribution	45	43	12	100	
	(N=582)	(N=560)	(N=162)		(N=1,304)

*During the past few years do you think our chances of staying out of war have been getting better, getting worse, or stayed the same?
Tau beta rank order correlation of .159.

in behavior, allows us to pinpoint some of the phenomena in which we are interested. We can now turn to the question of the relationship between the two kinds of short-run change.[3]

Between 1956 and 1960, 30 per cent of those who voted at least once changed their behavior: from vote to nonvote, nonvote to vote, from Democratic vote to Republican vote, or from Republican vote to Democratic vote. In the same interval, 49 per cent of the same group changed their report of personal concern about war. Our first analytic datum consists of the fact that these two forms of change were completely independent and unrelated (Table 6). If, in general, any change in the extent to which one is worried about war leads to some change in voting behavior, we should expect to find a higher than random incidence of both changes occurring together. Working from the two independent proportions of change, we should expect in our data 184 cases of change

3. Before proceeding, it is in order to specify precisely who is included in and who is excluded from the analysis. Inasmuch as our interest centers on voting we shall exclude all persons who voted for President in *neither* election, neither 1956 nor 1960. By allowing a vote in *either* election to bring a person into our analysis we permit not only the representation of the protest abstention, we also accommodate the variations in political involvement that may stem from perceived changes in the national or the world situation. All persons who participate in maintaining or changing the national electoral decision between 1956 and 1960 are included in the analysis. For other reasons, we shall exclude all persons who indicated in either year a lack of responsiveness to questions of policy or mood. Anyone who in either year "didn't know" whether he or she was or was not worried about war is excluded, as is anyone who had no opinion on two of the three foreign policy questions that were asked. Persons who "did not know" whether our national position had improved were not excluded, but anyone who was simply unable to respond to the query on national strength (whose answer was therefore categorized as "Not Ascertained") was excluded. In other words, we demand minimal evidence that a topic is within the comprehension of each person in both 1956 and 1960, but we do not limit our analytic population to the well-informed and involved. Within these two boundaries (including sometime voters who indicate comprehension of our queries about opinion) we shall first focus our attention on those who change on both attitudinal and behavioral dimensions.

in both dimensions (15 per cent out of a total of 1,235 cases); there are, in fact, 179 cases, not significantly fewer than we would expect if the two versions of change were unrelated—but certainly little evidence that a change in worrying about war *leads to* a change in voting behavior.

Our next question is, within the set of 179 changers, was one kind of change (increased worry about war, for example) associated with another kind of change (giving the Democratic candidate more, or less, support)? The answer, again based on expectations tied to the known proportion of each kind of change, is that no specific change on one dimension was associated with any specific change on the other. In seventy-four cases the person gave less support to the Republican candidate—or more to the Democratic—while exhibiting greater worry over the possibility of war; on the basis of a strictly random intersection of totally unrelated events we would have expected seventy-three such cases, and so on for the other combinations of change. There is no observable tendency for a given change in personal concern over war to be associated with any given change in voting behavior between 1956 and 1960. Although worry about war increased at the same time the Democratic vote increased, there is no evidence among persons who changed on both dimensions that this component of foreign policy mood was associated with Democratic prosperity.

Virtually the same pair of conclusions holds for the other indicators of the public mood. Concerning evaluations of the chances of avoiding war, there is no need for any qualification on the first and grosser point: stability in evaluation of chances of avoiding war is not associated with stability in voting for President. On the next level, however, there is a suggestion that increased optimism in 1960 was associated with greater support for Mr. Nixon. However, the basic relationship between optimism and a Republican vote is weak. It is also compromised by evidence that it may be a spurious relationship produced by joint association with Protestant-Catholic differences in world views. For the remaining items, the appraisal of our international relations and the

Table 6 — Stability and Change in Presidential Voting Behavior in Relation to Stability and Change in Perceptions of Parties as Agents of Peace, 1956–60
(in percentages)

	VOTING BEHAVIOR		
	No change	Change	
Perception of Parties:			
No change	46	15	(N = 754)
Change	23	16	(N = 496)
	(N=868)	(N=382)	(N=1,250)

Table 7 — Changes in Presidential Voting Behavior in Relation to Changes in Perceptions of Parties as Agents of Peace, 1956–60
(in percentages)

	VOTING BEHAVIOR		
	Democratic to Republican	Republican to Democratic	
Perception of Parties:			
Republicans more likely to avoid war in 1960 than in 1956	20	10	(N = 59)
Democrats more likely to avoid war in 1960 than in 1956	17 (N = 74)	53 (N = 124)	(N = 139) (N = 198)

assessment of our world position, there is again no evidence that they contributed one way or another to the change in political fortunes between 1956 and 1960. They apparently neither provoked nor repressed propensities to change the 1956 presidential vote.

In the face of this unbroken sequence of null findings, the first comparable datum concerning changes in more specific foreign policy preferences is something of a surprise. For all of our earlier comments on the perishable nature of popular policy preferences — as in 1952 and after — the sheer fact of change in policy preferences between 1956 and 1960 is apparently associated with the tendency to change one's presidential vote. The association is not strong but it does merit mention.[4]

On the other hand, we return to what has become familiar ground when we next note that the direction of change in policy preference is not associated with direction of change in the presidential vote. Increased support for internationalist policies (the predominant change) is not significantly more likely to be associated with movement either toward or away from either party. In sum, among those persons changing positions on both attitudinal and behavioral dimensions, voting behavior was not systematically associated with variations in appraisals of means nor with evaluations of the results of foreign policy.

In the entire portfolio of data we have examined, there is one set of findings that reflects a clear and unmistakable statistical relationship involving changes in voting behavior: Changing evaluations of the parties as agents of peace are apparently related to changes in the vote. (Table 6). There is a weak association involving the two measures of stability and change; there is a moderate association appropriately tying increased confidence that a party can avoid war to an increase in electoral support for that party (Table 7).

Unfortunately, we have no means of establishing a direct causal

4. Chi square value of 5.36 with one degree of freedom, .05 > P > .02 for simple random samples.

status for this specific appraisal of the two parties. Other analyses of change have indicated that factors of religion and party identification account for most of the 1956–60 change in voting behavior.[5] An inspection of the data now before us indicates that change in appraisal of the parties as agents of peace is also highly correlated with the same indicator of the religious factor, is highly correlated with change in party identification, and is very modestly correlated with stable party identification. Standing against the likelihood that this appraisal of the parties made a significant contribution to the vote in 1960, we have the possibility that the appraisal is little more than a *post hoc* rationale for a vote decision reached on other grounds.

We are not inclined to dismiss the relationship out of hand, however. At least three considerations argue its possible importance. Most pertinent to the election of 1960, independent evidence from other material in the parent study indicates a modest role for foreign policy in the election. A multivariate examination of free answer attitudinal materials supports the conclusion that voters' concern about foreign policy netted the Republican candidate about 2 per cent of the vote in that year.[6] The comparable datum from 1956, when problems of foreign policy occasioned less apprehension and concern but when the appraisal of the parties favored the Republicans even more heavily, indicates a 2.5 per cent increment in Republican strength attributable to public opinion on foreign policy.[7] The decline in the Republicans' foreign policy advantage between 1956 and 1960 is thus represented both in the analytic decomposition of the attitudinal components of the vote decision and in the relationship between the vote and the summary appraisal of party competencies in maintaining peace.

The surface comparison between these data and the null findings involving the other measures of public opinion on foreign policy invites a more extended and more involved discussion than time, space, and propriety will permit. Fortunately, the basic arguments have been well made elsewhere and we can be content with a brief application to our interpretive problem.[8] Our first argument is heavily methodological and

5. P. E. Converse *et al.*, "Stability and Change in 1960: A Reinstating Election," *American Political Science Review*, Vol. 55: 2 (June, 1961), p. 269–80.

6. The analysis was carried out by my colleague Professor Donald E. Stokes and is an adaptation of the method reported in Donald E. Stokes, A. Campbell, and W. E. Miller, "Components of Electoral Decision," *American Political Science Review*, Vol. 52: 3 (June, 1958), p. 367–87.

7. The same analysis performed on data from 1952 indicates a 3 per cent advantage to the Republicans that year.

8. P. E. Converse, "Attitudes and Non-Attitudes: Continuation of a Dialogue," paper read at Seventeenth International Congress of Psychology, Washington, D.C., August, 1963. P. E. Converse, "The Nature of Belief Systems in Mass Publics," in David E. Apter (ed.), *Ideology and Discontent* (New York: The Free Press, 1964).

is based on a growing awareness of the quality of popular evaluations of parties and candidates.

For all of its other shortcomings, the question asking our sample of the electorate for a choice between the parties as agents of peace moves directly to elicit a conclusion in which the partisan consequences of all the respondent's information, values, perceptions, and beliefs have been weighed, summarized by him, and made a matter of record. The familiar cues of party are explicit in both question and response. The object, war, is presumably within the ken of most people. The process of arriving at the summary can be as primitive, as chaotic, as informed, or as fanciful as the natural thought processes of the respondent.

The measurement of attitudinal components referred to above rests on even more natural data, with the partisan significance of each element built into the interviewee's response. At the same time, in telling us what is good or bad about the major parties and their candidates, a person can favor the Republican party for two apparently contradictory reasons; each of two people of opposite partisan persuasions can see exactly the same distinct virtue in his own preferred candidate; no norms for consensus on the meaning of policy are needed for the respondent and the analyst to comprehend the partisan implications of an attitudinal expression of approval or disapproval.

The result of such permissiveness in our measurement procedures is, of course, an analytic summary in which a thousand idiosyncratic and discordant views of the world can still add up to orderly sets of partisan preferences for each respondent. If the views among the individual members of the electorate are sufficiently lacking in the shared dimensions and understandings necessary to create a decision-maker's orderliness and coherence among attitudinal elements, an attempt to find shared order and coherence may well come to naught. Indeed, when one looks for systematic connections between opinions and behavior, one presumes common stores of information, common forms of cognitive organization and structure, and common applications of values, all of which are actually quite uncommon in the public at large, at least where politics is concerned. Thus it may be bootless or positively misleading to elicit specific policy preferences, array them along a dimension of internationalism, assess changes in individual positions on the demension over time, and then expect to find the changes systematically related to voting preferences.

The search for understanding of shifts in mass voting behavior is further compromised by the fact that when attention focuses on change it focuses on those members of the public for whom elite modes of thought are least common.[9] Certainly in the absence of crisis, and perhaps

9. P. E. Converse, "Information Flow and the Stability of Partisan Attitudes," *The Public Opinion Quarterly,* Vol. 26:4 (Winter, 1962), p. 578–99.

even in its presence, the ill-informed, slightly involved citizen is most likely to exhibit changes in political attitudes or behaviors. In the context of voting, "the probability that any given voter will be sufficiently deflected in his partisan momentum to cross party lines in a specific election varies... inversely as a function of the mass of [his] stored information about politics."[10] The voter who is cognizant of few political objects, has few beliefs about politics, and has little or no structure relating his fragments of knowledge, may respond sharply to a single new piece of information once it reaches him, but the response may be no more than random in its consequences for other attitudes and behaviors. The alert, informed, fully socialized, political man will become aware of many more new pieces of information and will behave much more predictably, usually by incorporating them into his prior system of values and beliefs.

The Suez crisis in 1956 stirred about one voter in ten to post-election comment about its influence on his vote. A full 95 per cent of those so moved actually voted as they had intended before the Suez crisis occurred. The common response of many such Eisenhower voters followed the line, "Well, like I told you before the election, you need a military man in the White House to handle a thing like Suez"; the Democratic voters unwittingly countered by saying, "Well, like I told you before the election, we will always be in trouble with a military man in the White House." For most of those alert enough to know about and respond to the crisis, response took the form of fitting new information into pre-existing belief systems rather than changing intended voting behavior to fit a "new" situation.

A final reason for maintaining an interest in the one element that tied foreign policy to 1956–60 vote changes derives from our view of the interdependence of behavior and opinion. Even if it can be demonstrated that the appraisal of the parties is a derivative and not an independent cause of voting behavior in 1960, the derivative may become a reinforcement, an anchor against further change in 1964. More generally, the relationship between opinions and behaviors is one of interaction and mutual influence. Party identification certainly influences voting behavior; voting behavior also influences party identification, since a vote across party lines affects the probable stability of tomorrow's party identification. Voters who switched sides in 1960 *and* changed their appraisals of each party's foreign policy potential, even as an incidental result, were doubtless different in 1964 from voters who made the same behavioral change in 1960 but did not bring their appraisals of party into line. The very essence of a "multivariate view" of the world of politics assumes a continuing interaction among an ex-

10. *Ibid.*

tended set of factors influencing each other and the vote, and being influenced by each other and the vote. The formal rules of the game may allow us to discard factors that are not involved in such a matrix of interrelationships; we know too much and too little to disregard situations of ambiguity. The observed relationship connecting appraisals of the parties as instruments of peace with changes in voting behavior is consistent with an independent assessment of the same phenomena: despite its ambiguous causal status in 1960, the relationship is based on the kind of information that could be expected to reflect meaningful attitudinal change, and its significance for future behavior cannot be ignored.

SUMMARY

By choosing to focus on the intersection of specific attitudinal and behavior changes we selected a sensitive but very partial approach to our topic. Even if we had unmistakably isolated the full set of vote changes inspired by foreign policy, the set whose net contribution was to reduce the Republican foreign policy advantage of 1956 by $\frac{1}{2}$ of 1 per cent of the total vote, we still might not have appraised the total contribution of foreign policy to the 1960 vote total. At the same time, more positive findings might have guided us to the location of more enduring contributions of foreign policy to the vote decision. Now we find ourselves uncertain about its contribution to change and thus still largely uninformed in detail about the mechanisms by which public opinion on foreign policy becomes related to voting behavior.

In the absence of comparable data from 1948, we cannot be certain about any change that occurred between then and 1952. Of course, we can be impressed with the conclusion that even the combination of the Korean War and General Eisenhower added up to little more than a 3 per cent net advantage for the Republicans in the latter year. This would seem to be of a piece with our general sense that World War II left surprisingly few marks on the electorate — certainly nothing equivalent to those of the Civil War or the depression of the 1930's. Coming up to 1956 and 1960, we can be sure of no more than that public opinion on foreign policy matters constituted a thin veneer on the basic structure of the vote decision. The contribution may have been much larger by way of an impact on changes in party identification throughout the postwar period; even a modest sensitivity to the perishable nature of evidence of such causal events cautions us against premature foreclosure on this possibility. It may also be true, however, that foreign policy issues made no basic contribution to the politics of the late 1940's and early

1950's. Even in 1956 and 1960 we may simply be observing the remnants of the steadily eroding impact of the single event of the Korean War.

The sense that voting behavior today is not acutely responsive to the issues of foreign policy should not be taken as uniquely characteristic of the content area. Comparable data pertaining to domestic policies in the social welfare and economic domains support a very similar analysis with identical conclusions about 1956–60 changes in voting behavior. Given the well-established correlations uniting partisanship and policy preferences in these domains, the null findings are the more striking. For example, comparable proportions of the analytic population changed their positions on a measure evaluating social welfare policy preferences; the changes resulted in an increase in support for social welfare action that was four times the increase noted for support of an internationalist foreign policy. Nevertheless, among persons who were also changing their presidential vote, there was no tendency for any change on the opinion dimension to be associated with a change in behavior.

To date, our studies of public opinion and voting have told us much that we need to know by telling us that much we once thought we knew is not so. To put a rather negative matter more positively, we have documented with greater elegance and in greater and greater detail the electoral consequences of a mass public that

> is uninformed about either specific foreign-policy issues or foreign affairs in general, [a public whose] members pay little, if any, attention to day-to-day developments in world politics. Being uninformed and without initiative, they lack structured opinions — that is, they are short of the cognitive and evaluative equipment which facilitiates comprehension of the ideas and information that are flowing through the circulatory system....The most predominant mood of the mass public is, of course, indifference and passivity. Except for acute peace-or-war crises (and not always then), the mass public is usually unmoved by the course of world events.[11]

There is a positive side. We are learning to study mass society through techniques of data collection that do not impose unnatural modes of thought (i.e., the analyst's mode of thought) and do not elicit nonexistent content. We have already collected data that can tell us more about how public opinion *is* formed than we now know. We are acquiring a better understanding of the functioning of the institutions of politics and government in the formation and selective transmission of public opinion. We have not yet thrown the baby out with the bathwater, and we may even be learning how to build better bathtubs.

11. Rosenau, *op. cit.*, pp. 35–36.

INTEREST GROUPS
AND
FOREIGN POLICY

Lester W. Milbrath

THIS paper addresses itself to the following questions: How can one conceptualize the process by which interest groups influence foreign policy? On which kinds of foreign policy issues are which kinds of groups likely to have influence? How should one classify groups vis-a-vis their posture toward foreign policy? Do groups act differently when trying to influence foreign policy decisions than they do when trying to influence domestic policy decisions?[1]

Since these questions make it plain that the concept of influence is central to my analysis, it is useful to start with a comment on how I

1. Foreign and domestic policies are distinguished in this way: the former are those whose direct consequences involve other countries, whereas the direct consequences of the latter do not extend beyond a country's borders. The direct consequences of an income tax, for example, are mostly limited to the country in which it is adopted. The direct consequences of a tariff cut, on the other hand, are immediately felt in other countries. Indirectly, of course, almost every policy has some impact abroad, so it is important to stress here that the foreign-domestic distinction is largely one of emphasis and holds only for direct consequences.

shall be using the concept. In order to assess fully the unique influence of interest groups on foreign policy, it would be necessary to trace all the influences at work and then to parcel out that influence which is unique to interest groups. Such a task is clearly beyond the capabilities of modern social science and will not be attempted here. Yet when discussing the relation of interest groups to foreign policy, it is difficult, indeed impossible, to avoid the influence problem. Interest groups, by definition, desire to influence the policies of government. In order to cope with this definitional reality, therefore, I shall pursue a middle course and attempt to specify some conditions under which influence could occur and others under which it is unlikely to occur. This exercise provides at least some perspective, if not a complete answer, to the influence problem.

I like to think of the influence process as a subcategory of the communication process. Not all communications transmit influence, some transmit only information; but all transmissions of influence constitute some form of a message. The basic principles of message transmission and reception, then, are useful in thinking about how influence occurs. Before any influence can occur, the influencee must receive *and consider* a message from the influencer. When I speak of influence in this chapter I mean only the process by which a decision-maker considers the content of a message as he makes his decision; I do not imply that the message must be the decisive factor as he makes his final selection among the alternatives.

INTEREST GROUPS AS INTERMEDIARIES

Concerned citizens, hoping to influence foreign policy decisions, must make some tactical choices about how they will try to communicate their policy desires to official decision-makers. They can take the simple and obvious tactic of dispatching a direct message to the official they hope to influence. In some instances that tactic may be effective, in others, not. However, citizens have many alternative methods for communicating policy desires to officials: they can ask a group to speak for them, they can work through a political party, they can use the mass media, they can cast a vote, and they can choose to do nothing that is overtly political (thereby communicating inertia). All of these actions constitute a message of some sort to the officials charged with making foreign policy. In most instances the citizen's choice of tactics is based on poor information about their effectiveness.

This chapter treats groups as intermediaries in communication between citizens and governments as those governments make foreign

policy decisions. The interrelationships of the actors constituting the communications network through which policy decisions are made are outlined in Figure 1.[2] In this figure, the heavy dark arrows represent the formal power relationships that tie together the actors in the system and that are usually specified in a constitution. The outputs from such a system are authoritative governmental decisions (laws, executive orders, judicial decisions, and so forth). These decisions are produced by elected and appointed officials who are placed in their jobs (directly or indirectly) by the votes of the body politic.

Formal constitutional relationships do not make a government, however; all such systems develop sets of auxiliary actors who are tied into the formal system by an elaborate communications network. Figure 1 suggests six types of auxiliary actors, their institutional bases, and the major channels of communication tying them into the system. These auxiliary actors are intermediaries in the sense that they transmit and interpret messages coming from public officials and directed to the body politic, and they also transmit and interpret messages flowing in the other direction, from the body politic to the officials. In another sense, of course, these auxiliary actors are more than intermediaries; very often they initiate communications directed elsewhere in the system.

This chapter focuses most directly on those boxes labeled "domestic" and "foreign interest groups." The mass media are covered by another chapter in this volume and political parties are dealt with in several others. When parties serve as channels of message transmission between the public and officials, with the messages intended to influence policy, rather than as institutions for getting officials elected, they are functioning very much like interest groups and can be subsumed under our discussion. When opinion leaders form themselves into groups or act as spokesmen for groups, they too can be subsumed into our discussion of groups; when they act individually, they may be thought of as part of the body politic. The latter were singled out for attention in the diagram mainly to allow for the so-called two-step flow of communications.[3]

Foreign governments and groups of citizens of foreign countries become part of the relevant communications network when decisions are to be made about foreign policy. This does not mean simply that information about the characteristics and probable reactions of these people are fed to officials by actors within the domestic system; it means also that many messages come directly from these foreign governments

2. Adapted from Lester W. Milbrath, *The Washington Lobbyists* (Chicago: Rand McNally, 1963), p. 181.

3. Cf. Paul F. Lazarsfeld, Bernard Berelson, and Hazel Gaudet, *The People's Choice* (New York: Columbia University Press, 1948), and Elihu Katz and Paul F. Lazarsfeld, *Personal Influence* (New York: The Free Press, 1955).

234

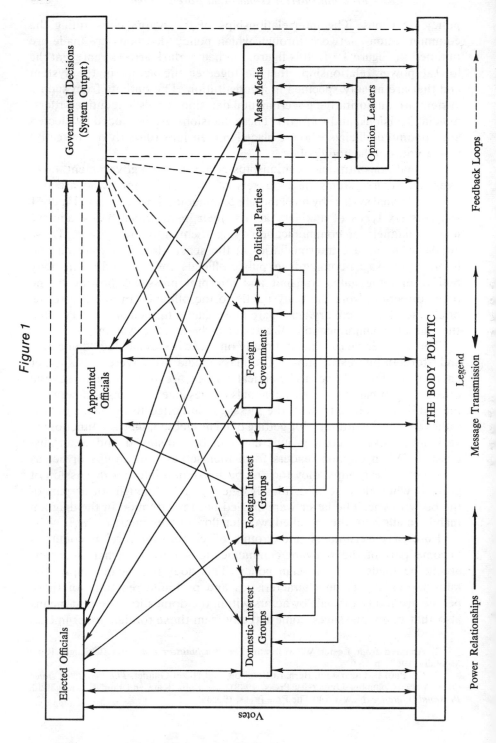

Figure 1

and groups, are aimed directly or indirectly at officials and are designed to influence their decisions. A message from a foreign government may be a formal diplomatic exchange, but it also may be informal or come via some intermediary such as the mass media. For example, in *The New York Times* of June 2, 1965, there appeared a letter to the editor from Prince Sihanouk of Cambodia that was clearly designed to influence the foreign policy of the United States. Messages from foreign interest groups are transmitted in much the same fashion as messages from domestic interest groups. Many foreign interest groups have registered lobbyists in Washington.

LOCI FOR FOREIGN POLICY DECISIONS

Before the role of groups in determining foreign policy decisions can be examined, it is necessary to locate where such decisions are made. It is wise to begin with those who are officially responsible for the making of foreign policy decisions and to define a decision-maker as one who is legally charged to make a final choice from among two or more alternatives on a policy question. Usually this power of final choice carries with it the power to commit the resources of the nation. In the United States, the President is preeminently charged with making these final choices in foreign policy matters. The import of this fact for understanding strategies of influence, although self-evident, is often inadequately appreciated. In contrast to domestic policy, where the President shares the authoritative selection of alternatives with many other officials (especially in Congress), in foreign affairs the President often is the sole authoritative decision-maker. To be sure, the President delegates quite a number of decisions, but he stands finally responsible for his delegation. The point here is that in seeking the loci of foreign policy decisions we look first to the President and then, if necessary, to the persons to whom he has delegated decisional power.

Certain kinds of foreign policy decisions require the concurrence of additional officials. Congress must concur in decisions requiring expenditure of money, declaration of war, treaty ratification, and the appointment of foreign affairs officials. Even in many of these cases, however, the requirement of concurrence often has the consequence of imposing a boundary on the decision latitude of the President rather than permitting actual participation in the selection of the alternatives.

Knowing where and when decisions are made is the central consideration for strategies designed to influence those decisions. It is a simple and significant fact that the President cannot attend to more than a minute fraction of the messages that people might wish to direct to

him. This means that the President has a relatively open choice in deciding to whom he will listen. Listen, in this context, does not mean simply that his ear picks up the sound; it means, rather, that he gives the message serious and thoughtful consideration. Perhaps more than any other actor in the system, the President has the power to decide to whom he will listen. The major limitation on this power is his desire to maintain political support. Since his constituency is the entire country, however, and since he has great potential for influencing public opinion, even this boundary imposes very few limits on his decisions as to whose messages he shall heed. There are two parts to the decision to listen: First, a message must pass through the organizational and perceptual screen that the President's staff erects around him. Second, he must sufficiently respect the sender to give the message serious consideration.

The scope and location of those in addition to the President involved in a foreign policy decision varies with the type of problem under con- sideration and, accordingly, so does the task of interest groups hoping to exert influence within the decision-making process. A decision about a bombing sortie in North Vietnam, for example, includes advisers in the Defense Department, the State Department, and the National Security Council; officials from other departments and from Congress are only peripherally involved and interest group messages are almost totally excluded. A decision to recognize a new country primarily involves advisers in the Department of State; those in other departments, other branches, and interest groups are, except in rare instances such as the recognition of Israel or China, outside the system. A decision pertaining to a tariff requires a much wider decisional system and the number of people the President must heed is extended to include advisers in the Treasury, Commerce, Agriculture, and Labor Departments, as well as State and Defense. In addition, the Congress has some authority in the tariff area. Thus the points of possible access which interest groups have to tariff decisions can be hundreds of times greater than is the case with diplomatic or military decisions, and since the legitimacy of their concern about such matters is also more obvious, interest groups are likely to be part of the decisional system that deals with tariff questions.

Serious attention from the President does not automatically follow from the mere fact that the agency or group has a right to be concerned with the problem under consideration. The President cannot listen to every would-be adviser, and he fully trusts advice from only a small circle of intimates. If he stops trusting information from an adviser, the latter and all of the people who work under him are out of the decisional system. If an interest group representative had close liaison with some person in that group, he too is cut out of the system. A new President restructures much of the foreign policy decisional system, even though

most of the agencies and the personnel who staff them remain the same. By the simple and necessary decision about whom to listen to, the President largely and effectively defines the actors involved in the foreign policy decisional process.

THE PROCESS OF DECISION AND ACCESS FOR INFLUENCE

The manner in which a decision is made is an important determinant of the likelihood that interest groups will have opportunities to influence it. Here a distinction can usefully be made between an intellective process in which the deliberations of the decision-making group are highly task-oriented and a social process in which the personal relations among the decision-makers are the dominant factor in the decision. Both processes are at work in nearly all decisions, but in some the intellective process predominates while in others the social emphasis prevails. In discussing intellective decision-making. Lasswell postulates the following seven functional steps: intelligence, recommendation, prescription, invocation, application, appraisal, and termination.[4] Not all steps are taken for every decision but, presumably, most of them are taken in approximately the order given. Bauer, Pool, and Dexter, on the other hand, challenge the notion that policy-making in Washington follows the highly intellective process postulated by decision-making theorists. They suggest instead that most policy decisions are "a social process and imbedded in a stream of social processes."[5]

Whether a decision tends in an intellective or social direction would seem to depend on the size of the decision-making group and on their perception of the weightiness of the task. If the decision involves many decision-makers who, in turn, are listening to many advisers (as in the case of tariff questions), it is likely to be made mainly through the social process, no matter how much importance is attached to the decision. On the other hand, if the circle of decision-makers is small and if they perceive that matters of life and death are at stake, the intellective process is likely to prevail. The U.S. decision to respond to the presence of Russian medium-range missiles in Cuba in October, 1962, is an example of what I mean here. If the stakes of the decision are not perceived

4. Harold D. Lasswell, *The Decision Process: Seven Categories of Functional Analysis* (College Park, Md.: Bureau of Government Research, University of Maryland, 1956).
5. Raymond A. Bauer, Ithiel de Sola Pool, and Lewis Anthony Dexter, *American Business and Public Policy: The Politics of Foreign Trade* (New York: Atherton Press, 1963), p. 479.

as high, the participants are more likely to allow, perhaps unconsciously, social considerations to enter their deliberations. The interaction of size and stake considerations can be sketched out as shown in Fig. 2.

Figure 2

		STAKES	
		high	low
NUMBER OF DECISION MAKERS	one or few	intellective	leans social
	many	social	social

It follows that interest groups are likely to find it easier to gain access to social process decisions than to those involving the intellective process. The latter do not foreclose group access, but I would hypothesize that they present many more difficulties in this respect than do social process decisions.

THE TASK OF GROUPS DESIRING TO INFLUENCE FOREIGN POLICY DECISIONS

With the above considerations in mind, it is now possible to specify some of the conditions that groups must meet if they wish to influence foreign policy decisions directly. First, it is essential that group leaders know the identity of the actors involved in a decision and the stages through which their deliberations must pass. The former point is obvious: messages can be influential only if they reach the persons who are making the decision. But timing a message so that it reaches decision-makers when it is most likely to be influential is also important. It is not easy for an interest group representative to know the most opportune time to send a message. Generally it can be said that a message that arrives before the problem is taken up by an official may become lost before he comes to consider alternative courses of action. At the opposite extreme, a message that arrives after an alternative has been selected will meet a reluctance from the decision-maker to reopen the question. Other, more subtle, considerations of timing are also relevant, but they are too specific to each situation to permit generalization.

Second, with a target audience in mind and the right time chosen, the group needs an open channel through to the target. This is generally more difficult to achieve than it may seem at first glance. The group leader can, of course, simply dispatch a letter or place a phone call, but

there is no assurance that the message will get through. The chances are, in fact, that it will be intercepted by some staff assistant who may or may not pass it on. If he does pass it on, it likely will be placed with many similar messages or aggregated in some way. At this point the message is surrounded by a good deal of noise and probably has undergone some distortion. The leader could seek an appointment in an effort to deliver the message in person, but such an appointment often is difficult to obtain. The closer the adviser is to the official or top decision-maker (usually the President), the greater the difficulty in obtaining the appointment with the adviser and the shorter the appointment's duration. The scarcity of opportunities to see officials means that groups store up their good will and try to get personal appointments only for the issues they consider to be most important. This importance is defined in terms of group goals and by the expenditure of scarce resources possessed by the group; it has little relation to what might be considered important for the nation or to a difference between foreign and domestic policy. Difficulties in obtaining a clear and open channel to an official stimulate many groups to try to send their messages through intermediaries who are presumed to have better access. A phone call from a friend, for example, will be put through to the official, and he likely will listen attentively. But friends who allow themselves to be used in this fashion are extremely hard to find. Furthermore, if they value their friendship, they will not be inclined to put much pressure on the official. If the decision-maker is a member of Congress, the group might find a constituent to transmit the message. The power connection, via the vote, between constituent and representative probably insures an open channel for the message. For those questions on which constituents can be stirred to take action, this is a viable means of message transmission.

The need for an open and clear channel for sending messages is the major reason why interest group representatives try to develop contacts. Contacts do not automatically insure favorable reception of messages, but they make it much easier to get messages through in undistorted fashion. The purpose of a call does not have to be extensively justified; the credentials of the sender do not have to be meticulously examined. Shared experiences in the past facilitate understanding between sender and receiver. The lobbyist with an excellent contact in every spot in which he might need one (an impossible situation to attain and maintain) would certainly have his work load lightened. A major difficulty with contacts is that they are so fragile and transitory. If they are overused, they wear out. If they are abused, the connection is broken. Connections naturally are between persons and not between roles; if a person moves, the connection to the role he played is likely to be broken even if the role continues. (In a few instances there is a natural

connection between roles, e.g., that between the President of the AFL-CIO and the Secretary of Labor.) The value of the contact (for influence) derives from the fact that the decision-maker is listening to, or is likely to listen to, the person one has contact with; if the decision-maker stops listening to the contact, any potential for influence that may have existed ceases.

Third, assuming for a moment that an open channel has been found for sending a message to the right place at the right time, how does the group achieve favorable reception of the import of the message by the decision-maker? This is the final step that must be consummated if the influence chain is to be completed, and most group leaders operate with very poor information and very little success in this realm. The perceptual screen that every human being possesses operates in a highly individualistic fashion. Many messages will be stopped and many others, distorted as they pass through that screen, and it is virtually impossible for any sender to know for certain how his message will fare. Busy public officials bombarded by a myriad of messages tend to select those that they wish to hear or to distort them so that they fit preconceptions. Being bombarded by so many messages, and therefore having an excuse for not listening to some or all of them, the public official can more readily stop listening and follow his personal predispositions than he could if he were the target of only a few messages. To a very great extent, officials determine the nature and amount of messages they will allow through their perceptual screen.

Despite the highly individualistic characteristic of message reception by officials, some generalizations can be stated about ways of making messages more acceptable. Nearly all messages are screened for legitimacy and credibility. A message will be considered legitimate if the official believes the sending group has a "right" to implore him on the matter. A demonstration of possible injury from a proposed action is one way of conveying a legitimate right to petition the government for redress of grievances. A firm that might be hurt if a tariff were lowered will be presumed to have a right to try to influence the decision. The legitimacy of the message might be questioned, however, if the firm approached a representative from another state rather than its own representative. A message that falls within the stated purposes of the group also will generally be considered legitimate. A message asking for negotiations to settle the Vietnam struggle would probably be considered legitimate if it came from SANE but illegitimate if it came from the American Margarine Manufacturers Association. The official receiving the message would probably say to himself: "Why should the margarine manufacturers wish to speak with a united voice that carries no direct consequence for them as margarine manufacturers?"

Officials receive many spurious and misleading messages and, therefore, they must seek to establish the veracity and credibility of all messages. The surest way to obtain credibility for an interest group message is for the group to establish a reputation for honesty and accuracy. In Washington lobbying, such a reputation is not easily gained and not lightly thrown away. Only repeated instances of honesty and accuracy of information in messages can build such a reputation.

Messages may also attain credibility because they contain unique facts that the sender's peculiar position enables him to know well. This tends to be true of facts ascertained by recognized experts. A group may also have unique facts about the consequences of a certain policy upon its membership, and credibility is likely to attach to messages containing these facts. Unique facts about the impact of a proposed policy upon group membership are more easily developed in the case of domestic policy issues than foreign policy issues. Domestic policies often have direct economic consequences for citizens; these consequences are fairly easily demonstrable in a message. Foreign issues, on the other hand, usually have more indirect consequences (tariff questions excepted) and it is difficult to demonstrate in a message how a certain group might be hurt.

A message may also attain credibility by the sheer force of the idea or argument it contains. Occasionally an idea comes along that is so cogent and important that it is immediately recognized as such by those who hear it. Such ideas usually are passed on by the staff to the decision-maker without delay. The probabilities are greater that such ideas will be generated by the executive bureaucracy than by interest groups. This is especially true of foreign policy issues, since planning and idea-generating groups for foreign policy questions are built into the bureaucracy. Still, it is certainly not inconceivable that new and cogent foreign policy ideas could come from an interest group.

Since style as well as content is important, interest groups are well-advised to present their message in an inviting fashion. If it is a personal presentation of the message, the sender should be pleasant and inoffensive; he should be well-prepared and well-informed. It is important that he personally be convinced that the message is "right." He should be succinct, well-organized, and direct; he should use the soft sell, and should leave a written summary of his message.[6] Since a message is always competing with many other messages for the attention of the decision-maker, the wise sender will try to find some way to convince the official that it is important for him to listen. The surest way to do this in the case of an elected official is to show him how he will protect himself or gain politically by listening. Demonstration that a given

6. For an elaboration of these points, see Milbrath, *op. cit.*, pp. 220–27.

measure is in the public interest or would serve the cause of justice also stimulates attention and concern. Unless this feeling of the importance of the message is created early in the presentation, there is a high probability that the entire message will be lost.

It should be apparent from the above discussion that it is no easy matter for interest groups and lobbyists to get messages through in such a fashion that they are likely to be influential. To help compensate for this difficulty, some interest groups have turned to "lobbying at the grass roots." They become propaganda agencies working on the opinion of their members or on public opinion in general. They may try to stir people at the grass roots to write letters, send telegrams, work for a candidate or party, or give money to a candidate or party. The implicit assumption of these tactics is that the number of messages directed to officials with the hope of influencing their decision can be enormously increased. Since each of these messages stands for potential votes, it is assumed that elected officials must listen and be affected by the messages. If the campaign to mold opinion at the grass roots is effective, and yet public officials do not make decisions in conformance with that opinion, it is presumed that the people will elect new officials who will follow public opinion.

Although the logic of this approach is unexceptionable, it is no easy task for interest groups to manipulate public opinion. In order for public relations campaigns to have a discernable effect, they have to be very large and very skillfully managed. A minimum of five million dollars has been expended in the few recent public relations campaigns conducted by interest groups that have had a clearly visible impact on public opinion (e.g., the campaign of the AMA to prevent adoption of compulsory national health insurance and the campaign of the margarine manufacturers to remove the ten cent a pound federal tax on their product.) Just as groups find it difficult to get officials to listen, they also find it difficult to get the attention of the public. Even on questions where some direct interest is apparent to anyone who cares to look (such as a job or a pension), many persons directly affected by the proposed policy will not be aroused by it. One would hypothesize, then, that it is especially difficult to engage the public on foreign policy questions, where its interests usually are much more indirect and general.

If an interest group tries to compete with the President to influence public opinion on any issue (foreign or domestic), most of the advantages are with the President. On foreign policy issues, where the President is considered to have privileged information, his advantages are even greater than for domestic issues. He commands the attention of all the news media; he is presumed to be better-informed and is presumed to have the interest of the whole country in mind. An interest group

acting alone would have no chance in such a contest. Only if it were able to attract the support of a substantial proportion of other public officials, could their combined campaign have a significant impact on policy outcomes. In such instances of collaboration between officials and interest groups, it is difficult to tell whether the officials are using the interest groups or vice versa. After examining the decisions over reciprocal trade renewal in 1955 and 1962, Bauer, Pool, and Dexter concluded that officials manipulated groups more than groups manipulated officials.[7]

If a group eschews an attempt to influence general public opinion (as most of them do) and concentrates on its own membership, it still has a formidable opinion formation task. Only a small portion of the membership reads the communications from the national organization; even a smaller proportion is willing to take action when requested. When the national leadership requests that messages of a given sort be sent to public officials, a certain proportion of the members will garble or distort the message. The leadership is on the horns of a dilemma here. If a standardized message is prepared so as to avoid distortion, it will be spotted as a "pressure campaign" and severely discounted; if the leadership tries to preserve a semblance of spontaneity in the origin and content of the messages, which facilitates a judgment by officials that the messages are credible, many fewer messages get composed and a higher proportion of them depart from the point of view the leadership is trying to promote. Frequently, public officials are tipped off that a letter or telegram campaign is in progress by some disgruntled member who sends the campaign instructions received from the group's national leadership to the official who is the target of the campaign. When this occurs, most of the campaign effort is wasted. These are the normal difficulties interest groups encounter when they are working on questions of domestic policy. On foreign policy questions, which tend to have a diffuse rather than a specific impact on individuals, it is even more difficult for them to mobilize their members and thus few interest groups attempt to mount large grass roots campaigns on foreign policy questions.

Even if an interest group focuses on attentive elites rather than on the mass (a somewhat more manageable task), attempts to manipulate elite opinions are difficult and unpredictable. Bauer, Pool, and Dexter suggest some very cogent reasons why:

> First, there lies latent in individuals a great collection of traces of previous communications. Any new communication may serve to change this massive structure only perceptibly, but it may at the same time set it into action in directions determined by the structure itself more than by the trigger stimulus.

7. *Op. cit.*, p. 477.

Second, the event triggered within the system may itself have more effect on the system than does the original stimulus. Arguing for one's own views in reply to a challenge may have more effect on one than does the challenge.

Third, within an individual many latent attitudes may be simultaneously present. The social controls and social relations may make some of them easier to express than others. Thus, even stimuli which have a persuasive effect on a man's thought may trigger quite opposite expressions.

Fourth, where a stimulus is addressed to a population of individuals, structural determinants may result in its mobilizing different proportions of those who agree and those who disagree with it. If it mobilizes more of those who disagree, the stimulus may boomerang...the communication is one input into a complex socio-psychological system. The effect of the communication on that system is, to a greater degree than is usually acknowledged, a function of the structure of that system. The impact of a given communication is of itself essentially indeterminate.[8]

To recapitulate, we have said that groups desiring to influence foreign policy decisions must know the optimum stage of the decision for delivery of their message; they must know the officials or their advisers who are involved in the decision and who are most likely to be receptive to the messages; they must find an open and clear channel to such persons; they must attract the attention of officials so that they will be heard; they must compose messages that are credible and legitimate. They may want to supplement these methods by stirring up messages from the grass roots or they may wish to concentrate on elites who are more likely to send supplementary messages. It requires a great deal of knowledge and skill to perform these tasks well. Many interest groups try to hire persons skilled in these tasks and send them as full-time lobbyists to Washington. Most lobbyists only partially fulfill the demands outlined here; many are frustrated by their inability to produce detectable results. This is not surprising, for the cards are stacked against them. Lobbying to influence foreign policy is no easy matter.

TYPES OF GROUPS INTERESTED IN FOREIGN POLICY

Persons who might wish to influence a decision on foreign policy live in many places and play many roles. Some may choose to act individually, but most would think that to be relatively futile. Only a citizen who had a close personal relationship with an official decision-maker (or who has power over an official) could hope to exert much influence

8. *Ibid.*, pp. 469–70.

through his individual action. Most citizens desiring influence form or join groups in the hope that the strength of numbers will increase their impact. Relatively few groups are formed solely to attempt to influence foreign policy; usually groups are formed for some broader purpose which incorporates foreign policy. Since the variety of groups that might wish to influence foreign policy is rather great, it is helpful to have a taxonomy of types of such groups. The one that follows (Figure 3) is oriented to our purposes and is very simple; it is not intended as an adequate classification for a general interest group study.

Figure 3—A Simple Taxonomy of Groups Interested in the Foreign Policy of a Government

INTERNAL GROUPS				EXTERNAL GROUPS	
Governmental Groups		Nongovernmental Groups		Foreign Governments	Nongovernmental Groups
Special Foreign Policy	General Interest (e.g. Congress) or specialists in matters other than foreign policy	Special Foreign Policy	General Interest Groups or specialists in matters other than foreign policy		

The first distinction presented in Figure 3, between internal and external groups, would not be necessary for strictly domestic policy questions. For questions of foreign policy, however, foreign governments and groups in foreign countries become important aggregates of persons desiring to influence the decisions of American foreign policy-makers. The interest of foreign governments in the foreign policy of the United States is obvious; it is the major reason for diplomatic representation in each other's capitals. The interest of private groups from other countries in American foreign policy is almost equally as obvious but is often overlooked. Several hundred agents are registered with the Attorney General under the Foreign Agents Registration Act of 1938. Foreign groups are not only interested in American policy, they also can have a significant influence upon it. Alger suggests that some "governments accept criticism and advice more willingly from foreign persons they perceive as private citizens than from the persons they perceive as governmental officials."[9]

9. Chadwick F. Alger, "The External Bureaucracy in United States Foreign Affairs," *Administrative Science Quarterly*, Vol. VII (June, 1962), p. 77.

A dramatic example from recent history of a foreign group influencing American foreign policy is the incident in which Buddhists committed suicide by fire in Vietnam and thus stimulated a change in the pattern of support from the United States government for the Diem regime. Both foreign governments and groups, then, are important factors in shaping and expressing world opinion which, in turn, has a significant impact on United States foreign policy.

The second level of distinction in Figure 3, that between governmental and nongovernmental groups, is essential to a complete picture of the groupings of petitioners who send messages to official decision-makers. In a large governmental structure like the Federal Government, it is helpful to think of the various branches and agencies as groups with a life and purpose of their own. Very often the fulfillment of the agency's goals requires another agency to make a coordinate decision, and hence, the first agency will try to influence the decision of the second agency. When agencies act in this fashion, and they regularly do, they are very similar to nongovernmental interest groups that try to influence governmental decisions. The problems of transmitting messages that are likely to have influence on official decision-makers are conceptually the same for governmental and nongovernmental groups, albeit governmental groups normally have an advantage in obtaining open channels and in legitimating their concern for the problem.

Thirdly, we can distinguish groups with special or exclusive foreign policy concerns from groups with more general concerns. In the U.S. government, the special foreign policy agencies would be the State Department, the National Security Council, CIA, USIS, and the Defense Department. Congress and the President have more general interests, as do such departments as Treasury, Agriculture, Commerce, Labor, and HEW. Certain branches and agencies have almost no foreign policy concerns, such as the Judiciary, and the Departments of Justice and the Interior. In the nongovernmental sphere, several types of groups have interests that include, but are much broader than, foreign policy. To use a common classification, they might be labeled as business, labor, agriculture, veterans, military, civic, women's, patriotic, and ethnic. It is difficult to decide whether the so-called China Lobby belongs in this category or that of special foreign policy interest groups or, for that matter, whether it is a group at all. Of course, some groups have no interest in foreign policy whatsoever and do not concern us here.

Groups specializing in foreign policy might be arrayed along a continuum stretching between government and the body politic (Figure 4). This notion pursues that expressed earlier that groups are intermediaries in the communication network linking the people to their government. Some foreign policy groups are so close to the government that it

Figure 4 — Special Foreign Policy Interest Groups Arrayed along a
Continuum Stretching between Government and the Body Politic

The Government			The Body Politic

Semi-autonomous study or advisory groups	Autonomous groups: economic and noneconomic	Ad hoc groups	World Affairs Organizations

is impossible to draw a boundary between them and the government.
The RAND Corporation, for example, receives most of its funds from
the government and does studies at the request of the government. The
Council on Foreign Relations, while not financed by government, works
so closely with it that it is difficult to distinguish Council actions stimulated by government from autonomous actions. These groups are used
by the government to float trial balloons, to help create public opinion,
and to consult on policy. Alger calls them "external bureaucrats" and
suggests that their role is very crucial indeed: "When governments are
unable to make crucial decisions, external bureaucrats are sometimes
called in to make them" and, equally important, "External bureaucrats
serve governmental needs by stimulating private persons or groups to
perform tasks that tradition or limited resources will not permit the
government to undertake itself."[10]

A relatively small proportion of autonomous groups specializes in
foreign policy issues. These groups could be further subdivided into
economic and noneconomic foreign policy groups. The former include
those interested in tariff questions (e.g., the Committee on a National
Trade Policy and the American Tariff League), groups interested in
international banking and investment, those concerned with international
fishing rights, the shipping industry, and groups interested in the allocation of quotas to import sugar into the United States. Often these groups,
representing economic interests that spill over into foreign policy, are
opposed by competitive interests in other countries: protectionists are
opposed by those desiring to export to America; American fishing
interests are opposed by fishing interests from other countries (Japan,
for example); American shipping lines are opposed by foreign shipping
lines (Norwegian, for example); and foreign sugar producers compete
with each other and with American producers for their share of the
American sugar market.

Noneconomic foreign policy groups tend to concentrate on broad
questions of war and peace. The groups are usually small, with a thin
financial base. Included here are such groups as the Women's Inter-

10. *Ibid.*, p. 78.

national League for Peace and Freedom, Committee for a Sane Nuclear Policy, the Peace Union, and so forth. Such groups are usually concerned with decisions where the President is the dominant or sole decision-maker. They concentrate mainly on the opinions of elites whom the President might consult. Their chances for getting clear channels through to the President or his closest advisers are relatively poor. Their chances for influencing broad general public opinion are also relatively poor. One would have to conclude that their impact on foreign policy is slight at best.

Now and then *ad hoc* groups spring up around an issue, an idea, or a particularly able leader. Sometimes *ad hoc* groups attract continuing support and turn into semipermanent organizations (e.g., SANE) if the issue which drew people together continues to be significant. A certain degree of institutionalization must set in before the group can develop a budget, rent an office, hire a lobbyist, and sustain a general lobbying effort.

Near the public end of the continuum described in Figure 4 are groups that make little or no attempt to communicate directly with governmental decision-makers; they concentrate, instead, on trying to educate the public about foreign policy matters. Some of their messages may flow through the public back to decision-makers, but little effort is made to direct or manipulate that flow. A world affairs study group, such as can be found in most communities, would be included here, as well as such national groups as the Foreign Policy Association, the United World Federalists, Atlantic Community groups, the Committee on World Peace through World Law, and so forth. These groups probably do have some impact on the opinions of the people who listen to them, but most relevant polls show that the proportion of the entire population who listen is not very great. It would be virtually impossible to trace their impact on any given foreign policy decision. Such groups can only hope for long-range effects in the form of persons exposed to their ideas who enter official foreign policy decision-making positions.

OVERALL EVALUATION OF GROUP INFLUENCE ON FOREIGN POLICY

With the foregoing considerations in mind, it is now possible to summarize by suggesting several hypotheses relevant to the influence that interest groups exert in foreign policy. Needless to say, considerable research would have to be carried out in order to test them.

I. The possibility for group influence on foreign policy issues varies with the issue.

A. Decisions made by social processes are more open to group influence than decisions made by intellective processes. Social process decisions have many more points of access and are more subject to interpersonal influences.

B. Decisions on foreign policies that involve direct, visible (usually economic) rewards and/or punishments to different sectors of the society generally tend to be shared by Congress and the President, to be social rather than intellective in process, and to stimulate more lobbying activities by groups at many points of access. Consequently, such decisions tend to resemble domestic policy issues more than those foreign policy problems that do not involve direct and visible rewards or punishments.

C. In general, it is easier for interest groups to compose and submit credible and legitimate messages to officials on domestic issues than on foreign policy issues. The direct impact of a proposed policy upon a group is usually more visible for domestic issues and thus the group's concern has greater legitimacy. Furthermore, on domestic issues groups often have unique and credible information about the impact of a proposed policy upon their memberships; comparable information is often lacking for foreign policy issues.

D. Assuming that the locus of decision is accessible to group influence, those issues that attract the attention of special publics, but that attract little general public attention, are more open to group influence than issues that attract wide and/or intense public scrutiny. The decision that foreign aid materials should, if possible, be shipped in American bottoms is an example of the former; the decision to send American troops into Vietnam is an example of the latter.

E. While the public pays relatively little attention to foreign policy issues, even to such a well-publicized issue as ratification of the test-ban treaty it does not follow that the public generally pays more attention to domestic than foreign policy issues. The over-all attention level to both kinds of issues is low and both kinds may receive increased attention if the press chooses to give them a play. Attention level does not seem to be a function of the domestic or foreign character of issues.

F. Robinson suggests a curvilinear relationship between group involvement in decisions and the crisis level of the decision.[11] At a very low crisis level only a few special groups are likely to be interested in the decision. As the importance, or crisis level, of the decision increases, the interests of more groups are likely to be at stake (as well as to stimulate more intense interest), and thus more groups will be inclined to try to exert influence. As the crisis level increases further, and especially as decision time shortens, there is relatively little opportunity for group interests to be taken into account (e.g., the Cuban crisis of October, 1962). In the latter instance, the President has enormous power to shape public opinion and receives little effective challenge from interest groups. This does not mean that groups are of no consequence for crisis

11. James A. Robinson, "Public Opinion in Lasswell's *Future of Political Science*," *Public Opinion Quarterly*, Vol. XXVIII (Fall, 1964), p. 399.

decisions, as their anticipated reactions may play some role and their subsequent positions may help set the stage for the next decision; but it does mean that groups are not likely to be consulted in the short decision time.

G. The less the importance of the issue, the greater the likelihood of group influence on its outcome; the greater the importance of the issue, the less the likelihood of group influence. This is a derivation from D and F above. Unimportant issues (in the total scheme of things) are less likely to attract public attention and are less likely to attract opposition groups. Public attention and conflicting positions by groups, which tend to accompany more important issues, serve as systemic checks on group influence.[12]

H. Decisions allowed to gestate over a period of several months are more open to group influence than decisions that must be made in a few days. If an issue is new, a group may not have a declared position, thus requiring the Washington staff to contact its policy-makers who, in turn, must confer and decide on a policy position. Furthermore, a few days is a relatively short time for a group to compose and transmit messages that are likely to be effective.

II. It is more likely that officials use lobbies as tools than that officials follow the bidding of such groups. This especially characterizes foreign policy decisions centering in the President, but it is also true of social process decisions involving a large number of decision-makers. As Bauer, Pool, and Dexter state.

> None of the lobbies we observed were the powerful monsters they are reputed to be. Underfinanced, they had to spend much of their time recruiting members and raising funds. Poorly staffed and overworked, they generally became effective, not as lobbies persuading public office-holders, but as service bureaus auxiliary to the efforts of those public servants . . . . The lobby became the congressman's publicity bureau. Indeed, without a congressman working with it, a lobby found it difficult to do anything the press would consider newsworthy . . . . The people who most actively form the issues to be discussed and debated are the symbolic leaders in Congress and the Executive. They generate the public concerns which come back as pressures on them.[13]

III. The ability of interest groups specializing in foreign policy to affect broad public opinion on foreign policy is severely limited. Compared to the power of the President in this respect, their direct impact on opinion is miniscule (although it should be noted that opinion-forming efforts of these groups may have second-order effects that social science cannot now measure). The basic difficulty is that few people listen to group propaganda. Only as part of a concerted campaign, in close collaboration with public officials,

---

12. Cf. Milbrath, *op. cit.*, Part IV.
13. Bauer, Pool, and Dexter, *op cit.*, pp. 477–79.

are group propaganda efforts likely to attract sufficient attention to have even a slight effect.

IV. The process by which groups respond to issues they may wish to try to influence is fundamentally the same whether the issue lies in domestic or foreign policy. In both cases they must find the locus of the decision and compose and transmit effective messages. The process within the group of arriving at a group position and of deciding on a strategy of action is also the same for foreign and domestic issues. Group leaders do not make a foreign-domestic distinction as they think about the way the policy will be handled within the group. The type of issue, foreign or domestic, probably affects their influence strategy to the extent that the locus and timing of decision is more confined for most foreign, as compared to most domestic, issues. Lobbyists, however, are accustomed to planning special strategies (with respect to locus and timing) for all issues and do not sort them into foreign and domestic boxes. In my research no lobbyist has ever indicated that he used a generally different strategy for foreign issues than for domestic issues.

In summary, I conclude that interest group influence on foreign policy is slight. In my earlier work I conclude that in general the direct "first order" effects of group influence on the policies of the federal government was slight.[14] Confining my gaze now to foreign policy, I would estimate that group influence is even weaker in that arena.

14. Milbrath, *op. cit.*, Chap. 17.

URBANIZATION, PAROCHIALISM, AND FOREIGN POLICY

Scott Greer

IN the beginning, foreign policy was the policy of cities. Transitory empires expanded to link them, then ebbed back to the walled stronghold. With the emergence of the nation-state, however, cities lost their walls and foreign policy dealt primarily with relations among rural territorial jurisdictions, in which cities, though command posts, held only a minority of the relevant population. Today, as the advanced societies become increasingly urban, international affairs and foreign policies are once more relations between urban complexes—though the complexes may be scattered over a continent.

Foreign policy is of major importance to any metropolitan complex because that complex lives in part by taking in international wash. And the exchange relation between nations is particularly sensitive to foreign policy, for the nation-state sets the boundaries of political space and these dominate physical space. This is apparent in the matter of tariffs, which determine the relationships between physical space and economic exchange space. It is no accident that the pocket matches of the British

West Indies are imported from Sweden, at several times the sales cost in the United States; we reciprocate by paying approximately four times the British West Indies going price for prime rum. Equally to the point, the metropolitan community may be concerned with foreign policy because it is essentially a worldwide producer (so the dominant employer in one large midwestern city sells 40 per cent of its merchandise overseas). In short, decisions concerning the relationships between states may shrink, expand, or deflect the flow of exchange among metropolitan areas and, in the process, may have major consequences for the economic fortunes of their residents.

Equally important to many metropolitan areas is the defense economy and its consequences for the locals. Whether or not getting a man on the moon helps us to stand up to Russia, it certainly improves the possibility of Boston's standing up to the San Francisco Bay area. American policy on the development of spacecraft thus becomes a domestic issue for Boston's economy. Even more bizarre, political-economic decisions on weaponry among the NATO countries may affect the economic state of the given metropolis. This was evident when relations between the United States and the United Kingdom resulted in abandonment of several expensive new British models in supersonic military aircraft. These will now be purchased, instead, from certain United States firms in certain cities partially supported by federal weaponry contracts. The metropolitan economy is increasingly a political economy.

International politics, meanwhile, impinges upon the politics of the metropolis. Relations with African nations bring out Negro pickets at various embassies; the "nationality groups" agitate for the freedom of their country from one or the other foreign yoke; and the Mayor of Boston visits the homelands of his constituency in Ireland, Israel, and Italy. At the same time, the WASPS (white Anglo-Saxon protestants) develop a new isolationism, based upon a thoroughgoing distrust of the new nations as well as their arena, the United Nations.

While these ideologies beat about the rock of city hall, other consequences are less noted. The greater the nation's investment in expensive foreign relations (whether aid or armament), the smaller the amount of the fisc devoted to domestic problems. Of the latter, some think urban problems to be the most critical. Thus we have an urban renewal program which is less costly than the funds sunk in Indochina since World War II. while we have tens of millions living in older central cities. We could "renew" the cities. By the present formulae, the cost would be approximately one trillion dollars to do this within a twelve-year span. This sounds utopian, yet Dyckman and Isaacs estimate that it could easily be done if the amount of the defense budget were so invested.[1]

1. John W. Dyckman and Reginold R. Isaacs, with the assistance of Peter R. Senn,

The costs and consequences of foreign policy come to rest, then, in the metropolitan communities. This is not surprising, for they are the organizational peaks and centers of our large-scale society. They are strange political quasi communities: seldom organized as meaningful units, they are in many other ways the most meaningful unit below the level of the nation-state. How do their interests and forces interact with those of the nation in the foreign policy nexus?

METROPOLITANIZATION AND SOCIETAL SCALE

It is doubtful that "metropolitanization" is the most useful term for what concerns us here. The sheer concentration of people in dense settlements has only an obscure theoretical or empirical generative power. Much more important is the set of linked processes making this desirable and inevitable: the increase in societal scale. This refers, not to the settlement of urban places, but to the organizational transformation of total societies. The size of a city is really no guarantee of its scale; though Accra and Kingston are fair-sized settlements, what we must be concerned with is their importance as sites for organizational head-quarters and the exchange of messages, men, and materials among organizations.

The term "metropolitanization" or "urbanization" conceals three quite distinct, though interlinked, notions. The first is the notion of increasing societal scale, the increased extensity and intensity of inter-dependency made possible by increasing energy turnover and organiza-tional innovation. It makes possible and, under certain conditions, desirable, the second meaning: urban concentration, the piling up of people in cities. The third meaning is the development of the *culture of cities*, the cosmopolitan style of life which rests on large-scale organiza-tion and results in wide intellectual horizons. (This has frequently been termed "urbanism.") The three concepts, once empirically linked, have come apart as we realize that cities exist outside large-scale societies, that farmers in large-scale societies may become "urbane," and that denizens of Boston may be comfortable in the role of "urban peasant."[2]

For this reason it is not useful to let our urban majority stand for that view of the world we evoke by the term "urbane." The broad, rational view of the world may be as foreign to the urban villager of the United States as to the higgler lady in Kingston, the market mammy in Accra. The contract planter in a village of the California Central Valley would

Capital Requirements for Urban Redevelopment and Renewal (New York: McGraw-Hill, 1961).

2. Herbert Gans, *The Urban Villagers* (New York: The Free Press, 1962).

have little to say to either. The key point is one's place in a larger network of action. Organizations vary in their scale, the spread and magnitude of their commitment in space and time; roles within organizations vary in their scope. Thus the low-level worker in a small plant may be as local in his outlook as a farmer, no matter how large his city of residence, while the professional or managerial worker in a national firm may be a true cosmopolitan though stationed in Butte, Montana or Fargo, North Dakota.

The key concepts for unraveling this situation are the *scale* of the society (and of the city within it) and the *scope* of the actor's role. There is a range of scale along which societies can be placed, measured by energy turnover and exchange transactions: it indicates the range of relations within which that society exists. Each city in it can be characterized, following the older notion of metropolitan dominance, by its relative scale.[3] And, since cities are bundles of organizations, each individual role can be evaluated by its place within an organizational structure. The larger-scale society would have more people with broader horizons, dependent on larger organizations with greater extensity. This would be more so in the large-scale urban centers. Separate from the simple spatial fact (but correlated), individuals with higher-level roles, and thus with access to the control and communications centers of large-scale organized groups, would have wider scope of action and broader perspectives. They are the cosmopolitans, whose true world extends far beyond the local scene. Their polar opposites, the locals, are immersed in the small, concrete, local group and local settlement.

The metropolitan complexes of the large-scale American society are differentiated by these criteria. Some are hardly more than overgrown marketing towns, invaded by a rural environment. Some are branch-plant towns, largely made up of locals, with a travelling circus of cosmopolitans. Others still are regional capitals, a few are national centers, and at least two are international capitals. The degree to which significant segments of their population are hooked into the national system of communication should vary considerably by such factors; their "urbanity" should covary.

I have denigrated the importance of the city, the "urban container," aside from its status as a center of large-scale society. This must be partially revised in light of two sets of attributes of cities. One is the impingement of their spatial structure upon interaction; the other is their social-political correlates.

With increasing size, American cities are generally more differentiated

3. Rupert B. Vance and Sara Smith, "Metropolitan Dominance and Integration," in Paul K. Hatt and Albert J. Reiss, Jr. (eds.), *Cities and Society* (New York: The Free Press, 1957).

by socioeconomic status, by ethnicity, and by lifestyle. Concurrently, as cities are increasingly larger they tend to be increasingly segregated by the same differentiation. In a small town the effective arena of action includes everybody. In the metropolis, birds of a feather flock together and interact with their own kind. Thus the metropolis is fragmented and divided, impeding communication and encouraging different definitions of events. Two clues to the consequences have emerged: (1) the smaller the city the greater the consensus in political matters;[4] (2) the smaller the city the more conservative and parochial the norms.[5] These probably interact, while small towns maximize the proportion of the "locals," their greater integration probably reinforces the conservatism of the average citizen. Deviants are urged towards the norm through social pressure.

On at least three dimensions, social rank, lifestyle, and ethnicity, large American cities vary internally in a dramatic way. Within specific neighborhoods, the local areas in a metropolis, these characteristics produce quite distinct subcommunities, differing one from another. Out of common ways of life, interests, and identities, neighboring and voluntary organizations are evolved, expressing the character of the area and, in the process, structuring its differences from other areas. At an extreme, as in the segregation of the ethnic poor on one hand, the rich "old Americans" on the other, spatial segregation fits with many other kinds of differentiation and produces sharp schisms in the body politic.[6] Such schisms are conducive to political views deviant from the average, i.e., extremism. Stable, integrated neighborhoods of black and white produce few Black Muslims or Minutemen. For these groups we look to Harlem and the Nordic White Protestant Suburbs. (The Ku Klux Klan probably reflects the combination of small town structure and strict racial segregation — the latter does not *require* a metropolis.)

At the same time that the metropolis differentiates and segregates, it also is conducive to inclusion and integration. The inclusive tendencies result from the mass media, available to all citizens alike and richer in content as cities increase in size. They also include the public educational system. Varied as its quality and content may be within the metropolis, its over-all quality is notably higher than that available for similar populations in less urban situations. Finally, the metropolitan ambit, with its freedom from surveillance and ease of movement among enormous

4. P. H. Ennis, "The Contextual Dimension in Voting," in W. N. McPhee and W. A. Glazer (eds.), *Public Opinion and Congressional Elections* (New York: The Free Press, 1962).

5. Alfred O. Hero, *Voluntary Organizations in World Affairs Communication* (Boston: World Peace Foundation, 1960).

6. Joseph R. Gusfield, "Mass Society and Extremist Politics," *American Sociological Review*, Vol. 27 (February, 1962), pp. 19–30.

populations, allows for a multiplication of what Gusfield has termed "cross-cutting" relationships.[7] These are relationships with many groups, various and often contradictory in their purposes, held by the same set of individuals. If Gusfield is correct, such relationships minimize the schism and extremism which "consistent" segregation maximizes.

Size is not, however, the critical aspect of the metropolis. More important is the rate of energy turnover (the wealth), and the organizational salience and complexity (the occupational status) of its population. While there may be enormous differentiation within a metropolis, the average for that metropolis may be much higher in social rank than for others, and this too is important. It is indicative of the city's rank within the larger society.

A second set of variables important to the cosmopolitan or urbane character of a metropolis is its age and rate of growth, proportionate to its size. Public discourse in a city is in part a result of its control and communications structure; in the mushrooming boom-towns of the Southwest and the West Coast, one suspects that a small control system appropriate to an earlier age has failed to grow allomorphically. It is flooded by the new in-migrants. In such a situation the trusted figures and groups (the "elite") become indistinguishable to the mass of newcomers. The mass media call the tune.[8] Thus Los Angeles dropped its Social Register in the 1920's at about the same time that Hollywood marriages began to dominate the society pages of the Los Angeles Times. In such a society, new money and new men gain a degree of prominence that stands as surrogate for civic leadership.

The importance of the boom-town today is that many of our metropolitan complexes are boom-towns, particularly the new metropolises of the West, Southwest, and South. Phoenix, moving from a few score thousand in 1940 to two-thirds of a million today, is an extreme; yet increases of several hundred per cent in the past twenty-five years are not rare. As boom-towns, both the rate of growth and the sheer friction of size and space in an increasingly horizontal settlement have tended to unite the networks of control and communication. While it is difficult to find a tangible "power elite" in most very large cities, I suspect it is equally difficult in smaller ones that have grown rapidly.

Under these circumstances, some observers have seen the problem as one of an uncontrollable mass society. It is a society of the incompetent, vulnerable to demagoguery, essentially alienated and dangerous. To these observers, political democracy is a portent and a reinforcing agent for decline. Others, however, relying upon recent empirical

7. *Ibid.*
8. Scott Greer, *Metropolitics: A Study of Political Culture* (New York: John Wiley and Sons, 1963).

research, see the metropolitan residents as typically engaged in everyday life, ebullient and confident rather than alienated and anomic, moving steadily from public school to job, family, suburbs, and taxpaying.[9] They also see a steady increase in the proportion of cosmopolitans, the persons who work in a large-scale world and whose intellectual scope is broad.

From this perspective there seems to be a kind of guerrilla warfare of political norms going on. The cosmopolitan point of view, oriented to the metropolis, the nation, and selected aspects of the world, is common among the well-educated who work with symbols and people.[10] Their business is the maintenance of the larger organizational systems. (In a recent study, the majority of executives in large business enterprises favored Johnson; small businessmen, with the significant exception of bankers, opposed him.) Against this point of view, however, stands an older American ethos, one which emphasizes the individual against the state, the state against the world.[11] Presumably appropriate to the agrarian democracy of the nineteenth century and the localized world of small town and open country neighborhood, it is perpetuated in the metropolitan complex and may become a genuine political force there.

Rather than speculate about the psychological correlation of such a perspective, it might be more useful to view it as essentially the *conservation* of an older culture. Should this be so, we would expect to find it strongest among the rural, the less well-educated, the segregated—all who are limited in their access to the emerging world of the twentieth century. Such an interpretation fits the data presented by McClosky: his isolationists are small businessmen, farmers, unskilled laborers.[12] It also fits the data organized by Hero with respect to "international behavior."[13] The fit is not perfect of course, for culture complexes serve many different purposes, especially when they are made explicit and converted into fighting ideologies. Pseudo-*gemeinschaft* is probably a constant attribute in a society undergoing rapid change.

Yet the trends of the times have been relatively clear. Increasing acceptance of an international role for the United States (as reported in a number of these chapters) and acceptance of an active role for the national government in once private affairs, seem to be long-run trends. Perhaps equally important is the declining strength of the Republican party when it is defined as standing for the isolationist and antigovernment

9. Scott Greer, *The Emerging City: Myth and Reality* (New York: The Free Press, 1962).

10. Alfred O. Hero, *Americans in World Affairs* (Boston: World Peace Foundation, 1959).

11. Cf. Herbert McClosky's findings in Chap. 3 of this book.

12. *Ibid.*

13. Alfred O. Hero, *Americans in World Affairs.*

position (the long-run drop in Republican party affiliations is impressive) and the spurt of strength where it is defined as opposing that position.

Under these conditions of ideological warfare, the structure of the local polity and the local communications system may be major intervening variables. The very looseness of both are, on the West Coast, conducive to loud noises from the radical right; initiative, referendum, and recall allow for considerable political effectiveness by well-organized minorities, while the press acts as a megaphone for their messages. Curiously then, areas of the country that in some ways maximize the cosmopolitan outlook may also maximize the extremely parochial—and this phenomenon may vary among the different areas of life, sometimes in the same people. (It seems to me that this syncretism was dramatically evidenced in the style of life and thought attributed to Senator Goldwater during his 1964 presidential campaign.)

Most of us are probably neither pure locals nor pure cosmopolitans. Instead, we are changelings, with the consequent unease about our past and future common to such. The political culture of the metropolitan American seems a mix of norms from the past and ideas from the present, not logical and often mutually contradictory. These norms can be activated by vigorous exhortation, by the shock of world events, perhaps by education. Whether they can be evaluated, changed, made orderly— whether their application rules can be more clearly specified—is another set of questions.

SOME TRENDS

The real income of the American people has doubled since 1900. Formal education is universal and the years invested rise steadily; both the norm and the range move upward. The counterpart of the decline in demand for unskilled labor is the increasingly demanding nature of the job. These could all be summarized as increasing the opportunity for social choice, as does the steady erosion of barriers based upon race. The argument of this chapter can be summarized as follows: (1) If increasing scale increases the average scope of the role; *and* (2) if increasing scope of the role increases average attention span; *and* (3) if increasing span of attention means increasing competence and concern for foreign affairs; (4) *Then* increasing societal scale = increasing competence and concern for foreign affairs. This would parallel intellectually an increasingly interdependent world order. It could result in the increase of communication and control to the point where they were congruent with increasing interdependence.

I have concentrated upon the society of the United States. The argument, however, is more general. But even if it holds for all societies, we must still keep in mind (1) the varying scale of societies; (2) their varying rates of increase in scale; and (3) rapidly increasing global interdependence.

ELECTORAL PUNISHMENT AND FOREIGN POLICY CRISES*

Kenneth N. Waltz

Not so long ago the point was often made, and rightly so, that the winning and losing of elections, insofar as issues are decisive, depends on domestic policies and problems and not on distant and evanescent questions of foreign policy. Problems of foreign policy are now no longer distant; they are constantly upon us. Almost always since World War II, matters of foreign policy have ranked highest among the concerns of the people at large.[1] Indeed, the old argument that foreign policy is electorally unimportant is revealed as misleading merely by rephrasing it as follows: Only those issues that people worry about will have electoral impact. Whether people care about foreign policy depends on time and circumstance. More often than not in the last quarter-century they have cared very much.

1. "With few exceptions, the international scene has dominated the thinking of the public over the years." Only occasionally has a matter of domestic concern crowded foreign policy out of first place, as did racial problems in July and October of 1963. American Institute of Public Opinion (AIPO) Releases, July 20 and October 1, 1963.

*Copyright © 1967 by Kenneth N. Waltz.

In terms of constancy of concern, international issues have been domesticated. Are there other similarities between domestic and international issues? Problems of governmental investment, the financing of research and development, urban renewal, highway building, programs for agriculture, for social welfare, and for education—all can be broken into pieces or parceled out to be handled at different government levels. Problems of foreign policy often appear to be different in type. They can be managed only by the national government, and it is often thought that they must be taken whole. When that great American experiment, Prohibition, clearly brought more bad effects than good, what had been done by altering the Constitution could be undone by repealing the earlier amendment. In international relations, however, an experiment tried and found wanting may bring changes in the world that no act of a single government can easily reverse. The United States fought World War II for military victory without giving much thought to the ways in which fighting the war would affect the subsequent peace. On the morrow of victory, it dismantled its military machine with breathtaking speed. The advance of the Soviet Union to the center of Europe was made easier by America's policies. No new policy, short of an aggressive war of liberation, could erase the effects that old policies had helped to produce.

The effects of foreign policies are hard to predict and difficult to control, for the forces involved are subject to the manipulation of two or more countries. The irreversibility of the result joined with the greater unpredictability of events serves to establish an important difference between the problem of controlling or influencing the external, as compared to the internal, world. Nonetheless, as foreign affairs have increasingly commanded the attention of government, foreign and domestic problems have taken on a greater similarity. The more closely the government is involved in the economy and society, the smaller is its opportunity to engage in whimsical legislative experiments. Because governments have become more deeply involved, continuity from one government to the next has assumed some of the importance in domestic policy than it must always have in foreign policy. And as the government's responsibility for maintaining full employment has increased, the need of greater executive flexibility in financial and fiscal affairs has come to be widely accepted.

In these characteristics—the irreversibility of the act, the importance of continuity, and the need for flexibility—domestic governance of the present has come to resemble more closely the discharge of foreign-policy functions in the past. Completing the pattern of convergence from the other side, foreign policy has acquired the attributes of domestic policy. Having become expensive, foreign policy now involves the politi-

cal problems of resource allocation and distribution that frequently plague domestic programs. Defense spending, in and after the Korean War, has taken about 10 per cent of the gross national product yearly and has accounted for 50 per cent or more of the federal budget. Foreign aid, small when compared with military expenditures, is larger than most domestic programs. Not surprisingly, it has been subjected to the pulls, strains, and threats of disruption that beset controversial items of welfare spending at home.

The fact that in many important ways the foreign and domestic problems of government have come to resemble each other does not necessarily lessen worry about the effect of opinion on policy. In nineteenth-century England, as political participation spread downward from the classes to the masses, voices of warning were raised. According to respectable opinion, the many poor and improvident, ignorant of political economy, would use their franchise to vote themselves a share of the wealth that they had not earned. Nor could they enrich themselves without destroying the capital treasures, accumulated by the industrious and thrifty, upon which the continued health of the economy was solemnly avowed to depend. The many, it was feared, would seek to control an intricate economy, which their educations had not fitted them to understand. Convinced of the danger, some sought devices to mute or modulate the voice of the masses, as did John Stuart Mill in espousing Hare's system of proportional representation. On questions of domestic policy, the edge of doubt was gradually dulled, though not deadened. In matters of foreign policy, comparable worries endure.

The fear of public opinion impressing itself upon foreign policy is necessarily great if elections go far toward determining policy and if the outcome of elections is determined by the inclinations of ill-informed voters. The fears become greater still if the dread voice of public opinion is able to dictate policy between elections, as well. On both counts, Walter Lippmann has written democracy's indictment with a telling eloquence:

> The unhappy truth is that the prevailing public opinion has been destructively wrong at the critical junctures. The people have imposed a veto upon the judgments of informed and responsible officials. They have compelled the governments, which usually knew what would have been wiser, or was necessary, or was more expedient, to be too late with too little, or too long with too much, too pacifist in peace and too bellicose in war, too neutralist or appeasing in negotiation or too intransigent. Mass opinion has acquired mounting power in this century. It has shown itself to be a dangerous master of decisions when the stakes are life and death.[2]

2. Walter Lippmann, *The Public Philosophy* (Boston: Little, Brown, 1955), p. 20.

All masters of decision are dangerous. Have the people been more dangerous than most of them? This question and many others are raised by Lippmann's statement. Does public opinion prevail in the Western democracies, as Lippmann argues? If it does, has the mass voice in and between crises been simply wrong? If the great undifferentiated public, which he describes and assumes to be decisive, has indeed been wrong "at the critical junctures," have others — professors and pundits, political leaders and highly placed officials — been more often and more nearly correct in their assessment of events and their estimate of policy requirements? If the democracies have erred consistently and disastrously as he says, have other types of modern government interpreted the world more reliably and acted more successfully upon their interpretations?

While Lippmann's harsh indictment is rejected by most students of politics, many would assent to a milder charge. Lippmann writes of democracy's inclination to "soft courses" of action, which are followed in order to "please the largest number of voters." Henry A. Kissinger finds that Americans have a "penchant for choosing the interpretation of current trends which implies least effort."[3] Lippmann writes of the public's impulsive commitment to appeasement and peace or to intransigence and war. Gabriel Almond, in a book first published in 1950, found that "an overtly interventionist and 'responsible' United States hides a covertly isolationist longing," that while interest in foreign affairs had increased, public responses remained "highly unstable."[4] Echoing the view a decade later, V.O. Key, Jr., doubted that "the new outlook toward the outside world has the same solidity and durability" as the isolationist opinion it had replaced.[5] Lippmann thinks of democratic leaders as followers. The ostensible leaders cannot actually lead, even though they may know what the situation requires, for the "great public" will impose its "massive negative" upon proposed new courses of action. Unable to act appropriately in times of crisis, leaders are deterred from preparing for trouble in moments of calm; for "with the massive veto" always latent, the political cost of preparing is likely to be great. Walt W. Rostow finds such a judgment borne out in one case at least, the presidential election of 1956. "There can have been few elections," he writes, "which reflect less credit on the democratic process than the uncandid projection and the self-indulgent public acceptance of the slogan of Peace and Prosperity in 1956."[6] Hidden by the calm that prevailed,

3. Henry A. Kissinger, *The Necessity for Choice* (New York: Harper, 1961), p. 7.
4. Gabriel A. Almond, *The American People and Foreign Policy* (New York: Praeger, 1960), pp. 67, 77.
5. V.O. Key, Jr., *Public Opinion and American Democracy* (New York: Knopf, 1961), pp. 256–57.
6. W.W. Rostow, *The United States in the World Arena: An Essay in Recent History* (New York: Harper, 1960), pp. 395–96.

storm clouds had gathered, but Republican leaders told the people what they wanted to hear rather than what should have been told. David Truman is inclined to spread the blame more evenly among a larger set of public figures. Presented with such challenges as the fall of China, the loyalty-security neurosis of the McCarthy era, and the Russians' first orbiting of a satellite, leaders of the press, of labor and business, and of other groups failed to respond boldly and courageously.[7] In replying to one of Lippmann's charges, Truman may be illustrating another: that leaders may be made timid by their fear of a hostile public reaction.

Three worries about the effect of democratic opinion on foreign policy are widespread. (1) Democracies will prefer the easy way. This is not to say that duties will always be shirked and dangers avoided. It is, for example, sometimes simpler to fight for "unconditional surrender" than to negotiate a limited settlement that is more likely to endure. (2) The public reaction to complicated international events is often unpredictable. Feelings, whether of patriotism or fear, supplant reason and produce a response based on moods of the moment rather than on solid and sensible analyses. (3) The opinions of the many override the wisdom of the experienced. Men of experience, by disguising their voices of wisdom when speaking to the untutored masses, compound the difficulty. Haunted by the memory of the democracies' failure to respond to the challenge of the totalitarian countries in the 1930's and dismayed by America's inability to adjust force to political purpose in and immediately after World War II, critics of democratic institutions found ample sustenance for a far-reaching pessimism. Although somewhat allayed by the rapidity and breadth of response to Soviet challenges in the period that began in 1947 and reached into the 1950's, pessimism reappeared in the Eisenhower years. Lippmann's critique, Emmet Hughes's description of the nation's plight conveyed in the title of his book *America the Vincible*, the officially sponsored investigation by the Gaither Committee, and the unofficial but highly authoritative studies of the Rockefeller Brothers' Fund, all reflected the fear that the 1950's, like the 1930's, were years of the locusts.[8]

Does the common citizen, one must wonder, have the fortitude to sustain costly military programs, the benefits of which are necessarily uncertain? Will the public permit the government the flexibility it requires

7. David B. Truman, "The American System in Crisis," *Political Science Quarterly*, Vol. 74 (December, 1959), pp. 481–97.
8. Emmet John Hughes, *America the Vincible* (New York: Doubleday, 1959.) The Gaither Report, which has not been published, was presented to the National Security Council in November, 1957. Rockefeller Panel Reports I and II, *The Mid-Century Challenge to U.S. Foreign Policy,* and *International Security: the Military Aspect* (New York: Doubleday, 1959 and 1958).

in dealing with a dangerous and changing world? Whether or not the citizenry is dogged and sensible, how closely is foreign policy controlled by the opinions of its citizens?

POLITICAL LEADERSHIP AND THE PUBLIC SUPPORT OF PROGRAMS

Often the person discussing the relation of opinion to policy is in the undignified posture of a dog chasing his tail. When it is charged that the people have been unduly complacent, the remedy prescribed may well be that their leaders should arouse themselves. Robert C. Sprague, co-chairman of the Gaither Committee, businessman, and self-styled conservative Republican, expressed his belief before Senator Jackson's subcommittee that the nation faced a threat to its survival to which it had not yet awakened. Who could awaken us? In the opinion of Sprague, there was one man alone "in the United States that can do this effectively, and that is the President."[9]

The thought is perennial. It was Plato who said in effect: the people are sick; their rulers must be cured. The question of leadership lies beneath the problem of the people's willingness to sacrifice and directly affects the stability of their opinions as well. When Churchill sought to awaken his countrymen to mounting dangers in the 1930's, few of the leading men of any party followed him. Are the people at fault when prime minister, foreign secretary, military officials, and others who bear a national trust assure them that armaments are adequate and that military preparations are proceeding at the necessary pace? The correspondence of the people's opinion to the position taken by their governors is strikingly illustrated by the rapid reversal of opinion on the controversial introduction of conscription in 1939, the first time Britain had ever adopted such a measure in peacetime. Before conscription was adopted, 39 per cent of the voters favored it, with 53 per cent opposed and 8 per cent doubtful. A week after the legislation was passed, 58 per cent approved, 38 per cent opposed, and 4 per cent were uncertain.[10]

The survival of the nation depends not only on fortitude in reacting to a threat that has at last become obvious, but also upon the people's willingness to pay and to serve when danger is not immediately visible. George C. Marshall, reflecting four years later upon his judgment of

9. Hearings before the Subcommittee of the Committee on Government Operations, *Organizing for National Security* (86th Cong., 2nd Sess., Senate, 1960), Vol. 1, p. 55.

10. Lindsay Rogers, *The Pollsters: Public Opinion, Politics, and Democratic Leadership* (New York: Knopf, 1949), p. 42.

1945 that the military force levels projected at that time were unrealistically high, explained in terms of public opinion the conclusion he had reached:

> When it comes to [military] appropriations in piping times of peace, I don't think America will ever learn its lesson, because the political pressures are tremendous. In the next place, my associates haven't lived through the education I had had in the 1920's and the immediate problems I had inherited in 1938, 1939, and 1940, when our degree of poverty was very trying. I could well understand that. They just thought I underestimated public opinion in the United States.
>
>   Well, I am a great respecter of public opinion, but, on the other hand, I am also a great respecter of the tremendous political influence of the budget and the fact that it almost gets beyond control when it relates to things that do not produce immediate results like good roads, agriculture matters, and such.[11]

Were American citizens, as Marshall thought, less willing to serve than to pay and not sufficiently willing to do either?

Before and after Korea, the marked tendency of American defense policy was to substitute machines for men in the demanding task of containing the Russian and Chinese Communists. The Truman-Bradley "old look" had meant reliance on air power and atomic bombs, with an army of minimum size. The insufficiency of such an establishment was demonstrated by invasion of the Republic of Korea from the north. With the Korean War ended, military policy slipped back to the old basis with a "new look" label attached. The army's vice-chief of staff, General Bolté, along with many others, despairingly tried to drive home the lesson that events had failed to teach. "Recent history has shown—and logic will sustain it—that the only way to defeat ground forces is by ground forces. The lesson of Korea should ever be before us."[12]

A strong inclination to keep defense costs low as measured in manpower is often said to be the military attitude of democracies. That democracy is alone the cause of the attitude is doubtful. The democracies that are thought to have this attitude are advanced industrial powers. For such countries to emphasize equipment more heavily than men may simply be an attempt to play from their strongest suit. In other fields, such a practice is accepted as mere common sense. A few words on "economizing" will help to make the proposition clear. Counting savings in terms of money easily obscures the importance of the question:

11. Quoted by Warner R. Schilling, "The Politics of National Defense: Fiscal 1950," in Warner R. Schilling, Paul Y. Hammond, and Glenn H. Snyder, *Strategy, Politics, and Defense Budgets* (New York: Columbia University Press, 1962), pp. 150–51.

12. General Charles L. Bolté, "Speech to United States Armor Association," Fort Knox, Kentucky, January 29, 1954, in *Armor*, Vol. 63 (March–April, 1954), p. 27.

In terms of what factors of production shall savings be measured? If arable land and machines are scarce and manpower is plentiful, for example, a country can increase to the maximum its return for money expended and acreage employed by adopting a system of intensive hand cultivation. Precisely this is done, so long as there is no choice, in Indonesia, Japan, and China, where the yield of crops per acre is markedly higher than it is in the United States.[13] Economic rationality requires substituting plentiful and cheap factors for scarce and expensive ones whether in agricultural or in military matters. Soviet leaders, so long as Russia had no nuclear establishment, proclaimed that the "permanently operating factors" rather than military technology or strategic surprise would determine the outcome of any contest with capitalist countries. With the maturing of Russian nuclear capabilities, however, Khrushchev announced, as the United States had earlier, that the deploying of rockets would permit simultaneously a reduction in manpower and an increase in military strength.[14] It is no more unusual that America, Britain, and other industrial democracies should seek to substitute machines for men in their military establishments than that they do so in agriculture, in dam-building, or in any of a number of other endeavors.

The proposition that democracies are unusually reluctant to keep large armies is questioned from one direction by noting that not only democracies are pushed or lured into the practice. It can be questioned from another direction by pointing out that not all republics have engaged in the practice. Athens and the Roman Republic in antiquity, Israel and Switzerland more recently, have conscripted large numbers of their citizens. The consonance of such practices with republican or democratic theory is indicated by Machiavelli's and Harrington's conception of military service as a school for civic virtue and in Juares's idea of the nation in arms.

One may nevertheless fear that political economizing—in terms of votes—will complement economic rationality in such a way as to make the preference for the machine difficult to undo even when international conditions would indicate its folly. Public pressure for rapid demobilization in 1945 and 1946 was strong and apparently effective. The conclusion frequently drawn is that at the outset of the Cold War public opinion placed the American government at a grave disadvantage. Those who reach such a conclusion have failed to bear in mind that civil and military leaders did not themselves urge upon the public the importance

13. Fred Cottrell, *Energy and Society* (New York: McGraw-Hill, 1955). His conclusion, supported by preceding analysis and data, is given on p. 143.

14. "Disarmament is the Path Toward Strengthening Peace and Ensuring Friendship Among Peoples," N.S. Khrushchev's Report at U.S.S.R. Supreme Soviet Session, January 14, 1960, in *Current Digest of the Soviet Press*, Vol. 12 (February 10, 1960), p. 3–16.

of remaining militarily prepared. Nor have they made the important distinction between enthusiasm for "bringing the boys home" and willingness to support a sizeable peacetime military establishment. The latter was not lacking.[15] The American public, in addition to supporting measures for improving our defenses in general, strongly favored the adoption of Universal Military Training. In nine surveys taken between December, 1945, and January, 1956, public support for the program, expensive in manpower, ran upwards of 65 per cent on eight occasions and only once fell as low as 60 per cent. Opposition to the measure never exceeded 33 per cent and only once rose above 25 per cent.[16] More generally, as Samuel P. Huntington has written and convincingly demonstrated, "Governmental policy and mass opinion on the level of military effort have frequently differed, but in every case the Administration has been in favor of less military effort and public opinion in favor of more." The statement applies, with variations that do not change the picture of broad and constant support, to all segments of the population and all sections of the country; and the pattern has been constant from at least 1937 onward.

When pollsters have asked where budgetary savings should be made, only small numbers of respondents have cited defense spending. As Huntington notes, one cannot say that the American people have put lower taxes or welfare programs ahead of an adequate national defense. At the same time the public in general, unsophisticated in matters of weaponry and strategy, looks to the Administration for a definition of adequacy. "If the critics vigorously and articulately attack the Administration for reducing military strength, the Administration eventually is forced to make a public defense of its policies. The public listens to the Administration, not the critics, and the reassurances of the Administration induce mass acquiescence in its policies."[17] The attitude of support and the implicit willingness to build the basis for a mass army have provided policymakers with a broad range of choice.

ELECTORAL SANCTIONS

Democracies have often been thought defective not only in their ability to sustain costly military establishments in time of peace but also

---

15. Samuel P. Huntington, *The Common Defense* (New York: Columbia University Press, 1961), pp. 33–39. H. Bradford Westerfield, *Foreign Policy and Party Politics* (New Haven: Yale University Press, 1955), pp. 196–202.

16. Huntington, *op. cit.,* p. 240.

17. The above quotations and summary are from Huntington, *op. cit.,* pp. 234–48, where many public opinion data on questions of defense are set forth and closely examined.

in their ability to move with speed and finesse in response to the shifting currents of international affairs. May one not say of the years since World War II that the close concern of the American people with problems of foreign policy has made it difficult for their government to conduct an international policy of feint and maneuver? Is it not likely that the more people care about foreign policy the more closely their opinions will limit the government? Such an effect has not been noticeable, partly because the concern of the public has outpaced its knowledge.

An international event ordinarily does not disturb the nation unless it has first obsessed the government. In the face of such an event, the people rally behind their chief executive, as one would expect them to do in any cohesive country. William Gladstone long ago commented in a letter to the Duke of Argyll that if the justification for the continuation of the Crimean War by England was that the people approved and supported it, then such justification could be given for any war that England ever waged, within eighteen months of its commencement.[18] A comparable statement, adjusted for the speed with which events are now publicly registered, can be made of America's reaction to crises. Franklin Roosevelt's popularity fluctuated in accordance with the recurrence of crises in Europe.[19] The outbreak of fighting in Korea gave a lift to President Truman's low standing with the public. In June of 1950, immediately before the attack, 37 per cent of those polled approved of the way Truman was doing his job, while 45 per cent did not. In July of 1950, the corresponding figures were 46 per cent and 37 per cent.[20] The invasion of Egypt by Britain and France, coming late in the American electoral campaign of 1956, apparently added a little to Eisenhower's wide margin of victory. A year and a half later, in April of 1958, the deepening of an economic recession, following upon Russia's lofting her first sputnik, drove Eisenhower's popularity down to 49 per cent, a low point. The following summer, a *contretemps* in Lebanon, which led the President to send American troops, boosted him to his 1958 high of 58 per cent.[21] The Cuban missile crisis of October, 1962, worked similar wonders for Kennedy. In April of that year, 77 per cent had approved of the way he was handling "his job as President." A gradual decline then set in, to 73 per cent in May following April's crisis in steel, to 71 per cent in June following a slump in the stock market, to 67 per cent in September after federal troops were sent to Mississippi, and to 61

18. Letter of October 18, 1855, reprinted in John Morley, *The Life of William Ewart Gladstone* (2 vols.; London: Edward Lloyd, 1908), Vol. 2, p. 610.

19. V. O. Key, Jr., *Politics, Parties, and Pressure Groups* (3rd ed.; New York: Thomas Y. Crowell, 1952), p. 596.

20. *Public Opinion Quarterly*, Vol. 15 (Spring, 1951), pp. 177–78.

21. Richard E. Neustadt, *Presidential Power* (New York: Wiley, 1960), p. 205n.

per cent before the confrontation with Russia in October. In December, however, 74 per cent expressed themselves as satisfied with the President's performance in office.[22]

The first effect of an international crisis is to increase the President's popular standing. One may wonder if this is so only when the response of the President is firm or he otherwise gives the impression of being able to deal with the situation effectively and without inconvenience to the public. It is, in fact, not necessary to add such qualifications to the statement that so far as the public is concerned the President in a moment of crisis has the widest freedom of action. President Kennedy, facing threats to Berlin, sent additional troops to Europe and in the summer of 1961 called up 150,000 reservists, an act usually thought to be politically dangerous. The political costs, on balance, were nil. Several months earlier, the United States had unofficially sponsored an invasion of Cuba at the Bay of Pigs. In the wake of the ill-fated attempt, President Kennedy's popular standing reached its highest point ever, 83 per cent as compared with an average of 70 per cent during his thirty-four months in office.[23]

At the moment of crisis, there is no time for dissension to develop. The public poses few problems for the President who acts deftly, or even clumsily, in a short and sharp encounter. If the crisis is prolonged and the blood of Americans is shed in carrying out the government's policy, should one not expect a different reaction? The experience of the Korean War seems to have led everyone to do so. In view of America's commitment of troops to combat on the mainland of Asia, questions debated since the early 1950's have once again become urgent.

America's military response in Korea had been prompt; it was also fairly effective. The North Korean and subsequently the Chinese invaders were met and thrown back; the line of the thirty-eighth parallel was restored and improved upon slightly; the United States and the non-Communist world were stronger at the conclusion of the affair than they had been at its beginning. Still, as the war dragged on, public support dwindled. Polls taken by the American Institute of Public Opinion from June of 1950 to November of 1952 found anywhere from 81 to 35 per cent supporting "President Truman's decision to send US troops to Korea," with 11 to 51 per cent opposed. Polls of the National Opinion Research Center showed from 80 to 51 per cent in support of the decision to send "American troops to stop the Communist invasion of South

22. AIPO: December 5, 1962.
23. AIPO: December 21, 1963 and November 30, 1963. The U-2 incident and the subsequent collapse of the summit meeting in May of 1960 were followed by a similar rise in President Eisenhower's popular standing.

Korea," with from 13 to 40 per cent opposed.[24] Different emphases in the wording of the questions may account for the discrepant results. No matter what poll one may look at, the line graph of President Truman's popular standing moved parallel to and consistently below the steadily declining popular support of America's fighting in Korea. In July, October, and December of 1950, 46, 39, and 36 per cent of those polled approved of the way the President was "handling his job." After 1950 and to the end of his term, approval fluctuated between 32 and 23 per cent.[25]

To take the full measure of the problem of executive leadership in a democracy, one must constantly bear in mind that a painful and costly policy may have to be long pursued, with the gains from the policy largely invisible. The rewards may be found mainly in preventing worse situations that might have arisen were the costly action not undertaken. It is clear that the decision to resist in Korea was widely approved and the execution of that decision over the next three years was not. If one dwells on the courage with which the decision was made to intervene in Korea, it becomes dismaying to notice that the party of the President who made it was punished in the subsequent national election. In the 1952 election, according to Key, "several million persons" voted against themselves "on domestic matters."[26] On grounds of domestic policy, these millions would have preferred a Democratic Administration. They were impelled to vote for Eisenhower by confidence in him as a man who could make peace, which was matched by distaste for the Democrats as a party that had taken their country into a war that the Administration was unable to conclude.[27]

In the 1948 election, a bipartisan truce on foreign policy questions had prevailed, for the most part, while economic and welfare questions were sharply debated. In the campaign of 1952, the Democrats played upon the people's interest in prosperity and, as ever, attached the depression label to the Republican party. Republicans drew political advantage from the higher taxes and prices that the war had brought and from the drafting of American boys to fight and to die in a war that was said to be useless. The loss of China to the Communists, the Soviet threat

24. AIPO: June, 1950; August, 1950; March, 1951; April, 1952; November, 1952. National Opinion Research Center (NORC): July, 1950 (100/287); September, 1950 (101/288); December, 1950 (105/295); January, 1951 (106/298); March, 1951 (107/300); April, 1951 (108/302); May, 1951 (109/307); August, 1951 (111/312); December, 1951 (115/315); March, 1952 (117/320); June, 1952 (121/327).

25. *Public Opinion Quarterly*, Vol. 15 (Spring, 1951), pp. 177–78. Neustadt, *op. cit.*, p. 96. Data in both of these sources are from AIPO.

26. Key, *Public Opinion and American Democracy*, p. 173.

27. Cf. the conclusion reached by Samuel Lubell: "the frustrations over Korea were the most important single propellent behind Eisenhower's sweep..." *Revolt of the Moderates* (New York, Harper, 1956), p. 265.

to Europe, and corruption in government were also prominent issues.[28] According to University of Michigan surveys, foreign issues worked almost entirely in favor of the Republican party. Twelve per cent of self-declared Democrats criticized the handling of foreign affairs, especially the Korean War, by their own party, as opposed to 6 per cent who had something good to say about the Democratic Administration in this field.[29] Twenty-two per cent of respondents mentioned being favorably impressed with Eisenhower's ability to handle foreign problems and particularly the Korean War, as compared with 9 per cent who spoke favorably of his ability to manage domestic affairs. The corresponding figures for Stevenson were 2 per cent and 7 per cent. In party rather than personal terms, 43 per cent referred favorably to the Democrats on domestic policies and issues, 33 per cent to the Republicans. On matters of foreign policy, preferences were reversed: 13 per cent expressed approval of the Republican party, while only 3 per cent had kind words for the Democrats.[30] By a different measure, the Republicans led as the party more likely to keep the country out of war by a ratio of more than two to one in the spring of 1952, while the Democrats continued to find favor as the "party of prosperity."[31]

Out of the military and political experience of Korea a conviction developed, widely shared by officials, commentators, and students of politics, that we ought not or could not fight another peripheral action, costly in manpower and without "victory" in sight. Charles Wilson, Eisenhower's first secretary of defense, once said, "We can't afford to fight limited wars. We can only afford to fight a big war, and if there is one that is the kind it will be."[32] Either we should not fight at all, such reasoning runs, or, in fighting, we should take every advantage of the modern means of warfare available to us in order to strike for victory. Where Wilson thought that militarily we ought not to fight another Korea, others concluded that politically we cannot. In 1951, following the congressional hearings that were prompted by the relief of General MacArthur, a Republican minority report declared:

---

28. In the Republican slogan of "Corruption, Korea, and Communism," Communism at home did not become an important partisan issue; Korea and corruption did. Just as the Great Depression had stimulated many to vote for the first time, so the "Korean War appears to have activated several million people who had sat out the previous elections." Angus Campbell, Philip E. Converse, Warren E. Miller, and Donald E. Stokes, *The American Voter* (New York: Wiley, 1960), pp. 50–51, 164.

29. Angus Campbell, Gerald Gurin, Warren E. Miller, *The Voter Decides* (New York: Harper and Row, no date), p. 51.

30. *Ibid.*, Table 4.12, p. 57, Table 4.3, p. 45.

31. AIPO: September 3, 1964.

32. Quoted by James M. Gavin, *War and Peace in the Space Age* (New York: Harper, 1958), p. 124.

We believe that a policy of victory must be announced to the American people in order to restore unity and confidence. It is too much to expect that our people will accept a limited war. Our policy must be to win. Our strategy must be devised to bring about decisive victory.[33]

Herman Kahn, drawing an electoral lesson from Stevenson's defeat, concluded "*that if there is another unpopular Limited War followed by the loss of the ensuing national election by the party in power, the ability of the United States to fight Limited War will be sadly impaired.*"[34] For their Korean venture, the Democrats were apparently punished severely at home; Republicans as well as Democrats presumably learned the electoral lesson. Some commentators were therefore tempted to say dogmatically that no President would ever again be willing to take the nation into such a war. Irving Kristol, for example, carried Kahn's qualified conclusion to such an extreme when he wrote:

The Korean War was unpopular to a degree that makes it inconceivable for any future Administration to contemplate that kind of limited, rigorously defensive military action. The scholars and the diplomats can continue to devise ingenious gradients of warfare, countering each enemy action with just so much (and no more) reaction. But they are indulging in a paper game. The American people cannot provide the kind of mercenary, professional soldiers such plans require.[35]

Students of politics seconded the impressions of public officials and underscored the worries that military strategists and political pundits entertained. It will be sufficient to cite two of the weightiest. Some years after the event, V.O. Key advanced the opinion that

the failure of the Truman Administration to make plain the reasons for American involvement in the Korean episode—a novel sort of enterprise for the United States—may have made it impossible to drum up public support for American participation in brush wars and thereby restricted us to atomic wars. At any rate, the successful Republican exploitation of the issue in 1952 will give statesmen cause for the greatest reluctance to engage in comparable enterprises, no matter what the need or provocation.[36]

33. Quoted in Morton H. Halperin, *Limited War in the Nuclear Age*, (New York: Wiley, 1963), p. 46.

34. Herman Kahn, *On Thermonuclear War* (Princeton: Princeton University Press, 1960), p. 418; italics in original.

35. Irving Kristol, "A Matter of Fundamentals," *Encounter*, Vol. 24 (April, 1960), pp. 56–57.

36. Key, *Public Opinion and American Democracy*, p. 261n.

Brzezinski and Huntington incline to a compatible conclusion:

> The normal and generally healthy play of partisan politics continually restricts an Administration's freedom of action. In times of crisis, restrictions may be supplemented by mass demands for quick victories and simple solutions. For almost two years the Truman Administration found itself boxed into a position where it could neither win the Korean War nor extricate itself from the war.[37]

A political system that makes it difficult for the government to contrive appropriate responses may threaten the world with its erratic actions or may doom itself to a gradually disintegrating position in international politics. It is important to re-examine the Korean case to see if the conclusions that have customarily been drawn are as depressing as many people have thought them to be.

It is true, as Key noted, that the reasons for American actions in Korea were never clearly explained. It is also true that what should have been done and why were not wholly and consistently understood at any level: not that of the President and his most intimate advisors, the executive branch generally, the Congress, the stratum of the public that is most concerned and best informed about public affairs, nor the people at large. Scarcely anyone in the United States, and not very many people elsewhere, had tried to figure out under what circumstances a country might wish to fight a limited war and how it should go about doing so. After the event, President Truman remarked to Richard Neustadt that on our way north in the fall of 1950 UN forces should have stopped "at the neck of Korea" as the British had urged. We knew, he said, that "the Chinese had close to a million men" at the Manchurian border. But, MacArthur was the President's man in the field, and as Truman himself remarked, he "had to back him up."[38] To make use of President Truman's homey saying, Truman belonged in the kitchen because he was able to take the heat. His political courage was inspiring and his loyalty to subordinates admirable, but in this case a different and better response would have been possible. Why should the President's statement not have been: Dean Acheson was my secretary of state, and, since military forces were fighting in Korea for political objectives, I had to back him up? If Secretary Acheson had recommended and President Truman had then decided that the neck of Korea was the right place to stop, the appropriate orders presumably would have been issued. There may be many reasons why such reasoning did not prevail in the difficult autumn of 1950. Among them, uncertainty is no doubt more important than

37. Zbigniew Brzezinski and Samuel P. Huntington, *Political Power: USA/USSR* (New York: Viking, 1964), p. 414.
38. Neustadt, *op. cit.*, p. 128.

civilian timidity. Not General MacArthur alone, but President Truman and Secretary Acheson, as well, tended to seek broad goals in Korea. When asked early in the war to describe America's and the United Nations' objectives, Truman and Acheson replied, in effect, to repel aggression and restore the *status quo ante*.[39] When the fortunes of war were reversed by the landing at Inchon and the route to the north lay open, however, official statements of purpose began to encompass the unification of all Korea by military force. In short, the goal was victory. Once Chinese troops entered the war in large numbers and the troops of the United Nations found themselves moving rapidly backward, the aim of the fighting was once again described as being to contain the enemy and to limit the war. But this modest goal was immodestly combined with a desire to secure a propoganda victory by saving from repatriation those prisoners of war who did not wish to return to their Communist homelands.[40] Unwilling to commit the forces that would make victory possible, the United States was also reluctant to fit her ends to the military means made available. The lure of success is difficult to resist.

Even if the foreshortening of goals had been firmly accepted, it would have remained difficult to say just how far one side could have gone without provoking the other to an unwanted enlargement of the war. If the Yalu bridges had been bombed on a line of flight parallel with them instead of perpendicular to them, would an important military advantage have been gained, or would the Chinese have retaliated in ways that the United States would not have preferred? The Chinese and the North Koreans never bombed the ill-concealed and unprotected bases south of the thirty-eighth parallel, nor did they interfere with America's shipping tons of materiel and thousands of men into Japan and Korea by sea. Should the United States have moved more daringly and imaginatively in the conduct of the war itself? Could she have used her superiority in materiel, her ability to produce grossly more than the Soviet bloc countries, her atomic power, and her ability to increase dramatically the extent of her mobilization in order to frighten the Chinese out of enlarging the war as the troops of the United Nations moved further north? Should the United States have used the threat to enlarge the war earlier in order to persuade her opponents to agree to a truce? Even uncertain answers were difficult to come by, especially since so few officials

39. Harry S. Truman, *Memoirs* (2 vols.; New York: Doubleday, 1956), Vol. 2, pp. 341, 359–60, 438–39; and McGeorge Bundy (ed.), *The Pattern of Responsibility: From the Record of Secretary of State Dean Acheson* (Boston: Houghton Mifflin, 1952), pp. 251–52, 263, 284.

40. Only about 70,000 of the 132,000 military prisoners agreed to return. Admiral C. Turner Joy, *How Communists Negotiate* (New York: MacMillan, 1955), p. 153. On the instability of American objectives during the course of the Korean War, see *ibid.*, pp. 173–74.

were attuned to the delicate process of action and reaction that characterizes the fighting of a limited war.[41]

Under the circumstances, it cannot be said that mass opinion tied the hands of officials. Instead, the mixture of firmness and vacillation in the government's policy was mirrored in the people's opinion. Military action was heartily supported at the outset. In the summer of 1950, upwards of 75 per cent of those who were asked for their opinions approved of President Truman's decision to send troops to Korea.[42] But what the decision might imply was wholly misunderstood. Just over half of those polled in July thought that we were "actually in World War III," while only 29 per cent thought that the fighting in Korea would "stop short of another world war."[43] As one might have expected, there was little appreciation of the possibility of fighting a limited war.

As the war dragged on, confusion grew and opinion broke into fragments. When people were asked to suggest a proper course of American action, they expressed doubt and bewilderment. In five polls taken in the year beginning in December of 1951, for example, from 16 to 24 per cent of those polled thought we should pull our troops out and send the boys home. Thirty to 43 per cent would have had us take the offensive against the Communist Chinese, while 27 to 37 per cent were resigned to carrying on the war while peace talks continued.[44] Early in March of 1951, 73 per cent of those polled thought that if we pushed "the Chinese back to the thirty-eighth parallel" we then should "stop fighting if the Chinese agreed." But in the middle of the month, 38 per cent of all respondents thought that if negotiations were to produce a comparable result, the outcome would be unacceptable.[45] The American tendency was to think that settlement at or near the thirty-eighth parallel would leave the Communists with greater gains from the war than we would enjoy. The idea of a truce nevertheless became increasingly attractive. The following question was asked in September, 1953: "As things stand now, do you think our government should have signed the Korean armistice, or should we have continued fighting?" Seventy-five per cent approved of our signing; only 15 per cent would have continued to fight.[46]

In sum, it can be said that the Administration did not explain its political strategy in the Korean War because it did not itself have a clear understanding of it — and therefore neither did the people. The Administration was constant in its determination to keep the war limited; it was

41. On the process of limitation, see Halperin, *op. cit.*, esp. pp. 55–57.
42. NORC: July, 1950 (100/287); September, 1950 (101/288).
43. AIPO: July, 1950.
44. NORC: December, 1951 (115/315); March, 1952 (117/320); June, 1952 (121/327); November, 1952 (125/333); December, 1952 (126/334).
45. AIPO: March 1, 1951, and March 18, 1951.
46. NORC: September, 1953 (134/348).

at times uncertain about the relation of its military and diplomatic decisions to that one clear goal. Unwilling to settle for a modest peace after the brilliant stroke at Inchon, unwilling to risk enlarging the war by striking for victory after China became engaged, the Administration appeared unable to wage war and unable to make peace.

Many have nevertheless thought that the Democratic party suffered electorally for waging a war that became unpopular in the course of fighting it. If this was the lesson learned from Korea, rightly or wrongly, then was it not to be expected that a future President would be reluctant to place restraints on the use of force in wartime. Wars that could have been limited would then be made into big ones in the manner that the previously cited statements of Secretary Wilson and Professor Key suggest. Or, the small-scale use of force by an aggressive state might remain unresisted, with the territorial position of the non-Communist world slowly wearing away. The first possibility has lessened. Any senator from Indiana who suggests now, as Senator William E. Jenner seemed to wish a dozen years ago, that we go all out for victory, will be inescapably aware that he may be arguing for a hydrogen bomb dropped on Gary.[47] Two can now play at the game of strategic nuclear retaliation with roughly equal ability, a condition that did not exist at the time of Korea. Without a system of defense effective against missiles fired in large numbers, the argument for keeping wars limited becomes politically as well as strategically much easier to make. But then why should the nation fight any wars at all? The other part of the argument becomes more difficult to make—namely, that it may sometimes be well to engage in small wars at considerable expense and with no prospect of "victory" in sight. No President and no party will wish to commit themselves to a difficult course of action with electoral punishment the likely result.

Even the policy that elicits a favorable response from a comfortable majority of the people may leave enough unhappy voters to tip the next election away from the incumbents. A dissident minority, bipartisan in composition, that finds itself badly put off by the policy associated with the party in power may cause the candidate of that party to lose the election. In controversial matters, even a policy popular with a majority of voters may be an electoral loser. The counsel of greatest caution may be to prevent issues from becoming prominent unless it is clear that action upon them will be overwhelmingly acceptable. One may then think that the habit that democracies will naturally develop is that of

47. Cf. the line of questioning persistently pursued by Senator Jenner in the hearings held from August through December of 1954 by his subcommittee of the Judiciary Committee. A summary is found in the Report of the Subcommittee to Investigate the Administration of the Internal Security Act and Other Internal Security Laws. *The Korean War and Related Matters* (84th Cong., 1st Sess., Senate, 1955).

obscuring situations that ought to call forth vigorous responses, in order to make those situations appear unimportant.

It is useful to take up the problem in its most difficult terms. The novelty of the Korean crisis was excuse enough for the vacillations of the Truman Administration. One can hope to learn from experience, and yet in international relations, it must be expected that each succeeding experience will be novel. It is impossible always to act wisely. Even wise actions may not preclude a gruelling and costly fight, and under such circumstances, the clear explanation of policies will not keep internal recriminations from growing. A president who does what the moment seems to require can then often expect that he and his party will have to pay the domestic political bill, however unjustly it may be drawn. Here again, foreign policy is not so very different from domestic policy. The Republicans, in office when the stock market crashed in 1929, still bear some onus as the party of depression. It would, of course, only be just to say that the crash and the succeeding depression were bigger than any party and that had Al Smith been sitting in the White House backed by an overwhelming majority of Democrats in both houses of Congress, he would not have been able to prevent these disasters, either. And so the Democrats, in office during the wars in which America has fought in this century, long remained in the public mind the party of war. While this is not surprising, it may be rather discouraging.

Actually, for several reasons it should not be. First, the election of 1952 was more a personal tribute to Eisenhower than a triumph for the Republican party, less a repudiation of the Democratic party than a conclusion electorally expressed that the Republicans had found a man who could see the country safely through a difficult international situation. On questions of foreign policy, Republicans were publicly favored, but the personal preference for their candidate was even more marked. Eisenhower was thought of as the man who would bring us peace with honor, who would end the fighting in Korea without weakening our position in the world. Varied and clear-cut evidence, some of it cited above, indicates that Eisenhower was chosen as President largely on grounds of imputed personal ability rather than as a reflection of party preference.[48] The war had lasted for two years. During the election campaign, small-scale fighting sporadically continued. It was difficult to see what the purpose of such fighting might be. In these unpleasant circumstances, large numbers of people treated the Korean War as an important political issue and were led, in doing so, to prefer Eisenhower to Stevenson. One may quarrel with their judgment but scarcely with the inclination to treat the issue as a major one that should have affected or even dominated the choice of a President. One might also think that the ability of

48. Cf. Campbell, Gurin, and Miller, *op. cit.*, pp. 57–58, 175–76.

the Republican party to come forth with a man who seemed to measure up to the demands of the crisis was a tribute to it. That Korea was a dramatically effective partisan issue should not be taken as evidence of a national desire to be quit of the world, to avoid all painful efforts, and to withdraw from all costly commitments, even if that were to mean creating situations of weakness in the world. That the Republicans won an election by running Eisenhower and laying great stress on the Korean issue may be evidence of some impatience with sacrifice long sustained. Their victory was also evidence of a feeling, which had some basis in reason, that someone could be found who would manage such difficult affairs with greater skill.

The second reason for not being deeply concerned that fear of being labeled the "party of war" will dissuade a party in power from standing firm in the face of aggression is that the reputations of parties are more fairly won and more easily lived down than is sometimes supposed. Traditionally, the Republicans have been viewed as the party of peace and depression. A Republican President, one must note, did conclude an honorable peace in 1953, which the Democrats for three years had been unable to do, and did avoid becoming militarily involved in Indochina in the following year. Republicans, at the same time, have been less willing to run a deficit in order to combat unemployment and less warmly in favor of social welfare programs. Democrats have long been viewed as the party of prosperity, but also as the party of war. For a decade, from 1951 to 1961, only 15 to 25 per cent of the public had thought of the Democratic Party as the "best" party to keep the country out of war, while from 26 to 42 per cent had, on this ground, preferred the Republicans. It is not true, however, that only the good fortune of having Barry Goldwater to oppose them in the election of 1964 enabled the Democrats to shed the unwanted reputation for bellicosity. In July of 1962, presumably because of Kennedy's performance in office, Democrats found as much public approval on the peace issue as did Republicans; and in February and May of 1963, Democrats were favored over their rivals by 32 to 23 and 31 to 26 per cent.[49]

Finally, harsh criticism of the party that is trying to carry out a given action does not necessarily indicate unwillingness to support other parts of the President's foreign policy. It may not even imply a disavowal of the policy criticized. A distinction must be drawn between critical attitudes, on the one hand, and the willingness or refusal to support policies, on the other. Republicans who, in the 1950s, criticized American policies in China, for example, were assigning blame for events that had already occurred. Their criticism did not indicate that they would withhold support from the President should he seek to undertake difficult

49. Data are summarized in AIPO Releases of February 5 and May 7, 1963.

international actions. Republicans in Congress did not deny the President the opportunity to carry out his policy. Indeed, because they had granted him the instruments he asked for, Republicans could more easily say that the ill-conceived policy of a Democratic President had opened the way for Communist conquest of China. Any party in opposition will try to lay the blame for national ills upon the party in power. It is then misleading to say that Truman erred in failing to associate the Republican party with his Far Eastern policy and wrong also to argue that if he had woven a bipartisan net around his China policy, as he did on European questions, his fall in popularity would have been cushioned.[50] No intelligently led opposition party would have bought shares in an American enterprise in China that looked as though it could be saved from bankruptcy only at a price that almost no one was willing to pay. In the very years when much political sport was had with the Truman Administration's troubles in the Far East, a majority of Republican legislators supported such radically new and far-reaching programs as the Truman Doctrine, the Marshall Plan, the Atlantic Defense Treaty, and such difficult actions as the Berlin airlift and even our military effort in Korea.

GOVERNMENTAL FREEDOM OF ACTION

The chances that a President will be unable to carry out even a controversial policy are slight, nor is it at all likely that he will be dissuaded from pursuing a difficult and possibly unpopular line of policy by fear that he and his party will be electorally punished. Parties and Presidents must care about losing a little of their popularity on one issue or another if democratic government is to be responsive to the wishes and worries of the people. At the same time, in politics as in all human affairs, there are situations in which one is damned if he does and damned if he does not. No man and no party can govern without accepting this truth. If the United States disengages in Southeast Asia and North Vietnam sweeps to the tip of the Camau Peninsula, the President in power and the party that he leads will be found to be at fault. But they will also be found at fault if the scale of American involvement is increased in order to hold what remains of the peninsula or to regain lost ground. In the most difficult matters, and international crises are certainly among them, there is no single policy whose widespread popularity would survive the test of action. If the world is a mess and the United States must act in it, then Presidents will often be in a position of deciding which of several unpopular policies they will follow. They will have no opportunity to pick a policy that will lose them no votes

50. Cf. Westerfield, *op. cit.*, pp. 266–68, 343–44.

at all. If timidity and quiescence were truly and clearly more popular than boldness and action, then one would rightly worry that democratic countries would always fall prey to the aggressive thrusts of others. If belligerence were always more admired, then one would live teetering on the brink of nuclear war. If either condition prevailed, Presidents would always experience pressure to act in one way whether or not it was appropriate to the situation at hand.

Brzezinski and Huntington suggested that a President steadily losing public support may find himself boxed in, as to a considerable extent Truman did. After months of costly and inconclusive fighting, withdrawal would have been humiliating, and to threaten the use of unlimited means in order to achieve a limited end, as Eisenhower and Dulles did later, would have failed of acceptance at home and lacked credibility abroad. The box, however, was not built by "mass demands for quick victories and simple solutions." As data previously cited make clear, there were no such demands, though as the war dragged on, impatience grew; and the country lost confidence in the competence of the government. Kristol, Kahn, and others thereupon concluded that the constraints of political competition severely limit America's contrivance and conduct of policy. Since World War II, foreign policy has usually been the most prominent of issues, but its electoral effect has nevertheless been diluted by juxtaposition with other problems and policies when voters made their decisions. One who bases his vote in part on performance in office must also ask himself how the competing candidate and party are likely to do. Numerous surveys have indicated that both parties are looked upon as competent to manage foreign policy. Furthermore, most people continue to vote in the present as they have voted in the past, whether or not the policies and programs of their preferred party have pleased them. When such countervailing factors are borne in mind, the fear that electoral punishment will dramatically affect foreign policy loses most of its force. International affairs have gone badly while Presidents of both parties were in power. Neither party has suffered any very deep political damage as a result.

The competition of two parties for the people's favor is sometimes said to lead both of them to espouse policies and programs that they know to be bad. In contrast, George M. Trevelyan, giving the Romanes lecture at Oxford forty years ago, strongly argued that the principal virtue of a two-party system is that where one party is weak, the other may be strong; where one party has failed, the other may succeed. "No one party," he asserted, "can cover all the ground." The party that reacted correctly to the French Revolutionary and Napoleonic Wars could scarcely have approached the questions of parliamentary reform with a proper attitude, "so powerful in the political mind is the instinct

to associate ideas not logically connected with one another." If Fox and Grey, in the 1790s, had joined Pitt in opposition to the Jacobins, Trevelyan averred, there would have been no Whig reform bill in 1830.[51] In much the same way, it may well have appeared that the Democratic Administration, having begun the war, was unable to end it either by military victory or diplomatic settlement. It is strange, then, that the Republican victory of 1952 has so often been described, in relation to the problem of limited war, as an indication of democracy's weakness rather than as a demonstration of its strength. "Weakness" would be an apt term only where the demise of the Administration meant the loss of its policy, even though conditions had not changed sufficiently to make a policy of different intent appropriate to the national situation. "Weakness" would also apply if the political system provided no routine way of discarding a leader or ruling group when its policy, once popular, had taken on a sickly hue and when the people had lost confidence in the integrity and competence of the Administration's leading members. Democracies permit a change of persons and parties to be easily and gracefully made. Because they do, policies that remain necessary though they have become unpopular can often more easily be continued. The situation found in a monarchy only upon the death of a king is the recurring condition of a democratic state. In the relation of crown prince to king, it was frequently thought by the people that the son would be saner and sounder and generally more pleasing than his father. In democratic countries, such a situation may be repeated every four or five years. It can then be said, and usually is by members of the opposition party, that the government has done everything wrong and that they, if elected, will do much the same things and, of course, do them much better.

One difficulty with Trevelyan's statement would seem to be this: it might just as plausibly be said that the constructive policies of one party may well be lost later when a party of contradictory tendencies gains office or that the weakness and confusion of one party will be reinforced by the uncertainty and stupidity of the other. The mutual reinforcement of the virtues of parties for the benefit of the state depends upon their policy positions being sensible and upon their being separated only by a harmonious third rather than by an entire octave or some dissonant interval. When such is the situation of parties, their alternation can be the glory of democracy. The election of 1952 is a good case in point. The Republicans stood for a policy of liberation, which was the Administration's aspiration in North Korea and which was, in reference to Poland, the promise of any politician who happened to be speaking in Buffalo, Hamtramck, or Chicago. The responsible leaders of both

51. G. M. Trevelyan, *An Autobiography and Other Essays* (London: Longmans, Green, 1949), p. 197.

parties and the vast majority of people in general wished to stand firm against the Soviet Union and Communist China, to set somebody free if that would not be too dangerous, and to avoid fighting and dying if that were at all possible. The Republican party won the election on a platform that was different from the Democratic platform mainly in tone and in emphasis.

The American government had apparently decided before the event that it would not meet force with force in Korea.[52] But it did. Numerous statements by Eisenhower, Dulles, and others indicated that in Indochina in the spring of 1954 the United States would fight or somehow retaliate if the Communists continued to drive forward.[53] In actuality, it did not do so. In neither case can it be said that fear of the people's opinion or of domestic political consequences noticeably affected the final decision. Nor had weariness with the war in Korea persuaded the public that giving way in other parts of the world would be preferable to fighting. Asked in May and September of 1953 and again in April of 1954 whether the American Air Force should be used if necessary to prevent Communists taking over all of Indochina, from 52 to 60 per cent agreed that it should. In all three of the polls, a larger percentage still, that is from 59 to 65 per cent, favored sending American troops, with always about a third of the sample opposed to either alternative.[54] For the next decade, as economic and military commitments grew, American policies in Indochina were viewed with a mixture of mild disinterest, mature skepticism, and judicial calm, with never an inclination to force the government's hand. Following the naval incidents of Tonkin Bay early in August of 1964, President Johnson proposed and the Congress overwhelmingly accepted a resolution that practically gave the President a free hand in Southeast Asia (Public Law 88–408). In February of 1965, the American bombing of North Vietnam began. In March of that year, 27,000 American troops were serving in Vietnam; in June, 54,000; in September, 128,500; by May of 1966, more than 250,000. Against the background of these events and in the presence of continued political unrest in South Vietnam, Americans, in their answers to pollsters, revealed themselves as being

52. John W. Spanier, *The Truman-MacArthur Controversy and the Korean War* (Cambridge, Mass.: Harvard University Press, 1959), p. 17. Trumbull Higgins, *Korea and the Fall of MacArthur: A Précis in Limited War* (New York: Oxford University Press, 1960), pp. 10–14.

53. Cf. John Foster Dulles, who in September of 1953 said, "There is the risk that, as in Korea, Red China might send its own army into Indochina. The Chinese Communist regime should realize that such a second aggression could not occur without grave consequences which might not be confined to Indochina. I say this soberly in the interest of peace and in the hope of preventing another aggressor miscalculation." Address by Secretary Dulles to the American Legion at St. Louis, Mo., on September 2, *Department of State Bulletin*, Vol. 29 (September 14, 1953), p. 342.

54. NORC: May, 1953 (130/340); September, 1953 (134/348); April, 1954 (137/355).

reluctantly willing to fight, amenable to settlement, anxious to negotiate, and, though obviously wary, worried, and confused, willing to give the President wide latitude.

Such a pattern of opinion persisted, even as the scale of American involvement increased and the toll of American lives rose. In the late spring of 1964, for example, of the 74 per cent who then knew of the fighting in Vietnam, 53 per cent opposed and 28 per cent favored "the United States getting out of the Vietnam war completely." At the same time, 46 per cent favored trying for some such "compromise agreement with Communist China" as "making all Vietnam neutral," with 29 per cent against doing so.[55] In January of 1965, the respondents of the Gallup Poll affirmed by a margin of four to one their belief that the Vietcong were defeating the South Vietnamese, and by a margin of two to one their opinion that the latter would not be able to form a stable government. Still, by a margin of almost two to one they subscribed to the statement that the United States was right to have become militarily involved. At the same time, 81 per cent expressed themselves in favor of President Johnson's calling an international conference with Chinese and Southeast Asian leaders to see if a peace agreement could be arranged, while only 11 per cent dissented.[56] In February and March of 1966, a group of behavioral scientists, most of them located at Stanford University, sponsored a survey to find what the deeper attitudes were. Though the questioning, conducted by the National Opinion Research Center, was more detailed, the attitudes uncovered were much the same as those previously reported. For example, 52 per cent would favor "a new government in which the Vietcong took some part," 36 per cent would not. Offered three choices, 49 per cent said they would continue to do in Vietnam as their government was then doing, 23 per cent would prefer to fight a major war, and 19 per cent would simply withdraw. Some 60 per cent would fight a major war if the only alternative to it were withdrawal of American troops. At the same time, 88 per cent favored "negotiations with the Vietcong if they were willing to negotiate," while 8 per cent opposed them. In general, President Johnson's actions in Vietnam were endorsed by 61 per cent and disapproved of by 29 per cent, while 10 per cent expressed no opinion.[57]

55. Council on Foreign Relations, *The American Public's View of U.S. Policy Toward China: A Report Prepared for the Council on Foreign Relations by the Survey Research Center, University of Michigan* (New York, 1964), Table 23, p. 42; Table 24, pp. 43–44. The survey was conducted, nationwide, in the late spring of 1964.

56. AIPO: January 31, 1965.

57. Sidney Verba, *et al.*, "Public Opinion and the War in Vietnam," (mimeo; no place and no date), App. I, Tables 1, 2, and 12. The report was summarized by Wallace Turner, "Public Backs Negotiations With Vietcong, Poll Says," *The New York Times*, March 15, 1966, p. 1.

What thoughts lay behind the answers? Did the public perhaps entertain the notion that delaying actions at low cost are worth mounting, that it is well to demonstrate that nothing is free for the taking, but that, all things considered, the time to leave had arrived if leaving could be gracefully arranged? While it is too much to attribute such intricacy, clarity, and precision of thought to the public mind, the state of the people's opinion permitted the President to fashion such an interpretation of America's position should he have wished to. It could not at any rate be said that public opinion constituted a pressing limit upon Presidential action, nor did the warning of the Korean experience lead the government to avoid military involvement. As difficulties in Vietnam multiply, criticism of the government will grow. Indeed, by the spring of 1966, disenchantment had begun to set in. In fairly steady progression, those approving of the way "Mr. Johnson is handling his job as President" declined from 69 per cent of those asked in July of 1965 to 66 per cent in early November and to 58 per cent in March of 1966.[58] If the public standing and moral authority of the Administration should gravely weaken, it will be time for a change, whether or not blame has been justly accorded. Obviously President Johnson has been keenly aware of the domestic political risks he was running. To have changed policies because of electoral fears for the future would not have been honorable. Examination of public opinion in periods of crisis has led us to the conclusion that it would not have been practical either. In their foreign policies, governments of all types have sometimes been fainthearted. One need not fear that pusillanimity is especially encouraged by the pressures of public opinion as it operates in the American democracy.

The fears born of the military and electoral struggles of the Korean era have faded. In the 1950s, it was fashionable to affirm that the American democracy would not sustain distant and indecisive military engagements firmly or long enough. In the 1960s it has become more common to suppose that the American government is impervious to criticism and has taken too free a hand even during protracted periods of crisis. Both worries are important; each has in its day been exaggerated. Two dangers threaten especially. With multiplication internationally of the arenas of major contention, it will become more difficult to remember that American security interests require military engagement only where the adversary is of such strength that he is or may become a threat to the nation. Beyond that, though the margin of power that America enjoys over any other contender may be a source of comfort to her citizens, it may also worry the observer. Powerful nations have often abused their power to the detriment of themselves and of others. More than has been the case with

58. Gallup Poll, *Philadelphia Bulletin*, July 11, 1965, and March 30, 1966.

any modern state, the restraint of the American nation must now be self-imposed. A nation as powerful as America may become impatient with the defensive pose it has struck and long maintained. Senator J. William Fulbright has detected in American foreign policy "signs of that fatal presumption, that overextension of power and mission, which brought ruin to ancient Athens, to Napoleonic France and to Nazi Germany." He has warned his country not to become "what it is not now and never has been, a seeker after unlimited power and empire."[59] Is Senator Fulbright premature in his pessimism and unduly alarmed by the experience of war in Vietnam?

In the case of Vietnam, spokesmen for the Administration have asserted the vital importance of showing that insurgencies are costly, damaging, and doomed to defeat; they have argued that China must be contained for a time as the Soviet Union was earlier. One may wonder if the assertion and the argument do not rest on an overestimation of Chinese capability, a failure to appreciate the penchant for independence of the Indochinese whatever the political orientation of their govern-ments, and an overlooking of the possibility that any increase in Chinese strength would be more of a worry to the Soviet Union than to the United States. The questions involved are, however, difficult ones on which no light can be shed by demonstrations and little by public debates. Nonetheless, with international restraints pressing less closely, internal correctives become all the more important. The American government is well supplied with them. To critics such as Senators Mike Mansfield, J. William Fulbright, and Robert Kennedy, the Administration pays the closest heed; for institutionally and politically their positions are strong. Fulbright's eloquent warnings are not misplaced. It is because of him and other powerful critics that the dangers of hubris are lessened.

One of the valuable qualities of the American political system is the persistence of effective criticism. Opposition to the President's foreign policy has most often since the war centered in the House of Repre-sentatives; on question of foreign aid, for example, it lodged in the Appropriations Committee. In contrast, the Foreign Relations Committee, strong enough to influence the whole Senate, soon converted its members, even those once isolationist, to support of the country's new policies.[60] That was the pattern until recently. In his first years of office, President Johnson showed an unusual ability to keep issues closed, to prevent arguments from occurring in publicly conspicuous places. From February of 1965 onward, from the time when American military forces were

59. "Excerpts from Fulbright's Speech on Vietnam War," *The New York Times*, April 29, 1966, p. 32.

60. David N. Farnsworth, *The Senate Committee on Foreign Relations* (Urbana: University of Illinois Press, 1961), pp. 151–155.

first committed to battle in Southeast Asia, however, Senator Fulbright reluctantly permitted his Committee to begin to oppose the President's policies—in Vietnam, with regard to China generally, and on matters of foreign aid. The function of opposing, like the task of providing leadership, sometimes migrates from one political institution to another.

CONCLUSIONS

There is no end to one's worries. One who is not busily worried about a possible absence of support for waging limited wars is liable instead to fear that the United States is politically prevented from acquiescing in defeat on those occasions when losing would be the least unhappy of all the unhappy choices. The American reaction to the Chinese Revolution after World War II supposedly illustrates one type of recurrent difficulty: an unwillingness to acquiesce in "necessary" defeats. Unwilling (and sometimes wisely so) to expend the manpower and materiel that a drive for victory would require, the government is also reluctant to say simply that the goal is not worth its price. One may then fear that the American people will be overly eager to fight, ever unwilling to compromise, and thus be able to press a government to rashly adventurous actions. Denis Brogan created a phrase that caught on when he attributed the McCarthyite hysteria of the early 1950s to America's "illusion of omnipotence," understandable in view of her history but unforgivable as the attitude of a country that stood as the leader of the "free world."[61] Internal political criticism first focused on the "loss" of China, grew with Representative Nixon's dramatization of the charges against Alger Hiss, became still more widespread when McCarthy made his flamboyant charges in February of 1950 that there were 205 or 57 or whatever number of Communists in the State Department, and reached a crescendo in the years of the Korean struggle. The frenzied frustration and self-indulgent hysteria of the McCarthy-Korea years could be interpreted charitably as a momentary reaction, a relapse after the vigorous and wholly unaccustomed activities in international politics that the Truman Doctrine, the Marshall Plan, and the formation of NATO represented. They could also be seen as the wild lungings of a bull who did not know how he was expected to behave in the international arena. Finally, of course, they could be and sometimes were taken as demonstrations of the proposition that her political institutions and national character make America unfit for a leader's role in the world.

Are the American people hopelessly naïve and in their naïveté a danger to the world? Is America given to vacillation between the poles

61. Denis Brogan, "The Illusion of American Omnipotence," *Harper's*, Vol. 205 (December, 1952), pp. 21–28.

of international commitment and national withdrawal? Is the American political system incurable without institutional surgery? Taking America's policy toward China as a difficult last example will enable us to suggest answers to these questions and, at the same time, to make summary comments on the present chapter.

Though opinion on the sensitive subject of China has often been contradictory, it has been neither rashly belligerent nor naive about the causes of our difficulties. Early in 1954, for example, the Gallup Poll asked: "What, in your opinion, are the main reasons that China went Communist?" Seventy-three per cent of those polled thought the reasons were the ignorance of the Chinese masses, the skill of the Communists, and the corruption of the Nationalist regime; 10 per cent blamed American policy and traitorous action; 17 per cent gave miscellaneous replies; and 23 per cent did not know.[62] Though multiple responses to the single question cloud the finding, it is nevertheless some evidence of maturity of political outlook that only 10 per cent of the replies ascribed to American officials responsibility for events in China. Asked in April of 1955 whether we should "be friendly to Red China and try to win her away from Russia," or should "treat her as an enemy," 47 per cent preferred the first alternative and 40 per cent, the second. At the same time, 78 per cent opposed China's admission to the United Nations and 65 per cent were against trading with her.[63] More recently, 53 per cent of those who realize that China's government is communist opposed her admission to the UN (31 per cent were in favor); but 75 per cent of the same sample would stay in the UN "if Communist China gets in" and only 5 per cent would thereupon leave. While distaste for the Chinese Communist regime is deep and persistent, 62 per cent oppose and only 10 per cent favor "helping Nationalists to attack Communists."[64]

If the American people in general are more sophisticated than is sometimes supposed, are they not still in their inclinations dangerously unsteady? Paul Ramsey has recently written that "perhaps because of the Calvinism gone to seed in the atmosphere, and the lack of any doctrine of the Two Realms in which a human destiny is played out, the American people are ill prepared for the self-discipline necessary for the limitation of warfare."[65] His conclusion may once have been true, though not necessarily for the reasons he suggests. William C. Foster,

62. AIPO: January, 1954.
63. AIPO: April, 1955.
64. Council on Foreign Relations, *The American Public's View of U.S. Policy Toward China*, Table 16, p. 30; Table 13, p. 23: Table 10, p. 19. Of those interviewed, 28 per cent were not aware that China is ruled by a Communist government (Table 1, p. 5).
65. Paul Ramsey, *War and the Christian Conscience: How Shall Modern War be Conducted Justly?* (Durham, N.C.: Duke University Press for the Lilly Endowment Research Program in Christianity and Politics, 1961), p. 151.

a man of both business and political affairs, clearly thought so. "We must," he once urged, "attempt to get away from the strange dichotomy with which we have traditionally viewed force, refusing to consider it except as last resort, then approaching it in a crusading manner with a 'punish the bandit' view which has been prevalent in our recent conflicts."[66] While religious beliefs have not changed noticeably since the Cold War began, America's notions of the place of force in foreign policy have evolved as her expectations of an easy international life have dwindled. Samuel Lubell, who is not the most scientific of pollsters but who may be the most perceptive, has drawn a sharp distinction between the typical American reactions of 1952 and of 1962. He reports that in 1952 he found people saying "I'm against this idea that we can go on trading hills in Korea indefinitely." In other words, his respondents implied that it may be well to strike at the enemy with all the power at our command. Early in 1962, in contrast, he reported the prevalent fear as being that "if we throw a nuclear bomb at them we'll get it back in this country." With the feeling that "all-out war" had become "unthinkable," acceptance of the likelihood of small wars has grown and so has the willingness to fight them. "It's just a little country," Lubell found some people saying, "but if we let the Reds walk off with it we will be lowered in the eyes of the world."[67]

Ever since 1948, 80 per cent or more of those polled have replied affirmatively to such questions about Berlin as this one: "Should we stay in Berlin even if doing so means war with Russia?" Should the audacity of the reply cause fear that the President may order shooting so that by doing what the people seem to want he will look something like a leader? Or should one think of such responses as indicating a reluctant willingness to fight in situations of tremendous risk if the President with the support of the Congress should decide that other policies would be riskier still?

For several reasons, it is the latter question that merits an affirmative answer. (1) In an era of Cold War, the American people have not, despite what is frequently said, demanded either victory or withdrawal, though occasionally articulate minorities and highly placed politicians have done so. (2) Reluctance to retreat and willingness to fight in order to avoid retreat are more the product of the international condition of bipolarity than of internally generated political pressures.[68] People and Presidents, the public at large and the dominant elites have united in

66. Quoted by Arthur Krock, "In the Nation," *The New York Times*, December 20, 1957.

67. Samuel Lubell, "Ideas Change About Small Wars," Philadelphia *Bulletin*, April 2, 1962, p. 5.

68. Cf. Kenneth N. Waltz, "The Stability of a Bipolar World," *Daedalus*, Vol. 93 (Summer, 1964), p. 881–909.

their belief that the United States must stand firm in the face of aggression abroad. (3) One must ask what it means to "stand firm." The actions and words of the President, more than of any other, will define for the public this difficult term. To put it crudely: defeats will be described as unimportant and compromises, as triumphs, if it is at all possible to do so. The Cuban confrontation in October of 1962 was said to be an American victory over Khrushchev — he removed the Russian missiles. But Castro remained in power and a number of the Soviet Union's technicians remained in the country. Khrushchev was able to retreat, which is said to demonstrate that dictators enjoy freedom from internal constraint. But the United States, it should also be noted, was able to settle for something less than the achievement of ends that had earlier been widely proclaimed.

The people react to what the President does, and some of them, at least, form an opinion of how well he does it. If a President says that we need not fight, as Eisenhower in effect did when the French were beseiged at Dienbienphu, no spontaneous rush to the colors is likely. Willingness to fight should not be identified with eagerness to do so. Reluctance to give way should not be confused with a stubborn unwillingness to compromise. It would seem from the record that the mass of the American people have learned to live with danger, to tolerate ambiguity, to accept setbacks, and to understand that victory is sometimes impossible or that it can only be gained at a price the wise would refrain from paying.

MAKING DEMOCRACY
SAFE FOR THE WORLD:

National Politics and Foreign Policy

Theodore J. Lowi

THERE are at least three modern schools of thought on the structure and functioning of American politics. All three are supported by a considerable body of doctrine. All three are grounded legitimately early in political history. All three are illustrable in a considerable range of contemporary cases and events. Each involves quite distinctive moral consequences. Each represents itself to be the American political system.[1]

One school, what we shall call Theory 1, begins with the fragmentation of society and economy and concludes that the polity is no different. The popular basis of sovereignty builds the fragmentation into the polity, leading to both constitutional and informal decentralization. Walter Lippmann, the modern prophet of this school, sees in this a "devolution

1. For a full, critical treatment, see my "American Business, Public Policy, Case Studies and Political Theory," *World Politics*, Vol. XVI (July, 1964), 677–715, and the essays of Dahl and others cited there.

of power" down into the constituencies and a derangement of relations among institutions.[2] E. E. Schattschneider's work offers much empirical support as well as further theoretical justification. Political relationships are seen largely in terms of logrolling, the pork barrel, and so on. These are inescapable in a world of extreme particularism. They are the inevitable means of building up consensus for decisions at the national level.[3] In his later work, Schattschneider began to view party as the essential means for saving the system from devolution. But that is only a more or less realistic solution to the problem, not a fact about this system. Decentralization characterizes the politics of this system; the basis of relationships among the participants in this system is logrolling. The outcome may often manifest itself in a fairly stable centralized "power structure"; but this a congeries rather than an elite, a leadership based on conspiracy more than consensus.

The second of the schools, or Theory 2 is more self-consciously a school. It has a name, *pluralism*, and it has for some years been the prevailing ideology among American political scientists. It begins upon the same factual base as the first system—fragmentation, or social pluralism. But to the pluralist, the system is not fragmented and decentralizing. It is fragmented and self-correcting. It represents classical economics applied to the political system. Bargaining among directly conflicting interests is the basic pattern of politics, and the "power structure" is dynamic as well as rational. Logrolling is not basic but is merely one occasionally used strategy, usually employed among interests on the same "side" of the conflict in order to extend and intensify the conflict. A coherent system as well as a public interest are produced out of the fragments. But there is no center of the system, no elite, no meaningful order below the order of the system itself. The system is "multicentered." There may be an elite for each center, but it is not stable and legitimate as an elite. The reality, instead, is an interaction among leaders. The political process is one of bargaining among like or comparable interests. The "power structure" is the coalitions that are the outcome of the bargaining, and public policy is the mere ratification.

The third major school of thought, Theory 3, recognizes the fragmentation as a societal fact but treats it as largely irrelevant to the political system. All the activity in the fragmented society simply helps ensure the legitimacy of the elite. This approach has never been popular among political scientists but is very much alive as the prevailing ideology among American sociologists. To some, the political elite is derived from a socioeconomic class whose members hold all the "command posts" and

2. Walter Lippmann, *The Public Philosophy* (Boston, Little, Brown, 1955).
3. E. E. Schattschneider, *Politics, Pressures, and the Tariff* (New York, Prentice-Hall, 1935).

make all the "key decisions." To others, perhaps the more sophisticated, the elite is comprised of the holders of the command posts whose members ultimately constitute a class. In either (or any other) case, power is centralized and power relations are highly stable. They are based on consensus. Thus, agreement on the most important issues can often be reached with ease, without publicity, and yet highly legitimately because conflict tends to be managed by regular, hierarchical means ("through channels"), and the ultimate settlement of conflict can take place by relatively informal means among like-minded gentlemen, without debates and votes.

It is not necessary to go at length into each school of thought as a theory.[4] It is only necessary first to point to the existence of the multitude of inconsistencies among them and then to decide how to operate as an analyst in face of those inconsistencies.

One way to deal with the extraordinary degree of inconsistency among the prevailing schools of thought is to abandon all three. But that is all too likely to involve rejection of an extremely valuable feature common to them all, and that is their focus on real institutions and real decisions in the real political system.[5] Another way is to embrace them all and then to try to find the limits of the applicability of each. This I have done and, as I have argued elsewhere,[6] each theory turns out to be an extremely rich (and truthful) source of logically related, empirically grounded propositions. In short, once each puts an end to its claim to universality and contents itself with being a theory for only a subsystem, it approaches the standards of scientific theory. The empirical support associated with each as a subsystem becomes stronger rather than weaker.

In sum, therefore, the American system is not all of a piece but is composed of several fundamental subsystems. Internally, these have developed around the most fundamental functions of the state. When public policy is facing the *redistribution* of resources, the system is elitist in very much the theoretical and empirical terms laid down by Mills and others. When public policy is facing the *regulation* of resources, the system is pluralist in all of the specific issues fought out and decisions

4. Some of this can be found in Lowi, *op. cit.*, and in the excellent criticisms representatives of each school cast upon the others.
5. The "transactional" approach offered by Raymond A. Bauer and associates in *American Business and Public Policy* (New York: Atherton Press, 1963), p. 460, does not recommend anything but rejection of Theory 2, the "pressure-group model" as they call it. But more than that is implied, as with other communications approaches, such as Milbrath's in *The Washington Lobbyists*. (Chicago: Rand-McNally, 1963). Likewise for most who use the so-called decision-making approach, where single organizations are taken as systems. Cf. R. C. Snyder, et al., *Foreign Policy Decision-Making* (New York: The Free Press, 1962), pp. 86ff.
6. Lowi, *op. cit.*, esp. p. 686 ff., and also *Arenas of Power*, a book now in progress.

made. A system very much like the one Lippmann disdainfully describes develops around public policy that deals in the *distribution* of resources.[7] Since each of these three types of public policy is a function of the state, and therefore an ongoing process, it is not inconceivable that each becomes a subsystem with a distinctive political structure, process, and morality. This is also perfectly consistent with our present notions about differentiation in modern politics. After all, this is a form around the basic functions of the state; and it is highly adaptive: (1) On the occasional issues (redistribution) that can trigger revolutions and class warfare, the political structure is highly centralized, and the participants are the holders of the most highly legitimate and highly prized statuses in society. The prevailing political relationship is, thus, one of hierarchy or management. (2) On the more frequent occasions when directly coercive restrictions (regulation) must be placed on alternative uses of resources, there is a subsystem that is decentralized and open, usually resulting in the application of general rules or precedents to conduct. Here the prevailing political relationship is one of bargaining. (3) On by far the most frequent occasions, when existing public domain must be "divvied up," decisions can be made quite amorally (without application of a general rule). However, the result is highly co-optative and stabilizing without need of consensus.[8]

In this chapter it is assumed that the "domestic political system" is of the tripartite nature described above. There is much ground for controversy about the assumption that three functions of the state or areas of policy — distribution, regulation, and redistribution — are the essential determinants of the three subsystems. But that need not deter us here. The important point is that there is ample evidence for the existence of the three subsystems and that each would clearly have consequences for American foreign policy if it were also the dominant power pattern in foreign policy making.

The question is, then, what sort of a power pattern can be found in foreign policy? Is it elitistic, pluralistic, or massified? What kind of a subsystem is it? This is a proper enough academic subject. But it is also merely a more academic way of asking (or perhaps answering) two more

7. See my article cited above for a more detailed distinction between distribution and redistribution. Suffice it here to say this: In the long run, all governmental decisions either redistribute or threaten to redistribute resources. But in the short run some decisions can be made involving resources already on hand, e.g. public land, franchises, tariff privileges. In this case, the participants obviously bear a quite distinctive relation to one another.

8. The distinction between bargaining and logrolling is a conventional one that is simply taken more seriously here than usual. Bargaining refers to relations among men bearing common or tangential interests in which each expects to give in somewhere in the expectation of net gain. A logrolling relation is not one borne of tangential interest in which direct conflict and compromise are expected, but, on the contrary, is a relation among men who have absolutely nothing in common.

immediately significant questions: (1) To what extent do domestic political factors influence the making of foreign policy? Put another way, to what extent does our politics change as the interests of the whole country are involved? (2) More normatively, to what extent do our own institutions facilitate or hinder the most rational use of the country's resources toward realization of its vital interests?

In one way or another, each of the papers in this volume has something to offer on these questions, but in all such cases the dimension involved is that of the relation of the formal leadership to the mass, or mass public opinion, in one form or another. Assessments differ on the amount, direction, and virtue of the influence exercised, but the assessments are no less those of elite-mass relations. Thus there remains untreated the other dimension: By this I mean *the actual relations among the formal leaders and among the institutions of foreign policy making that create the formal leadership positions.* Only by inspecting relations among the formal leaders and the governmental units they control can we hope to settle the questions posed above. Ultimately, this would reconcile the various points of view toward the relationships between the foreign policy leaders as elite and the informal forces of groups and mass opinions. A reconciliation would be found by discovering the conditions under which one or another power pattern prevails. These conditions will be found in (1) events, (2) institutions, (3) policies, and (4) types of policies.

Before proceeding to the inquiry into the events, institutions, and policies that explain our foreign policy establishment, it might be useful to state in a few brief propositions the terms of discourse. These propositions may also serve to summarize and conclude this introductory section:

1. A modern, highly differentiated state generates conflict that cannot altogether be taken care of by mere elite management but must necessarily involve, under varying circumstances, a great deal of bargaining and logrolling.

2. These three fundamental political relations—hierarchy or management, bargaining, and logrolling—form the basis for three distinct subsystems within the American political system.

3. These three types of political relations are indexes to the pattern of power in any political institution or unit of government.

4. Evidence for these relations can be found in the ordinary workings of the institutions and units, and the workings of these units can be found in the nature and impact of their outputs. That is to say, the statute (or other policy expression) properly understood is a valid source of data on institutions and processes; therefore, we can know about the political system through the policy outputs of its units without need of "inside dope."

EVENTS AND ELITES

Events shape foreign policy making in any number of ways. Events in Asia intensify or relax our diplomatic, military, and economic activity there. Certain events intensify economic over military or military over diplomatic activities. And so on. But the most important aspect of the event in the operation of our foreign policy establishment is the time dimension. Is the event a crisis or is it not? Does the event allow time for consideration of alternative policies or time only for a conditioned reflex? Are we on the brink of violence, civil or military, or are the events taking place at some point away from the brink where responses rather than reflexes, preventives rather than cures, may be appropriate?

In regard to events or situations of the first type, crises, the foreign policy record of the United States has been outstanding.[9] Postwar examples of United States behavior in crises include Greek-Turkish aid, the Berlin airlift, response to the Korean invasion, the 1956 Arab-Israeli intervention, the Cuban missile crisis. Due to our relatively poor record in most noncrisis situations, our adversaries consistently underestimate our capacity to react in time to crises.

Crisis situations are special conditions underlying special operations of the foreign policy establishment. The aforementioned crisis decisions involved less bargaining than discussion preceding consensus. Only command-post positions were involved; the public and its institutions were far removed; the decisions made by the elite were highly legitimate; public and semipublic responses were largely ceremonial and affirmative.[10] In sum, there was hardly any politics at all.

Each of these decisions in crisis seems, therefore, to portray the foreign policy establishment much in the image offered by Mills as the whole truth about the United States: "Within the higher circles of the power elite, factions do exist. But more powerful than these divisions are the internal discipline and the community of interests that bind the power elite together..."[11] But on further inspection, Mills did not go far enough. As is well known, Mills defined his power elite as all the holders of the top "institutional positions" in the military, in the executive branch of national government and in industry. In crisis decisions, inspection shows that actually the participants have always constituted an elite *even*

9. I make such judgments frequently throughout the essay. In all instances the judgment is grounded in these assumptions: (1) that the United States has vital and legitimate interests abroad; (2) that the United States is acting rationally when it pursues these interests; and (3) that rational foreign policy is good foreign policy and irrational foreign policy is bad foreign policy. Since I will so often be critical of our establishment, my description of its attributes and patterns should be called a pathology rather than a physiology. However, this is more an issue of language than of science.

10. See, for example, the data on public responses to presidential actions in chapter 10.

11. C. Wright Mills, *The Power Elite* (New York; Oxford, 1959), p. 283.

smaller than the elite identified by Mills. Even when the crisis offers a small grace period, such as was true for instance even of Dienbienphu in 1954 and aid to Greece and Turkey in 1947, rarely has more than a small proportion of the standard power elite been involved in the making of the decision, and it was a very special segment.

These facts suggest the more accurate proposition that *crisis decisions in foreign policy are made by an elite of formal, official office-holders.* Rarely is there time to go further. Apparently rarely also is there need to go further, except immediately after the decision through ceremonies of affirmation and perhaps long after the decision, through criticism and "electoral punishment." Thus, a corollary to this obvious, albeit often overlooked, first proposition is that the people who make decisions in times of crisis are largely those who were elected and appointed to make such decisions. That is to say, *in foreign affairs crises our government has operated pretty much as it was supposed to operate.* There is a normative corollary as well: Since our record of response to crisis is good, then the men in official positions have been acting and are able to act rationally.

So far, then, all we have established is that foreign policy making is influenced by events and that critical events produce a distinctive type of process and leadership. But this statement is clearly true of only one type of situation — crisis — and not necessarily of all foreign policy decisions. It would be a serious mistake to assume that all important foreign policy decisions occur at moments of crisis just as it would be a mistake to a assume that the existence of a crisis is irrelevant to the pattern of politics in foreign policy.

This leaves us with the study of the entire noncrisis dimension of foreign policy decisions, and it will not be so easy to analyze as the crisis dimensions because noncrisis decisions involve institutions. So far nothing has been said of institutions. Indeed, a fundamental feature of crisis decisions is that they involve institution leaders (holders of the top posts) *without their institutions.* Only when time allows does the entire apparatus of the foreign policy establishment come into play. And when men and their institutions are involved, the decision-making process is bound to differ from when only the men are involved. Thus the long section on noncrisis decision-making which follows is basically an analysis of institutions.

INSTITUTIONS IN SEARCH OF AN ESTABLISHMENT

Most people would prefer a foreign policy establishment working regularly and normally as it works in crises. Most would also agree that this is not the case, that the establishment falls far short of that ideal

whereby responsible officials work together without outside hindrance, in a context of immediate support and ultimate accountability. Since the United States' plunge into the hostile waters of world leadership, much effort has gone into the creation of a special establishment that would work as an extension of the system of crisis politics. After World War II, for instance, much was done, in the interests of peacetime, to capture the spirit and perpetuate the organizational innovations of the war. However, possibly because of our peculiar tradition in foreign affairs or because of the immediacy of our new role, we ended up instead with an extension of domestic processes, practices, and values. As a result we have the reverse of Wilson's problem. We have not yet succeeded in making democracy safe for the world.

Only a few selected cases of noncrisis policy decisions will be examined here. Those included were chosen because they are decisions concerning our basic instruments of foreign policy and foreign policy formulation. Each, then, has double value. Each case is, first, a set of decisions that produced the instrument; thus each case was a major policy decision and can be taken as a reflection, in and of itself, of the political process in foreign policy. Second, once created, each instrument becomes a part of the foreign policy establishment as one or more institutions contributing, for better or worse, to the political process of later decisions.

Upon examination each tells nearly the same political story with about the same moral: When there is time for planning there is time for disagreement. Since there is nothing (short of violence) in American culture, values, or habits to limit the course of disagreement, disagreement spreads. Disagreement spreads the area of involvement toward all individuals who possess or represent resources that would improve the positions of the initial combatants. More and more individuals, values, and institutions become involved as the stakes increase and the time allows. As the area of involvement spreads it also decentralizes to include the more public resources and strategies. As involvement spreads there is an increase in the uncertainty of the outcome (in policy).

Each case was an effort to create the instruments for the most rational use of a particular type of American resource in realizing our interests abroad. Presumably each of the instruments, once created, was to be available for use with, not against, other instruments. Men who act rationally in concert during the vital periods of crisis are men who desire the same working relationships when the stakes are high but the pressures are less intense. One of the most important points to be made in this chapter is that, despite the rationality of individual members of the elite, action in concert and consensus was the rare exception. Whether this is admirable or reprehensible, it is a reflection of a particular kind of political process, a political process so decentralized as to be almost completely

susceptible to domestic political influences. What these are, how they work, and to what consequence they work will be the subject of the final section of the chapter. First it is necessary to analyze the cases for evidence of the type and degree of decentralization to be found in noncrisis foreign policy formulation.

Marshall Plan: Toward an Establishment in Economic Policy

The story of the "opening of America" in the passage of the Economic Cooperation Act has been told often and well.[12] It has usually been taken as an instance of the American foreign policy establishment working at its best, because the Act was economically timely and close to adequate. The reassessment here is not for the purpose of judging its economics, but for analyzing the kind of politics it reflects and the kind, after passage, it contributed to.

The structure of the Economic Cooperation Administration (ECA) cannot possibly be understood except in terms of domestic style conflict and its regular influence on foreign decisions. That is, everything about the Act and its administration was the outcome of adjustment (either through compromise or logrolling) of a multitude of independent interests, and was not a decision following consensus among a narrow elite of public and private power holders. The most compelling evidence in the case for the type of political process involved lies in the creation of the second State Department. In sum, United States' peacetime involvement was achieved at the price of setting up an independent ECA.

The State Department draft of European Recovery Plan (ERP or Marshall Plan) called for an administrator "whose every function, especially those involving foreign policy, would be performed 'subject to direction and control of the Secretary of State.'"[13] Ultimate State Department control was something even the great Marshall had insisted upon. But Vandenberg, along with many other members of Congress, was dissatisfied, even though he had been aware of the problem of having dual responsibilities in foreign affairs.[14] Vandenberg, with the help of The Brookings Institution, sought and found the compromise eventually accepted by Truman, Marshall, and Congress.

Essentially, Congress won. Bipartisanship had been a means of congressional co-optation of the executive rather than the other way around.

12. See especially Joseph Jones, *The Fifteen Weeks* (New York: Viking, 1955).

13. Arthur H. Vandenberg, Jr., *The Private Papers of Senator Vandenberg* (Boston; Houghton-Mifflin, 1952), p. 388. See also President Truman's message to Congress, December 19, 1947: "The Administrator must be subject to the direction of the Secretary of State on decisions and actions affecting our foreign policy." *State Department Bulletin*, (December 28, 1947), p. 1243.

14. On Marshall, see H. B. Price, *The Marshall Plan and Its Meaning* (Ithaca; Cornell University Press 1955), p. 69; on Vandenberg, see *Papers, op. cit.*, p. 388.

In the Act, the Administrator was given a fully independent agency and the authority and status of Cabinet rank. Since it would be bad form to have two Secretaries of State, there would just have to be "successful liaison"[15] between the Administrator and the Secretary. Optimistically, Section 105 (b) of the Economic Cooperation Act provided that the Administrator and the Secretary were to keep each other "fully and currently informed on matters, including prospective action...pertinent to the duties of the other." Somewhat more realistically and very much in point is Section 105 (b) (3) which provided that "...if differences of view are not adjusted by consultation [between Administrator and Secretary], the matter shall be referred to the President for final decision."

If there had been any doubts about the likelihood of such an arrangement becoming a second State Department, all actions following passage should have dispelled them. Marshall's choice for Administrator was his Undersecretary, Will Clayton. This appointment Vandenberg successfully opposed on the grounds that the "overriding Congressional desire [was] that the ERP Administrator come from the outside business world with strong industrial credentials and *not* via the State Department.... [T]his job as ERP Administrator stands out by itself — as demonstrated in all of the Congressional debates — as requiring particularly persuasive economic credentials unrelated to diplomacy."[16] On similar grounds, President Truman's initial proposal of Dean Acheson was also vetoed. Paul Hoffman suited the requirements of business administration to a T.

Hoffman's operational code for ECA was based upon a profoundly political decision to be nonpolitical: "I believed that in fighting communism in Europe, we would lose all our moorings if we adopted the Machiavellian philosophy that the ends justify the means. Therefore I insisted on confining ourselves to the recovery field....I had a strong belief that no pattern imposed by a group of planners in Washington could possibly be effective....Coming into this with a business background, I thought that if we in the ECA adopted a new role — as a kind of investment banker — that would be the right approach."[17] It is only necessary here to observe that such an approach was rife with "matters...pertinent to the duties of" the Secretary of State.

The statute also provided for a Special Representative to Europe, with rank of Ambassador Extraordinary and Plenipotentiary (Section 108). It provided that he be "representative of the Administrator" and also "chief representative of the United States Government" for any recovery activity in all of Europe. The Act also provided that the Special Representative direct the special ECA missions, which were to be

15. Vandenberg, *op. cit.*, p. 393.
16. *Ibid.*, p. 393. Emphasis in original.
17. Quoted in Price, *op. cit.,* pp. 73–74.

established in each country independent of the regular diplomatic mission (Section 109). In any disputes with the diplomatic mission, the chief of the ECA mission and the country ambassador were considered equal parties in consultation that could be carried up to Administrator and Secretary of State as provided for under Section 105 (b) (3), as described above.

The staffing of ECA definitely made it the second State Department allowed for in the statute. Averill Harriman, appointed Special Representative, had been Truman's Secretary of Commerce. He had served as an ambassador, but in his experience in foreign affairs he was more accustomed to dealing directly with the President. William C. Foster, named Deputy Special Representative, had been Undersecretary of Commerce. The Deputy Administrator was Howard Bruce, a Baltimore industrialist-financier and formerly Director of Materiel, Army Service Forces. Others in offices close to Hoffman included: three professors of specialties important to ECA; two New York attorneys, one of whom was also President of *Time*, Inc; a onetime President of the Export-Import Bank; the chief of Foreign Agricultural Relations in the Department of Agriculture; and a couple of professional administrators. There was some experience in foreign affairs among them, but there was not a single professional from the State Department in the entire company (unless Harriman's very special experience is counted). The list contains several important departures from Hoffman's principle of business administration, but no departures from an unspoken rule of independence from the "other" State Department. Among the first chiefs of ECA missions were: Thomas K. Finletter, executive, attorney, air expert, to the United Kingdom; David Bruce, Assistant Secretary of Commerce, 1947–48, to France; J. D. Zellerback, San Francisco businessman, to Italy; and Roger Lapham, former Mayor of San Francisco, to China. Only Bruce had had State Department experience prior to appointment, and that was as a vice-consul in Rome, 1926–28.

The political, and therefore foreign-ministry, character of such an agency ought to be too close to the inevitable to require much documentation. Let these brief observations suffice. The initial expectation for ECA was that it would be a small agency whose staff would be essentially a few experts in agriculture, industry, and procurement.[18] But once in operation, ECA began to grow, not merely in obedience to some Parkinson's law of bureaucracy, but in a politically significant manner. The staff turned immediately to analysis of economic conditions in order to

18. Price, *op. cit.*, p. 75. See also Truman's ECA message, *op. cit.*, p. 1242: "... I expect that the Economic Cooperation Administration will need only a small staff. No vast new agency or corporation is needed to perform functions for which government facilities now exist." The facts in this section are taken largely from Price, Vandenberg's *Papers*, and Robert Asher's *Grants, Loans, and Local Currencies* (Washington: Brookings, 1961); however, none of these authors would necessarily agree with my interpretations.

have independent means of assessing the plans of the Organization for European Economic Cooperation (OEEC). Although the autonomy of OEEC and the self-execution of the program were stressed from the very beginning (see Hoffman's attitude above, for example), it is impossible to believe that the framers of the aid agency were naïve enough to think they could make the whole process self-executing and nonpolitical. In any case, if ECA was not going to accept OEEC plans as final, it was going to have to make value judgments. That is the implication of their "analyses of economic conditions." If only to that extent, ECA had to become a second State Department.

A second aspect of this expansion of the political character of ECA was early growth and elaboration of the Special Representative's Office in Paris, despite the fact that it was expected to be a mere staff for the Special Representative himself: "Never before had an overseas regional office been set up to play so large a part in a peacetime operation of the United States government."[19] This separated still further our economic aid from our central political arms, while at the same time it further guaranteed that political considerations would be involved in ECA's "economic" decisions. Finally, the Administrator set up an Office of Labor Advisors for propagandizing European unions on the commitment of American labor to the democratic point of view.

The foreign policy inherent in this series of compromise and partial decisions and the proliferation of the units of government, was, in effect, "You can give money but you cannot use money as a means of realizing our interests abroad." Congress was not altogether at fault but fed upon the confusions and conflicts of the Administration leaders. In any case, the Marshall Plan was a sort of "*partial decision*" that is so typical of decisions in domestic policy. Often, in fact, domestic decisions are so partial as to be nugatory (e.g., the Employment Act of 1946), or to be confusing beyond use (e.g., three or four different ways left open to the President to end strikes), or to be self-destructive (e.g., some programs to get people off the farms and others to keep them on). This is called "slack in the system;" through such means we buy time, displace conflict, and avoid the costs of planning. Obviously, the United States can afford it. Partial decisions also occur in foreign affairs, but we probably cannot afford them. And when they occur, as in ECA, they are evidence either of the total irrationality of the participants or of a highly decentralized bargaining-logrolling system. The Marshall Plan under State Department (central political) control would inevitably have involved decisions on the particular goods or amounts that would be allowed to go to particular countries at a particular time following upon fulfillment of particular conditions. There would probably have been no objection to lodging so

19. Price, *op. cit.*, p. 76.

much power in a State Department to manipulate Europe. *The objection would be to lodging so much power in a State Department to regulate our own society for purposes of manipulating Europe.*

Placed outside the State Department, economic aid pure and simple offered little threat of enhanced internal controls. In fact, aid could then be seen as a set of opportunities to be created by a significant expansion of our trading domain. On a matter of that sort, there would have been little political controversy, and the decision would then have been an example of low-pressure policy-making rather than one of elite control of foreign affairs. But there was ample controversy, and it is significant that it took the form of controversy over the independence of the agency itself and not, for example, over the amount of money, the conditions attached, problems of repayment, or even problems of "buy American" or "trading with the enemy." Thus, the key sources of conflict in formulating the Marshall Plan were domestic in nature. Essentially, the political question in the Marshall Plan was, "What sorts of disciplines do we want or need to impose upon our system in order to realize our external interests?" To save it from sure congressional burial, the answer had to be "None." That answer robbed the program of much of its value as an instrument of foreign affairs because in avoiding internal regulation the state also willfully deprived itself of its resources. More to the immediate point, the *formulation of the Marshall Plan is not a reflection of elite control, but of the inability of an elite to formulate an effective and clear policy.* Once in existence, the aid agency contributes in turn to further inabilities in future issues.

Toward a Defense Establishment

Following World War II, virtually everyone seemed to desire "unification." If it had worked dramatically in the form of the new Joint Chiefs of Staff, then it could be made to work after the war in a unified and rational defense establishment. This would be necessary as well as desirable because the practical problems in the postwar period demanded it: Occupation policy and operation required it. Bipolarity required it by constantly pushing marginal decisions upward toward high policy. Proper strategic planning to meet those same bipolar conditions made unification the more compelling with the rise of collective security arrangements that were expected to be collective in terms of the separate military services as well as of the sovereign countries. Finally, unification was also supposed to solve the problem of development, control, and use of atomic energy.

But, of course, that desire for unification meant different things to different people.[20] The National Security Act of 1947 is well known as a

20. See Paul Hammond on Navy's approach in "The National Security Council As a Device for Interdepartmental Coordination: An Interpretation and Appraisal," *American Political Science Review,* Vol. 54 (December, 1960), pp. 899–910.

bundle of compromises, although the significance of such knowledge as an insight into political structure might be better appreciated. The extent of conflict in this national security area of foreign policy was certainly no less than in the economic area. And there is reason to believe the conflict was even more intense, protracted, and widespread. After the war the stature of the military was at its highest; "key" decisions were at stake, and as with the Marshall Plan there seemed to be consensus on principle. Yet, it would be hard to imagine a statute less reflective of consensus.

The National Security Council (NSC), core of the concept, was set up as an ex officio body with very little in the way of arms and legs. Essentially it was a subcommittee of the Cabinet with the representativeness of a committee but not the coherent apparatus of a department.[21] The intelligence functions of the Central Intelligence Agency (CIA) belonged to NSC, but even so, all intelligence activities of all other departments were left, by the statute, totally intact. CIA was given access to all their data, but not even through NSC could CIA affect the organization or work of these other intelligence agencies (Section 102a). And except for CIA there was no true organizational arm to make NSC a real establishment.

The alternative core to NSC in a defense establishment would be the Department of Defense. In the statute, however, it was not a department; there was only a small Office of the Secretary.[22] Everything else resembles a confederation. Section 202 of the Act provided the Secretary with some general powers but further provided that each of the respective services "shall be administered as individual executive departments by their respective Secretaries, and all powers and duties relating to such departments not specifically conferred upon the Secretary of Defense by this Act shall be retained by each of their respective Secretaries." That is the "tenth amendment" of the Department of Defense constitution. The powers left to the Secretary of Defense were largely fiscal, and, although this changed after 1958, and especially with McNamara, he was basically a procurement officer.[23]

The Secretary of Defense (and therefore NSC also) was deprived of

21. Hammond in *ibid.* offers still another type of assessment which is in point here: "...the existence of two different 'cabinets,' the traditional one which is to deal primarily with domestic affairs and the NSC, which is supposed to specialize in national security, or foreign, affairs, with dual membership for some, has left an obvious means of maneuver—the choice of the most favorable forum—with results about which we can at least speculate." Reprinted in Andrew Scott and Raymond H. Dawson, *Readings in the Making of American Foreign Policy* (New York; Macmillan 1965), p. 360.

22. In the 1947 statute no provision, not even for the name, was made for a Department of Defense. There was to be a "National Military Establishment, and the Secretary of Defense shall be head thereof" (Section 201a).

23. More in a moment on post-1958; but here, I should say, the fact that so many of the Secretaries have been out of Wall Street and big industry is to me more a reflection of the true function of the office than of the "power eliteness" of the incumbents.

the backing not only of his civilian departments, but also of the military services as well. As the tenth amendment above suggests, neither Congress nor the military expected real unification—only coordination, "a distressingly frequent word"[24] in the Act. Lack of unification in the peacetime Joint Chiefs of Staff (JCS) is a phenomenon that needs no recalling. As a body, they were constituted "the principal military advisers to the President and the Secretary of Defense," totally brushing aside the civilian counterparts. Internally, the statute was crystal clear on the integrity of the members and their services. The original statute provided for no chairman, and relations among the three members (or four, if the President had his own chief of staff) were derived from their respective service positions: "The Chief of Staff, United States Army, the Chief of Naval Operations, and the Chief of Staff, United States Air Force, shall take rank among themselves according to their relative dates of appointment..." (Section 208b). This is all the more an interesting outcome considering that the scheme favored by President Truman (the Collins Plan) called for a single Chief of Staff of the Armed Forces responsible to the Secretary.[25] The Navy Department won not only on this point but succeeded in getting insurance of real implementation by getting its patron, James Forrestal, the appointment as first Secretary of Defense.

We might leave the Defense Department with Millis' judgment that the JCS "were almost constitutionally incapable of resolving the major problems which the National Security Act had confided to them..."[26] But, continues Millis, since no other agency could probably do better, "there was something to be said for leaving them to an agency which, rather than resolve them wrongly, would not resolve them at all."[27]

Some evidence suggests improvement in political control since 1958, capping efforts in that direction beginning with the National Security Act amendments of 1949. Over the years, the Secretary's role was strengthened, first by creation of the Department of Defense and then by enlargement of the Office of the Secretary, particularly with additions of an undersecretary and several assistant secretaries. However, it is easy to overemphasize this help, because of two basic restrictions imposed by law upon their use. First, the Secretary was forbidden to encroach upon the "combatant functions assigned to the military services."[28] Second,

---

24. Walter Millis and Harvey Mansfield, *Arms and the State* (New York; Twentieth Century Fund, 1958), p. 179.

25. Paul Y. Hammond, *Organizing for Defense* (Princeton: Princeton University Press, 1961), pp. 213 ff.

26. Millis and Mansfield, *op. cit.*, p. 183.

27. *Ibid.*

28. Gene M. Lyons, "The New Civil-Military Relations," reprinted in Scott and Dawson, *op. cit.*, p. 414. After quoting the passage, Lyons observes that "Congress deliberately used this basic prohibition to maintain the essential identity of the individual services, a tactic that has been retained in subsequent major reorganizations in 1953 and 1958."

the assistant secretaryships were established with the understanding that "they should not be in the direct line of administrative authority between [the Secretary] and the three military departments, but instead should assist in developing policies, prescribing standards, and bringing to the Secretary of Defense information on which he may base his decisions."[29]

If the Secretary's position has been improving in relation to his confederate units, it has been due less to conscious actions of policy-makers than to general and unplanned developments that have simply facilitated the role of Secretary of Defense. First, changes in the technology of national security have enabled him to flank the services. Weapons development has not in any direct way very deeply involved the specific roles and missions of the services. Thus, through skillful financial management, direction over R and D, and assignment of weapons systems with due regard for the exercise of influence, a Secretary can, in the 1960s, impose some modicum of will upon the far-flung defense establishment.

The Secretary's role may have been further improved by a second and a third general development, both negative. The second is the decline of the civilian secretaries that most historians agree has taken place.[30] Having civilian aids to the Secretary, who were often special pleaders, was always a problem. So, demotion from Cabinet status was followed by reduction in the status of the incumbents, which was accompanied by the expansion of another dimension of civil authority, the Assistant Secretaries of Defense. Finally, in 1958, the Secretary was given authority to delegate powers to his assistant secretaries, in partial contravention of the earlier restriction on direct lines of authority to the services. The third development is the continuing decentralization of the Joint Chiefs of Staff. The unwillingness of Congress to centralize JCOS under a true chairman, and the consequent inability of the chiefs to come to and hold to military agreements have given a succession of Secretaries many of their opportunities to get, informally and through legislation, increases in their own central power.[31]

In sum, then, recent developments, although showing operational improvement, are not evidence for much of a fundamental change in the political process of national security. The 1960's Secretary of Defense is a more powerful figure, but his enhanced power rests upon the subterfuges of budgetary and materiel controls and on the perhaps temporary advantages of his Office being slightly less in disarray than the three

29. Quoted by Lyons in *ibid.*, pp. 414–15, after which, his understated judgment that "Under these terms, the authority of the assistant secretaries was ambiguous."

30. In all of this I am indebted to Lyons, to Hammond, and to Millis-Mansfield (*op. cit.*) for vital factual assistance, but they would not necessarily agree with my interpretations.

31. Lyons picks this as the most important reason for increase in civilian authority (*op. cit.*, 415).

services. To this one observer, the main point in the most recent developments is that the defense establishment is different in many respects from
what it was but not so different in fundamental character. That is, *cohesion around and responsibility toward the Secretary and the President
have not been institutionalized. The greater accountability of the units to
the center in recent years is due to bargaining advantages; therefore, the
bargaining feature of the establishment remains, and the advantages
must be treated as possibly ephemeral.* Secretary McNamara's very
strength may be the undoing of his successors. In getting influence for
himself through the initial assignments of weapons, for example, he may
be using up the options (therefore the bargaining advantages) of future
Secretaries. How many assignments and transfers can be made before
precedents are established and binding, through the help of Congress,
upon future decisions? In this sense, then, the powers of the Secretary
remain, albeit greater, essentially fiscal. Improvement has come through
wiser use of these fiscal powers to influence other types of decisions. But
this hardly paints a picture of hierarchy, management, efficient execution
— in a word, elite.

Much more can and should be said of conflict in the formation and
conduct of the Defense Department. But there is more to be learned from
looking at the prevailing relations between Defense and other working
parts of our defense establishment. Of these the most fascinating is the
Atomic Energy Commission (AEC) and its relation both to the defense
establishment and to central political control. If there was ever any
ambiguity in the evidence for the argument that no consensual, nonconflictive, managerial defense establishment exists, relations between
Defense and AEC ought to dispel it. Relations here have been so loose as
to leave as quite plausible the interpretation that the United States has
no discernible national interests at all.

The Atomic Energy Commission's powers in its vast domain exceed
"those of any department of the government ever before established. The
Commission has, in effect, a plenary charter to do anything in the field of
atomic energy that will promote the public safety and welfare."[32] Section
4 of the Act of 1946, for instance, turns over all ownership of fissionable
materials and control of all production facilities. Decisions on fissionable
material released for research or as irrelevant to bomb production are
left to the Commission. The Commission was set up deliberately and
legally as a monopoly.

There was probably never any issue over whether atomic energy and
its production would or would not be a government monopoly. The
issues, rightfully in my opinion, revolved around how the monopoly

32. James R. Newman and Byron S. Miller, *The Control of Atomic Energy* (New York;
Whittlesey House, 1948), p. 27.

would relate to the rest of the government. Naturally it became a question of control. But the significant thing here is the alternative control features debated. In high-sounding tones the fate of atomic energy was defined as passing to "civilian control" or to "military control." This made for simplification for purposes of adversary proceedings and debate in Congress and in the press; and, better, this definition of the problem gave everyone a point of reference by fitting the perplexing atom into established (prewar) liberal-conservative alignments.[33] But obviously, it had very little to do with the problems that made the Act, for better or worse, one of the significant decisions of our time.

The real question of control was probably whether scientists and the universities or the military and military-related industries would have the easiest access to the materials and the decisions on their use. But it is clear from the debates and from a straighforward reading of the statute that at no time did either side expect that control should be in neither set of hands; none of the interested parties expected that control would rest in the hands of the political executives who would run the defense establishment. Dahl and Brown are left to ask only five years later whether the Commission should or should not be placed within the Department of Defense. Since the overwhelming proportion of its work has been in military and strategic uses, why should the program be anything more than one part of the arms program?[34] The question is not supposed to imply an answer. It is to emphasize the fact that the separation of AEC from the executive was almost a foregone conclusion and, further, a foregone conclusion hardly suggestive of a consensual foreign policy elite, but rather one in which further conflict has been institutionalized.

Thus, AEC became its own boss. It was made independent, and apparently continues to be just as independent, of State and of Defense and, therefore, of the presidency. In security affairs, AEC is a coequal partner of Defense. AEC-Defense disputes, like ECA-State disputes, have been settled, according to the Act, by the President. At first this arrangement may appear to be a sound principle of insuring presidential involvement, but that would be mere rationalization of the inevitable. During the formative years, through 1951, only one dispute — the custody of atomic weapons — was taken to the President, and that one would have gone up to him regardless of AEC location. More important is the fact that the President decided this one in favor of AEC and that, given the spirit of the Act, that was really the only decision possible.[35] So long as AEC

    33. Cf. Byron S. Miller, "The Atomic Energy Act of 1946," in Theodore J. Lowi (ed.), *Legislative Politics U.S.A.* (Boston, Little, Brown, 1962 and 1965), p. 267.
    34. Robert A. Dahl and Ralph S. Brown, *Domestic Control of Atomic Energy* (New York; Social Science Research Council, 1951), pp. 25–26.
    35. Cf. *ibid.*, p. 24.

possessed a monopoly of the secrets[36] along with its monopoly of the materials, it would also possess most of the bargaining advantages with the President. There is paraphernalia inside the AEC for military representation and joint consultation, but that was put in largely to guarantee access for the separate services, not particularly for the highest echelons. The fight among the services for operational control of the bomb affected the structure of the AEC as it would the National Security Act institutions of the following year and the entire establishment for the indefinite future thereafter.

This left (and leaves) the Secretary of Defense as simply the biggest customer of AEC, but having no statutory rights of direction, not to speak of control. In stark contrast, Congress gave to itself an extremely strong statutory right to participate in, with the distinct possibility of controlling, AEC decisions. This means that all the arguments about the novelty and the unique significance and the international security importance of atomic energy are largely empty rhetoric. The setup is essentially like every other independent agency created since the ICC. H. L. Nieburg, in an excellent paper on the AEC,[37] has detected several spiritual ages in the life of the Commission, roughly paralleling the tenure of the AEC chairmen. In the first age, under Lilienthal, the orientation was primarily executive.[38] The second age, the late Lilienthal period and then Gordon Dean's, was one of congressional (that is, Joint Committee on Atomic Energy) collaboration. The third, Strauss, age was a stormy one of attempted extrication from the Joint Committee and also from established executive alliances. Strauss' failure led to his resignation in such an air of unpopularity as to prevent his later appointment as Secretary of Commerce. And his replacement as chairman led to the fourth age, a congressional *rapprochement.*

Were there really four distinct ages? Or were there simply variations in one basic pattern of Congress-AEC relations? Strauss' unhappy tenure suggests that the latter is closer to the truth. Nieburg characterizes atomic policy in the last years of Eisenhower as "not congressional predominance in its simplest form," but rather as an alliance between AEC and the

36. Section 10, in which the Commission was given power to "control the dissemination of restricted data" and also to decide what were "restricted data." [Sec. 10 (b) (1) defined "restricted data" as all data having to do in any way with fissionable material for bombs or power, and then it left the Commission to decide what data could be published.]

37. "The Eisenhower AEC and Congress," *Midwest Journal of Political Science* (May, 1962), pp. 116–17.

38. Nieburg compares the AEC of that period to an "independent commission," The quotes were, I hope, meant to suggest that the typical commission was not particularly executive-oriented either, but that it simply played at being independent as a strategy against Congress on occasion, against constituency on other occasions, against the president at other times. Then it would be like other independent commissions.

Joint Committee[39] against President, Treasury, Budget, and State. The change of Administration and the restoration of common party majorities in both Branches has not changed this pattern very much. In a later publication, Nieburg observed that Chairman Seaborg has "not yielded to Congressional direction, but through the graceful maneuvers of politics, his boss the President (Kennedy) has."[40] Only the rhetoric seems to be different.

AEC is the result of a series of partial decisions, wrought out of the same conflict and compromise or displacement of that conflict that inevitably seems to characterize American political decisions. In accommodation to industry and military service interests, the AEC was made "independent." As a result, however, atomic energy, atomic weaponry, and information regarding both, are not a direct part of the resources of diplomacy or of strategy. In war, of course, AEC separatism, like all agency and group particularism, disappears. But that is in war.

The unusually strong congressional relation to the atomic energy aspect of survival need only be noted here as special and significant. Further attention will be paid to it presently. What I hope the foregoing illuminates is the extent of conflict and the degree of decentralization in the original Act, and the significance of the AEC, once created, as an additional aspect of fragmentation in the defense establishment. This was offered, in turn, as a reflection, an index, of the degree and types of continuing conflict in the total establishment for foreign policy. Fragmentation and conflict perpetuate themselves in separated agencies, each with statutory integrity, none enjoying many rights to intervene in the processes of the others. *The instruments — and the policy implications underlying them — were shaped by the momentary requirements of getting agreement, not the ultimate fact of making decisions toward the realization of foreign objectives.*[41] This must seriously impair efforts to put these instruments to the service of political strategies. More academically, it should destroy any claim that foreign policy-making is a fundamentally different policy-making system, or one that is in any considerable way insulated from domestic political forces.

In sum, all the efforts to create a set of rational instruments in a separate, integrated foreign policy establishment seem to have resulted in partial decisions. Each instrument was created but always with a vital element missing. We could get the commitment and many of the activities and much of the appropriations attendant to the commitment. But we could not so fashion commitment or activities to perform the over-all

---

39. Nieburg would go so far as to include all congressional Democrats (*op. cit.*, p. 116).

40. H. L. Nieburg, *Nuclear Secrecy and Foreign Policy* (Washington, 1964), p. 36.

41. Cf. Samuel P. Huntington, "Strategy Planning and the Political Process," *Foreign Affairs*, Vol. 38 (January, 1960), p. 291.

function of serving our interests abroad: economic activity outside diplomacy and power politics; military procurement, R and D, atomic energy activity outside military diplomacy, and power politics. These results are more understandable, although not any more tolerable, if we see foreign policy as a mere variant of domestic.[42]

POLICIES: OVERSELL, NOT OVERKILL

The institutions of foreign policy formulation and coordination created after World War II were essentially policies, as well as being instruments for making policies. Thus, in analyzing these institutions we have already had a look at some policies and have found, through them, many significant indexes for the analysis of the establishment itself. But there are many other policies that are not also institutions and were shaped by the institutions already analyzed. Analysis of some of these policies and the continuities in the manner of their formulation will provide further evidence and more useful indexes for our final assessment of the politics of foreign policy. Put in the most concrete, operational terms, the question here is: What are the policy consequences of the "separation of powers" prevailing among the units of foreign policy formulation? The policy consequences will be viewed primarily from their most fundamental perspective — the presidency.

Somehow a President must try to make a ministry out of what is at best a coalition. Any man who can engineer his own nomination in one of our national conventions and then hold together his winning cadre for election victories in a large number of states, has an impressive array of political skills. The requirement of possession and use of such skills is a reflection of the dispersed, coalitional character of political power in America. The presence of such behavior in the formulation of foreign policy ought then to offer an additional set of dependable indexes for the patterns of power in this particular issue-area.

Presidential behavior since World War II can be summarized as "oversell": the President has been forced to (1) oversell the crisis and (2) oversell the remedy. These are the continuities in the formulation of foreign policy. In reverse order, each of the types of oversell will be analyzed and illustrated.

42. Colleague Waltz disagrees with the stress put on fragmentation on the grounds that the U.S.S.R. and even Great Britain also have lived with institutional diversity, and that the American cases do not constitute a special American question of unity versus disunity. Granted, most advanced states are highly differentiated (fragmentation being reserved for differentiation one doesn't like); but the United States, in great contrast to the other two countries, has no other *centripetal* institutions. Thus, the proliferation of units means something quite different in the United States.

Overselling the Remedy

The United Nations was an instrument and a policy the United States was determined to fashion after World War II, if only as repayment for our role in destroying the League of Nations. Enormous care was taken to insure its passage—and its passage without crippling amendment or even embarrassing debate. So well was the UN sold that when the Charter came before the Senate for advice and consent, almost no opposition remained. As Bertram Gross recorded it: "Since little defense of the Charter was needed, few Senators planned to speak on its behalf and there was genuine danger that an impression of disinterest would be created. As a last-minute measure...Senator Connally...was seen walking around the floor with a pad of paper in one hand and a pencil in the other, buttonholing one Senator after another and beseeching them to speak on behalf of the United Nations."[43]

What seemed politically appropriate and successful for the occasion proved to have been almost too heavy a price to pay, for many in the most attentive public had become convinced that the UN would be a real instrument of our foreign policy. Thus, when the critical emergency of aid to Greece and Turkey arose, the possibility of a timely response by the United States ran into serious difficulty from unexpected as well as expected sources. Once the news of direct United States action in Greece and Turkey became known, "the overwhelming attachment of the American public to the United Nations made itself felt in no uncertain terms, and many of the staunchest supporters of the President's policy, who were at the same time backers of the United Nations—including Walter Lippmann, Marquis Childs, Barnet Nover, and Anne O'Hare McCormick—were deploring the failure of the President to notify the United Nations and to adopt other procedures that would have brought his proposed action 'within the spirit of the United Nations.'"[44]

Hands were burned, but apparently no lessons were learned, for Administration leaders treated Greek-Turkish aid and the larger ideas created to package this aid as though it would be the last time Congress and the public would ever have to be faced. These programs were "proposed and accepted with panacean overtones"[45] for quickie rebuilding of Europe, righting the wrongs in underdeveloped lands, and containing the Communists once and for all. So, the original Policy Planning Staff memorandum prior to Marshall's Harvard speech stressed that "the program must contain reasonable assurance that if we support it, this will be the last such program we shall be asked to support in the foreseeable

43. Bertram Gross, *The Legislative Struggle* (New York: McGraw-Hill, 1953), p. 368.
44. Jones, *op. cit.*, p. 181.
45. Gabriel Almond, *The American People and Foreign Policy* (New York: Harcourt, 1950), p. 88.

future."[46] President Truman stressed this "get it over with" theme in his December, 1947, special message on aid.

Two years later when the pressures for expansion of economic and military involvement were so great — note NSC 68 alone[47] — the Korean outbreak must have come as a considerable relief to those who had to face Congress with what would have appeared as broken pledges otherwise, rather than mere reassessment. One other important aspect of oversell in the aid programs was the stress the public was allowed to put upon the doctrines of (1) self-help and (2) anticommunism. Soon after passage, the Administration got into hot water over the glaring inconsistencies of resistance to helping Spain (anti-Communist and ready to help itself) and eagerness to help Yugoslavia (Communist).

Examples of oversell can just as easily be found in noneconomic policies, and they serve even better as indexes to the politics of the foreign policy establishment. The most interesting is the case of the Administration's perjury on American troop commitments under the NATO treaty. At the time of the treaty ratification, there was intense opposition to the degree of entanglement implied in NATO. To the treaty unanimously reported by the Foreign Relations Committee, Senator Wherry, for himself, Taft, and Watkins, attempted to attach the reservation that none of the parties was committed "morally or legally to furnish or supply arms . . ."[48] Due to unequivocal assurances made publicly and privately at that time, the reservation was withdrawn and the treaty was allowed to pass unamended. A year later, when we did become committed to stationing troops abroad, these early assurances hurt.

In April, 1949, Senator Hickenlooper asked Secretary Acheson, "are we going to be expected to send substantial numbers of troops over there as a more or less permanent contribution to the development of these countries' capacity to resist?" Acheson's reply was: "The answer to that question, Senator, is a clear and absolute 'NO'."[49] In the 1951 hearings, Acheson, when reminded of 1949, attempted to get out of his embarrassment with a labored definition of a word. He explained that if the "expected to" in the 1949 question meant that under the treaty we had undertaken a commitment, the answer was "NO"; however, that did not mean an absolute "NO" to a question whether we intended to send them.[50] His

46. Quoted in Jones, *op. cit.*, p. 250.
47. Millis and Mansfield, *op. cit.*, p. 256.
48. Quoted in Bradford Westerfield, *Foreign Policy and Party Politics* (New Haven, Yale Press, 1955), p. 332. See also *Hearings* cited below, pp. 119–20.
49. Committee on Foreign Relations, *Hearings on the Assignment of Ground Forces of the United States to Duty in the European Area* (Washington, 1951), p. 111. For further reference to "absolute assurance," see p. 120. These extraordinary hearings were held pursuant to the Wherry Resolution discussed below.
50. *Ibid.*, p. 112.

testimony was accompanied by an elaborate brief showing that the President, in his role as commander-in-chief, needed no congressional authorization for sending the troops, and that the treaty had not affected this power one way or the other.[51] No one questioned this, but many felt that such a brief would have been more appropriate in 1949.[52]

It is beside the point now to question the wisdom of assigning the troops before or after Korea or the wisdom of perjury as a political strategy. What is significant is the lack of a proper conspiracy among leaders in the pursuit of the national interests of the United States as an "interest group" in the world system. Administrative perjury in the presentation of the package is a strong example of oversell. And even without the charge of perjury, there is still the undeniable fact of a sense of misrepresentation felt by the Congress that made the introduction of the 1951 Wherry Resolution necessary. The Wherry Resolution declared that no troops would be stationed in Europe under NATO "pending the adoption of a policy with respect thereto by the Congress."[53] This incredible expression would have forcibly pried open the foreign policy establishment for congressional reentry; and it did achieve part of this goal, because the extraordinary hearings referred to here were held pursuant to the Resolution. These hearings achieved the following, according to Senator Russell: "It is the first time, I suppose, in such a critical international situation that any great power has laid all of its cards on top of the table not only to be seen by our allies but by our potential enemies."[54] This is a result of the reaction of a consumer who discovers he has been oversold.

Overselling of package doctrines has been repeated over and over again in the years since the postwar formation of our establishment. Eisenhower's personal diplomacy ("I shall go to Korea," "spirit of Camp David"), Dulles' brinkmanship, and Wilson's "bigger bang" were necessary parts of the task of selling the New Look—the marketing language for making the downward budgetary adjustments absolutely necessary in the post-Korean period. Since so much of foreign policy between Korea and Sputnik involved implementation and amendment of basic instruments already in existence, naturally much of the process in these years landed in the fiscal area. Consequently, Congress enacted fiscal versions of the Wherry Resolution as a means of dispelling for itself the fog of oversell, because the use of oversell did not abate. In 1951, Congress enacted a requirement that military departments must "come into agreement"

51. *Ibid.*, pp. 88 ff., and p. 110. This contrasts with the Administration's 1949 assurance that the treaty would be resubmitted if troops were contemplated (p. 120).

52. *Ibid.*, p. 120.

53. *Ibid.*, pp. 38–39.

54. *Ibid.*, p. 87.

with the Armed Services Committees on virtually all transactions involving real estate for military installations.[55] Eight years later it was repealed through constitutional (Attorney General) construction, and only after that, by Congress. But it was immediately replaced by another "fiscal Wherry Resolution," the Russell Amendment. This stated: "No funds may be appropriated after December 31, 1960, to or for the use of any armed force of the United States for the procurement of aircraft, missiles, or naval vessels unless the appropriation of such funds *has been authorized by legislation enacted after such date.*"[56]

It seems then that one special development in foreign policy since the formative years has been the institutionalization of second thoughts in Congress. This is the mentality of "Stop the world, we want to get on" that has arisen out of the failure of leaders to find means of dealing with each other frankly, yet confidentially. And the Kennedy and Johnson Administrations have given no signs of change. The Common Market was so far oversold to Congress as to imperil the Trade Act. The Alliance for Progress was packaged to sound like an attempt to revolutionize the hemisphere. The lack of coherency in the establishment that makes oversell necessary caught President Eisenhower in an outright lie on the U-2 incident. But it caught the more sophisticated Kennedy in one of the most disastrous blows to national prestige in our history. The Bay of Pigs catastrophe is the classic case of partial decision: "You may go into Cuba but you may not have the support necessary to succeed." No wonder the President must propagandize his colleagues.[57]

However, if overselling remedies is a bundle of indexes for the level and degree of conflict in the politics of foreign policy, it is also a syndrome in the pathology of foreign policy. Few policies — major instruments or minor tactics — have been all bad; many have, no doubt, succeeded even beyond the claims of the salesmen. But no policy has escaped injury to

55. See Raymond H. Dawson, "Innovation and Intervention in Defense Policy," in Robert L. Peabody and Nelson W. Polsby (eds.), *New Perspectives on the House of Representatives* (Chicago: Rand-McNally, 1963), p. 283. This was vetoed by Truman and then passed as a rider to another bill.

56. *Ibid.*, p. 273. Italics added.

57. Here is how two apologists (for Cuba in particular and American policies in general) explained the Bay of Pigs: "In Cuba, these two principles collided head-on. According to the dictates of the Monroe Doctrine, we could not endanger American security by standing aside as Communist power expanded in the Western Hemisphere. The principle of non-intervention, however, prevented us from acting on any all-out full-scale basis within the jurisdiction of another sovereign state" (Joseph E. Black and Kenneth Thompson [eds.], *Foreign Policies in a World of Change* [New York: Harper and Row, 1963], in an essay by Black and Thompson, p. 711). Note how seriously and uncritically these doctrines are taken as definable objectives. But even so, one must either believe that doctrines (not men) can "collide," or one must sense the extreme intensity of conflict in the Kennedy Administration behind the collision of principles. One must also sense how these principles have persisted as packages of doctrines for purposes of oversell after one side or the other has won out.

itself and therefore to national interests and public (including congressional) expectation by the requirement that each policy be oversold in order to become a policy and to avoid being a "partial policy."

The current situation in Vietnam is another instance of this point. It has been just one more crisis made out of the decentralized system. The outbreak of fighting in Vietnam itself was not of our making; the crisis was. It was sold by American policy-makers and image-makers as a case of unambiguous aggression and as a case of the need for unambiguous victory. It may be a case of both of these things, but to sell it on the front pages as that sort of a package left diplomats almost no options. Add the Rusk Doctrine of the total involvement of our credibility throughout the world, the rigidity becomes almost complete for the United States and also for its allies, whose choice now seems only to be whether to be or not to be an official ally. Under popular pressure, magnified by congressmen who rightly feel they have not been properly treated in the matter, the extremities of oversell are exceeded over and over again. Finally, in order to justify everything else, the Ky regime itself is oversold for its strength and legitimacy. We spread it on so thick, topping it off with Presidential bearhug, that the regime itself came perilously close to a fall and may still bring itself and our shaky justification down with it.

When experiments must be sold as sure things and limited sure things must be sold as cure-alls, frustration and failure are inevitable. An experiment can be partially successful; but after oversell partial success can only be defined as failure. Failure leads to distrust and frustration, which lead to more oversell and to further verbal excesses, as superlatives become ordinary through use. Since international politics is special in the amount of risk involved, these responses become especially intense. All of which leads to the worst possible abuse of oversell, the rhetoric of victory. While it has been resisted, with exceptions, up to now, the rhetoric of victory is constantly on the verge of gaining ascendancy. It is the last stage before the end of politics.

Overselling the Threat

The second type of oversell is essentially the attempt to create the moral equivalent of war. It is the conversion of cues into incidents, incidents into challenges, and challenges into crises for the purpose of imposing temporary and artificial cohesion upon the members of the foreign policy establishment. It is the escalation of meanings. When peace is in peril, all Presidents have found it necessary to create that sense of self-restraint, self-sacrifice, and devotion to higher causes that seems to come about so naturally in war. For modern Presidents, this tactic has become necessary, compelling, and regular whether there is a true crisis or not.

Typically, a Britisher provided us with our most important concepts. In the vocabulary of oversell no doctrines have been as important as "cold war" and "iron curtain." (Also typically, the British proceeded to take it all less seriously than we.) There were, of course, varying amounts of truth underlying both terms. Perhaps there is a total but unseen war. Perhaps there has been a communist devil who will "get you if you don't watch out." But the analytic value of the terms was lost to their hortatory value: We can get some cohesion in a power elite if we can only attribute to our enemies a singleness of purpose and a perfection of rational means to achieve it. These two themes proved to fill basic psychological and political needs in our system, and they have been used to help oversell crises ever since.

"Containment," first seized upon to help provide a package for Greek-Turkish aid, was also found to be generally valuable. Thus it became a significant American contribution to the more pervasive themes of cold war and iron curtain. It helped show that all local wars, guerilla actions, *coups d'état*, and other types of upheaval were interrelated and cumulative.[58]

Along with these pervasive themes are the more specialized, *ad hoc* emotions whipped up for campaigns on more specific issues. President Eisenhower had an important oversell mechanism in McCarthyism. Functionally, McCarthyism was the internal equivalent of containment, and it helped bring the twenty-year Democratic, tea-sipping, and Soviet-friendly State Department into line as well as to silence much independent opposition. Late in his Administration, Eisenhower found over-selling of foreign crises increasingly valuable as his personal prestige declined. Dulles became famous for such talk as the "brink of war" and "massive retaliation." The latter was particularly good because it helped oversell the positive value of atomic over conventional arms, and at the same time helped create the sense of the seriousness and the

58. Compare Lippmann, in an article which appeared after the first draft of this chapter: "All the postwar Presidents have taken it for granted that they had to create the majority they needed [for unpopular foreign policies], and that, while some...might respond to argument, the others had to be scared into joining up....As a result, it has become part of the established procedure of American foreign policy to invoke the threat of Communist take-over whenever American opinion is divided. As the practice has grown, the formula has been generalized. Now we are accepting the unique burden of resisting the advance of Communism everywhere..." Lippmann refers to this as the "all-purpose myth" despite the "essential fact" about disorders like Vietnam and the Dominican Republic that "they are at bottom indigenous to the countries where the social order is broken down, not originally, not essentially, conspiracies engineered from the centers of Communist power" (*Newsweek*, May 24, 1965, p. 23). Lippmann goes on to argue that the myth will be used to "reassure our people that Mr. Johnson is not going to take part in an unending series of wars," because we can teach the "masterminds of a universal conspiracy" a lesson in only one or two encounters. My argument is a variant based on the attribution of worldwide conspiracy, or at least interconnection.

immediacy of the threat that made retaliation necessary. Dulles opposed containment as "negative, futile and immoral" and implied its replacement with rhetoric that (especially for Europe) verged on preventive war. But he continued to sell all outbreaks the world over as interrelated and cumulative. Finally there was the use of Sputnik for a variety of issues in the arms race during the "Sputnik age."

Much of the activity in Kennedy's short span was of the same nature. In fact, Kennedy spent more of his earlier months on creating a moral equivalent of war than on just about anything else. The "ask not" passage of his inaugural address was a suitable transition from missile gaps to something more substantial (and truthful). The idea of man-on-the-moon-by-1970 had all sorts of value besides the increasing of space appropriations. The Bay of Pigs, once survived, became an excellent means for creating a sense of unity, then some real unity, on a host of defense-related items. (It is hard to forget the Kennedy-MacArthur, Kennedy-Hoover, Kennedy-Truman, and so forth, unity pictures.)

Again it should be emphasized that any criticism expressed or implied is subsidiary to the essential point, which is how these themes are reflective of the system and fulfill needs in the system. Overselling the nature of the crisis is not as specific and selective as the techniques of overselling the cures. This is why themes have been stressed. But it is no less a reflection of the conflictive system. Facing real political stress, and committed to real goals about which there is usually a great deal of consensus, the President is impelled into domestic strategies that may give him the means of realizing the goals without having to mortgage so much as to make the means eventually fashioned (the partial decision) useless to him. There is always hope, as we must judge from his actions, that he can reverse the aphorism, "He who mobilizes the elite mobilizes the the public." What has become important to the President is the possibility that "He who mobilizes the public mobilizes the elite."

Turning again to pathology, overselling the crisis is dangerous precisely because it is so nonspecific. Even if it may provide the proper setting for putting the important policy across, it can create expectations of war that can falsely affect business, alienate the attentive publics and allies, or, more gravely, reduce the President's own flexibility at a later point when he would like the crisis to "be over." He might, in other words, wish it on at will, but he cannot so easily wish it off (e.g., McCarthyism). Given the regular use of oversell despite such obvious dangers, the need for oversell must be enormous.

All the more significant is the fact that the tactic seems to be so unsuccessful. While this cannot be proven conclusively, it is possible to observe that all the other forms of political interaction continue unabated. The President continues to manufacture an occasional crisis out of a

minor challenge, but he still gets partial decisions. He must still mortgage large parts of trade control as an instrument of politics in order to get any trade act at all. He must still expect to be forced into an occasional war, be forced to fight it one-handed, and then be expected to win an unambiguous victory. In diplomacy, the only thing worse than unambiguous defeat is unambiguous victory. That is the Scylla and Charybdis of presidential power in survival politics.

CONCLUSIONS

Regardless of ideology or context, conflict tends to decentralize power. Decentralization is a function of continuous conflict. In answer to the iron law of oligarchy, there is an equally ferrous law of democracy. They are merely converse expressions of the same law, each being a statement for its appropriate extent and degree of conflict. For each experimental situation like Michels' oligarchy in socialist labor parties, there is probably one like Lipset's typographers union or Brooks' New York Central Railroad.[59]

There is conflict in foreign policy politics. Separated agencies, each with constitutional or legal rights to independent identity, access, and participation, guarantee the continuity of conflict. The President's efforts to propagandize all his colleagues and his publics through the risky tactics of oversell attest to the extent of conflict and consequently to the broad base of participation and relatively extreme decentralization of power in the foreign policy establishment. We have seen the process largely through the instruments so fashioned and the actions so taken. The process of conflict-and-conflict-resolution in some form was the only explanation for most cases, because rational men could never have arrived at these instruments or actions through reason and consensus. In most cases it is difficult to conceive of instruments or actions more poorly designed for the rational pursuit of any rationally defined (self-interested) goals. Democracy is, of course, unsafe for the world so long as democracy is not set up for consistently rational action, because the enemy can too easily miscalculate. And instruments and actions cannot be rational or consistent so long as they are arrived at as simply the outcome of a meandering process. However, the prospect of rationality is less important here than the system that has made its prospect so dim. What remains to be done, therefore, is to make more explicit and theoretically relevant my basic arguments about the system.

59. Robert Michels, *Political Parties* (New York: The Free Press, 1949); S. M. Lipset, *Union Democracy* (New York: The Free Press, 1956); John Brooks, *The Seven Fat Years* (New York: Harper, 1958); and, of course, Madison in Federalist No. 10.

Looking back over the cases and illustrations used in the chapter, it seems that *the only instances in which the makers of foreign policy were truly separated and insulated from broad publics and worked truly in unison, even if not always in harmony, were crisis.*Here it is easy to cite reasons, among which are anxiety and insufficient time. But can we do better than isolate merely this one important subsystem of foreign policy behavior? What about other subsystems? It would be possible to let the matter rest here, with the sufficiently weighty and far from unanimously accepted contention that in all other situations, foreign policy is "pluralistic." This would imply two things, both fairly close to the truth: (1) that inside the "elite" there is much organized bloc actions, not unlike domestic patterns of pluralism; and (2) that American foreign policy is subject to domestic political forces to a degree unknown to other modern democratic or nondemocratic states. But I think it is possible to take another step beyond this position toward a more elaborate notion of foreign policy as an "issue-area" or "arena." This is to identify the type of policy involved.

From the cases above, and one or two others cited below, it is possible to identify two distinct subsystems within the general field of noncrisis foreign policy-making. To summarize, this gives us three predictable subsystems of foreign policy-making, although they are not identical to the three domestic ones earlier described. The first is the elitist subsystem (although involving a much smaller elite than the "power elite") that prevails (a) in crisis and (b) in any noncrisis situations in which in the short run no internal resources are involved at all. Recognition of a country with no immediate United States commitments beyond mere recognition might prove such an example; however, it is difficult to imagine many noncrisis situations of any great importance where no internal resources are involved. Thus it follows that there is little eliteness in noncrisis foreign policy politics.

The key factor, once internal resources are involved, is not how much involvement there is (which would push us toward *post hoc* and truistic propositions), but what kind of involvement. This means classifying foreign policies in terms of their impact upon the United States. Thus, subsystem 2 is a logrolling pattern. The logrolling pattern is decentralized and nonconflictive just as the elitist pattern is centralized and nonconflictive. This subsystem gives the appearance of being elitist only because it is nonconflictive. This subsystem is similar to the domestic pattern I have called distributive politics, and for the same reason: It develops around policies that can be disaggregated into a multitude of isolated, small units.[60] Subsystem 3 is decentralized and conflictive—in a word,

60. See Lowi, *op. cit.*, p. 690 and pp. 692 ff., for further discussion of the political significance of "disaggregation."

pluralistic. When foreign policies depend for their success upon direct and relatively coercive regulation of internal resources, it is impossible to avoid conflict. It is also impossible to disaggregate the issues into their many negotiable parts. Such situations are the most decentralized and the outcomes are most unpredictable. Foreign policy considerations are least insulated from domestic forces.[61]

Now let us look at three different noncrisis situations to see how much is to be gained from the imposition of distributive and regulatory categories upon them. The test is whether political relations among participants could have been predicted from knowledge of whether the foreign policy was distributive or regulatory in its involvement with internal resources.

The Tariff. The best example of the relation between technique and process, and therefore the best introduction to the theoretical value of the approach, is the tariff. It is a good example because it has undergone a redefinition from a distributive to a regulatory type of policy in recent times and thus provides an experimental situation.[62] The traditional tariff was a classic case of distributive techniques. The scope of tariff coverage could be expanded indefinitely and the schedules could be broken up into smaller and smaller items almost infinitely. The inevitable conflicts among participants could be accommodated without ever requiring face-to-face conflict by simply giving to each a portion of what he wanted. Even potential combatants could find a basis for cooperation: logrolling.[63] Eventually, someone has to pay the piper; but this moral equation could be balanced easily by the simple process of displacement onto the world system and onto the future.

The politics of the traditional tariff, so clearly captured by Schattschneider, was neither pluralistic nor power elitist. There was an elite, but it was not based upon an upper class or the command posts, but was specifically a congressional committee (House Ways and Means). Relations among participants were highly stable around the committee, but it was a stability among uncommon interests rather than one of consensus. There can hardly be said to have been a "group process" at all; nor does there appear to have been any executive control whatsoever.

Beginning with 1934, and increasing after World War II, tariff underwent very significant changes in the manner of its use as the United States emerged as a regular world participant. Even before the outbreak of war, the United States had entered into agreements affecting over 1,000 major

61. In light of the earlier discussion, it is interesting to note the absence of a foreign policy variant of redistribution. This might be due to my incomplete coverage rather than to a datum about the system. Devaluation might be an example of a redistributive use of resources in foreign policy.

62. Cf. Lowi, *op. cit.*, p. 699.

63. See Schattschneider, *op. cit., passim.*

tariff items. Reciprocal trade renewal in 1945 established 1945 rates as a new standard below which the President could reduce rates by still another 50 per cent. Under the most favored nation clause, the tariff had obviously become a means whereby we could affect world trade and also bargain for nontrade concessions *if we were willing to bargain with our own rates.* Thus it was only a matter of time before tariff became the reverse of its earlier form. Earlier it was a means of manipulating international affairs for domestic purposes. Now it had become a means of regulating the domestic economy of international purposes.

Without arguing cause and effect, it is possible to observe significant political changes in the tariff during the same period.[64] The field shifts from committee to Congress in classic interplay with the executive. The "group process" emerges.[65] Larger and larger categories of commodities (rather than single items) become involved, until they are formally incorporated into the Trade Expansion Act of 1962[66] and the Tariff Classification Act, passed earlier in 1962. The entire story becomes a great deal more public.

Aid, Not Trade. I have already made a great deal of the proposition that an important aspect of the Marshall Plan was whether or not it was to be a set of powers granted to the State Department. I conceived of this largely as an issue over whether the State Department or any other department would be granted powers that amounted to the regulation of our economy for international purposes. The politics of ECA appeared to be one of consensus; but it was neither consensual nor elitist except in superficial appearance. Once ECA was set up independently, it became simply a new segment of public domain available for distribution. The politics of aid could be predicted, because aid looks pretty much like the politics of the traditional tariff, of water resources,[67] or of agriculture subsidy.[68]

ECA did not actually engage directly in the purchase of supplies (making the imposition of regulatory disciplines an all the more remote threat). Procurement was left to recipient countries buying almost completely through regular private trade channels. Each application for a commodity —by a government, a firm, or an individual—was reviewed by ECA,

---

64. See Lowi, *op. cit.,* p. 701; Raymond A. Bauer, *et al., op. cit.,* pp. 26 ff. and other page references cited in my paper.

65. See, for example, *Congressional Quarterly Almanac,* 1962, pp. 291–94. For the first time in many years even the Chamber of Commerce was able to take an unequivocal stand on tariffs.

66. Under Section 211, the President may disregard the Smoot-Hawley schedules and make out a new, comprehensive classification for all commodities of which the U.S. and Europe account for 80 per cent of the export value.

67. See Arthur Maass, "Congress and Water Resources," *American Political Science Review,* Vol. 44 (September 1950), pp. 576–93.

68. See Theodore J. Lowi, "How the Farmers Get What They Want," *The Reporter,* (May 21, 1964) pp. 34 ff.

which in turn issued a "procurement authorization" to a cooperating bank guaranteeing reimbursement once the purchase from the American firm was made. When ECA decided a loan was more appropriate, it was authorized to turn over the funds to the Export-Import Bank, which was to administer the loan according to the terms set down by the ECA administrator (Section 111 (c) (2)). However, the difference between loans and grants has been politically unimportant because (1) in most cases the recipient had to put up the equivalent of the grant in local (counterpart) funds; (2) there were many strings tied to grants and many types of loans were very "soft"; and (3) ultimately the individual American supplier faced a customer with cash no matter what the customer had to do about the cash later on.[69]

A formal reading of the Act and official interpretations reveals the meaning of ECA as a bundle of techniques. In the short run, essentially no governmental regulations at all were imposed upon the resources of the United States. There was an expansion of domain that attracted the support of industrial and financial interests facing postwar recession.[70] The prospect of sales to totally trustworthy (U.S. guaranteed) foreign accounts is bound to have had a major impact on how businessmen related to each other and to Congress and the executive. It is not necessary to know what each man's motives were to know that his political relations with all others having Marshall Plan interests in common were quite different from what these relations would have been if, for instance, the Act had involved such lend-lease techniques as direct presidential and Army-Navy procurement decisions, "set-asides" for particularly desirable commodities, or discretion in the use of ECA goods as items in bargaining and diplomacy with Marshall Plan countries. As a consequence, and as predictable, the politics of Marshall Plan was quiet, appearing to be almost without conflict. Far more than the published accounts say explicitly, the process centered in Congress, particularly in the Senate Foreign Relations Committee. Bipartisanship was a harness designed strictly for Chairman Vandenberg, but he was as often the driver as the driven.

There is some experimental value in a brief look at the more recent history of "foreign aid." The dollar gap was closed during the early 1950s, and not too long afterwards the opposite problem emerged, which became the gold flow. As a strategy, foreign aid remained more or less the same, but its national politics undoubtedly changed. Insofar as aid is responsible for an unfavorable balance of trade and a gold outflow, it is

69. See Price, *op. cit.*, pp. 78 ff.; Jones, *op. cit.*, pp. 241 ff.; and esp. Robert E. Asher, *op. cit.*, pp. 6 ff.

70. See, for example, Secretary of State Marshall's speech to the Pittsburgh Chamber of Commerce, January 15, 1948, in the *Department of State Bulletin* (January 25, 1948), pp. 108–11.

responsible to that extent for direct contraction of the domestic economy (actually by a multiplier of as much as five times that amount). This has a fiscal impact on the domestic economy that requires adjustment among many individual firms. This impact, in turn, has brought about an interconnection of aid decisions that hitherto were taken up one at a time and in isolation. For example, President Eisenhower's directive of November 16, 1960, to reduce to "the lowest possible figure" the amount of commodities purchased abroad with ICA funds[71] required (1) a contraction that in turn required (2) ICA to make hard choices among claims that triggered (3) competition among claims. No longer could the aid program enjoy being merely a set of expanded opportunities.

The political changes associated with these changes in the relation of foreign aid to the domestic economy are consistent with the theory. Increasingly in the late 1950s, reaching a climax in 1964; conflict began to develop around almost all aspects of foreign aid. This contrasts to the tendency of most American policies to become part of the consensus after being around for a long time.[72] Probably for the first time in American history an "independent commission" lost its statutory independence and became incorporated in a department—in this case the dreaded Department of State. In Congress, aid became conflictive rather than consensual. Control of aid moved dramatically away from committee; the floor came to have real functional value. The President had to return, after over a decade, to the public, in hopes of mobilizing the elite.[73] Otto Passman has been more a reflection than a leader.

Thus, the politics of foreign aid changed because foreign aid as a policy changed. Many leaders no doubt began to oppose foreign aid in the late 1950s because of dissatisfaction with the experience of foreign aid programs abroad. But that would be sufficient explanation only for revival of aid *as an issue*. The concern here is not to explain why, when, and what people become dissatisfied. It is, rather, to explain why certain kinds of political relationships develop and to speculate on the consequences of each, once the question is raised. In the case of aid, the first decade was distributive policy, and the political patterns developed accordingly. More recently, for many reasons, aid programs are related to our own resources in a much more regulative way, and the politics of aid has begun to be quite different from before.

Arms and Armaments. Unification had worked during World War II because there was a war and because resources could be treated as though they were unlimited. After 1945, there was neither war nor unlimited resources. Setting hard budgetary ceilings in the pre-Korean period inten-

71. In Asher, *op. cit.*, p. 33, note 8.
72. Cf. Robert E. Lane, *The Regulation of Businessmen* (New Haven, 1953).
73. See President Kennedy's argument that aid was better than B-58s at defeating Communism, *New York Times*, June 17, 1961.

sified interservice rivalries beyond all reason. The ceilings made clear that there was a pie that had to be sliced three ways. This made relations among the services a zero-sum game; and the absence of war removed most restraints on how to respond to it. On the other hand, the size and scope of the decisions each service had to make in the postwar period meant that it would be impossible for President or Budget Bureau or Congress to break up the issues into small, negotiable units. The most spectacular battle among the services, the so-called B-36 controversy, was so large a procurement item that it basically involved a decision on "a theory of war."[74] Thus, conflict could be displaced neither through expansion of available resources nor through further and further disaggregation of the existing resources. All decisions were elevated to a degree of inclusiveness as great as could be achieved by compromise and coalition — i.e., the level of the Service and whole sectors of the economy dependent on that Service. Decisions, therefore, tended to be so inclusive and also so conflictive that some kind of doctrine (a "theory of war") was almost a requisite. Like domestic regulatory decisions, the politics of tight budgets or of contraction, or of major changes in roles and missions, takes place among large, organized sectors and bureaucracies in a classic interplay with Congress. Conflict and compromise, not logrolling and not elite consensus, describe the process that inevitably expands beyond the original parties (e.g., Air Force vs. Navy). To emphasize the point, the politics of disarmament cannot be the same as its opposite, an arms race. Ironically, the latter is politically much more peaceful.

The politics inside each military service is typically one of dramatic contrasts to that between and among the services. Here, to carry out its policies once the big decisions requiring doctrine have been made, each service operates as a distributive arena. Contracts can break up the total budget into units of almost any size and can accomodate to the conflicts among industrial and local claimants, just as the Corps of Engineers and the Public Health Service can. Whatever the substance at issue, this kind of activity is basically co-optative. The politics of intraservice activity is consequently quieter, more elitist (to the level of the service), more stable, centered less in Congress and more in congressional committee.[75]

---

74. Cf. Millis and Mansfield, *op. cit.*, p. 248, especially the Radford testimony; also Paul Y. Hammond, "Super Carriers and B-36 Bombers: Appropriations, Strategy, and Politics," in Harold Stein (ed.), *American Civil-Military Decisions* (Tuscaloosa: University of Alabama Press, 1963).

75. See, for example, Dawson, *op. cit.* (pp. 283–84). Intraservice decisions have been made largely between each service and the Armed Services Committees, especially during the 1950s under the "coming into agreement" clause touched upon earlier. However, the issue between Army and Air Force over Nike versus Talos immediately expanded (beginning with leaks to the press) beyond the authorizing and appropriating committees, to the floor, conference, presidential veto, and back again until Congress effected a compromise (pp. 287 ff.). This is a regular and predictable difference between the politics of distribution and of regulatory policies.

external relations are truly of an agency-clientele nature. The distributive politics of *intra-service* activity, of course, is significant in itself but doubly so because it in turn supports and provides the resources for the regulatory politics of *interservice* struggle.

A major problem in the study of politics, especially the politics of foreign policy, is that of escaping the uniqueness of events. The ultimate data are policy decisions, and their great relevance is also their greatest shortcoming. Faced with policy-making cases, theory becomes a set of afterthoughts tagged on to untheoretical chronicles, unless we develop conventions for answering the ultimate question: Of what class of cases is this case?

There may be several useful directions away from the unique event toward theory, several bases of classification. The classification formulated here for noncrisis foreign policy is derived from an understanding of that limited number of means by which men can use government to control other men and their environment. Properly categorized, these techniques of control are the functions of the state. Therefore it is not too much to expect that political relationships among political participants will be determined in large part by what technique of control they have in common. In domestic affairs, two men may appear to have "agriculture policy" or "education policy" in common. But that only describes and predicts their political interests. Their political relations will be determined and structured according to whether agriculture, for example, is to be manipulated by subsidies, by licensing, by marketing controls, or by credit; or, concerning education, whether by loans, grants, tax rebates, building programs, or "aggregate demand." Such an analysis does not attempt to tell all about either agriculture or education. Its purpose is to reveal the essential political ingredient of the issue: How is the object to be controlled? This is simply an attempt to characterize policies for purposes of analysis just as we often take ideologies, interest groups, or roles as the relevant aspect of broader and larger phenomena.

In foreign affairs such an effort seems equally useful. An approach to noncrisis foreign policy politics through the techniques of internal control does not tell all about any decision or development. But it does tend to clarify one vital dimension of foreign policy and helps avoid the confusion of trying to deal with several dimensions at once. Such an approach emphasizes the domestic sources, strengths, and limitations of foreign policy. It may be even more useful in establishing stronger continuities, academically speaking, between foreign and domestic theories of politics. The effort here resolved itself into three subsystems or arenas of power in domestic politics and two subsystems in noncrisis foreign politics, because only three categories of control techniques (functions of the state) could be identified. Congressional and executive roles,

relations between Congress and its committees and between committees and interest groups, degree and type of group involvement, degree and type of public and mass involvement — all these seem to vary according to conditions created by the type of technique involved.

However, the principle of analysis — classifying the techniques of control and predicting political relations for each technique — is more important than my particular realization of it. The superior realization of the principle of analysis will arise not out of more elaborate cases or technically superior data but rather out of a superior understanding of the functions of the state as the source of politics.

INDEX

Abelson, Robert P., 142, 142n
Acheson, Dean, 277, 278, 304, 317
Adorno, Theodore W., 58n, 79n, 139n, 158n
age, 212; and content of issues, 186
aggressiveness, 65n, 67, 68, 103, 104
agriculture subsidies, 326
Alger, Chadwick F., 245, 245n, 247
alienation, 73–75
Alliance for Progress, 319
Almond, Gabriel A., 3n, 28, 28n, 29, 53n, 63n, 76n, 79n, 92n, 266, 266n, 316n
America First Committee, 54
American Medical Association, 30, 242
American people, 292; education of, 260. *See also* mass public, United States
American politics, theories of, 295–98, 324–25. *See also* United States
American Tariff League, 247
Angell, Robert C., 161n
anomy, 74n
anti-Semitism, 80
anxiety, 71–73, 76, 106
approach-avoidance conflict, 126
Apter, David E., 78n, 226n
Archibald, K., 65n
articulates, 78
Asher, Robert E., 305n, 327n, 328n
Atlantic Community groups, 248

Atomic Energy Commission, *see* United States
attitudes, 52, 55–56, 58, 92–93, 107, 111, 127, 146; and foreign policy, 92, 112, 118–19, 221; and personality, 158; and social position, 179–84; change of, 126, 133–34, 137, 138, 139, 141, 142, 144–48; defined, 132; measurement of, 227; of groups, 156–58; of mass publics, 132; theories of, 115–16, 131–46, 166–73, 177–78; toward Cold War, 154
authoritarianism, 158
Awareness scale, 76

B-36 controversy, 329
background variables, 162
Barth, Ernest A. T., 20n
Barton, Alan, 155n
Bauer, Raymond A., 20n, 42n, 93n, 211, 211n, 237, 237n, 243, 244, 250, 297n, 326n
Belknap, G., 79n
Bella, Ben, 34
Bensmans, Joseph, 41n
Berelson, Bernard, 165, 165n, 233n
Berkowitz, L., 65n
Berlin, airlift to, 283, 300; issue of, 48, 203, 273
bipartisanship, 25, 303, 327
Black, Joseph E., 319n
Black Muslims, 257

BOOKS PUBLISHED FOR THE
CENTER OF INTERNATIONAL STUDIES

Published by Princeton University Press, Princeton, N.J.

The Appeals of Communism, Gabriel A. Almond (1954).

Military Policy and National Security, William W. Kaufmann, ed. (1956).

The War Potential of Nations, Klaus Knorr (1956).

Guerrilla Communism in Malaya, Lucian W. Pye (1956).

The Political Process and Foreign Policy: The Making of the Japanese Peace Settlement, Bernard C. Cohen (1957).

Theory and Reality in Public International Law, Charles de Visscher, trans. by P. E. Corbett (1957).

Party Politics in India: The Development of a Multi-Party System, Myron Weiner (1957).

Law in Diplomacy, Percy E. Corbett (1959).

NATO and American Security, Klaus Knorr, ed. (1959).

Economic Integration: Theoretical Assumptions and Consequences of European Integration, Rolf Sannwald and Jacques Stohler, trans. by Herman Karreman, Foreword by Klaus Knorr (1959).

The Politics of the Developing Areas, Gabriel A. Almond and James Coleman, eds. (1960).

On Thermonuclear War, Herman Kahn (1960).

Tojo and the Coming of the War, Robert J. C. Butow (1961).

The International System: Theoretical Essays, Klaus Knorr and Sidney Verba, eds. (1961).

Deterrence and Defense: Toward a Theory of National Security, Glenn H. Snyder (1961).

Small Groups and Political Behavior: A Study of Leadership, Sidney Verba (1961).

The Civic Culture: Political Attitudes and Democracy in Five Nations, Gabriel A. Almond and Sidney Verba (1963).

The Press and Foreign Policy, Bernard C. Cohen (1963).

Peace-Making and the Settlement with Japan, Frederick S. Dunn (1963).

National Leadership and Foreign Policy: A Case Study in the Mobilization of Public Support, James N. Rosenau (1963).

Nigerian Political Parties: Power in an Emergent African Nation, Richard L. Sklar (1963).

Communism and Revolution: The Strategic Uses of Political Violence, Cyril E. Black and Thomas P. Thornton, eds. (1964).

Britain and the European Community 1955–1963, Miriam Camps (1964).

International Aspects of Civil Strife, James N. Rosenau, ed. (1964).

The Third World in Soviet Perspective: Studies by Soviet Writers on the Developing Areas, Thomas P. Thornton, ed. (1964).

Security and Disarmament, Richard A. Falk and Richard J. Barnet, eds. (1965).

Conflict and Decision-Making in Soviet Russia: A Case Study of Agricultural Policy, 1953–1963, Sidney L. Ploss (1965).

The Ecological Perspective on Human Affairs, Harold and Margaret Sprout (1965).

Political Development in Pakistan, Karl von Vorys (1965).

On the Uses of Military Power in the Nuclear Age, Klaus Knorr (1966).

Published by Frederick A. Prager, Inc., New York.

Limited Strategic War, Klaus Knorr and Thornton Read, eds. (1962).

A Theory of Strategic War, George Modelski (1962).

Guerrillas in the 1960s, Peter Paret and John W. Shy (1962).

Peace-Keeping by United Nations Forces: From Suez Through the Congo, Arthur L. Burns and Nina Heathcote (1963).

Law, Morality, and War in the Contemporary World, Richard A. Falk (1963).

French Revolutionary Warfare from Indochina to Algeria: The Analysis of a Political and Military Doctrine, Peter Paret (1964).

Published by The Free Press, New York

Internal War, Harry Eckstein, ed. (1964).

Published for the
Princeton Center of International Studies

A list of other Center publications appears at the back of the book

DOMESTIC
SOURCES
OF
FOREIGN
POLICY